The Best of *Anthropology Today*

Anthropology Today has been, and remains, extremely influential in anthropological studies. Between 1974 and 2000 its articles placed it in the thick of a turbulent period for anthropology. Reacting to current research interests and launching what were often heated debates, the journal set the agenda for disciplinary change and new research.

Once described by the American Anthropological Association as creating 'a strong voice for anthropology in the public arena', the Founder Editor, Jonathan Benthall, introduces here a personal selection of articles and letters with his own candid retrospect, arguing that the discipline's greatest strength and potential lies in testing and refining the ideas of other disciplines. A vast array of topics are covered both by well-established anthropologists and young scholars, including:

- feminine power
- indigenes' rights
- fieldwork as intervention
- anthropology in the mass media
- war and civil strife.

Among the many highlights are a remarkable exchange from the mid-1970s between a young graduate student, Glynn Flood, who was undertaking fieldwork in Ethiopia, and an expert on development in Africa, A.F. Robertson. Shortly after its publication, Flood was murdered by Ethiopian soldiers. The exchange brings out clearly a number of issues which are still vigorously debated today.

Articles from *Anthropology Today* are already widely used for teaching purposes. The editorial policy of encouraging sharp, concise writing will make this collection essential for teachers and students as well as for all those with an interest in anthropology.

Jonathan Benthall was Director of the Royal Anthropological Institute (1974–2000) and Founder Editor of *Anthropology Today* which succeeded *RAINews* (1974–84). In 1993 he was awarded the Anthropology in Media Award by the American Anthropological Association.

The Best of

Anthropology Today

Edited by

Jonathan Benthall

with a preface by

Marshall Sahlins

London and New York

First published 2002
by Routledge
11 New Fetter Lane, London EC4P 4EE

Simultaneously published in the USA and Canada
by Routledge
29 West 35th Street, New York, NY 10001

Routledge is an imprint of the Taylor & Francis Group

Typeset in Bell Gothic and Perpetua by
Florence Production Ltd, Stoodleigh, Devon
Printed and bound in Great Britain by
TJ International Ltd, Padstow, Cornwall

British Library Cataloguing in Publication Data
A catalogue record for this book is available from the British Library

Library of Congress Cataloging in Publication Data
A catalog record for this book has been requested

ISBN 0–415–26255–0 (hbk)
ISBN 0–415–26256–9 (pbk)

Contents

PART SEVEN: Human Sciences in Authoritarian States

PART EIGHT: The Technology of Enchantment

PART NINE: War and Civil Strife

Figures

Contributors

Jon Abbink is Senior Researcher at the African Studies Centre, University of Leiden, Netherlands, and Professor of African Ethnic Studies, Free University of Amsterdam.

Abigail E. Adams is Co-Director of Women's Studies, Central Connecticut State University, New Britain, Connecticut.

Marcus Banks is Reader in Social Anthropology, University of Oxford.

Jonathan Benthall is Honorary Research Fellow in the Department of Anthropology, University College London.

Anne-Marie Brisebarre is Director of Research at the Laboratoire d'Anthropologie Sociale, Centre National de la Recherche Scientifique, Paris.

Lionel Caplan is Professorial Research Associate, Department of Anthropology and Sociology, School of Oriental and African Studies, University of London.

Pat Caplan is Professor of Anthropology, Goldsmiths College, University of London.

Christopher Clapham is Professor of International Relations, University of Lancaster.

John M. Coggeshall is Professor of Anthropology in the Sociology Department, Clemson University, Clemson, South Carolina.

Stephen Corry is Director-General of Survival International, London.

Veena Das is Krieger-Eisenhower Professor of Anthropology, Johns Hopkins University, Baltimore, Maryland.

Bartholomew Dean is Assistant Professor in the Department of Anthropology, University of Kansas, Lawrence, Kansas.

Mary Douglas CBE, FBA has held numerous chairs in anthropology.

Glynn Flood (1948–1975) was a research student in the Department of Anthropology, London School of Economics, University of London.

Alfred Gell (1945–1997) was Professor of Anthropology, London School of Economics, University of London.

Gustaaf Houtman is Editor of *Anthropology Today* and Deputy Director of the Royal Anthropological Institute.

Arne Kalland is Professor of Social Anthropology, University of Oslo, Norway.

Anatoly M. Khazanov is Ernest Gellner Professor of Anthropology, University of Wisconsin-Madison, Madison, Wisconsin.

Danièle Kintz is a consultant with a number of aid organizations and is attached to the Laboratoire d'Éthnologie et de Sociologie Comparative, University of Paris X – Nanterre.

John Knight is Lecturer in the School of Anthropological Studies, Queen's University, Belfast.

Liliane Kuczynski is a researcher in the urban anthropology section of the Centre National de la Recherche Scientifique, Ivry, France.

Charles Leslie is Emeritus Professor of Anthropology at the University of Delaware and Adjunct Professor of Anthropology at Indiana University, Bloomington, Indiana.

James Lewton-Brain (1923–1996) was Professor of Anthropology at the State University of New York, New Paltz.

Lucy Mair (1901–1986) was Professor of Applied Anthropology at the London School of Economics and author of many books on social anthropology.

J. Anthony Paredes is Courtesy Professor of Anthropology, Florida State University, Tallahassee, Florida.

Mark Allen Peterson is Assistant Professor of Anthropology, The American University in Cairo.

Sarah Pink is Lecturer in Sociology, Loughborough University, Leicestershire.

Johan Pottier is Professor of Anthropology with reference to Africa, School of Oriental and African Studies, University of London.

Elizabeth D. Purdum is Courtesy Professor of Anthropology and a Research Associate in the Institute of Science and Public Affairs, Florida State University, Tallahassee, Florida.

Declan Quigley is Lecturer in Anthropology, University of St Andrews, Scotland.

A.F. Robertson is Professor of Anthropology, University of California at Santa Barbara.

Silvia Rodgers (Lady Rodgers of Quarry Bank) has published her memoir *Red Saint, Pink Daughter: A Communist Childhood in Berlin and London*.

Marshall Sahlins is Charles F. Grey Distinguished Service Professor of Anthropology Emeritus, University of Chicago.

Jane Schneider is Professor in the PhD Program in Anthropology, Graduate Center, City University of New York.

John Sharp is Professor and Head of the Department of Anthropology and Archaeology, University of Pretoria, South Africa.

Cris Shore is Head of the Department of Anthropology, Goldsmiths College, University of London.

Slawoj Szynkiewicz is a Fellow of the Polish Academy of Sciences and a specialist in the anthropology of the Far East.

Julie Taylor is Professor of Anthropology at Rice University, Houston.

Michael Thompson is Professor in the Department of Comparative Politics, University of Bergen, Norway, and Senior Researcher in the Norwegian Research Centre in Management and Organization.

Katherine Verdery is Professor of Anthropology in the University of Michigan, Ann Arbor, Michigan.

Alex de Waal is a Director of Justice Africa, London.

Alex Weingrod is Professor of Anthropology, Ben-Gurion University of the Negev, Beer-Sheva, Israel.

Preface

■ MARSHALL SAHLINS

Anthropology Today is not yesterday. Its pages are not given over to arcane studies of kinship, witchcraft or ceremony of the kind that used to fill the academic anthropological journals. Of course, there is still some place for that. But it isn't *Anthropology Today*. What Jonathan Benthall assembles here – thus continuing his invaluable services to the Royal Anthropological Institute – reflects the discipline's awakening to what's going on in the world, especially to the many bad things going on, and the responsibilities anthropologists have assumed to witness them. Maybe even to ameliorate them.

Well over a hundred years ago, E.B. Tylor, the great founding ancestor of anthropology in Britain, said it was a 'reformer's science'. We also learned from Tylor and the other ancients that if there is culture anywhere, there is culture everywhere. The current implication is something more than it is time to 'bring anthropology home', to study *us* and our problems, although that is part of it, and there are many instructive examples in these pages. Globalization has given a new, literal meaning to the anthropologists' received sense of the ubiquity of culture. Now we are all culturally connected, and increasingly so. The old Maori proverb, 'the troubles of other lands are their own', has hardly been true since we became their problem. If there is one argument of this book, it is that anthropology is the discipline best endowed to know and to relate the struggles between cultural diversity and cultural hegemony that are affecting us all, peoples everywhere. We are best endowed to know the afflictions of modernity because of a century spent in perfecting the practices of ethnography. And we are best endowed to relate them because, as a number of articles in this book will testify, we have learned to reflect on these ethnographic practices, to situate ourselves and our knowledges in relation to the peoples with whom we interact. True that this self-reflexivity is sometimes paralysing. But it usually saves us from the hubris of development economists, international-relations realists and end-of-civilization pundits who, in dealing with other peoples, too often assume the missionary position of knowing what's best for them: that they ought to think and be happy just like us!

If there is one fault in the book, it is Jonathan Benthall's modesty in describing anthropology as a small and rather obscure discipline whose future may well be in doubt. Of course the current follies of bottom-line accounting by the captains of university and higher political authorities would hurt anthropology along with a lot of other academic fields whose true worth is not measurable in such terms. But if we are talking of value to learning over the long haul, we should neither discount anthropology's utility nor fear for its destiny. This collection proves that.

Figure (a)   Anthropology yesterday: a dancer in *makishi* costume photographed by Max Gluckman, *c.*1940, probably in the grounds of a Zambian museum. The *makishi* rites were associated with male circumcision among the Wiko tribes.

Acknowledgements

The editor and publishers wish to thank the following for their permission to reproduce copyright material:

The Royal Anthropological Institute for permission to reproduce all the articles in this collection which are from the journal *Anthropology Today* and its predecessor *RAINews*; for the individual articles, the authors or their executors; for Chapter 32, *The Times Higher Education Supplement*, 8 March 1974; for Fig (a), The Royal Anthropological Institute Photographic Collection; for Fig 0.1, The Royal Anthropological Institute Photographic Collection; for Fig 0.2, Musée d'ethnographie, Neuchâtel, Switzerland, photo Alain Germond 'Tu seras rose: le fort et le faible'; for Fig 1.1, Private Collection/Bridgeman Art Library, ZAL 151144; for Fig 2.1, Associated Press, 'Illinois Prison', Y13142, 15 October 1971; for Figs 3.1 and 3.2 Abigail Adams, 1993; for Fig 7.1, DISAPPEARING WORLD/ Granada Television Ltd.; for Fig 8.1, Bartholomew Dean; for Fig 10.1, David Lawson from a draft by A. F. Robertson; for Fig 10.2, Mr and Mrs Harry Flood; for Fig 14.1, Laurence Burns; for Fig 16.1, Courtaulds; for Fig 16.3, Associated Press/Mark Lennihan, 'Fashion Kamali', NYR137–2309408, 11 March 1997; for Fig 17.1, Jeremy Panufnik; for Fig 17.2, Associated Press/Vadim Ghirda, 'Romania People Hagman', BUC101–4106414, 11 August 1999; for Fig 20.1, DISAPPEARING WORLD/ Granada Television Ltd; for Fig 22.1, Associated Press/Fluor Daniel, 'Hanford cleanup', KEN101–2493421, 27 January 1998; for Figs 24.1 and Fig 24.4, Arne Kalland; for Fig 24.2, the *Daily Star*; for Fig 24.3, British Columbia Lottery Corporation; for Fig 26.1, Anne-Marie Brisebarre; for Fig 28.1, Associated Press, 'Transkei election, South Africa', N19700, 26 November 1963; for Fig 29.1, Associated Press/ Fotokhronika TASS, 'Khrushchev visits Baku', 202, 26 April 1960; for Fig 30.1, Burma government web site: www.myanmar.com; for Fig 32.1, Private Collection/Christie's Images/Bridgeman Art Library, CH 89261; for Figs 34.1 and 34.2 (c) Phil Sears 1989; for Fig 35.1, Associated Press/Adil Bradlow, 'Lesotho Coronation', MAS191–2302515, 31 October 1997; for Fig 35.2, Associated Press/Jerome Delay, 'Crowds queue to sign condolence book for Diana', 1 September 1997; for 36.1, Associated Press, 27 January 1993; for Fig 37.1, Associated Press/Jean Marc Bouju, 'Rwanda soldier', K1G102, 23 May 1994; for Fig 40.1, Associated Press/Kathy Willens, 'Buenos Aires man reading newspaper', KAW22205stf, 14 June 1982; for Fig 41.1, Associated Press/Liu Heng Shing, 'Mourning Brother', AGA12–2316659, 5 March 1992; for Fig PP3, Royal Literary Fund; for Fig PP7, The Royal Anthropological Institute Photographic Collection.

Every effort has been made to contact copyright holders. Any omissions or errors will be rectified in any subsequent printings if notice is given to the Publishers.

Thanks are due to all the authors for allowing their material to be republished here on the understanding that all royalties go to the RAI.

I am grateful to two anonymous readers for Routledge who supplied stimulating suggestions; to Hastings Donnan and Ray Abrahams, who kindly read drafts of the Introduction; to the Esperanza Trust for a grant to cover the expenses of compiling this anthology; and to Hilary Callan, Jean Fairweather and Arkadiusz Bentowski of the RAI for administrative support; also to Routledge's outstanding editors.

For help over a longer period I would like thank three part-time Deputy Editors, Gustaaf Houtman (now an excellent Editor), John Knight and Sean Kingston, with each of whom it was a privilege to work. Gustaaf's contribution in particular has been innovative and sustained ever since the final year of publication of *RAINews* in 1984.

Thanks are also due to many advisers to *RAINews* and *AT* over the years, and especially to the late Sir Edmund Leach, who warmly supported the venture from the beginning. I am also grateful to the RAI Council for consistently respecting the vital principle of editorial independence.

A number of the articles were originally based on papers given at the annual meetings of the American Anthropological Association.

Introduction

■ JONATHAN BENTHALL

T HIS IS AN ANTHOLOGY OF *Anthropology Today*, more precisely of *RAINews* – which preceded it from 1974 to 1984 – and *Anthropology Today* from 1985 to 2000. I was invited by the publishers to hold a mirror up to an intellectually turbulent quarter-century in anthropology's history. I have written before that editors should see themselves as like earthworms aerating the soil, rather than as divine gardeners. This is a view from the humus.

This Introduction sets out some general themes. The emphasis is on anthropology in Britain; but this bias is balanced in the selection of articles, the majority of which are by American or other non-British authors. Each of the nine sections is preceded by some editorial linking material.

Anthropology as queen of the social sciences, or the misfit?

By 2050, will anthropology still survive as a university discipline, or will it have been asset-stripped into sociology, political science and development economics? When I was appointed Director of the Royal Anthropological Institute is 1974, after employment at the Institute of Contemporary Arts, I naïvely assumed it to be a vessel for a unified 'science of the study of man', as its legal constitution proclaims. Now, only a few heroic individuals still cling to this ideal, which was never as potent anyway in Europe as in the USA. But this Introduction is not another death notice for anthropology.

Much excellent scholarship has been devoted to the history of anthropology, yet if one considers the objects of study which counted as anthropological during the first half of the last century – including the cranial measurements of living populations, hominid fossils, folk tales, comparative religion, patterns of sexual behaviour, kinship charts, tribal artefacts, and archaeological sites not accepted as representing literate civilizations – it looks like a residual category, a receptacle for topics that did not fit into the major disciplines. This was also true of the material objects allocated to the ethnography department of the British Museum, which came to include such diverse things as Central American archaeological finds, almost everything brought to the Museum from Africa, and eastern European folk costumes.

Hence, in part, anthropology's fascination, especially for practitioners and students who by temperament prefer to embrace rather than shun marginality. The archetypal anthropologist is everywhere an 'odd man out', and this can lead to a particularly generous sense of humanity. At the individual level, it is widely recognized – as a result of centuries of Western religious and philosophical thought – that self-realization in an individual life derives from engagement with other persons, or face-to-face reciprocity. One can go further and suggest that the same is true of engagement at the level of other human collectivities and appreciation of their values.

Having no formal training as an anthropologist but given the job of running the Institute, I was in a good position to appreciate the advantages as well as the drawbacks of marginality. The editor's own marginality enabled the bi-monthly *Anthropology Today* to be more successful than most other anthropology journals in holding up a mirror to the discipline, candidly exposing its flaws as well as displaying its strengths.

Anthropology with and without the magic touch

During the second half of the twentieth century, social and cultural anthropology – hereafter to be called 'cultural anthropology' for the sake of simplicity, though a bygone generation of social anthropologists no doubt turns in its graves at the conflation – acquired an impressive momentum and influence. (Physical – now more commonly known as biological – anthropology has largely pursued its own course, adopting a straightforward natural science model and barely troubled by agonizing dilemmas of method and intent, so that the links with cultural anthropology have weakened over the period.) During my twenty-six years as Director of the RAI, I ingested an appreciation of the mystique of cultural anthropology. In retrospect, this had been built up by its forebears such as Frazer, Boas, Malinowski, Radcliffe-Brown and Lévi-Strauss, with a strategic flair only surpassed by that of the founders of psychoanalysis.

I always tried to stress those qualities that made anthropology different: to sum up its exciting combination of intellectual distinction with a whiff of subversiveness: its challenge to the ethnocentric and the parochial. I never knew Evans-Pritchard or Gluckman (to go back no further in the history of the discipline), but this is what Lévi-Strauss, Raymond Firth, Audrey Richards, Edmund Leach, Meyer Fortes, Mary Douglas, Rodney Needham, John Blacking and Julian Pitt-Rivers all seem to have in common, whatever their divergences. That aura of being attached to established tradition but somehow apart from it was more fascinating to me than the alternative, 'shaggy' or 1960s image of the anthropologist who simply tries to dramatize a rejection of Western values. And the RAI – being Victorian and Royal and customarily labelled as either 'august' or 'dusty' or both, but at the same time host to some of the most radical thinking available – seemed to encapsulate this ambivalence. So did the theatrically acrimonious rivalry between Mary Douglas and the late Edmund Leach, two careers with a strongly gendered parallelism, woven around the basic notion of categorical anomaly or 'matter out of place'.[1] The colonial origins of leading figures such as Max Gluckman, Isaac Schapera, Meyer Fortes (South Africa) and Raymond Firth (New Zealand), and the distinctiveness of some major non-Western figures such as M.N. Srinivas and Stanley Tambiah, also seemed to help to keep the anthropological sensibility de-centred.

The spirit still flourishes in some brilliant up-and-coming anthropologists, but heavy institutional pressures now bear down to blur anthropology's singularity. There are the university bureaucrats intent on quantifying academic standards; there are school-leavers hoping to pay back their student loans through planning more lucrative career paths; there are larger disciplines which can plausibly allege, in the competition for resources, that anthropology is a relic of imperial times. In the recent past, British anthropology gained an unearned advantage in this competition, resulting from the decline in the 1970s of the academic reputation of British sociology; and in that intellectual vacuum a whole sub-discipline, the cultural anthropology of Britain, has been developed by a few anthropologists under the inspiration of Anthony Cohen. The extreme position is articulately held by Nigel Rapport, who holds that this should be the core of the discipline since 'all of human life is there', that is in Britain.[2] If a genuinely comparative and broadly based sociology should re-emerge in future, it is likely to do so by appropriating this tradition for itself, which would in turn weaken cultural anthropology.

As regards Rapport's position, I support the view held by the majority of anthropologists, which is that though the discipline has much to offer as an oblique perspective on the forms of life that we find most familiar, it depends indispensably on a constant stream of new information and ideas from overseas fieldwork. If that were to be lost, it would become incorporated in amorphous departments of 'social research', ceasing to attract adventurous minds ready to be challenged by difficult languages and sometimes arduous living conditions. Self-sufficiency or extraversion? There is much to ponder in the metaphor of the anteater and the jaguar, which we owe to the Sherente Indians of central Brazil (see Pot-pourri five).

I got to learn about cultural anthropology from the early 1960s through reading Lévi-Strauss's *Tristes Tropiques* – excerpts from which appeared in the influential monthly *Encounter,* Evans-Pritchard's BBC radio talks, Leach's Reith Lectures, Douglas's *Purity and Danger.* Then there were the popular American books by Margaret Mead, Ruth Benedict, Ashley Montagu. (Much of this ground has been covered in MacClancy and McDonaugh's collection *Popularizing Anthropology.*)[3] Anthropology went through a period of being fashionable. In Britain, the weeklies *New Society* and *The Listener* gave it regular space. It seems that intellectual 'sex appeal' is correlated with media attention and with the ability of academics to exploit a public demand for novelty which the media stoke up.

During the 1980s and 1990s, British cultural anthropology became less successful in satisfying this demand. The last British anthropologist who was also a major public intellectual was Ernest Gellner – and he was better known as a social philosopher. Gellner was to die in 1995 while still in his prime, and Mary Douglas has devoted her years of retirement to important but specialized research on the Hebrew Bible. Leach died in 1989 after some years of illness. In the USA Clifford Geertz, Marshall Sahlins, Nancy Scheper-Hughes and a few others still have a comparable presence in public debates.

In a few countries, such as France and India, leading anthropologists often write articles for the daily press. But in Britain, the museum curator Nigel Barley, a witty iconoclast, is one of the few anthropologists with regular access to the media. Some are known as regional specialists, such as I.M. Lewis on Somalia, or Akbar Ahmed (now moved to the USA) on Pakistan and the Islamic world, while others such as Jean La Fontaine on child sexual abuse, or Alex de Waal on humanitarian aid, have carved a niche in policy-related research. The baton of public intellectual has passed to biological pundits such as Richard Dawkins, Steven Pinker and Lewis Wolpert, while others in disciplines related to anthropology such as (in America) Chomsky and Edward Said have engaged in a passionate political rhetoric, given prestige by their respective academic achievements but not always directly related to them.

By contrast, Britain has excelled in producing 'anthropologists' anthropologists'. Students now enter a discipline dominated by these indoor cult figures rather than by public intellectuals, with the result that it has become rather involuted. This tendency has been aggravated by the sporadic popularity – though not nearly as much in Britain as in the USA – of literary reflexivity, extreme cultural particularism or extravagant political posturing.

Anthropologists' anthropologists have always been vital to the discipline. Their current doyen is Dame Marilyn Strathern, whose deliberately unfocused literary style is much admired and imitated and who (as was Edmund Leach) happens to be an outstanding academic leader as well as a scholar (see Pot-pourri seven). From the recesses of that style have nonetheless emerged some remarkably original insights into issues of public policy: in particular, into the social and ethical implications of the New Reproductive Technologies, and into the need to scrutinize the claims to Intellectual Property Rights. There is a trickle-down into public debate. Anthropologists can be good at locating objects of study which are not, from the standpoint of common sense, obvious or important – and turning them into gold. But the alchemy of intellectual innovation is not often combined with the ability to communicate.

If we may discern a dialectic between the anthropologist as public intellectual and the 'anthropologist's anthropologist', RAINews/AT has tried to make up for the dearth of public intellectuals by reaching out to the wider context. At the beginning of the 1980s, I editorialized in RAINews (no. 36, February 1980) that 'with the same aims as a good salad, to be slim and crisp, RAINews seems fit to survive "the decade of scarcity"'. I could not have been more wrong about the aesthetics of scarcity in the 1980s – a decade which in British middle-class circles would have been more aptly symbolized by lobster Newburg and *crêpe Suzette* than a crisp salad. Perhaps my prediction was merely two or three decades too early. But I added that 'most things worth saying in the 1980s can be said in a short article with references'. Contributors were asked to 'emulate the style of Maine or Lucy Mair rather than those of Frazer or Lévi-Strauss'. Social anthropology's influence had not been strong enough. 'Some of the weaknesses are institutional: *RAINews* ought to be able to help anthropological institutions become stronger, both in Britain and worldwide'. Also – and here I turned out to be more right than I knew – anthropology needed to do more to correct the bias in the other social sciences towards analysing the Third World in purely secular terms.

Ethnographic film

In reaching out to the public, the exception throughout the period under review has been ethnographic film, because of the patronage of television; this was almost unique to Britain and has now come to an end. *RAINews* pioneered the serious critique of anthropological films and television programmes, before the foundation of two specialist journals of visual anthropology. The halcyon days began in the early 1970s with the launch of Granada Television's series *Disappearing World*, which was joined later by the BBC's *Face Values*, *Other People's Lives*, *Worlds Apart* and *Under the Sun*, and by Central Television's *Strangers Abroad*. Some of the Granada films, in particular, achieved surprisingly high viewing figures at peak times such as 9 p.m., which would be unthinkable today. A survey of first-year British undergraduates carried out by *Anthropology Today* in 1990 (6.1, February) revealed clearly that more students were making the decision to read anthropology after seeing films or television programmes than as a result of reading books or journals. The RAI Film Committee, a harmonious consortium of academics and film-makers, provided some leadership during this period in promoting high standards and making ethnographic films more widely available, especially through its biennial film prizes and film festivals.

The halcyon days came to an end in the early to mid-1990s with the beginnings of deregulation of British television. We tried to put moral pressure on the broadcasters to carry on what we regarded as a proud tradition, but in vain. With hindsight, it is now clear that anthropology had benefited from the presence in powerful positions of a few individuals, notably Sir Denis Forman of Granada Television. They – looking back to the great days of early British documentary film and being aware of similar movements in France and America – were temporarily able to override market forces and introduce what must have seemed to their middle managers some strangely esoteric material. It is also true that the formula of ethnographic films on television became rather tired, and the genre is now out of fashion. The last ambitious series was the well-meaning but disappointing series *Millennium* hosted by David Maybury-Lewis and sponsored by the Body Shop.[4] The crowning insult is that the label 'anthropology' is now sometimes used by television programmers to indicate fly-on-the-wall and run-of-the-mill journalistic programmes with a titillating element. For instance, a documentary about a professional gigolo in Sydney will be described as belonging to an 'anthropology strand'. Genuine ethnographic film has retreated to the relatively closed world of anthropological film festivals and conferences. Some commentators consider that the British dependence on television, during what I have called the halcyon days, was a false trail.

Ethnographic film and 'visual anthropology' have been the subject of a number of books, and in this anthology I have limited its coverage to a review by Pat Caplan of a masterpiece of ethnographic film, Tone Bringa's *We Are All Neighbours*, and a sour-ish comment by Marcus Banks published in 1999 on the treachery of British television. Its ambitions have in general declined still further since he wrote his article.

Pure and applied anthropology

Ever since the publication of Douglas's *Purity and Danger*, it has been difficult to keep a straight face when any claims to intellectual purity are advanced, for we have learnt to recognize the symptoms of punitive boundary maintenance. Yet the term 'applied' anthropology has more or less stuck, as if there were really a pure form analogous to pure mathematics. It is not surprising, then, that working, for instance, as an adviser to government or private companies is still commonly seen as second best by professional peers, and that anthropologists who work outside the universities are sometimes made to feel they do not 'belong' – though they may be better paid.

One of the innovations during my directorship of the RAI which I hope will have a lasting impact is the foundation of a new annual award in 1998 to stand alongside its traditional academic awards: the Lucy Mair Medal for Applied Anthropology, which recognizes excellence in using anthropology 'for the relief of poverty or distress, or for the active recognition of human dignity'. The high intellectual standard of the medallists so far has been such as to refute any suggestion that applied anthropology is only for the less gifted.

There was an element of personal tribute to the late Lucy Mair when I persuaded the Council to name the medal after her, for she was made Honorary Secretary of the RAI at the same time as I was appointed Director. Cannily suspicious of the more buccaneering and speculative careers in anthropology, she introduced me to a more 'nuts and bolts' version of the discipline than that which had first excited me. Though far from being a philistine herself, she told me once 'You come from an arts background, and you think man cannot live by bread alone. I say that first of all he needs bread' – a proposition that seemed to me, and still seems, indisputable.

An early exchange in the long, still ongoing debate about applied anthropology and economic development is reprinted in this collection. Glynn Flood was an LSE doctoral student who argued in 1975 that the Ethiopian government's agricultural schemes were ignoring the interests of a nomadic group, the Afar or Danakil, to the extent that they created a 'man-made famine'. A.F. Robertson, a prominent Africanist, replied that Flood's position was meritorious but one-sided, and he offered

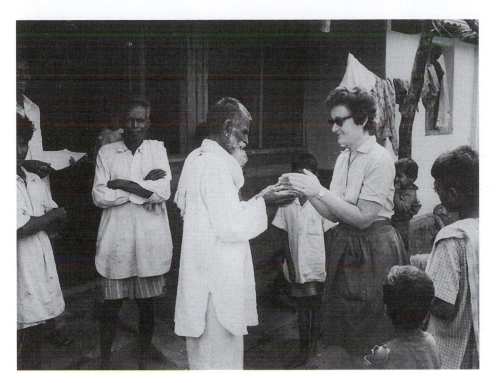

Figure 0.1   Scarlett Epstein, the development anthropologist, doing fieldwork in Mysore, India, 1970s.

a qualified defence of the development scheme. Flood was murdered in the same year by Ethiopian soldiers in the course of their suppression of Afar dissidents. The topical background to this episode – which is bound to be glossed as a cautionary tale for fieldworkers, even if the facts are more equivocal – is that Ethiopia was still much in the news, following the fall of Emperor Haile Selassie the previous year and gruesome television coverage of famine in other parts of Ethiopia.

RAINews – RAI News – started as a tentative affair (partly for in-house reasons explained in an article in MacClancy and McDonaugh's *Popularizing Anthropology*),[5] but the breakthrough came when I attended the World Anthropology Seminar 1977 organized in Houston by Sol Tax and others, under the patronage of Margaret Mead – my first introduction to the messianic strand in anthropology, for Sol Tax believed that 'anthropology can save us'. *RAINews* published as its lead article in February 1978 (no. 24) a piece by Dorothy Willner, an American anthropologist, entitled 'Anthropology and public policy', together with an editorial by myself on Development Anthropology, and another article by one of the few British social anthropologists then working as a freelance development consultant, which argued that anthropologists were taking refuge in over-finicky ethics rather than getting their hands dirty. The editorial noted the promise of medical anthropology because the ethical difficulties presented were relatively minor (shortly afterwards, the RAI was to initiate the very successful biennial Wellcome Medal for Anthropology as Applied to Medical Problems, and medical anthropology has expanded rapidly, especially in the

USA). But it went on to argue that anthropology must get more involved with public policy issues: 'Professional self-interest and altruism appear to coincide. If this is not recognized, social anthropology will become an intellectual mandarinate like Oriental Studies.' I was told by Lucy Mair that this was a 'cheap shot', but in retrospect this was the point at which *RAINews* began to find its feet.

Whereas the debate about anthropology and Third World development has intensified since then, making a convincing contribution to the British economic revival has been rather less easy. When I attempted to stimulate British anthropologists' participation in Industry Year in 1986, I found little in their work to impress hard-nosed industrial journalists, and when one of the latter asked me whether perhaps the best anthropologists did not go into studying industry, I had to admit that this was probably the case. This is a pity because early American industrial sociology was much influenced by the work of Radcliffe-Brown and Malinowski, and in the 1950s and 1960s some outstanding fieldwork in the industrial workplace was done in Britain, for instance Sheila Cunnison's *Wages and Work Allocation: A Study of Social Relations in a Garment Factory*.[6]

Anthropology and journalism

RAINews was the first anthropology journal, or equal first with the short-lived American *Studies in Visual Communication*,[7] to use illustrations as an integral part of the design. More generally, the major innovation of *RAINews* was to introduce quasi-journalistic values into the organ of an academic institution. For instance, in the second issue, an article 'Lying and Deceit' by Mary Douglas (p. 288) was accompanied by a reduced reproduction of a 1973 issue of the *New York Daily News*, showing the recently disgraced Vice-President Spiro Agnew raising his finger defiantly, with the caption '"DAMNED LIES," SAYS AGNEW'. In 1982 we published a lead article by an Argentine anthropologist, Julie Taylor, highly critical of British conduct of the Falklands/Malvinas war (p. 341).

This policy was enhanced when the decision was made to abandon the rather esoteric acronym *RAINews* and the modest printed format, in favour of the new title, explicitly underlining the topicality of the intended subject-matter, and an upgrade of the typography and presentation. Some anthropologists felt it was almost treachery to follow the fashions set by the media. Should not anthropology give special attention to regions and issues which are *neglected* by the media? Some of the most influential 'anthropologists' anthropology' over the last thirty years has been done in Melanesia, for instance, which has been prominently represented in the RAI's flagship journal *Man* (now *JRAI incorporating Man*) but much less in *RAINews/AT*.

There is a problem here. All narrative material from the South – especially of disaster and misery and conflict, but also of the glamorously exotic – may be conceived of as exports to the North, subject to unpredictable shifts of consumer fashion, to political manipulation, and to control of the channels of communication by Northern intermediaries. Anthropology certainly has a responsibility to resist the propagandistic function of the mass media — as powerfully attacked by Chomsky. But if it confines itself to discussing groups and movements that few Western readers have heard of, its audience remains very restricted.

Changes in our micro-climate

During the period we are dealing with, anthropology underwent a number of intellectual transitions, some of which will be seen reflected in this anthology. However, the practical problems of funding also affected its development in Britain. Anthropology has fared no worse than other comparable academic subjects since 1980, when government began to seek to control the universities more closely and to strap down salaries. But anthropology had a privileged position which it lost. An anonymous editorial in the December 1981 issue of *RAINews* foreshadowed major concerns in the discipline ever since.

Early warning in the 1970s was given to social scientists by the now forgotten Senator William Proxmire in the USA, who specialized in drawing the Senate's attention to some of the apparently outlandish social science projects on which taxpayers' monies were being spent. (His first Golden Fleece Award was given in 1975 to the National Science Foundation for spending $84,000 on a study to find out why people fall in love.) Until 1981, the UK's Social Science Research Council had a social anthropology committee which exercised control over its own budget, even if this was small by comparison with the 'big' social sciences such as economics. This committee was abolished in favour of a system of policy-driven committees, and the Council's name was later changed to the Economic and Social Research Council.

Until 1981 British social anthropology was like a family which squabbled internally but closed its ranks against outsiders. In proportion to academic employment prospects, it was over-producing PhDs in large numbers. The loss of its own funding committee was a turning point. The third decennial conference of the Association of Social Anthropologists at Cambridge in 1983 seemed paralysed by the challenge of the new adverse funding climate, and was criticized at the time for sacrificing intellectual content to a preoccupation with careers and employment. But soon anthropologists were forced to turn outside: towards interdisciplinarity, towards more imaginative planning of conferences and workshops, towards new developments in teaching techniques, towards new employment opportunities, towards defending their position more formally as a collectivity. When one thinks of the outstanding 'anthropologists' anthropologists' in Britain, as I have called them, the cult figures, they have nearly all been associated with a few departments of anthropology whose prestige and access to non-state sources of income has kept them relatively insulated from these financial pressures.

Defence of the anthropological patch has been quite successful, but it has resulted in a threat to anthropology's uniqueness. As Editor of *Anthropology Today*,

I tried to maintain a sense of that aura surrounding the discipline which had earlier so impressed me, looking for it particularly in new and unknown authors, and I hope that in the following pages you will find some of it intact up to the present.

Anthropology as a service discipline

Theoretically, anthropology ought perhaps to be queen of the social sciences. In practice, given the peculiar marginality of its traditional subject-matter, it will probably continue to fascinate a few thousand people all over the world and leave the vast majority indifferent. Only in the USA does it have a large professional association to promote it, the American Anthropological Association, and the impression of wealth and power given by its annual meetings in luxury hotels is somewhat illusory. Even in the USA it is a marginal discipline in proportion to the whole of academia, except at the undergraduate level.[8]

It will be argued later in this book that, effective as it may be in colonizing new subject-areas, if anthropology abandons its traditional subject-matter – 'indigenous' peoples, roughly defined – it stands at great risk of being absorbed into political science and development economics. Nonetheless, some influential figures regard the traditional subject-matter as an anachronistic embarrassment. I might have thought this a plausible point of view twenty years ago, but now I am convinced of the opposite.

Chris Hann, writing specifically last May of what he calls 'transitology' – the study of the post-Cold War world, post-socialism, the expansion of the European Union, and so forth – says that 'if economics, political science and sociology form the Premier League . . . anthropology is well down in Division One' (*TLS*, 4 May 2001). For John Gledhill and several other senior members of the profession, the remedy is to seek greater 'institutional clout' through getting across 'the big message about the potential of anthropology', abandoning elitism and getting the subject into schools (*AT*, Dec. 2000). For others, the way forward is getting more anthropologists to appear on television as experts.

My own bitter experience in trying to do all this has persuaded me that it would be best to turn on its head the idea of anthropology as a master discipline. It is better thought of as a service discipline, remaining small but exercising its intellectual power, and its unique access to the marginal and culturally unassimilated, to influence and sometimes infiltrate other, more mainstream disciplines, offering consultation and cooperation. This point of view is not original but indebted to conclusions reached by two of the most sophisticated British exponents of anthropology in an interdisciplinary context, Mary Douglas (see p. 290) and Ronnie Frankenberg, who in 1992 argued at a conference that 'rather than trying to compete with other, larger disciplines . . . anthropologists should select promising lines of research, and move towards consultation and complementarity with other disciplines.' (Frankenberg added that 'it is essential that there should be no compromise on the needs for work in traditional ethnographic sites outside Europe, or for adequate time-depth in designing research programmes so that processes of transition can be tracked'.)[9]

Anthropology has been wonderfully fertile in generating new ideas – compared to its big sister, geography, which has produced practically none – but it has also borrowed voraciously from other disciplines. (Kluckhohn, the American anthropologist, called it an intellectual poaching licence.) It has also influenced other disciplines extensively, and helped in the formation of new disciplines such as women's studies and Black studies which have then overtaken it on the Left. Might we not see it as a kind of ideas processor, which takes theories from other disciplines – biology, sociology, psychology, philosophy, linguistics, cybernetics, literary criticism . . . and subjects them to the fiery ordeal of fieldwork, returning them in a new shape for consumption? In other words, it is an academic *rotisserie* or kiln, depending on which metaphor you prefer.

Let other disciplines aspire to pontificate and dominate institutions. Anthropologists may reflect, with the Anglican Book of Common Prayer, that sometimes in service there can be perfect freedom.

However, I do not expect this point of view to be popular. Clannishness, sectarianism, or what has sometimes been called pseudo-ethnicity, are as rife within the academic world as in all other walks of life. Marshall Sahlins, the American anthropologist, has satirized these tendencies in his pamphlet *Waiting for Foucault*.[10] The 'my Father knew Evans-Pritchard' notion survives, assuming anthropology to be a kind of lineage by apprenticeship – in which students are linked to ancestors through their teachers and teachers' teachers, as in the Church's apostolic succession or the Islamic chain of authorities known as *isnâd*. It is not a scientific notion, valuable as apprenticeship may be in passing on the 'craft' elements in anthropology such as fieldwork techniques.

And I see no reason why anthropology should not adhere to its self-definition as a social science – provided that the term 'science' is defined broadly, both to include the study of meaning and values, which are so central to anthropology, and to do full justice to anthropology's great trump card – which is that it is the only social science which continuously subjects all its own preconceptions to radical interrogation.

The invention of gender

A huge gap separates the anthropology of the early 1970s from today, and that is the invention of gender – a term which until then, when applied to anything other than grammar, tended to have jocular overtones. Even such an excellent introductory text as David Pocock's *Understanding Social Anthropology*, published in 1975, seems heavily dated today in ignoring gender (a problem which MacClancy has tried to deal with in his introduction to Athlone Press's new 1998 edition).[11]

It would be wrong to suggest that *RAINews* and *AT* made a major contribution to the development of feminist anthropology. Marilyn Strathern and Ruth Finnegan, two women editors of the senior journal of the RAI, *Man* – despite its benighted title, which was not neutralized into *The Journal of the Royal Anthropological Institute* until 1995 – made a much more positive contribution. However, having worked at the determinedly progressive Institute of Contemporary Arts in

Figure 0.2 'Spaces in contrast: the strong and the weak': a display in the exhibition 'Les Femmes', Ethnographic Museum, Neuchâtel, 1992.

the early 1970s and organized a mixed media programme there called 'The Body as a Medium of Expression', which explored the use made of non-verbal communication by social minorities, I was sympathetic to feminism in general.

In 1974, I saw feminism as a matter of sexual politics, and as far less significant than ethnic politics. Now I can appreciate the centrality of gender to anthropology, which has been specially well put by Michael Peletz:

> [I]ndeterminacies, paradoxes, and contradictions in representations of gender, are, at least potentially, the most profoundly subversive challenges to all ideologies of social order . . . Such is the case partly because gender differences are among the earliest, least conscious, and most fundamental differences internalised in all societies . . . [C]hallenges to these ideologies necessarily constitute deeply unsettling threats to the most basic categories through which we experience, understand, and represent our selves, intimate (and not so intimate) others, and the universe as a whole.[12]

Without trying to do justice to the intricate mutual relationship of anthropology with the rise of feminism over this period, I would claim that this was linked to a broader sensitization to issues of representation, which may be summed up as the critique of exoticism. Elderly anthropologists, however distinguished, who were left behind by feminism were left behind on the issue of exoticism as well.

The insight in common is that glamorization and subjugation are two sides of the same coin. In an early issue of *RAINews* (no. 14, May/June 1976) Rosemary Firth explained how Edwin Ardener sought to solve the puzzle that women have great saliency in the symbolism and literature of the West, but this is not matched by their position in the structure of social life. Today this no longer seems a puzzle. Women are glamorized or idealized or valued as objects of desire or as close to 'nature', and at the same time often called on to lead more demanding lives than men and not to complain about it. In fact, women are less expendable than men insofar as the reproduction of society is concerned.

Similarly, the way in which 'we' in metropolitan countries picture colonized or formerly colonized peoples betrays an anxiety about our expendability and a fear of unsettling forces such as poverty and mass migration. As John Knight observes in the article about Colin Turnbull reprinted in this collection: 'When Turnbull wrote *The Mountain People* [in 1972], it was generally assumed that the sentimentalization of traditional societies and their depreciation were contradictory processes. We now see them more as reciprocal inversions.' This is an insight that is obliquely indebted to the feminist movement in anthropology.

Fieldwork as intervention

One of the last rolling themes introduced in *Anthropology Today* under my editorship, assisted by Sean Kingston and Alma Gottlieb, was that of the relations between ethnographic fieldworkers and their hosts, especially what we characterized as 'gift relationships'.[13] Earlier issues had explored such topics as whether anthropologists should pay their informants, and the tradition of using local assistants who, in the colonial context, were sometimes given inadequate credit and confined to the status of 'native informants'.

The articles selected here cover the issue of fieldwork as intervention in a wide context. As this anthology goes to press, it seems that the future of grassroots ethnographic fieldwork will be an increasing problem for the discipline, because of a new factor resulting from '11 September 2001': the certainty that covert intelligence services, led by the USA but assisted by its military allies, will teem all over the world more than ever before, especially in Muslim or partially Muslim countries. Suspicion that an ethnographer may be a spy is by no means new (one need only read Rudyard Kipling's *Kim*). American anthropologists such as Ruth Benedict, Margaret Mead and Gregory Bateson worked for their government during the Second World War – and to general approval. But since the controversial Vietnam War, and the ill-fated 'US Army Project Camelot' intended to assist governments in quelling subversion, the professional bodies of anthropology have strongly deprecated such use of anthropological expertise. Will a significant number of anthropologists disregard their professional norms and lend their services to governments in the 'war against terrorism'? Even if they decide not to, will host communities believe in their truthfulness when spies are increasingly disguising themselves as journalists, aid workers and sometimes anthropologists? In case anyone might think I am fabricating this threat, while I was preparing this Introduction for publication I heard Jeremy Paxman, the well-known British broadcaster, in conversation with Nigel Barley on BBC Radio Four's *Start the Week*, ask with his familiar leer: 'What then is the difference between anthropology and espionage, exactly?'[14]

The achievement of most successful ethnographers has been to get past the public lineaments of society, which may or may not be masked, and describe either the neutral parts – society's own back, as it were, which it cannot see itself, except in a mirror – or, with even more difficulty and sensitivity, the areas of highly charged emotional intimacy. To do so necessitates a relationship of trust. The trust which enabled a television team to film *We Are All Neighbours* in Bosnia during the Yugoslav civil war (see p. 179) is just one of countless examples that could be chosen. But now the twenty-first century has taken a new turn. The last quarter of the twentieth century will be looked back on as, in some respects, an age of innocence for the discipline that is committed to reaching the parts the other social sciences don't reach.

Pot-pourri

Rather than reprint those of my own editorials which tried to steer interest towards promising topics, from child-focused ethnography to undocumented immigration, I have made a selection of short pieces by my own hand which attempted a lighter touch. These have been grouped under the heading Pot-pourri – 'a collection of unrelated or disparate items' – and scattered throughout the book.

Editorial note

Misprints and trivial errors have been corrected in this anthology without indication. No attempt has been made to standardize the system of bibliographic references, since it has been the editorial policy to allow authors flexibility in this regard, while generally following the bibliographic guidelines recommended for the Institute's other journal, the quarterly *Journal of the Royal Anthropological Institute*.

Some time in the 1980s, the use of he/him to mean he or she/him or her went out of favour in academic writing. The older usage has not been corrected.

Notes

1   See Richard Fardon's *Mary Douglas: An Intellectual Biography* (London: Routledge, 1999) and the introduction to Volume 2, *Culture and Human Nature*, of *The Essential Edmund Leach* (ed. Stephen Hugh-Jones and James Laidlaw, New Haven, CT: Yale University Press, 2000).

2   See '"Best of British"? The new anthropology of Britain' by Nigel Rapport, *AT*, 16.2, April 2000, 20–2. For dissenting views, see the correspondence columns in the June and August issues.

3   Routledge, 1996.

4   For critical reviews which dwelt on *Millennium*'s glamorization of the primitive see John Knight, 'Making a tribal difference in the modern world', *AT*, 9.1, February 1993, 22–4, and Jonathan Benthall, 'Charisma in cashmere', *New Statesman and Society*, 8 January 1993, 33–4.

5   'Enlarging the context of anthropology: the case of *Anthropology Today*', pp. 135–41 in Jeremy MacClancy and Chris McDonaugh (eds) *Popularizing Anthropology*, London: Routledge, 1996.

6   Tavistock Publications, 1966.

7   Founded in 1974 as *Studies in Anthropology of Visual Communication* by Sol Worth, then co-edited by Jay Ruby and Larry Gross from 1977 to 1986 (title changed to *Studies in Visual Communication* in 1980).

8   As shown in James Peacock's Presidential Address to the American Anthropological Association, Washington, DC, 1995. At his own university (North Carolina, Chapel Hill) the proportion of anthropology to the whole university was on every count less than 1 per cent, except that students taught were more than 15 per cent.

9   Conference report, 'Child-focused research', *AT* 8.2, April 1992, p. 24.

10   Prickly Pear Press, 2000 (3rd edition).

11   David Pocock, *Understanding Social Anthropology*, London: Hodder and Stoughton, 1975; new edition with Introduction by Jeremy MacClancy, London: Athlone Press, 1998.

12   Peletz, Michael (1995) 'Neither reasonable nor responsible: contrasting representations of masculinity in a Malay society', in *Bewitching Women, Pious Men: Gender and Body Politics in Southeast Asia*, ed. Aihwa Ong and Michael G. Peletz (Berkeley: University of California Press), pp. 112–13.

13   *AT* 13.6, December 1997, p. 27.

14   8 October 2001.

PART ONE

Feminine Power

■   JONATHAN BENTHALL

ANTHROPOLOGICAL THEORY tends to date rapidly, so I have chosen
to represent the 'invention of gender' by four articles with strong ethnographic
content, all emphasizing feminine power in one form or another. I hope the juxtaposition will encourage readers to develop their own readings of the data.

The first three articles give evidence of the symbolic power of the feminine in
various all-male Euro-American institutions: ships of the Royal Navy, the Virginia
Military Institute in Lexington (VMI, thinly disguised by a pseudonym) and an
American all-male prison. Of these institutions, the first two have since opened up
to women, in 1990 and 1997 respectively. But prisons, in the USA as nearly everywhere, remain firmly segregated by gender.

Silvia Rodgers had an unusual vantage-point for her doctoral study of the
launching of British naval ships. She first became interested in the tradition when
she was invited to perform a launching ceremony herself – as the wife of the then
Minister for Transport, Bill Rodgers. A specially intriguing observation in her article
is the embarrassment of the Church of England about the naming ritual, analogous
to a Christian baptism but unsupported by any orthodox theology, since a ship is
only metaphorically a female entity and has no actual soul ascribed to her. Proof
of this embarrassment is that, though a high-ranking lady launches the ship, it is
the humble local vicar who provides the blessing, never a bishop or a naval chaplain.

At the time when Rodgers wrote her article, in 1984, women were not allowed
to go to sea in the Navy, or even to spend a night on board. From September 1990,
this changed and they are now eligible for service in all ships except submarines,
mine-clearance diving and commando units. An interview study by the University of
Plymouth, published in 2000, suggests that over the last ten years:

> women at sea have become progressively more integrated into mixed
> manned ships and there is now far greater acceptance of women at sea.

> The majority of those interviewed felt either that the operational effec-
> tiveness of a ship is not adversely affected, or, that it is actually improved
> by having women in a ship's company.[1]

As far I know, no ethnographic research has been carried out.

John M. Coggeshall's '"Ladies" behind bars' is a highly original contribution to the ethnography of prisons – a small but select body of literature pioneered by Erving Goffman. As Coggeshall has written elsewhere, 'prisons . . . provide evidence for the overwhelming strength of culture to modify and supersede oppressive environmental conditions'.[2] In this article he shows how inmates in southern Illinois prisons reconstitute a dual-gender society in a single-gender environment, with a variety of gendered roles: 'daddies', 'kids', 'girls', 'ladies', 'queens', 'gumps' and 'punks', while female guards and staff are reclassified as 'dykes' or inauthentic women.

We may note his entrée: he taught university level courses in two medium-security prisons, which enabled him to conduct participant observation with guards and staff. A resident inmate, instructed ad hoc in ethnographic data collection, then assisted him by conducting further interviews. Coggeshall concludes that 'gender roles and attitudes in prison do not contradict American male values, they merely exaggerate the domination and exploitation already present'. In the absence of follow-up or comparative studies, one can merely recall that 'American culture' is neither as homogeneous nor as static as a cursory reading of Coggeshall's article might suggest. One also wonders whether a study of the Royal Navy pre-1990, conducted by less elevated a personage than a launcher of naval ships, might have revealed a similar re-partition of gendered roles, if in a covert or sublimated form, since at that time open homosexuality was illegal in the British armed services.

Abigail E. Adams gained her access to VMI while teaching at a nearby women's college, and it was a senior officer at the Institute as well as her own students who prompted her to study this copybook rite of passage. As in the naval and penal examples, feminine power seems to pervade all-male institutions.[3]

Adams contributes a brief update on developments at VMI since 1993, when the article was published. I have noted myself that the Ratline is still a source of controversy and emotion, for at the beginning of the 2000–1 academic year two cadets were dismissed and one suspended for disciplinary offences relating to it. The authorities also had to clamp down on illegal 'group protests' of an undisclosed nature (VMI website, 26 September 2001).

The fourth article deals with feminine power in a different way. Conventional feminism often seeks to reduce the differences between men and women, and abhors the segregation that is typically found in African and Islamic societies. **Danièle Kintz** did fieldwork in West Africa, where local forms of Islam are strong, and she shows how the Fulani or Peul take pleasure in dramatizing rather than playing down the difference of gender. Kintz does not accept that Fulani women are economically exploited. More subtly, she shows that whereas the men tend to present stereotyped, serious and rigid models of their society, it is the women who have a more sophisticated, nuanced and humorous view – that social sensitivity to which the anthropologist aspires. We may guess that Kintz's rosy picture of gender segregation may be partly due to her having enjoyed convivial relations with some of the more well-to-do Fulani women.

Kintz's position is that the 'gender' dimension to anthropology, indispensable because of its earlier neglect, does not always take enough account of the opportunities which gender offers for gamesmanship. In another article,[4] she describes the recurrent practice, among elderly Fulani men, of nostalgic lament for the past: 'The world is going to the dogs!' – the unseemly behaviour of women being one of their complaints. The participation of women in development projects becomes much in demand, often by means of more-or-less fictive voluntary associations, in order to satisfy the requirement of external aid agencies for a 'gendered approach'. Meanwhile the women retort, 'Do you hear what lies they [the men] are telling?'

All four articles represent the contribution of anthropology over the last quarter-century to a more subtle understanding of gender than that to be found in old-fashioned 'women's studies'.

Notes

1   Wreford, Commander Katrine (Royal Naval Reserve), 'The integration of women at sea', *Broadsheet 2000* (Ministry of Defence, London).

2   Coggeshall, John M. (1996) 'Prisons' in *Encyclopedia of Cultural Anthropology*, ed. D. Levinson and M. Ember, New York: Holt, pp. 1032–3.

3   I must admit that when accepting this article by Adams, I thought of my own experience in an all-male English secondary boarding school in the 1950s, when the institution of 'fagging' – abolished not long afterwards – facilitated personal relationships between seniors and new boys. New boys were required to run errands, make beds, toast bread, and perform other chores. 'Fagmasters' were expected to take a brotherly interest in their designated fags. (Consistently with the observations of Coggeshall on all-male prisons, at this school a particularly good-looking new boy tended to be labelled a 'tart' by some of his age-group regardless of his personal behaviour.)

4   Kintz, Danièle (1999) 'Le monde est gâté, un example peul de chronophilie'. In *Les Temps du Sahel: En hommage à Edmond Bernus*, Paris: Institut de Recherche pour le Développement.

Chapter 1

Silvia Rodgers

■ FEMININE POWER AT SEA,
RAINews 64, October 1984, pp. 2–4

THE CEREMONY THAT ACCOMPANIES the launch of a Royal Navy ship is classified as a state occasion, performed more frequently than other state occasions and to an audience of thousands. But until now it has never been the subject of research, either historical or anthropological.

If the ceremony of launching looks at first sight like the transition rite that accompanies the ship as she passes from land to water, it soon becomes clear that the critical transition is from the status of an inanimate thing to that of an animate and social being. From being a numbered thing at her launch, the ship receives her name and all that comes with the name. This includes everything that gives her an individual and social identity, her luck, her life essence and her femininity.

My research into the ceremony sheds light not only on the nature and development of the ceremony itself but also on the religious beliefs of sailors, on the symbolic classification of a ship by sailors, on the extensive and reincarnating power of the ship's name, and on the relationship between women and ships and mariners. It is the last aspect on which I want to concentrate here.

Most of us know that sailors refer to a ship by the feminine pronoun. But the extent of the metaphor of the ship as a living, feminine and anthropomorphic being, is not, I think, appreciated. Furthermore, it is this metaphor that shows up the quintessential and extraordinary nature of the launching ceremony. I say 'extraordinary' because this ceremony is unique in our society and any of its auxiliary societies in that it symbolically brings to life an artefact. It looks more like a case of animism than of personification. Its status in the Royal Navy as a state occasion makes all this even more remarkable, particularly as it is accompanied by a service of the established Church.

There are of course other new things that are inaugurated by secular or sacred means. But in none of these instances does the artefact acquire the properties of a living thing, let alone a feminine person. There is the proclivity to personify virtues and institutions in the feminine, but these are not conceptualized as living and human

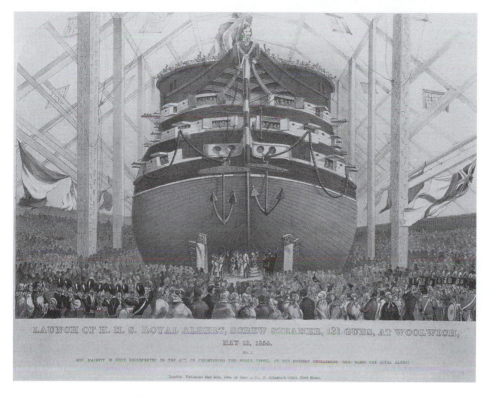

Figure 1.1 Launch of HMS *Royal Albert*, Screw Steamer, 131 Guns, at Woolwich, May 13th 1854 (colour engraving) by English School (19th Century).

beings. Personal articles are given human attributes, with a name and even a gender. But this is not a social rule, nor a rule of grammar, as in the case of the personified ship. Nor is life, name and gender instilled through the public enactment of a prescribed ceremony.

Members of the Royal Navy, and indeed the merchant navies, talk about a ship as having a life, a soul, a spirit, a personality and a character of her own. These notions are not necessarily differentiated, and the terms are used interchangeably. Whether the word 'soul', 'life' or 'spirit' is used depends on the informant. What is constant is the gender of the ship. In the English language, which allows gender only to human beings and animals of determinate sex, it is the rule to refer to a ship as 'she' or 'her'. While reflecting the strength of the metaphor, the rules of grammar also indicate its limit. The linguistic boundary lies in the region of the relative pronoun. According to Fowler it is correct to say: 'The ship that lost her rudder' and 'the *Arethusa* that lost her rudder' or '*Arethusa* who lost her rudder'. Sailors frequently drop the 'the' in front of the name of a ship. They explain that if I went to see a friend I would not say 'I am going to see the Sally' but 'I am going to see Sally' and that this applies to a ship.

The image of the ship as a fictive woman is established in diaries and chronicles, is legally encoded in naval and legal documents, and celebrated in poetry and prose. It survives masculine names, figureheads and the labels East-Indiamen and men-of-war. In the current Royal Navy, as I have indicated, the metaphor is as strong as ever. But what kind of woman is she? A ship is represented as possessing the attributes of more than one category of woman. All are stereotypes that are idealized by sailors. Two images predominate: the all-powerful mother who nurtures and offers womb-like protection; and the enchantress of whom a man can never be certain. Other images intrude, but all inspire romantic and consuming love, awe and constant devotion. When Conrad (1960) writes of 'the mysteries of her [the ship's] feminine nature' and how the love of a man for his ship 'is nearly as great as that of man for a woman, and often as blind', he expresses the sentiments of modern sailors.

Conrad not only depicts vividly the ship as a woman, but brings out the whole environment of being at sea. My informants frequently explain to me, with some emotion and with interesting detail, the reality at sea. It is disorienting, frightening as well as awe-inspiring. This environmental context is crucial when we look for reasons for the feminine nature of the ship. In an environment which is not the natural habitat of human beings, a man may feel himself to be especially vulnerable if as a species he is incompletely represented. That vulnerability could well account for the partnership of an all-male crew with a feminine ship. It is significant that the male and secular principle is complemented not by a secular and natural woman, but by her metaphysical and metaphorical manifestation. Needham (1980) has gathered enough ethnographic evidence from diverse and land-based societies to suggest that the complementary opposition men:women::temporal:mystical is widespread if not archetypal. It is easy to understand that the oceanic environment exacerbates the need for mystical protection that emanates from women. In addition, in circumstances where uncertainty and the likelihood of sudden death is increased, the symbol of rebirth in the form of the mother would be particularly welcome. Nor should we omit to look at the metaphor from the point of view of the archetypal figure of the mother and the mother goddess which according to Neumann is deep within the human psyche. Neumann (1974) also explains how the ship has served as the symbol of the mother, of rebirth, and salvation for many cultures over many periods; and not only for people who go to sea.

It comes as a surprise to find that, unlike the life essence of the ship, the universality of the ship as a symbolic woman is undermined by some ethnographic data. Nevertheless it is very widespread and historical, and cross-cultural material helps to underline the supernatural power of women in the oceanic domain. Hornell (1946) finds that, from the Mediterranean to the Pacific Ocean, and from Ancient Greece to the 20th century, 'ships are generally considered to be feminine'. He believes that the feminine principle is often introduced when the ship is dedicated to her tutelary goddess at the launch. He describes such cases from the coast near Madras. Hornell (1946) points out that sometimes there is an identifiable icon of the deity. Malinowski (1932) relates how the Trobriand canoes are closely associated with the Flying Witches, whose power is on occasion concentrated in the carvings at the prow.

In western societies, from the coasts of pre-classical Mediterranean to Catholic Europe, patron saints of mariners are usually feminine. Figureheads, now no longer extant on British ships, were particularly efficacious if the image was a woman, especially if she was bare-breasted (Kemp 1976). There is some ground for concluding that this icon symbolized the mother who suckled the infant god, and that this made her a powerful intercessor, especially against the devil. However one hardly needs this evidence to recognize the existence of a special relationship between women, ships and mariners in British fleets.

First and foremost is the irrefutable feminine nature of the ship. Then there is the launch at which the two most important personages are both feminine: the ship and her sponsor. It is the role of the sponsor, a woman of high rank by ascription, to exercise her mystical powers to imbue the ship with luck and life by naming her in strict adherence to the ritual detail: the bottle must move, the ship begin to move, the name (the generator of the luck and life) be pronounced – all at the same moment. Anything else augurs bad luck for the ship. Unfortunately, a ship at her launch is hypersensitive towards her sponsor and may react with self-destructive wilfulness to any lapse by the sponsor in her manner of dress or rendition of the formula. There are many accounts of instances when a ship has refused to move or moved too soon, making it impossible for the bottle to break at the right moment. When a ship behaves in this way she puts her own luck at risk, but it is always the sponsor who is blamed. The sponsor's power to bless has inadvertently turned into the power to curse.

There are several ethnographic examples where positive power coexists with negative power in one and the same person: a coexistence that had been spotted earlier by Jacob Grimm (in Briffault 1927). But negative power, where ships of the Royal Navy are concerned, usually emanates from ordinary women. Strict taboos attempt to restrict this harmful influence. A woman on board a ship at night is regarded with particular misgiving. She is bound to bring bad luck, and sophisticated technology is no proof against this. On the contrary, it may itself be a target. This is nicely demonstrated by the true story of the Rolls-Royce engine of a destroyer that blew up when a woman computer programmer had spent the night on board. It was perfectly true that the manufacturers had omitted to drill a critical hole, and the engine could have blown up at any time. But why, the officers wondered, had it blown up on the one night that a woman was on board? (The reasoning is Azande, the granary is water-borne.[1]) The taboos excluding women from critical areas extend to the part of the dockyard where ships are under construction. We know that equivalent taboos are described in a host of ethnographies. They also operate on oil rigs and down coalmines in Britain, and are very stringent in fishing communities here and across the world.

With modern technology no match for the vicissitudes of luck, it is not surprising to find that the ceremony of the launch is as indispensable as ever, and part of the regulations of the Royal Navy. Nor is it surprising that it is still believed that if the bottle fails to break at exactly the right time, the fate of the ship is in doubt.

At the launch of a destroyer in 1975, a distinguished naval officer was alarmed when he thought that the sponsor had failed to break the bottle across the bow. 'After all', he told me, 'I might be in command of her one day'. The role of the sponsor has if anything increased. Advanced technology has made it possible for her to be seen to control not only the mystical but also the technical part of the launching. From 1876, engravings in the *Illustrated London News* portray Royal sponsors setting the ship in motion and releasing the bottle with just a touch of the finger. It may have been coincidental that this overall control mechanism was installed at the same time as the Christian service was added to the ceremony.

But the very existence of a Christian service presents a puzzle. The critical part of the launching ceremony is concerned with imbuing the ship, an artefact, with luck and the soul and personality of a feminine entity — hardly in accord with Christian doctrine. Although this naming ritual has always been called a 'christening', the term is misleading: the subject of the ritual is not a human being but an artefact; the liquid is not water but wine; the celebrant is neither ordained nor male. The duties of the sponsor (or godmother as she is sometimes referred to) are in any case not consistent with that of a Christian godmother, apart from the secular obligations that start after the launch.

The puzzle comes no nearer to solution when one looks at the varying attitudes of ministers of the Church to this ceremony. Some clergymen in the 19th century voiced strong disapproval of the naming ritual and of its being called a baptism. Today, incumbents of parishes local to the shipyards are happy to conduct the service at a launch. The only aspect that continues to baffle them is that no higher-ranking ministers are ever invited to officiate, not even when the Queen Mother is the sponsor. Although the service was inaugurated by the Archbishop of Canterbury in 1875, since then it has been the rule for the local incumbent to conduct it. But if the ceremony of the launch seems to bother the main body of the Church, for naval chaplains the problem is even more complicated. Among the duties of the Chaplain of the Fleet is the keeping up to date of the launching service, and approving the minister chosen to conduct it. Yet, as a senior naval chaplain was at pains to point out to me, according to the Naval Chaplaincy no naval chaplain should himself ever take part in a launching. Incidentally, this same chaplain shares, and with conviction, the view of sailors that the ship is a living and feminine entity, though he does deny the ship her soul, that hallmark of a Christian being.

To understand the religious beliefs of sailors one has to look beyond the tenets of Christianity. The power of a ship's name, the naming ceremony, the metaphor of the ship as a fictive woman, the taboos relating to women: all are part of the beliefs of sailors which they themselves call 'superstitious'. It is well known in our own society that sailors are superstitious. What is not appreciated is that when sailors describe themselves as being superstitious, and they do so frequently, it has none of the usual pejorative connotations. They explain it as a natural consequence of life at sea, which makes them see things in a different way. An acceptable part of their syncretic religion, it comes near to the sense that adhered to *superstitio* in early Classical Rome: a valued and useful quality (Benveniste 1973).

Historical investigation shows that this so-called superstition has always existed in British navies, though specific manifestations may have changed. A ceremony to mark the launch of a new ship seems to have been imperative for centuries. But it has undergone such transformations that it is unrecognizable from, for example, the one performed in Pepys's time. The ship has always been feminine, but the relationship between women and ships had shifted over time. That the power of women has remained confined to the supernatural plane will come as no surprise.

With so much emotion invested in a ship, one may well ask why the demise, unlike the launch, of a Royal Navy ship, is marked only by routine, and not by ritual. The answer must surely lie in the name through which the life, luck and personality survive the body of any one ship. The choice of names is vast, but the same names recur time and again: the present *Ark Royal* is the fifth ship of that name;

the first belonged to Elizabeth I. If a name is outstandingly lucky and illustrious, it is reincarnated more frequently than others. The name as the keeper of life, as integrator into society and its history, has ethnographic parallels. Mauss draws on North American Indian material to show that the name of a person is part of the stock of the tribe, and that it reincarnates the original ancestor ([1950] 1979). When Gronbech describes the power of the names in *The Culture of the Teutons* (1931) he could be writing about names of Royal Navy ships. But unlike the societies studied by Mauss and others, the Fleet, or the society of Royal Navy ships, consists entirely of feminine personages.

Note

1   This is an allusion to Evans-Pritchard's *Witchcraft, Oracles and Magic among the Azande*. Oxford: Clarendon Press (1937). *Editor.*

References

Benveniste, Emil. 1973. *Indo-European Language and Society*. London: Faber.
Briffault, Robert. 1927. *The Mothers: A Study in the Origins of Sentiments and Institutions*, 3 vols. New York: Macmillan.
Conrad, Joseph. 1960. *The Mirror of the Sea*. London: Dent.
Gronbech, V. 1931. *The Culture of the Teutons*. Oxford: Oxford U.P.
Hornell, James. 1946. *Water Transport*. Cambridge: Cambridge U.P.
Kemp, Peter. 1976. *The Oxford Companion of Ships and the Sea*. London: Oxford U.P.
Malinowski, Bronislaw. 1932. *Argonauts of the Western Pacific*. London: Routledge.
Mauss, M. (1950) 1979. *Sociology and Psychology* (trans. B. Brewster). London: Routledge.
Needham, Rodney. 1980. *Reconnaissances*. Toronto: Toronto U.P.
Neumann, E. 1974. *The Great Mother* (trans. R. Manheim). Princeton, NJ: Princeton U.P.

Chapter 2

John M. Coggeshall

■ 'LADIES' BEHIND BARS: A LIMINAL
GENDER AS CULTURAL MIRROR,
Anthropology Today, 4.4, August 1988, pp. 6–8

'**Y**OU HERE TO SEE THE SHOW?'' the inmate leered. The focus of attention was the tall blond then receiving her food in the prison cafeteria. The workers filled her plate with polite deference, and as she walked between the tables her fine blond hair bounced over her shoulders. 'Make you want to leave home?' the guard next to me teased. His joke clarified the significance of the episode I had just witnessed. The object of attention was genetically a male, reconstructed as female according to the perception of gender within the cultural rule system of prison. Behind bars, certain males become redefined as 'ladies'. I have not been able to discern any correlation between assigned gender and the type of crime for which an inmate was sentenced. The process by which this transformation occurs reveals not only clues about gender construction in prison culture, but also suggests perceptions of gender identity in American culture in general.

Prison culture involves one predominant theme: control. To establish identity, males profess a culturally defined image to defend themselves from oppression by guards and other inmates. Men define themselves as males by juxtaposing maleness with femaleness, fabricating gender identity from the reflection. For inmates, the concept of female emerges from the concept of male. To borrow a well-known metaphor, the rib for Eve's creation is taken from Adam's side, and draws both its cultural significance and social status from the extraction. Woman is defined in contrast to man, and takes a lesser place at his side. In prison, males create females in their image, and by doing so, dominate and subjugate them.

The fieldwork upon which this study is based was conducted in two medium-security prisons in southern Illinois between 1984 and 1986.[1] Within that time span I taught three university-level courses to about thirty adult inmates, constituting a range of racial group and criminal record diversity representative of the overall prison population. Their perceptions provided a portion of the field data, supplemented by my observations of and conversations with guards and staff. After having received some instruction on ethnographic data collection, a former student and

Figure 2.1 A guard watches a group of prisoners walking inside Stateville Penitentiary, Illinois, 1971. Aaron Carey 'says he maintains the delicate guard–prisoner relationship by impartial enforcement of rules, impartial treatment and disinterest. He makes it a point "never to concern myself in the slightest with any inmate's personal life".'

then resident inmate, Gene Luetkemeyer, volunteered to collect additional information on 'ladies' behind bars. His nine detailed interviews of various categories of inmates, identified in the text by pseudonyms, significantly enhanced the scope of detail of the study.

Prison culture is extremely complex, and deserves much more detailed study by anthropologists (see for example the treatment by Goffman 1961, Davidson 1983, and Cardozo-Freeman 1984).[2] Even my relatively brief 'incarceration' has suggested numerous leads for future research. Gender identity in prison could be explored in much greater detail, describing for example the abusive context whereby young males might become pawns for an administration concerned with pacifying gangs. Another productive line of inquiry might explore the overall cultural context of gender identity in prison culture, for themes of sexuality pervade prison, indicating its cultural significance for staff as well as inmates.

Gender perceptions of convicts

Here the research concentrates on the gender perceptions of convicts, i.e. the long-term residents (Davidson 1983). Convict attitudes towards homosexual behaviour vary considerably from one individual to the next. Not all participate, and not all do so with the same self-perception or with the same purposes. A subtle distinction is made by many inmates between individuals who engage entirely in submissive, recipient homosexual intercourse, and those who participate in mutual exchange of pleasure. Further distinctions also exist. Certain types or categories of homosexuals, some of which are discussed below, provide a ranking of these attitudes. Despite intra-cultural variation, widespread agreement prevails on cultural definitions of masculine and feminine gender identities.

Inmates have provided various estimates for the amount of homosexual activity in prison.[3] All agree that long-timers are more likely to engage in such practices, for they have less of a future to anticipate, more opportunities for sexual pleasure to utilize, and relatively lenient punishments for violations. For example, Paul and Sandy, homosexual lovers, and Frank, Paul's straight friend, believe that about 65 per cent of their prison population engages in homosexual activity, an estimate supported by Dr B, an incarcerated medical doctor. While such numbers reveal the amount of control and coercion in prisoner culture, they also reveal the 'need for love, affection, [and] intimate relationships' denied by the system, another inmate observes. Some ties are based on affection, but these are relatively rare.[4] Homosexual behaviour fulfils numerous functions in the social and cultural system of prison. Thus most inmates see it as at worst a repugnant necessity and at best a tolerable alternative.

Despite varying views on prevalence, prisoners agree on the general gender constructs in prisoner culture. Males in prison adopt a 'masculine role', inmates assert. Robert describes 'a big . . . macho weight-lifting virile Tom Selleck type guy' as typical of the stereotype. Weight-lifters, in fact, seem to predominate in the category, for strength suggests masculinity. Real men vigorously protest sexual advances from other males by exhibiting a willingness to fight. Men are also seen as preoccupied with sexual gratification, and will obtain it at all costs.

Real men in prison are perceived as those who can keep, satisfy, and protect 'women'. The dominant sex partner is termed a 'daddy', who watches out for and protects his 'kid' or 'girl'. For some men, the acquisition of sex partners strongly resembles courting, where the pursuer flirts with and purchases commissary (snack foods, cosmetics and similar items) for the object of his interest. Others acquire submissive sex partners by force. Ultimately, with either type, sexual partnerships are based on power and control, the complete domination of one person and one gender by another. In fact, domination defines the structure of the relationship which distinguishes the genders in prison.

However, in prison, since the culturally defined females had been males at one time, this presents 'real' men with a gender identity problem: reconciling having sexual intercourse with males while maintaining a masculine self-concept. This adjustment is accomplished by means of a unique folk explanation of the origins of gender development and orientation. Basically, males in prison redefine selected males as females.

In direct contrast to these self-perceptions of males, men portray women in a painting of their own creation. Males see females as passive, subordinate, sexual objects. According to Robert, women are 'sweet and charming', 'fluid of movement', with 'seductive gestures'. Dr B believes that he himself exhibits such effeminate qualities as 'mild manners' and a 'passive demeanour'. Women are also viewed as attractive, and they use that allure to their advantage by feigning helplessness; this allows women to maintain a 'certain power' over men, Paul feels. A woman might 'use her charms' to 'get what she wanted', while at the same time she might not 'put out' sexually, according to Dr B. Women often tease to coerce men, and sometimes withhold what had apparently been promised, he adds.

Of course, nearly all female staff in prison culture do not meet these stereotypes. By inmate definition, then, they must not be women. Such 'non-women' do not challenge gender constructs but reinforce them further. Female guards and staff occupy positions of power and authority over inmates, decidedly atypical for women from a prisoner's perspective. Moreover, most of these women dress in ways to deliberately de-accentuate anatomical differences and to resemble their male counterparts uniformly. Because these women dress as 'non-women' and control men, they cannot be women and must therefore be homosexuals or 'dykes', as the convicts term them. To inmates, this can be the only explanation for women who do not act like women. Cultural reality persists as potentially disruptive anomalies disappear through redefinition.

Trapped between male and female roles

The process by which certain males become redefined as females in prison provides an example of Victor Turner's (1969) concept of liminality. Prisoner culture perceives certain males as being trapped in between male and female, thus necessitating the release of their true gender identities. The period of incarceration provides the 'time out of time' necessary for the transfiguration to occur. In fact, inmate terms for the metamorphosis reveal this gender ambiguity: males 'turn out' these non-males, transforming them into the cultural equivalent of females. The liminal gender is actually 'male as female', betwixt and between both. Such individuals figuratively 'turn out' to be females, reconstructed according to the prisoner cultural stereotypes of 'female'. They thus become their 'true' selves at last.

This duality creates additional complications in self-identity for such men. Goffman (1961) noted the struggle inmates have in reconciling the staff's perception of them from their own self-concept. Inmates readjusting a sexual orientation share a similar problem. Dr B explains that individuals who make the transition from male to female must reconcile past heterosexual behaviour with their present homosexual identity. The homosexual in prison must convince herself that this new self-perception had been her true identity all along. Thus she now has adopted the normal role befitting her identity and gender adjustment.

Vindication for the transformation comes as those forced to become homosexuals remain as such. The acceptance by the homosexual of her new gender identity and associated behaviour justifies the conversion in the eyes of the rest of the prison population. If the 'male becoming female' had no natural proclivity or had not been submissive by nature and thus also female, she would never have agreed to have adopted a feminine identity. As Frank (an inmate) explains, those who surrender are weak, and females are weak. Therefore, those who surrender must be female by nature.

Folk conceptions of the origins of gender further support this perspective.

Tommy (another inmate) notes that all humans are 'conceived as female, then either, as foetuses, develop genitalia or not'. Some individuals perpetuate, even unconsciously, this dualistic foetal identity into adulthood: they can be transformed or 'turned out'. Not resisting, or not resisting aggressively enough, merely validates this gender liminality. In a sense, it is only appropriate that those trapped betwixt and between be released, to unfetter their true natures. Even coercive gender conversion restores the natural order.

Prisoner culture divides homosexuals into several types, each defined on the basis of degree of sexual promiscuity, amount of self-conceptual pride, and severity of coercion used to turn them out. Generally, status declines as sexual promiscuity increases, self-concept decreases, and the types of intensity of coercion used in the conversion process increase.

The highest-status category of homosexuals in prison is that of 'queens' or 'ladies', those who had come out both voluntarily and willingly. Prisoner cultural belief suggests that these individuals had been homosexual on the outside but may have lacked the freedom to have been themselves. Prison has provided them with a treasured opportunity to 'come out', and they have accepted the freedom gratefully. Such individuals maintain a high status by remaining in control of their own lives and of their own self-concept.

Other individuals volunteer to be females, transforming themselves in order to acquire material comforts or social prestige. Terms for this general category vary, depending on the amount of coercion or force needed to 'turn out' the female image. 'Kids', 'gumps' or 'punks' describe individuals who in effect have sold their male identities, surrendering their culturally defined masculinity to be redefined as females.

Many other inmates, however, are forced to become homosexuals against their initial will. According to Wadley (another inmate):

> everyone is tested. The weak – of personality, personal power, willingness to fight, physical frailty, timidity – are especially susceptible.

'Respect is given to one who can control the life of another', he adds. Those unwilling or unable to control others are thus themselves controlled. According to the cultural rules of gender identity in prison, those who dominate, by natural right, are males, and those who submit, by natural temperament, are females.

A forced female role

Individuals forced to adopt a female role have the lowest status, and are termed 'girls', 'kids', 'gumps' or 'punks'. Kids are kept in servitude by others, as a sign of the owner's power and prestige. Gumps are generally owned or kept by a gang, which collects money by prostituting the sexual favours of the unfortunate inmate. A gump may at one time have volunteered to come out to her feminine identity, but due to lack of personal status or power she has been forced to become sexually promiscuous for money or her physical survival. A punk, most agree, initially hesitates, and is turned out by coercion.

However transformed, most homosexuals in prison take on a feminine persona and appearance, even assuming a feminine name and requesting feminine pronouns as referents. The external transformation from male to female often is remarkable. Despite the formal restrictions of a dress code in prison, clothing styles may be manipulated rather patently to proclaim gender identity. Hair is often styled or curled and worn long. Even cosmetics are possible: black felt-tip pens provide eye liner and shadow; kool-aid substitutes for blush; and baby powder disguises prominent cheekbones. The personal appearance of homosexuals enhances their identity by demarcating them as obviously different from men.

Homosexuals perform numerous functions depending upon their status and relative freedom. Generally, the higher the status the more control one has over one's activities and one's life. High-status individuals such as Sandy select their own lovers. These couples live as husbands and wives, with the 'little woman' providing domestic services such as laundry, cell cleaning, grooming and sex.

Those with less status perform much the same tasks, but less voluntarily and with less consideration from their daddies. Once an inmate has been forced to adopt a submissive lifestyle, the nightmare of domination becomes more intense. For example, gumps might be forced to pleasure a gang chief, or may be passed down to soldiers in the gang for enjoyment. A particularly attractive kid might be put 'on the stroll', forced to be a prostitute, for the financial benefit of the gang. Business may prove to be so lucrative that some homosexuals must seek protective custody (solitary confinement) to get some rest.

According to Dr B, some homosexuals actually prefer to be dominated. The prevalent value system in prison suggests that those 'females' who resist sexual attacks vicariously enjoy being dominated physically and sexually by more powerful individuals.

Hated and abused, desired and adored, ladies in prison occupy an important niche: they are the women of that society, constructed as such by the male-based perception of gender identity. In prison, females are termed 'holes' and 'bitches', reflecting the contempt that Dr B believes to be characteristic of society's view of lower-class women in general. In prison, he adds, a homosexual 'is likely to receive much of the contempt [and] pent-up hostility that would otherwise be directed at women . . .'. Herein lies the key to unlocking the deeper significance of gender construction in prisoner culture.

Gender construction in prison

Recall the general inmate perception of this liminal gender in prisoner culture. Homosexuals are owned and protected by daddies, who provide for their material and social comfort. In exchange, they provide sexual gratification. They often sell themselves and their bodies for material objects, promiscuously using their allure to manipulate men and to improve their social status. They feign helplessness in order to control their men. Ladies are emotional, helpless and timid, while at the same time petulant, sassy and demanding, nagging their men for attention. Best suited for certain tasks, homosexuals provide domestic and personal services for their daddies, serving their every whim.

Most fundamentally, homosexuals are sexual objects, to be used, abused and discarded whenever necessary. Passive recipients of male power, they even enjoy being dominated and controlled. Males do them favours by releasing their 'true' female identities through rape. In prison, sexuality equals power. Males have power, females do not, and thus males dominate and exploit the 'weaker sex'.

Ultimately, in whose image and likeness are these 'males as females' created? Genetically female staff and administrators do not fit the stereotypical view, and thus provide no role models for ladies in prison. Males themselves draft the image of female in prison, forming her from their own perceptions. Males 'turned out' as females perform the cultural role allotted to them by males, a role of submission and passivity. In actuality, males produce, direct, cast and write the script for the cultural performance of gender identity behind bars.

In prison, woman is made in contrast to the image and likeness of man. Men define women as 'not men', establishing their own self-identity from the juxtapositioning. Gender as a cultural construct is reflexive; each pole draws meaning from a negation of the other. As in Monteros (Brandes 1980: 205, 207), folk concepts reinforce the differences, emphasizing maleness at the expense of femaleness and the powerful at the expense of the powerless. By means of sexual domination, women remain in a culturally defined place of servitude and submission.

Prison culture as a distorting mirror

It is precisely this concept of gender identity that has proven most disquieting about the status of homosexuals in prison. Granted, prison culture fosters a terribly distorted view of American culture.[5] Nevertheless, one sees a shadowy reflection in the mirror of prisoner culture which remains hauntingly familiar. As ladies are viewed by males in prison culture, so are females perceived by many males in American culture. Gender roles and attitudes in prison do not contradict American male values, they merely exaggerate the domination and exploitation already present. In prison gender constructs, one sees not contrasts but caricatures of gender concepts 'on the street'. Thus, the liminal gender of ladies behind bars presents, in reality, a cultural mirror grotesquely reflecting the predominant sexism of American society in general, despite initiatives by women to redefine their position and change gender relationships.

Notes

The author also published 'Those who surrender are female: prisoner gender identities as cultural mirror', in *Transcending Boundaries: Multi-disciplinary Approaches to the Study of Gender*, ed. Pamela Frese and J.M. Coggeshall, New York: Bergin and Garvey, 1991.

1   A slightly shorter version of this paper was presented at the 1987 American Anthropological Association meetings in Chicago, IL.
2   In my other writings I have discussed various ways in which inmates successfully retaliate to maintain a sense of identity. Much more could be explored, but space constrains discussion.

3   There are obvious implications for study of the spread of the AIDS virus. From my research it seems that most inmates had not yet thought about acquiring AIDS, probably on account of a low self-concept paralleling that of intravenous drug users. Since homosexual behaviour in prison cannot be eliminated, education and protection should be stressed.

4   I do not mean to suggest that homosexual relationships in society at large are similar. In this article, I do not deal with homosexuality outside of prison, nor with affectional homosexuality inside prison, which does exist.

5   Racial distinctions become exaggerated in prison. Some research indicates that prison administrations sometimes deliberately exacerbate racial antagonism to 'divide and conquer' gangs by rewarding leaders with homosexuals of the opposite 'race'.

References

Brandes, Stanley, 1980. *Metaphors of masculinity: sex and status in Andalusian folklore*. Publications of the American Folklore Society (n.s.) Vol.1. Philadelphia: U. of P.P.

Cardozo-Freeman, Inez. 1984. *The joint: language and culture in a maximum-security prison*. Springfield, IL: Thomas.

Davidson, R. Theodore. 1983. *Chicano prisoners: the key to San Quentin*. Prospect Heights, IL: Waveland P.

Goffman, Erving. 1961. *Asylums: essays on the social situation of mental patients and other inmates*. Garden City, NY: Anchor Books.

Turner, Victor. 1969. *The ritual process*. Chicago: Aldine.

Chapter 3

Abigail E. Adams

■ DYKE TO DYKE: RITUAL REPRODUCTION
AT A U.S. MEN'S MILITARY COLLEGE,
Anthropology Today, 9.5, October 1993, pp. 3–6

THE U.S. MILITARY NOW TRAINS women combat pilots (and even closeted homosexuals), but two military colleges are in court to defend their right as state institutions to accept only heterosexual men. This article examines the resistance to enrol women at one of these colleges, which I will refer to as 'South East Military Institute' (SEMI), by analysing the institution's rituals known as the 'Ratline' and 'Break Out'.

SEMI is one of two remaining state-supported men's colleges in the United States, both of which are Southern 'military' schools, although not official U.S. armed service academies (which have been coeducational since 1976). SEMI and its state's government were ordered by U.S. federal courts to either admit women, cut state funding, or create a SEMI-style program elsewhere in the state. The U.S. Supreme Court refused in May to consider SEMI's appeal, and SEMI's governing board this Fall will announce the plan that complies with federal courts – but keeps women from enrolling (Associated Press, 8 August 1993).

SEMI had won an initial 1991 case against the U.S. Department of Justice when a district federal judge accepted SEMI's argument that provides valuable diversity for the state's higher education: 'Excluding women is substantially related to this mission . . . [SEMI] has set its eye on the goal of the citizen-soldier, . . . and I will permit it to continue to do so.'

The decision was an innovative application of political correctness, but was condemned by SEMI's opponents as the work of an 'anachronistic' yet 'powerful old boys' network' (Goodman, 1991), devoted to keeping women out of business, politics and the military. Yet the issue was not about excluding women generally – just excluding them from SEMI. One cadet (student) wrote me, 'Why do women want to open all doors closed to them? . . . Women belong in the military but not at "SEMI".'

'The very thing that women are seeking would no longer be there' if women were admitted, said SEMI's 1992 senior class president. Alum were more adamant:

Figure 3.1   Break Out at the military academy, 1 March 1993.

Figure 3.2   Break Out at the military academy, 1 March 1993.

'The first moment any woman enters [SEMI], she will be fooling herself – because SEMI will cease to exist.'

I stumbled into SEMI's controversy while teaching anthropology at a nearby women's college. My students mentioned SEMI when we studied Melanesian rites of passage. SEMI's Commandant of Students sent our class a videotape of SEMI's freshman or 'Rat' year, and later visited as our guest informant. I found he shared 'the anthropological romance with initiation rites' (Herdt, 1982: xvi). SEMI had won its first case the day before, and both the Commandant and I were intrigued by what ritual analysis would reveal about SEMI's 'uniqueness'. The Commandant asked me to lecture on ritual process at SEMI, and to attend SEMI's major ritual, Break Out. I welcomed the opportunity to leave the armchair – as far as my gender would permit – and study this ineffable 'thing' that women would destroy at SEMI.

SEMI's opponents and supporters have also focused on SEMI's famous regime of 'bizarre psychological and physical ordeals', as distinctive as the cadets' crisp uniforms and buzz cuts (Yoder, 1991). As I watched Break Out in 1993, the ritual seemed less of a 'bizarre ordeal' than a metaphorical birth, an impression which the SEMI cadets corroborated when we analysed the ritual later. I was further struck, not by the intensity of 'hazing', but by the tenderness of the seniors, who are called 'dykes'. Why, at a school dedicated to heterosexual men, would its major ritual recall childbirth and its central role, female homosexuality?

Men's rituals: here, there but not everywhere

My students were right: SEMI's 'Ratline', Break Out, and 'dyke' system fit perfectly with Van Gennep's tripartite scheme of separation, liminality and re-aggregation (1960). SEMI's method for creating the 'citizen-soldier' includes three missions of military discipline, academics and athletics, but at its heart is the Ratline. In SEMI parlance, the Ratline is 'the longest distance between two points', exaggerated routes around campus that freshmen had to follow, but in general it refers to the seven months of initiation they must endure to become cadets.

The question of why men need and participate in initiation rituals has re-emerged along with the 'men's movement'. Previously, arguments centred on the psychoanalytic, such as the thesis that these rites break boys from identifying with and depending on mothers (Whiting et al., 1967), or Bettelheim's idea that men express and resolve 'womb envy' by culturally creating ritual analogies of what women do 'naturally': create people (1954).

Why then don't *all* societies have male cults? Robert Bly (1990) suggests that U.S. men particularly need initiation rituals in post-World War 2 society, because as fathers left the home for work, boys lost their male role model.

It was the early literature on the male cults of Melanesia and Amazonia that initially reminded my students of SEMI's rituals. These writings described these societies as having unilineal descent systems that emphasize sexual polarities, in which one sex forms the core of a local group, and the Other sex are the affines, aliens, spies, possibly enemies (Murphy, 1959; Allen, 1967). SEMI was conceived of in 1834, the beginning of the Victorian era, certainly a period of sexual polarities. The antebellum upperclassmen took pride in winnowing out the 'weak' and creating manhood for the survivors, claiming, 'Give us your boy and we'll send you a man.' They also invented some of the harshest hazing methods of the Ratline: the 'company room', a nightly session of corporal punishment and exercise; 'sweat parties', a company room conducted in a steam-filled shower room; 'straining' and 'finning out', which are taxing postures that Rats must hold; and 'fagging', or menially serving upperclassmen (Wise, 1978).

It was only after the World War 2 era that Break Out was created as a formal culmination to the Ratline experience. Originally it was called 'Bloody Sunday', and Rats had to run a gauntlet of the bodies and fists of upperclassmen, including seniors. Later classes of Rats 'ran the stoops', fighting their way up the barracks' flights of steps over mattresses, juniors and sophomores, but aided by seniors.

Today, by contrast with the Melanesian and the Victorian era SEMI cults, secrecy and cruelty are not so important (President Reagan starred in a 1938 Hollywood movie about SEMI, *Brother Rat*). Many of the techniques resemble Outward Bound, EST and other 'New Age' consciousness-raising programs. However, like other male cults, the predominating metaphors of SEMI's Ratline still emphasize and transform sexuality, childhood and family.

Separation: SEMI's unique method

From the first day 'in barracks', the entering class is separated from previous life, but also from SEMI as 'rats' (the epitome of a liminal animal), 'the lowest form of life . . . but still higher than anything *outside*' stated a cadet. They enter an upside-down world of unpredictable rules, space and time. The Ratline is administered by the upperclassmen in the barracks: the four floors of unlocked, spartan dormitory rooms, organized in balconies, outside staircases and communal bathrooms around a central courtyard, which are ranked by class from the ground floor of the senior class to the fourth floor of entering class. This is 'home' for 1,300 cadets. Right away the new students find it is *not* like home:

> When the class of 1980 arrived in August, it was greeted by veterans [who] were polite and friendly and put the new [students] to bed that night without introducing them to the rat system. But the same night they hauled them out of bed . . . (Wise, 1978).

The Rats are stripped of young manhood and infantilized: put to bed, yelled at in baby talk, told how to eat, how to bathe, how to walk, how to talk. Like babies, their bodies are not their own. They are reduced to the 'sucklings' that Victor Turner described in *The Ritual Process*.

The 'suckling' imagery is used as well by SEMI cadets to subordinate. Classmates resist and insult each other and lowerclassmen with 'You suck' or 'Suck it in'. Another tradition is called the Rape of the First Sentinel. When the first Rat marches 'guard detail', he is attacked by the seniors, who rip off parts of his clothing, spray him with shaving cream, and throw days-old food and used chewing tobacco on him. Said 1990s Rat sentinel '*It* sucked' [emphasis mine], successfully externalizing the 'rape'. His accosters reported, 'Pretty good rat. He took it like a man' (*The Cadet* 1990).

Before 'Break Out', some one-third of the entering class has left, either drop-
ping out or not meeting the requirements. Those who remain have dissolved into
the mass of 'good rats . . . low profile, subservient, doesn't stand out'. This is the
epitome of the highly valued 'Rat Unity', a bonding and levelling said to be essential for survival. But each also has a special Rat Daddy or 'dyke', a senior who serves
as his mentor and advocate. The Rat/aide helps his senior 'dyke (deck) out' or
dress, and, previously, did 'light fagging such as running a few errands', making the
dyke's bed, shining his shoes. The Rat receives advice and haven from his senior
dyke, whom he had the privilege of visiting 'informally' (Wise, 1978: 298).

Liminality: Break Out

Break Out is announced during the last month of winter. After morning classes end,
the upperclassmen 'resurrect' Rat discipline, and have one hour to 'purge' themselves using the harsher measures. Juniors and sophomores taunt the Rats, while
the seniors encourage them: 'You'll make it.' The Rats are marched to an audito-
rium where the senior class president tells them to do well, because after graduation,
'all we leave behind is you'. Then they run to Break Out field, on the 'outskirts'
(Nelson, 1993) of the campus, which the town's firetruck has sprayed to create a
medium of mud.

The Rats crawl on their bellies through the mud some 50 yards to a first 10-
foot high bank. As they crawl, upperclassmen of juniors and sophomores attack
them, shout at them, push them to their bellies, sit on them, pull them back by
their legs, fill their faces and clothes and 'all orifices' with the mud. By the time
the Rats reach the first bank, their eyes and ears are filled with mud, and they can
barely grope their way along. Many Rats have lost their pants. They cannot tell who
is friend, fellow Rat or foe. At the base of the bank, they scramble over each other
towards the top, but are pushed down by sophomores and juniors. Some Rats try
to help each other in an effort at 'Rat Unity'; however, it is largely their seniors
who help them up. At the top of the first bank, the sophomores and juniors toss
the Rats into a water ditch, pull them out and push them up another bank of brush.

Integration: dyke to dyke

Only when they have gotten to the top of the second bank is the ordeal over. The
seniors rush to greet them, tenderly wash the mud out of their eyes and ears,
and wrap them in their own blankets. At this point, dykes embrace each other, take
photos and pose for the professional video cameraman. The Rats run back to the
rear of barracks, where their dykes hose them down *en masse*, and give them dry
clothes. According to my cadet informants, the moment when the seniors wash
away the Rats' mud is their 'incorporation' into the corps of cadets.

Several alumni and parents anxiously wait on the path returning from Break
Out field, although they are urged not to attend. 'Go get 'em, Killer!' shouts one.
Upperclassmen lead them in cheers and exercise chants about impregnating local
women. As night falls, the entire 'corps of cadets' assembles in the barracks' court-

yard. Each class gives their cheer, including the freshmen. They are no longer called Rats, except Brother Rat by classmates. They are 'part of the SEMI *corps* of cadets', but not until graduation will they become 'SEMI men'.

Engenderings: monstrous mothers and dyke fathers

Break Out struck me as a birth from which the newborn emerges blinded and covered by birth fluids, to be cleaned up and blanketed. One observer commented how the Rats in their belly-scramble across the mud field resemble the cartoon sperms in the old health class movies, competing to overcome the vagina's obstacles, penetrate the egg and conceive life. Given the metaphor of the ritual as birth rather than conception, one could almost see the ritual as a Super-birth, in which all the sperms have won and all the babies are born. The Super-birth has an accelerated gestation of seven months and delivery of one to two hours. In the Super-womb of SEMI (always referred to as 'She'), the Super-foetuses are actively conditioned and will 'labour' their way to their daddies, after 'breaking the water' of the ditch.

Break Out also transforms the Ratline's gender benders in which the Rats are sterile, effeminate, and subordinate: babies, dyke 'wives', and 'passive' homosexuals. Immediately after their birth, they become virile, active, even 'Killers', whose first feeding will be a special steak dinner from their Rat Daddies.

If the seniors are the fathers, who are the mothers? The mud identifies them: the juniors and sophomores who become one with the womb/field, as their bright yellow sweats become caked with the medium created by the phallic fire-engine spray that the seniors have arranged. I suggest that the Rat 'line' symbolizes ties with mothers, or at SEMI, with the juniors and sophomores, who deliver most of the hazing. It is the umbilical cord connected to monstrous mothers, who rule over a childhood of rules one doesn't write, punishment one doesn't deserve, and a hier-archical enmeshment that one can't break.

The upperclassmen also use the imagery of rapists: sexual, sterile, but powerful. Ethnographers have documented how the threat of homosexual rape sets hierarchies in all-male settings like prisons and fraternities (Sanday, 1990; Blake, 1971). But juniors and sophomores lose their power in Break Out, their ability like mothers or rapists to hold 'the corps'/the body from manhood. They will only regain power by becoming 'dykes' as seniors.

'Dyke' refers to SEMI's dress uniform, and to the Rat himself. 'A rat often takes on the traits of his dyke' (Wise, 1978). For Break Out, many Rats shave into their buzz cuts their class year and the year of their senior dykes. The term 'dyke', then, is a clear example of teknonymy[1] in which the reciprocal term denotes how the Rat and the Senior create each other.

'"It is the first classmen's most important relationship", stated a former Commandant of Students, "until they are married and have children of their own"' (Wise, 1978). In fact, a senior told the SEMI counsellor that being a dyke 'is like having my own child'. 'They feel a paternal instinct towards them', the counsellor concluded. In 1990, when a group of Rats attacked a rival school's mascot at an off-campus football game and broke several spectators' bones, the senior class took full responsibility like parents for minor children (*The Cadet*, 1990).

The parenting may be paternity, but it is also ambiguous. Rat Daddy is in fact 'a *combination* of your mother, father, and older brother' (*The Bullet*, 1990). The Rat Daddies' role in Break Out is both the doctor's work of delivery, and the nurses' 'dirty' work of washing and eventually feeding the newborn (Ortner, 1974).

The role's ambiguity is highlighted by the term, 'dyke', which since the 1920s commonly refers to homosexual women (Mills, 1989). In fact, this current usage may derive from the military term, and the domestic nature of the military officer's aide. One may argue that the word doesn't carry the modern – and negative – connotation within SEMI's tradition-laden world of meanings. But a 'dyke' may also be seen as someone who can bear and nurture children, participates in same-sex relations, and does not have subordinate or subordinating sexual relations with men.

Perhaps the seniors are best seen as 'dyke midwives' in the ritual, mediating between and transforming these parallel series of sexual roles: infant/mother/father; cocksucker/homosexual rapist/dyke; wife/mother/midwife. The dyke midwife is the powerful mediating point, who creates 'mothers' out of wives, and their own redeeming 'dyke' paternity. SEMI cadets 'matriculate' into wifehood and motherhood and graduate into 'SEMI manhood' and grandpaternity.

Ritual reproduction and unilineal descent

The question still remains: why can't women attend SEMI? SEMI does socialize its cadets to be 'gentlemen' with explicit instructions on how to treat 'ladies'. Cadets are taught to set women apart, rather than to mentor, lead or work with women. This paternalism infuriates those who view SEMI as a patriarchal institution. In fact, given SEMI's emphasis on creating mentors out of teenagers, women might do quite well, given their head start in relational skills.

The most informative statement was from the thoughtful cadet who stopped telling me what women could or couldn't endure and said simply '*I* could never do "it" [the hazing?] to a woman.' At SEMI, a 'gentleman does not so much as lay a finger on a lady', states the Rat Bible. Instead, SEMI's procreation is monosexual, establishing a patrilineal descent kinline through an inversion of childbirth, in which the foetus and father can take control of the generating body. Women are peripheral to SEMI and have no maternal rights, although they are necessary to establish the cadets' heterosexuality. In Ring Figure, the formal dance when the juniors receive their class rings, the cadets and their dates (no one attends 'stag', alone) create the 'figure' of their class year on the dance floor.

I propose that the fight is not over keeping women out of men's domains; there *is* a 'woman' (in fact several) in SEMI's body/corps (cf. Martin, 1987) and rituals. SEMI has created a unilineal descent system of fictitious kin through its alliance with the state. But now SEMI's men are fighting for their reproductive rights and family welfare, even after being turned down by the Supreme Court in 1993. In an interesting twist, SEMI and the old boys have joined the pro-choice battle.

Notes

I would like to thank SEMI's Commandant of Students, the professors of its Behavioral Science and Leadership Department, and its corps of cadets, particularly the juniors and seniors. They invited me to attend Break Out, freely shared their insights on the ritual and the court case, and critiqued my initial ritual analysis. Nancie S. Gonzalez urged me to write up the SEMI ritual analysis. Thanks also to Susan McKinnon, Fred Damon and Sandra Bamford at the University of Virginia, Belle Edson of Hollins College, and the Hollins and University of Virginia students of my Symbol and Ritual courses.

I owe special thanks to 'fellow' graduate student Anna Lawson and husband Tom Lawson. Without their combined expertise in anthropology, SEMI and editing, this process would have been a lot less interesting.

1   Teknonymy: the custom of identifying a person with a name which marks him/her as parent of a child.

References

Allen, Michael. 1967. *Male Cults and Secret Initiations in Melanesia*. Melbourne: Melbourne U.P.

Bettelheim, Bruno. 1954. *Symbolic Wounds: Puberty rites and the envious male*. New York: Collier.

Blake, James. 1971. *The Joint*. New York: Doubleday.

Bly, Robert. 1990. *Iron John: A book about men*. Reading, MA: Addision-Wesley.

The Bullet. 1989. 'South East Military Institute.'

Goodman, Ellen. 1991. *Washington Post* 22 June.

Herdt, Gilbert H., ed. 1982. *Rituals of Manhood: Male initiation in Papua New Guinea*. Berkeley: U. of California P.

Kiser, Judge Jackson L. 1991. 17 June decision.

Martin, Emily. 1987. *The Woman in the Body: A cultural analysis of reproduction*. Boston: Beacon P.

Mills, Jane. 1989. *Womanwords: A dictionary of words about women*. New York: Free P.

Murphy, Robert F. 1959. Social structure and sex antagonism. *Southwestern Journal of Anthropology* 15(2):89–98.

Nelson, Diane. 1993. 'Rigoberta Menchu Jokes', Paper presented at 13th International Congress of Anthropological and Ethnological Sciences, Mexico City.

Ortner, Sherry. 1974. 'Is Female to Male as Nature is to Culture?' in *Woman, Culture and Society*, ed. M.Z. Rosaldo and L. Lamphere. Stanford: Stanford U.P.

Sanday, Peggy Reeves. 1990. *Fraternity Gang Rape: Sex, brotherhood, and privilege on campus*. New York: New York U.P.

Turner, Victor. 1969. *The Ritual Process*. Chicago: Aldine.

Van Gennep, Arnold. 1909 (1960). *The Rites of Passage*. Chicago: Chicago U.P.

Whiting, John et al. 1967. 'The function of male initiation ceremonies at puberty', in *Personality and Social Life*, R. Endelman, ed., New York: Random House.

Wise, Henry A. 1978. *Drawing Out the Man*. Charlottesville: U. of Virginia.

Yoder, Edwin. 1991. *Washington Post*, 22 June.

Update by Abigail E. Adams, 2001

The Virginia Military Institute (VMI) has now admitted – and graduated on May 2001 – its first women citizen-soldiers, but only after a legal battle leading to the U.S. Supreme Court and to the founding of an all-women's program elsewhere.

After the U.S. Justice Department challenged VMI's single-sex admission policy in 1991, VMI was ordered to admit women, cut state funding, or develop a 'creative/parallel program elsewhere'. VMI chose the third option. The solution as stated by VMI was to 'provide to college-age women in Virginia a state-supported, single-sex educational program whose graduates, like the graduates of the Virginia Military Institute, have been educated and trained as citizen-soldiers', but based on the 'physiological and psychological differences between men and women'. Thirty-five miles up the road, tiny Mary Baldwin College, a woman's college, opened the Virginia Women's Institute for Leadership Studies (VWIL) in Fall 1995, with an initial class of 42 women.

Mary Baldwin's VWIL program continues, but it did not save all-male VMI. On 27 June 1996, the Supreme Court ruled that VMI must admit women or give up public funds. The VMI Board of Visitors announced the following September that it would develop a public coeducational programme, but that 'we do not anticipate any changes at all, with the single exception of changes necessary to accommodate the needs of physical dignity'. And so, on 18 August 1997, thirty women lined up to receive the exact same buzz cut as their brother Rats.

There have been ups, downs, and drop-outs of VMI women students since (just as there have always been for VMI's men students), but nothing approaching the targeted public humiliation of Shannon Faulkner, the first woman matriculant, who left early in her first semester, Fall 1995. As I predicted in a June 1996 interview, VMI has adapted to the entrance of women students – as it has adapted in its long history to including non-Virginians, foreigners and African-Americans. Indeed, VMI's upper-class students, who run the Ratline, have now replaced Break Out, as the culminating event for the first year students, with a 'long weekend' in physical and field challenges, including an overnight forced march to the site of the Civil War battle of New Market, in which ten VMI lost their lives helping to turn back the Union forces. Today the numbers of applications are on the upswing, and over 100 women applied for the class of 2005.

References

Adams, Abigail E. 1997. 'The "military" academy: VMI and metaphors of masculinity or pedagogy and public life', in *Wives and Warriors: A Study of Women and the Military in the United States and Canada*, Laurie Weinstein and Christie White, eds. Westport, CT: Bergin and Garvey.

Brodie, Laura Fairchild. 2000. *Breaking Out: VMI and the Coming of Women*. New York: Pantheon Books.

Chapter 4

Danièle Kintz

■ FORMAL MEN, INFORMAL WOMEN: HOW THE FULANI SUPPORT THEIR ANTHROPOLOGISTS,
Anthropology Today, 5.6, December 1989, pp. 12–14

THE TERM *FORMAL* ALLUDES primarily to form or appearance as opposed to matter or content. But in English (and increasingly in French too) the word 'informal' (*informel*) has taken on the secondary meaning of 'unofficial'; and we can describe persons, and not simply acts or situations, as being formal or informal. The distinction helps me to explain how my informants, male and female, in the Central African Republic in 1988 managed to present me with their society on a plate.

Fulani societies,[1] spread as they are throughout the Sahel from Mauretania and Senegal to Sudan, and also in all the coastal countries of West Africa as well as in part of Central Africa, are similar but different, showing a strong unity but no uniformity. It is as if certain Fulani groups but not all of them – that would be too simple – had decided to help their anthropologists, who would be otherwise be lost, by proposing to them a model of Fulani society set out clearly, perfectly visible, including also an explanatory notice for those who would like to investigate the functioning of the model. To make things even clearer, it is the men – who have a look quite different from that of the women, admitting of no error – who present the model and the women who provide the notice.

The chic of segregation

All societies provide some form of segregation, social in general and by gender in particular, even those which deny and disclaim it. (In France, examples are legion, one of the best I know being that of a woman such as myself going to buy spare parts for a car. The scale of the transgression is measurable from the movements and the words of rejection and quasi-refusal from the so-called salesman. Try it . . .)

The Fulani have developed their segregative system with a hierarchy of social value. To each given social position corresponds some degree of gender segregation;

if one increases this, one can receive in exchange an equivalent in social esteem. But watch out! You must know up to what point you can exaggerate: adopting the segregative attitudes of chiefs when one is not a chief leads only to ridicule.

Gender segregation among the Fulani presents the following traits which I shall analyse in turn:

1.   It must be proportional to social position, each influencing the other.
2.   It is always ostentatious, for why put on airs when there are no witnesses?
3.   It governs everyday behaviour and organizes its space according to complicated procedures whereby everyone's art of living is expressed.

In all Fulani groups, there exist forms of organized segregation, at least among the chiefs and, to a less systematically marked degree, among the marabouts. For segregation is chic, elegant, important. However, the wives of chiefs have, like their husbands, more prestige than most of their fellow-citizens and they receive many visitors of both sexes. One cannot therefore take the view that they are hidden from the domains of political power. Nor do they present themselves as constrained by men to keep their distance: I have never heard this opinion, and we must beware of the ethnocentrism of Northern countries which is so quick to interpret phenomena against its own grid. How does gender segregation become chic? A high-status Fulani woman will sometimes say, with visible satisfaction, 'I never go out of my courtyard.'

That shows three things. First, in fact she does go out of her courtyard less than most other women do, but there is nobody who never goes out: there are always *some* opportunities to go out: for religious duties, or for health (one's own or other people's), or for visits of congratulation and condolence, or the organization of social, economic or family activities. Second, there are people who can carry out obligatory visits for her – to the well or the market – and so she has a large domestic entourage of descendants of captives, servants, dependants, children. And, finally, her social status is such that others visit her at her home, and there are very few visits that she must make herself.

Let us add that in the hot countries where the Fulani live, countries where much time is spent out of doors night and day (even if only in one's own courtyard), European notions of 'taking the air', 'going for a walk' or 'going out' have no meaning or interest. Value is given to showing oneself only on rare occasions and in certain conditions, and above all to not having to go out to do the vulgar tasks which the majority of people under the sun of Africa are tied to.

Whatever the Fulani group under consideration, it always includes at least some women who 'never' leave their courtyards. But these women are more numerous among the urban or wealthy Fulani or among fervent (or ostentatious) Muslims, and especially among Fulani who possess two or three of these characteristics.

In the Central African Republic, where I did my most recent fieldwork, the Fulani are rich in cattle and trade compared to either the Fulani of the Sahel or the other peoples of the CAR. Fulani women in villages or towns, sometimes rich in cattle themselves on their own account, have their domestic staff. Thus it is possible to cross a Fulani village in the CAR without ever seeing a single Fulani woman. The only Fulani women whom one sees there sometimes in the streets, markets or villages are those who have come from the encampments to sell milk where there are some customers. These women are the most peasant-like in their way of life and their economic activity, and also in the attitude of the other women towards them. They can in some cases be rich in cattle themselves but their tradition is not urban: they follow directly the circuits of animal production in the countryside.

How to make gender segregation apparent? How to be sure that it escapes nobody's attention? It is not enough that women avoid being seen in public: they must be seen not to be seen. For example, if surprised, they make off in an agitated manner, not furtively as they would if they hoped not to be seen. When a woman's husband entertains male friends, he does so in a room used for that purpose opening onto the outside, so that the wife brings food to the limit of her segregative space, and her husband serves it to the guests. The husband *could* go and fetch the food from right inside the courtyard, the wife *could* decide not to show herself at all but to send a child to announce that the dishes have been put down behind the fence. Generally she chooses to show just a little of herself so that it escapes none of her guests' attention that she disappears immediately.

It is important that the practice of segregation is visible because it is a sign of social prestige: for the whole family, men and women. The more numerous and highly regarded the guests, and the larger the village, in other words the more there is of a public, the more segregation is practised and ostentatiously underlined. It is a way of life where protocol matters, and in the absence of a public it loses its meaning and utility in terms of social prestige. The less this public is known, and the less frequent its visits, the less strong are bonds of kinship and alliance, and the more carefully put into practice is segregation. Certain members of the family are honoured by an identical treatment to that given to strangers, especially a man or a woman's parents-in-law; for when these are present, one has to show them how well-brought-up and so how segregated one is.

Double circuits

Segregation is certainly not more difficult to live with than mixing of the sexes (and of course, these very notions are culturally determined), but it is more complicated to organize, especially in space. Double channels of circulation for individuals must be provided for: this duplication being required for women who 'never' go out and who cannot be seen in public, on roads and paths or in markets.

So a small Fulani village in the CAR (or the Fulani part of a polyethnic village, the Fulani part being called 'Hausa', which in this case means 'trader') is generally crossed by a road or path along which are found public places: shops, mosques, communal wells, markets. All Fulani courtyards include a shelter, a place for conversation, a shop or porch giving onto a road: you only see men there and it is they who receive visitors, Fulani and other, who are generally men. When a Fulani woman has to come by way of this male space, for instance when she arrives by car, she crosses as quickly as possible – ostensibly – and those men who know her, or are related to her, and can pay her a visit, do so afterwards inside the courtyard.

This men's space is separated from the rest of the family courtyard by a fence of plaited straw, much more rarely by a cob wall, which is more socially prestigious.

Of the building materials, straw is the least valued, having a peasant look, then comes cob, but cement blocks are the most prestigious of the three. In the court-yard, each woman has a personal house for herself and her children. Normally a Fulani man does not have his own house. He stays in his wife's house – in peasant surroundings where the houses are straw huts, these are built by women, but the cob and cement houses are put up by men – or in his wives' houses if he is poly-gynous. However, sometimes men, especially the oldest and richest ones, build a personal house for themselves as well.

All courtyards have a way out on the side of the open countryside (opposite the way out that leads into the road) and women use it when they have to devote themselves to occupations of an agricultural, pastoral, domestic or social kind. These ways out leading to the countryside are sometimes also used by men who do not wish people to see from the road where they are going. Thus, if a man uses these ways out, it is clear that he wants to be discreet, which results in discussion inside the courtyard about where he may be going.

Moreover, the courtyards all communicate with one another and women go frequently to one another's houses by a circuit parallel to that of the road. If the village is grouped on the two sides of the road, there are two circuits parallel to the road, which hence must sometimes be crossed. This is done furtively, or *appar-ently* furtively, at a half-run, or for preference at night (if one is not seen, there is no crossing).

Gender segregation results then in a particular organization of the way indi-viduals circulate, to which both men and women bring a good deal of care, and which gives everyone an evident pleasure in the form of a social game, where good upbringing is expressed in the art of knowing how to play it and how to break the rules when the opportunity arises.

The material form of the distinction between the men's domain and the women's is a fence. This is never a hermetic closure: you can see very well between two blades of straw, and walls of cob or cement rapidly develop faults, which can be expanded. Moreover, you hear everything on either side of the fence, and that is why women go away from it when speaking to one another.

But the fence is at the same time a materialization of (among other things) distinct social and intellectual behaviours and of modes of expression which are also inverted.

The support that the Fulani give to their anthropologists

Men are committed to a social façade, a serious demeanour, a stereotyped discourse about their society: these are the phenomena which one has access to from the road and which are shown externally. Here we find descriptions of chiefships, their official role, the organization of a society and its methods of production. Here we find ideological notions of patrilinearity, virilocality,[2] the *essential* function of men in their society. Anthropologists must begin with these themes and affirmations, and, when the anthropologist is a woman, she will be perceived above all as an anthropologist.

By contrast, the anthropologist can shoulder her status as a woman, and cross the fence – when everything changes. Joking and warmth win the day. On the women's side of the fence, we learn that patrilinearity is modified by the fact that lineal and familial endogamy is very strong, so that all individuals claim a lineage from their fathers which is also that of their mothers. Virilocality is much called into question too because it is not unusual for women to refuse to follow their husbands in their moves, whether seasonal or permanent. As for the necessity of the male role in every society, it provides an inexhaustible topic of conversation. And among the Fulani, both men and women, it is often said that family and society can function only where the women are intelligent.

The Fulanis in the CAR are not the only group to champion gender segregation, which is also found in northern Nigeria, for example, and in certain restricted circles in every Fulani society. It would be tempting for the Western or westernized anthropologist, man or woman, to study this segregation from a feminist angle which values highly either mingling or equal opportunities for both sexes. CAR Fulani society, and especially its more prestigious parts, sets a high value on the opposite: a maximum of gender segregation which everyone strives for, at least in public, giving much effort to it, for avoidance is probably more difficult to cater for than meeting.

Whatever opinion one many have on gender segregation in general, or the Fulani's in particular, two linked points seem to me clear. First, Fulani women are not economically exploited. They possess their own cattle which are at their disposal, whereas they have far fewer economic obligations than men. Second, this kind of dichotomization of society, with its contrastive discourses and attitudes, is a precious aid to the anthropologist. Our female informants devote themselves to explaining the real functioning of the ideological model provided by our male informants outside the fence. During the Muslim *ramadan* in 1988 I spent whole nights on the other side of the fence discussing human societies and their complications, without which the anthropologist's job would lose its interest. Isn't it exactly the role of the anthropologist to go the other side of the fence?

Notes

1   The Fulbe are a major African people, called by the French 'Peul' (from the singular word in their language for 'man or woman', *Pullo*), and by the British 'Fulani', from a name for them borrowed from the Hausa language.

       They are specialists in raising cattle but they also practise agriculture and, in some countries, trade and other urban work. They are nearly all Muslim, and have been so since the beginning of the 19th century or earlier. They engaged in a huge campaign of conversion to Islam, sometimes by force (*jihad*), which has remodelled the political and religious patterns of the Sahel. Fulani states survive in the form of provinces within modern nation-states.

       Fulani society and culture are known to us from numerous texts, the oldest of which date back to the 11th century, and from oral traditions which remain vigorous today. British studies focus largely on the Nigerian Fulani. A *Bibliographie générale du monde peul* (Christiane Seydou, *Études nigériennes* 43, Niamey IRSH et Paris Laboratoire d'anthropologie sociale) gives exhaustive references up to 1975.

This article first appeared in French in *Chercheurs et Informateurs* vol. 2, Bulletin no. 34 of the Association Française des Anthropologues, December 1988. The translation is by Jonathan Benthall.

2   In a *virilocal* society, women move to their husbands' area on marrying. *Editor*.

Towards a Radical Reform of Education

■ *RAINews*, 26, June 1978, p. 4

This was published anonymously. Some at the time read into this verse scurrilous allusions to individual personalities in Cambridge, but they were not intended.

Towards a radical reform of education

See Goody's print[1] dispel the verbal fogs,
Praise honest toil, disrobe all pedagogues,
Disband the common school, whose slates and inks
Teach budding clerks that sweaty labour stinks.
We know for radical reform he hopes,
Else how distinguish Goody's line from Pope's?
'Worth makes the man, and want of it, the fellow;
The rest is all but leather or prunella'.[2]

But hold! here's no defence of rank and caste;
In Goody's scheme, the first shall be the last.
Let pleasant work be its own recompense,
Let Cambridge bookworms lucubrate for pence,
But dustmen find from slops a princely gain,
And steeplejacks and miners swill champagne.
Inverted be the pyramid of pay,
Rotated be our duties day by day;
Let pleased academicians harvest yams,
Let sportsmen set, and gaolers mark, exams;
The courtesan, retired from wear and tear,
Waits till the music stops, then grabs a Chair.

Most blessèd Goody, light-years distance thee
From the just grumblings of the A.U.T.[3]

Notes

1   An article by a famous man of science, Professor Jack Goody, published in *New Society* on the 20th of March, 1978, and unfairly travestied in the following verses.
2   An Essay on Man, IV, 203.
3   The Association of University Teachers.

Jonathan Benthall

PART TWO

Indigenes' Rights, Anthropologists' Roots

■ JONATHAN BENTHALL

L UCY MAIR'S PITHY ATTACK in 1975 on what she saw as the woolly
concept of ethnocide was prompted partly by **Stephen Corry**'s article on ethnocide in Colombia – here reprinted together with ripostes from Corry and Mair again
– and partly by an earlier, more philosophical article on 'Ethnology and history',
published in *RAINews* 3, July/August 1974, by Robert Jaulin, an extreme critic of
imperialism and campaigner for indigenous rights in the Americas. It had in fact
been Jaulin who popularized the use of the new word 'ethnocide', though it first
appeared in print in 1965 in a book by another French anthropologist, Georges
Condominas. The term does not appear in most dictionaries, being still restricted
to the technical vocabulary of anthropology,[1] and it has no generally accepted
definition.

Jaulin – whose article was preceded by some introductory comments by Julian
Pitt-Rivers – maintained that modern western civilization was actually 'deciviliza-
tion', the destruction of our own culture by ourselves, deriving from the denial of
the existence of others, which for him was the equivalent of death. Just as an individual life can realize itself only through others, so the same is true – he argued –
at the level of collectivities. 'The History of the west is not the struggle of warring
factions . . . the internal contradictions are secondary. The *apparent* adversaries
were always within the same camp. Their *joint* campaign was aimed at the destruction of multiple human civilisations, and it partly realised that destruction.'

Whereas Jaulin's rhetoric now seems in retrospect overblown,[2] Corry's has
provided the basis for an exceptionally effective career as a practical defender of
indigenous causes through the organization Survival, of which he was to become
Director-General. Lucy Mair's donnish position has probably been more representative of academic anthropology in Britain. While in the USA and Scandinavia,
anthropologists have been in the forefront of 'indigenist' causes, only a small minority of British anthropologists[3] have allied themselves actively with organizations

such as Survival during this period. A revival of interest in human rights, including indigenous rights, may now be observed among younger anthropologists.

The term 'indigenous' derives from European settler societies and is notoriously imprecise; like the word 'culture', it is one of anthropology's hot potatoes. The UN Working Group on Indigenous Populations defines its subject-matter as simply those peoples whose leadership represents them as indigenous. The official view in India, Indonesia, Malaysia and much of Africa is that the whole of their respective populations is indigenous.

Social anthropology has developed many other regional and thematic interests since the mid-1970s. And intellectual fashion moved sharply away in the 1980s and 1990s from the assumption that primitive tribes are primordially and mystically bonded with their ecosystems, which still characterizes some popular anthropology. The Iban of Borneo, now considered indigenous, were formerly expansionist. The 'tribals' of Bastar, India, may have chosen their detached way of life to escape the tax-collector. The Transjordanian Bedouin are vital to the modernizing King of Jordan because of their military loyalty needed to keep the kingdom's Palestinian majority in their place. And so on. An extreme academic position has been to argue that the 'pre-modern' condition is merely a modern construction. Dare one add the practical point that fieldwork in 'indigenous' contexts is on the whole an arduous personal challenge that not all of us are up to?

But there are signs of a revival of interest in the traditional concerns of anthropology, with a new sophistication. I asked the question in a 1998 issue of *Anthropology Today* (April, 14.2, pp. 18–19):

> does a renewed interest in indigenous rights mean that social anthropology, after spreading freely like ivy, is rediscovering its roots? Some would say yes – provided that it incorporates genuine analytical advances such as the understanding of the mass media, representations of the exotic, and the global economy. ... Moreover, such a swing back in fashion might make it less likely that anthropology will become absorbed by cultural studies, political science and development economics. It may well be that the rights of the world's indigenes and the roots of a small, tradition-conscious discipline are congruous.

In **Bartholomew Dean**'s article about the Frenchman Pierre Clastres' *Chronicle of the Guayaki Indians* of Paraguay, an outstanding young American anthropologist with a strong commitment to indigenous rights reflects on a classic ethnography of the early 1970s – but not translated into English until 1998 – , finding in it a romantic primitivism. Writing in 1999, Dean finds Clastres' *Chronicle* 'acutely anachronistic', essentializing the Guayaki's cultural identities in ways that make it virtually impossible to imagine a place for them in 'modern' Paraguayan national society. Dean sees anthropology's legacy of 'pristinism' as a restricting intellectual burden. **Jon Abbink** responds with the charge that it is Dean who is anachronistic because he is unhistorical. Clastres was an engaged, anti-imperialist scholar in the idiom of 1972. If he emphasized the cultural autonomy of the Guayaki, it was to attack arrogant Western modernization programmes. But along with many other anthropologists and others in the early 1970s, he wrongly believed that peoples such as the Guayaki would 'disappear'.

Notes

1   Corry, Stephen. 1996. 'Ethnocide' in *Encyclopedia of Cultural Anthropology*, New York: Henry Holt, 405–7.
2   Among his major books were *La Paix Blanche* [The white peace]. Paris: Seuil, 1970.
3   Among the exceptions have been Audrey Butt Colson, Olivia Harris, Paul Henley, Stephen Hugh-Jones, Robert Layton, Stephen Nugent and James Woodburn.

Chapter 5

Stephen Corry

■ **ETHNOCIDE: A REPORT FROM COLOMBIA,**
RAINews, 6, January/February 1975, pp. 1–2

TYPICAL OF SOUTH AMERICAN COUNTRIES which include an indigenous population within its boundaries (as all do except Uruguay), Colombia since the earliest Spanish colonies has represented an ethnocidal force for the sixty or so Indian groups who live there. The widespread massacres of the Spanish invasion are well known, the brutality of the 'Casa Arana' (the British Peruvian Rubber Co. Ltd.) less so. During the first quarter of our century this company ransacked the South Colombian rain-forest as far north as the banks of the Caquetá. About 50,000 Indians were controlled by the company, which forced them to work the 'black gold' as the rubber was called. They were maltreated, beaten, tortured and murdered. Many groups were completely annihilated, others merely decimated. In the eastern grass-lands of Colombia, Indians are still occasionally hunted today. In the Cauca and the Sierra Nevada de Santa Marta Indian land is still being stolen. Virtually everywhere Indians are exploited economically. The Catholic Church still maintains large territories under its control. Although some missionaries are enlightened and are actually a positive force as far as the Indians are concerned, most are still perpetrating forms of education which degrade and eventually destroy the Indian culture and some are outright crooks. The U.S. Protestant and supposedly scientific missionary organisation, the Summer Institute of Linguistics, has little actual effect on most groups but it is at present keeping a watchful eye in the areas which are difficult of access. The written law cannot quite make up its mind if the Indian is to be 'integrated' or 'protected'; but it makes little difference, as the individual's ability to bend or ignore the law depends directly on how much power or wealth he has and how far he is from the cities. The central government worries little about the Indians (it has many other concerns); through the Agrarian Reform Institute it has begun to create some reservations for some groups. In most cases these are of little effect as the land is already settled by 'whites'.

At first sight the Indian's position may seem hopeless. Surprisingly it is not. The Indian in Colombia is beginning to demand his rights and is making his voice heard. At the head of the movement is the entirely Indian organisation, the CRIC (Regional Indian Council of the Cauca) who, based in the Andean hills in the south-west of the country, are very slowly winning back land to which the Indians hold ancient titles but which has been stolen from them. CRIC's fight is entirely within the law. Its bitterest enemies are the local politician landowners. Its leaders are killed every so often in strange circumstances. The influence of CRIC is gaining ground outside its homeland of the Cauca. Indians from the other end of Colombia, from the Sierra Nevada de Santa Marta and from other areas, are coming to the national meetings organised by the CRIC. Amongst them tribal differences count for little as they realise that their problems are similar. All are both Indians and peasants and are proud of it.

CRIC's influence is even beginning to reach the tropical forests of Amazonia, but here the level of political awareness of the Indian groups is less than in the hills; communication is difficult and few Indians travel great distances. Tribal identity is still stronger than ethnic identity in dealings with non-Indian society. Here it is principally a small handful of Colombian anthropologists, working individually with different groups, who are acting as mediators between Indian and non-Indian society. Their action is exemplary; they have put their knowledge of the non-Indian world at the disposal of the groups they live with and study.

One anthropologist has helped the Andoke group in getting a reservation drawn up and in finding the necessary finance (supplied by Survival International and Aborigines Protection Society) to enable the group to begin rubber-work indepen-dently of the white boss who kept them in a cycle of debt-bondage. The Andoke, reduced from 10,000 at the beginning of the century to a group of 20 by the end of the 1940s, now number about 100. The group have reinstated many of their traditions, have re-built the traditional long-house ('*maloca*') and have even ritualised the departure of the canoe filled with *their own* rubber for the first time in their history.

Another anthropologist, Horacio Calle, is conducting a number of projects with the Murui and Murui-Muinane Indians. Together with his wife he has set up a health post and bilingual education programme (Spanish/Indian language) and is helping the Indians to secure their own independent economic base.

In none of these cases are the anthropologists forcing their own ideas on the Indians; they are acting as advisers and, at most, catalysers. They are making sugges-tions which the Indians themselves decide whether to accept or not. The Colombian Anthropological Institute is giving these people a free hand in their own forms of applied anthropology and its liberal foresight is only to be recommended.

It is work of this kind that will enable the Indian to become a useful member of Colombian society, in a way of his own choosing which does not involve the loss of his own identity or pride as an Indian and as an individual. To quote one anthro-pologist, this is the 'only justification for anthropological research'.

I am not referring to the 'preservation' of Indian societies. These are, like all societies, in a process of movement, change and adaptation as they have been since long before the coming of the white man. There is no such thing as 'static culture'. The World Population Year has adopted a motto 'Take care of the people and the population will take care of itself'. Similarly, help the Indian to take care of himself and his culture will take care of itself. If he is given the chance to survive then he will adapt his way of life to suit his new situation. In many areas of the world, as well as in Colombia, he is no longer waiting to be given that chance: he is making it himself.

Optimism and hope about the 'new Indian' should not take the place of action. In areas of Colombia not mentioned above the situation of the Indian is much the same as it has been for years. A slow but seemingly inexorable movement towards a loss of tribal and ethnic identity, a drift towards the lowest level of South American poverty and humiliation, means that over the next generation some groups will, almost certainly, cease to exist. Against this trend, the reassertion of group/tribal/ethnic feeling is coming from areas all over the world where it has long been considered dormant or dead.

By way of conclusion, I would like to give my own view of the concept of 'ethnocide', a concept which is sometimes criticised as excessively loose or emotive. 'Ethnocide' is a descriptive term which refers to a continuing process rather than specific incidents; for this reason it is usually more fruitful and valid to examine the situation of particular groups than to lay down universal definitions or recommendations. As a generalisation, 'ethnocide' can be said to be the destruction of an ethnic group by a dominant ethnic group by means other than deliberate killing (which would constitute genocide, although ethnocide and genocide often go together). This does not necessarily imply that the individual members of a group are killed, but that the *group itself*, as a social and cultural unity, is destroyed. 'Enforced acculturation' amounts to ethnocide, although the level of 'enforcement' is often subtle and complex and needs to be closely examined, as does the degree of 'deliberation' on the part of the dominant group. 'Culture' does not exist separate from the society which generates it, and it is, in my view, incorrect and somewhat naïve to regard ethnocide as the destruction of 'culture'.

Note

1   Stephen Corry [then] Projects Director of Survival International, [had] recently returned from a visit to some of the Indian areas of Colombia.

Chapter 6

Lucy Mair

■ 'ETHNOCIDE', *RAINews,* 7, March/April 1975,
pp. 4–5

'ETHNOCIDE' IS A WORD recently coined on the analogy of 'genocide', a rather less recent coinage. The latter word was intended to describe something quite precise: the deliberate destruction of a 'race' – the Jews – at which Hitler aimed in the territories that came under his domination. Genocide was described as a crime in a United Nations Convention which called for its punishment. Hence political points can sometimes be scored by making accusations of genocide at the UN Assembly, and the word has been somewhat devalued. It was much used in the Nigerian civil war, when the Biafrans taxed their enemies with it. It might be more correctly applied to the refusal of famine relief to Tuareg men while their women and children are assimilated into the majority populations of African states: this is a deliberate act of policy intended to eliminate the 'white' Tuaregs.

'Ethnocide', however, has had no clear meaning from the start, because the people who use the word to condemn a kind of destruction have not made up their minds what it is they are condemning. English, unlike French, does not have the word *ethnie*, which refers to a population with a common language, sometimes a common culture, and a belief in a common geographical origin; we say 'ethnic group'. Both 'nation' and 'tribe' have been used in this sense, but both these words are commonly used with other meanings. 'Ethnicity' means the attachment of a population to cultural or other symbols which differentiate them from their neighbours. 'Ethnocentrism' is the attitude that assumes there is something wrong about any behaviour or values that diverge from those of one's own ethnic group.

What then does 'ethnocide' destroy? Those who use the word refer without discrimination to two quite different kinds of victim, people and cultures. The word became current along with the latest invasion by peoples of advanced technology of the habitat of populations whose techniques are still primitive, the forest-dwellers of the remoter parts of Latin America. Some of these peoples have been treated with appalling cruelty or equally appalling negligence. Settlers in their country, who have cleared for ranching the forests where they get their livelihood, have deliberately killed some. One tribe was exterminated by an epidemic of measles. As was described in Christopher Hampton's play, *Savages* [a play first performed at the Royal Court Theatre, London, in 1973 – *Ed.*], the last survivors of another were brought to Brasilia in an un-pressurised cargo plane; they did not survive this final journey.

Such events have happened in earlier centuries, as prospectors and other pioneers encroached on the territory of weaker peoples. Settlers in South Africa hunted the Bushmen like animals. The entire Aboriginal population of Tasmania was wiped out, as were some North American tribes. Elsewhere in Australia poisoned meat was put out for Aborigines to find, as poison might be laid for rats. Such actions may well lead us to question what there is in the claim of 'civilisation' to be superior to 'barbarism'. There is an answer, though; it is that voices were raised in protest against them, and that one of the many motives, though certainly a minor one, that combined to produce the extension of European rule to other continents, was the belief that organised government could control the worst excesses of individual pioneers; and sometimes it did.

When a population is exterminated, whether by negligence or deliberately, it is finished; its collective life comes to an end with the individual lives of its members. What shocks us, or logically should do so, is the number of deaths; and perhaps, for the more imaginative, the thought of the agonies that the last survivors must have experienced. Few thinking people would hesitate to condemn 'ethnocide' in this sense, or to do anything they could to prevent it.

But the word is also used in a sense in which its implications are much more equivocal. An ethnic group is a population the members of which have, or claim to have, a common culture. In fact it is not always true that they have; though it is true of the food-gathering populations whose fate has inspired contemporary discussion of 'ethnocide'. Some people speak of 'ethnocide' when what they mean is the abandonment of their previous way of life by populations which have continued to live and to reproduce themselves through the generations and indeed the centuries; this in fact is the history of the vast majority of the present inhabitants of the world. We were all food-gatherers once.

Robert Jaulin (*RAINews* no. 3)[1] would seem to imply that world history is one of continuous decline, as does Lévi-Strauss in his *Tristes Tropiques*. Did the 'civilisation' that Jaulin calls a fatal infectious disease begin at some later date than the 'neolithic revolution' of which archaeologists tell us? This is a question to which I shall return. For the moment I want to ask whether a word that refers to killing, and has been deliberately chosen because it does, is appropriate to describe the process of cultural change. Who is it that sees murder done when nomad herdsmen yoke their cattle, teach them to plough and plant land on which they can live in settled homesteads? Many have done so in the past; if they had not, the history of Europe as we know it would never have been. Of course it is necessary that the environment should offer grazing all the year round; to force nomads to settle in areas where this is not the case might indeed be called 'ethnocide'.

To bring the story further up to date than ten thousands years ago, we might consider the Eskimos who today are using motorised sledges to travel over the snow in greater speed and comfort than they did with their dog-teams. It is outsiders, not the Eskimos, who mourn the destruction of their *culture*. This is, in fact, the very attitude that has been ascribed to anthropologists almost ever since the subject became a serious study – the wish to keep exotic peoples in 'human zoos' for the aesthetic pleasure to be derived from looking at them. The *apartheid* policy of South Africa has been described in the same way, as a denial to the African peoples of access to a culture which they seek.

Now it is true, and we are becoming alarmingly aware of the fact, that man's mastery over nature has led to a reckless destruction of the world's resources the consequences of which we must all expect to suffer. In the relatively circumscribed world of the Eskimos their new mobility has made possible an over-fishing which threatens the basis of their life. But does this fact authorise someone outside to decree that Eskimos are not to have technical devices which they, as shortsighted as the rest of us, have chosen to use and enjoy using? Would not such a decision be paternalist or even colonialist? How would it be enforced? By forbidding the manu-facturers of motorised sledges to sell them? And would not such a restriction, in the name of the conservation of world resources, be like saying to the Eskimos, 'The party's over before you have even had a bun'?

Anthropologists for some generations now have thought it their duty to combat ethnocentrism as I defined it earlier: to show how world-views and institutions which differ from those of the industrialised world do not represent some kind of failure to catch up, but are often the best adaptation to a difficult environment, and are always deserving of an interpretation in terms of their meaning for the peoples who live by them. But we do not, I think, feel any obligation to argue that the life of a hunting and gathering community is *better* than our own, still less that a return to it would solve the problems of the present century.

Let me conclude by asking whether civilisation is really a disease that has already infected most of the world and brought no benefits to anybody. If this is true, it is certainly unlikely that the few people still out of contact with it can be effectively quarantined; but let that pass. It really is time to ask whether it has had no value at all, and whether, even if it is now threatened with destruction, it would have been better if the capacity for invention which distinguishes man from other animals had never developed. The food-gathering cultures that can still be observed have themselves superseded the way of life of the cave-dwelling first tool-makers. Why should we not be asked to go back to that? The cave-dwellers must have begun to destroy their environment as soon as they discovered how to make fire. So perhaps we should regret that *homo sapiens* ever appeared at all.

It seems to be assumed, however, that the cut-off point in the advance of 'civil-isation' should have come, not within the last thirty or forty years when we began to consume resources at a rate faster than ever before, and to use chemical substances that dangerously pollute the atmosphere; nor when the peoples of Europe began to colonise other continents; nor when the Romans spread their culture through the Mediterranean; nor, even earlier, when the Greeks did; but at the moment when settled agriculture became possible, with its corollary in the growth of cities and the invention of writing. Even before the growth of cities there were differences in wealth and power; such benefits as may be ascribed to these new forms of social structure were certainly not equally shared.

Is this to say that they were worthless? I think not, and one of my strongest reasons is that, ever since there have been such inequalities, there have been men thinking about them, asking what justifies the claim to obedience, or the right to dispose of great possessions; not always answering in terms that disguise self-interest under appeals to principle either. As far back as their thoughts are recorded, people have concerned themselves with questions of ethics: justice and the good life, and how these values could be attained. And others have looked at particularly disadvantaged sections of society and sought to alleviate their lot.

One does not find this critical attitude among food-gatherers or nomad herdsmen. The answer could no doubt be made that they do not need it. The next question would then be whether the injustices and inequalities that have gone with advances in technology outweigh whatever benefits they may have brought with them. The answer here must be a matter of opinion; it is certainly permissible to hold that a benefit that is not equally shared is of no value. This would not be my answer, however. I would rather say that any addition to the enjoyment of life that is not demonstrably bought at the cost of a greater loss to those who do not receive it is a bonus. I grant that the calculation is hard to make, and that different people would give different answers.

Then I would ask what benefits these have been. The first, which is generally valued, as can be seen from the study of religious belief and ritual, is the extension of the life-span that comes from medical knowledge. Next are the devices that reduce hard physical toil and the expenditure of energy in travel on foot; if proof is sought that people dislike hard physical toil, it can be found in the flight from agriculture that is swelling the urban population in all the developing countries. In the course of the centuries huge numbers of people have enjoyed these enhancements of life. Even the remotest peasants today use pots and pans that last longer than those they used to make of clay; and Indians (in India) who can get it like the electric light that so displeased Lévi-Strauss in Lahore.[2] Certainly these artifacts are less satisfying to sophisticated connoisseurs than the products of unmechanised crafts, but is that the most important consideration?

No doubt it is elitist to value those products of the human mind to which so many humans are indifferent. Yet, for some reason, there are folk whose life has been enhanced by contemplating (and even sometimes sharing) ingenuity of thought, rigour of argument, scientific enquiry, patient scholarship, and the elaboration of literature and the arts. How could the great Lévi-Strauss himself, that deplorer of civilisation, have evolved his theory of myth as a code without the centuries of scientific and scholarly tradition?

Perhaps humanity is facing its end. When this comes, there will be no one to ask whether the world would have been better with no Homer, no Botticelli, no Mozart, no Taj Mahal – no Jackson Pollock perhaps? But equally, no one will ask whether it would have been better if the work of man's imagination had been confined to cave paintings and Zulu praise-songs.

Notes

1   See introductory notes above. *Editor.*
2   The reference is to the end of Lévi-Strauss's *Tristes Tropiques*. *Editor.*

Chapter 7

Stephen Corry and Lucy Mair

■ ETHNOCIDE AND ETHNOCENTRICITY:
  CORRESPONDENCE, *RAINews*, 9,
  July/August 1975, pp. 16–17

LUCY MAIR'S MAIN ARGUMENT (as expressed in *RAINews* 7, p. 4f.) sems to be that the word 'ethnocide' is often used in an excessively loose and emotive way. This is true; emotions do tend to be aroused in the face of gross and obvious injustice, especially when that injustice is perpetrated against such people as North American Indians or Bushmen (which examples she give) – people who have no effective means whatsoever of defending themselves or even of having their complaints heard.

But the criticism that 'those who use the word refer without discrimination to two quite different kinds of victim, people and cultures' is worth examining. It does not need anthropological training to see that if you kill all chickens you won't have any eggs and if you smash all eggs . . . If you destroy the people what happens to the 'culture' (if it's 'lucky' some of its material manifestations wind up in the Museum of Mankind)? If you destroy the 'culture' what happens to the people (if they're 'lucky' they end up as servants and prostitutes)? What is meant by saying that these are 'quite different'? In putting this question I am referring quite concretely to the destruction of a group and not to cultural change which is coming about because the group want it to (what any group 'wants' or 'does not want' when it comes to interaction with a different society is, of course, a very complex question). In South America – as Lucy Mair states, it was the situation of South American Indians which generated interest in the subject and the coinage of the word 'ethnocide' – there is usually no doubt that the acculturation of Indian groups is very much enforced, either physically or by continual psychological pressures which are no less effective. The two examples of 'non-ethnocide' given in the article (nomad herdsmen and Eskimo motor sledges) do not come from areas where ethnocide is so evident. Expressed as they are, these two examples can hardly be said to constitute an ethnocidal situation; they are, however, irrelevant if we are discussing what is, or is not, ethnocide.

Having criticised the term as being emotive and loose, her article itself suffers from just such faults. Although she states 'Anthropologists . . . have thought it their

Figure 7.1　The wife of a Meo soldier feeds her child sitting on top of American artillery shells in Laos in 1972, when the Indo-China war was at its peak. Photographed during the filming by Brian Moser and Chris Curling of *The Meo*, a much acclaimed Granada Television *Disappearing World* film.

duty to . . . show how world-views and institutions which differ from those of the industrialised world do not represent some kind of failure to catch up . . .', it would appear that her description of South American Indians (and other tribal groups) relies exactly on the assumption that they are somehow 'behind'. She calls their techniques 'still primitive', says that she does not feel obligated to argue that a 'return' to a hunting and gathering life would solve our problems, and announces that 'we were all food gatherers once'. She goes on to say that 'civilisation' is really not so bad and is rather superior to 'barbarism' because 'voices were raised in protest against' the inhumanity of civilisation, and that 'one does not find this critical attitude among food-gatherers . . .'. 'Ingenuity of thought, rigour of argument, scientific enquiry, patient scholarship and the elaboration of literature and the arts' are essentially described as being the attributes of 'civilisation'; but does not tribal man often have his own forms of all of these?

Devices that reduce physical toil are also given as among the benefits of 'civilisation'. The proof that people dislike such toil is, Professor Mair argues, the flight from agriculture to the cities in the developing countries. This is no 'proof' for anything. There are a hundred reasons why people move into cities; the principal ones are probably poverty, exploitation and the lack of land.

The final paragraph of her article carries its own, barely concealed, implication that Zulu praise-songs are inferior to Mozart.

That 'civilisation' has brought greater happiness, or whatever, to a greater number of people and that it is therefore arithmetically valid, despite its destruction of the few unfortunates, may be Lucy Mair's own opinion. Such an assertion must remain, however, an 'opinion', as she acknowledges. It is as emotional an opinion as Robert Jaulin's declaring that Western civilisation is a 'decivilisation' and that it is self-destructive in that it lives essentially on the destruction of others. Ethnocide, genocide and enforced acculturation are all real factors in the lives of many tribal groups in South America and elsewhere, and they are factors which lead to sadness and suffering. The anthropologist is often in a position to see all this. My own emotional opinion is that he should try and act on what he knows to be true.

Stephen Corry
Survival International

Lucy Mair writes:

Stephen Corry tells us that all populations whose present culture is different from that of their ancestors are servants or prostitutes. This is a very remarkable statement to make, not only about the society of the present day but about all those of which we have historical record, all of which are descended from food-gatherers. I cannot conceive why he thinks it offensive, let alone emotional, to mention this indisputable fact. Is he a servant and am I a prostitute? I don't think so.

If the word 'ethnocide' was used only of the peoples with whom Survival International is concerned, it would be pedantic to discuss it. But once a word has been launched on its career, its use cannot be confined to specific situations, and it is the wider use of this word, and a number of ideas that have come to be associated with it, that I criticise. Of course the Eskimos are not in the same situation as the Amerindians, but the same tears are shed about the disappearance of their cultures.

One of the ideas that I think needs rational scrutiny is that nothing has been achieved in the course of centuries in which knowledge and invention have been gradually built up over the generations. Anthropologists do indeed write of 'primitive' techniques. I prefer the word 'simple'. The difference between the simple and the complex is surely an objective one. When we use these adjectives we refer to technology and not to supposed advances in morals or in intellectual capacity.

The past is behind us; therefore, to return to it we should have to 'go back'. Would Stephen Corry think it was derogatory to London if I talked of someone leaving London and coming back to it?

On such questions as intellectual rigour I refer him to Robin Horton's eloquent expositions of the similarities between African religious speculation and western science, in which he does not hesitate to say that the achievements of the latter have been greater.

Like Sweeney, I gotta use words when I talk to you, and 'civilisation' is a part of the outfit available. I *do* think it is worth something. We are all entitled to our own values, but we can defend them either by mere shouting or by rational argument. I chose the latter. I see no logical reason why justified indignation on behalf of the Amerindians should lead me to abandon mine.

Update note by Stephen Corry on the Corry–Mair exchange, 2001

My 1975 article about the situation of Indian peoples in Colombia ended with a brief explanation of 'ethnocide', defined as 'the destruction of an ethnic group . . . by means other than deliberate killing'. In my subsequent exchange with Lucy Mair, she criticised the thinking of those who oppose cultural change, focused on a lack of rigour in using 'ethnocide', and wrote that 'civilisation' has benefited the world more than 'cave paintings and Zulu praise-songs'.

She was right on the first point. Popular thinking often clings to an image of the untainted 'noble savage', which is ultimately unhelpful to real tribal peoples. Lucy Mair assumed that I espoused this idea, whereas in fact I didn't, and still don't. My problem was never with cultural change as such, but with changes enforced by outsiders, against the will of the people, and damaging both to individuals and the people as a whole – making nomads settle, for example.

I also now believe that she was right on the second point. The term 'ethnocide' was not the one to use: both because it is capable of misinterpretation along just these lines, and because there is a better one – genocide. Current interpretations of the crime of genocide do embrace the notion of 'cultural genocide', and it is defined in the UN Draft Declaration on indigenous peoples' rights. Moreover, it has become accepted that genocide need not involve 'deliberate killing', as long as destruction of the group is a foreseeable consequence of deliberate actions. In campaigning against less extreme cases, existing principles of human and tribal peoples' rights – such as the right to land ownership and so on – prove perfectly adequate.

On the third point, however, I still think Lucy Mair's position was muddled. She clearly thought that tribal peoples are the same as our distant ancestors, and therefore backward: she classes cave paintings together with Zulu praise-songs, and contrasts them with Homer and Mozart. But they are not the same, and nor is their situation. Saying that we are all descended from hunter-gatherers tells us as little about modern tribal peoples as noting that we all walk upright. Zulu or Oxfordian, we are all contemporary peoples. I too find Botticelli and Mozart enriching, but to claim that they show how advanced 'we' are is ethnocentrism.

I have yet to come across a tribal people whose 'techniques' have seemed 'simple'. On the contrary, I am not alone in being repeatedly struck by their genius. Successfully hunting eland in the desert is, I suggest, no less skilful than flying a jet (or being an anthropologist!).

Returning to Colombian Indians: the situation there today is not so different from that in 1975. The principles I set out then, supporting their right to their lives and lands, has seen successes. The recognition of the lands of recently contacted Maku, a direct result of a Survival International campaign in the 1990s, is reason for celebration, as is the now widespread acceptance of Indian rights in legislation. On the other hand, attacks by left- and right-wing paramilitaries have worsened, as they have for everyone. A very few of the heroes of this struggle are anthropologists, the vast majority are not.

Chapter 8

Bartholomew Dean

■ CRITICAL RE-VISION: CLASTRES' *CHRONICLE* AND THE OPTIC OF PRIMITIVISM, *Anthropology Today*, 15.2, April 1999, pp. 9–11

PIERRE CLASTRES' EVOCATIVE *Chronicle of the Guayaki Indians* (1998) stands as an enduring testament to a bygone era of anthropological sensibilities and imperial exploration among putatively 'pristine' peoples in remote corners of the globe (see for instance Masterman 1870; Grubb (1911). Aside from early Jesuit accounts (e.g. Pedro Lozano's historiography, circa 1750s), the Aché Guayaki of Paraguay remained poorly documented until well into the latter half of the twentieth century: a time when the Stroessner dictatorship's brutal pacification campaign drove many groups of Guayaki to settle permanently in government-sponsored encampments. Written in lucid and direct prose, Clastres' *Chronicle* recounts the subtle intricacies of Guayaki culture, paying special attention to life-stage ordeals, cosmology and the group's daily struggles for survival.

Readers are treated to lively accounts of how the Aché Guayaki hunt for coati and forage for honey and grubs; told in great detail about their sexual lives (including why girls are flagellated with tapir penises); and warned of the dangers of vultures, venomous serpents and demonic forest spirits. Starting with childbirth, and continuing through descriptions of initiation ceremonies, hunting adventures, matrimony, gruesome retaliatory violence, sickness, death and mourning, Clastres concludes his *Chronicle* by pondering the nature of Guayaki anthropophagy. At times, Clastres' depictions of nature, such as his vivid accounts of pouncing *baipu* or jaguar, tend to eclipse his representation of society. Nonetheless, his experience of the shared hardships and joys of life enables Clastres to eventually recognize the Aché for their 'piety, the gravity of their presence in the world of things and the world of beings' (p. 347).

The victim of a fatal automobile accident, Clastres was only 43 at the time of his death in 1977, yet he was widely acclaimed as an innovative and thoroughly creative anthropologist. His *Chronique des indiens Guayaki: ce que savent les Aché, chasseurs nomades du Paraguay* appeared in 1972, but a chain of fluke publishing derailments resulted in the two-decade delay of its publication in English. American

Figure 8.1 A Urarina headman surrounded by some of the legal documents on which indigenous peoples must increasingly rely in order to establish and maintain their claims to ancestral lands. Pangayucu River, Peruvian Amazonia, 1998.

novelist Paul Auster's beautifully rendered translation of Clastres' close-up and haunting description of the Aché Guayaki does justice to the text whose appeal lies in its claims to universal truths, particularly for a world seemingly inured to violence and unbridled consumption. Perhaps what makes Clastres' now classic account so seductively compelling is the author's rare gift of communication, which, as Auster admiringly contends, combines both, 'a poet's temperament and a philosopher's depth of mind.' However, in design and content, Clastres' *Chronicle* is an old-fashioned monograph detailing heroic encounters with the exotic Other. Unlike the numerically dominant peasant (*caboclo* and *ribereño*) societies of lowland South America, indigenous peoples such as the Aché Guayaki have occupied the imagination of ethnologists, explorers and missionaries for centuries. Anthropological research and writing on the region have long been concerned with the micro-study of the area's putatively primordial and hence 'authentic' social formations. Clastres' account is no exception to this tendency.

Firmly rooted in the shared experience of daily life, Clastres' path to knowledge of the Other is a mix of exoticism and profoundly self-assured empiricism (albeit tempered by an empathetic and perceptive view of the most agonizing and humble truths of human existence – such as the cosmic perils of childbirth, the fears of death and the traumas of bodily affliction). Clastres' book can be read as a response to our discontent with Western modernity. It chronicles encounters with subjects whose 'savagery was formed of silence', and details how Clastres sought 'to break through the Strangers' passive resistance, interfere with their freedom, and make them talk' (p. 97). Such an approach has obvious limits, which become readily apparent when the anthropological interlocutor reflects on the unwillingness of an informant to enter into dialogue. This triggers Clastres to recall his mentor (and fellow Paraguayanist) Alfred Métraux's (1946) counsel: 'For us to be able to study a primitive society, it must already be starting to disintegrate.' This inspires Clastres to declare:

> Hardly touched, hardly contaminated by the breezes of our civilization – which were fatal for them – the Atchei could keep the freshness and tranquillity of their life in the forest intact: this freedom was temporary and doomed not to last much longer, but it was quite sufficient for the moment; it had not been damaged, and so the Atchei's culture would not insidiously and rapidly decompose. The society of the Atchei *Iroiangi* was so healthy that it could not enter into a dialogue with me, with another world. (pp. 96–7).

Not only does Clastres describe an immense cultural gulf, but so too does he envision great temporal distance dividing him from the subjects of his ethnological inquiry. While living among the Guayaki, Clastres could easily imagine that he 'was living several centuries earlier, when America had not yet been discovered' (p. 138). The rudimentary communication he established with a Guayaki upon his arrival in camp prompts the narrator to observe that, '[s]tanding before me, speaking to me, was a Stone Age man (a description that turned out to be more or less accurate)' (p. 77). Clastres' rendition of the Guayaki as morally superior, 'living fossils, throwbacks to a distant period' (p. 113) displays what Geertz (1998) aptly notes is a

'Rousseauian primitivism' – the nostalgic perception that the free and unfettered 'noble savages' are radically unlike us moderns. This invariably makes for a good read, but the cumulative force of Clastres' ahistoricism, rhetorical romanticism, and museumification sadly obscures the ongoing challenges facing indigenous peoples like the Guayaki.

Known as the Atchei Gatu in the *Chronicle* – or 'good Aché' as they call themselves – the Guayaki speak a Tupian dialect of the Tupi-Guaranian language family. Traditionally, they inhabited the densely forested, upland region between the Paraná and Paraguay rivers of eastern Paraguay. Before the 16th-century arrival of Europeans, they led a relatively settled, agrarian existence. But this all changed with the encroachment of colonists and other indigenous peoples in the region. Like other mobile societies of lowland South America, such as the Sirionó of eastern Bolivia, the Urarina of Peruvian Amazonia, or the Nambikwara (Nambicuara) of Mato Grosso, Brazil, the Aché Guayaki have long faced the pressures of state-sanctioned cultural assimilation, not to mention the systematic pillage of their homelands.

Though the backdrop and context for ethnic conflicts are intimated by Clastres (and completely neglected in Auster's prefatory comments), the processes that have precipitated the violence against the Guayaki are much less clearly elaborated in his *Chronicle*. Instances of ethnocide and genocide have proximate and specific historical causes. Beginning at the turn of the century, a steadily advancing agro-extractive frontier forced the four primary Tupi-Guaraní speaking groups (Pai-tavy-terá, the Mbya-Guaraní, the Ava Chiripa and the Aché Guayaki) of eastern Paraguay to seek refuge in the more inaccessible forested regions of the area. Previously, the Aché had suffered violent attacks by predatory bands of professional slavers, like Pichin Lopez and other *montaraces* – or strong men of the forest – who ruthlessly besieged Guayaki compounds, and chased the group 'into the forest to steal their *kromi*, their children' (p. 65). As the forests were clear cut for multinational mining, timber and cattle concerns, and to make room for landless peasants, expulsion and forced resettlement became a standard part of the state's genocidal 'development' policy (Münzel 1973; Arens 1976).

By 1959, 'the forest had become more a prison than a shelter for them' (p. 75). Diminished, the Aché Gatu entered into a Faustian bargain. They relinquished their nomadic freedom in return for the 'protection' of a local farmer and former 'Indian hunter' whose *hacienda*, fittingly called the 'White Stream' (Arroyo Moroti), abutted the ever receding forest. The Guayaki's benefactor's motives were far from humanitarian: in addition to taking advantage of the young girls, he had economic interests in becoming the group's officially recognized protector. For every native castaway residing on his property, the Paraguayan chief received government rations – flour, lard, powdered milk and sugar – much of which he predictably diverted for sale to the local peasant population. To maximize his profit margin, he persuaded the refugee Atché Gatu to assist him in resettling their historic adversaries, the *Iroiangi* ('the Strangers'). Sheltered yet trapped, wasted by tuberculosis, despair and depression, the two rival groups of Guayaki descended into an awkward coexistence.

It was exactly in this context that Clastres – the promising young apprentice in Lévi-Strauss' *laboratoire anthropologique* – set out to live with the Guayaki, a society he goes to great length in describing both as primordial and on the brink of extinction. It is true that when Clastres appeared on the scene in 1963, the Guayaki's number had dwindled to around a hundred people, and their culture appeared to loom precariously close to the edge of annihilation. By the time Clastres departed from their midst – never to return – he believed that they, like the other 'tribes' of the New World, were inevitably condemned to oblivion. In what he calls the Guayaki's 'tragic festival of their end', Clastres pessimistically contends that '[t]here was nothing ahead of them but death' (p. 255). Nonetheless, more than three decades later, the Guayaki still survive (albeit in wretched conditions), and tenaciously continue to clamour for their voices to be heard.

Clastres' account of the Guayaki is out of step with an increasingly critically engaged anthropology whose practitioners actively collaborate with indigenous peoples in their struggles, helping them make sense of the ineluctable pull of modernity and development. Notwithstanding the surge in popular interest in 'primitivism' – thanks in part to the New Age movement – Clastres' *Chronicle* now seems acutely anachronistic a quarter-century after its first public appearance. While Clastres portrays the Guayaki in a romantically positive light, his *Chronicle* essentializes their cultural identities in ways that make it virtually impossible to imagine a place for them in 'modern' Paraguayan national society.

Politicization of indigenous organizations, and increased accessibility to the media have made the plight of subordinated peoples more apparent to the general public. Fortunately, the growing recognition of group rights, corresponding to decolonization, and an increasing global awareness of the plight of subaltern peoples has provided the impetus for the re-imagination of how indigenous peoples are portrayed in ethnographic and popular accounts. As a result, private and public organizations are now providing critically needed financial support and technical support for the creation and on-going operation of indigenous advocacy organizations. These efforts are by and large not aimed at trying to freeze in a time warp or conserve indigenous 'societies in aspic' (Geertz 1998); rather they are designed to give indigenous peoples a voice as formidable stakeholders in determining their future (for the case of Paraguay, among others, see Maybury-Lewis and Howe 1980; Stahl 1993; Kidd 1995; Reed 1997).

The risk of being heard and *viewed* as indigenous peoples illustrates what some call a 'post-identity politics' that is inescapably 'about displacement and relocation, the experience of sustaining and mediating complex affiliations, multiple attachments' (Clifford 1998: 369). The challenge now remains one that translates the re-imagined view of the Other in ways that facilitate the reconfiguration of regional, national and international policies and beliefs adversely affecting the lives of indigenous peoples and ethnic minorities worldwide. For anthropology, this quest involves articulating, not simply transcending, the various components of cultural identity constitutive of social being in ways that encourage multiple attachments and facilitate complex, and at times deeply contradictory affiliations. Anthropological defence of the rights of indigenous peoples presupposes a rediscovery of the discipline's roots, as well as a frank examination of the mass media, the global economy (Benthall 1998: 19) and the various motivations underpinning representations of the exotic Other. Given its unabashed pristinism, Clastres' *Chronicle* is valuable precisely because it reminds us of anthropology's intellectual legacy of primitivism, which needs to be checked before the discipline can continue to fulfil its mission as a critical voice in the shaping of contemporary local and global affairs.

References

Arens, Richard (ed.). 1976. *Genocide in Paraguay*, epilogue by Elie Wiesel. Philadelphia: Temple U. P.

Benthall, Jonathan. 1998. Indigenes' Rights, Anthropologists' Roots? *Anthropology Today* 14(2): 18–19.

Clastres, Pierre. 1998. *Chronicle of the Guayaki Indians*, trans. by Paul Auster. New York: Zone Books.

Clifford, James. 1998. 'Mixed Feelings' in P. Cheah and B. Robbins (eds), *Cosmopolitics: Thinking and Feeling Beyond the Nation*, Minneapolis: U. of Minnesota P.

Geertz, Clifford. 1998. 'Deep Hanging Out'. *The New York Review of Books* 45(16): 69–73.

Grubb, W.B. 1911. *An unknown people in an unknown land: an account of the life and customs of the Lengua Indians of the Paraguayan Chaco, with adventures and experiences met with during twenty years' pioneering and exploration amongst them*. London: Seeley and Co.

Kidd, Stephen W. 1995. 'Land, politics and benevolent Shamanism: the Enxet Indians in a democratic Paraguay' *Journal of Latin American Studies* 27(1): 43–65.

Lozano, Pedro 1754–55. *Historia de la Compañía de Jesús en la provincia del Paraguay*. Madrid: Imprenta de la viuda de Manuel Fernández.

Masterman, George Frederick. 1870. *Seven eventful years in Paraguay; a narrative of personal experience amongst the Paraguayans*. 2d edn. London: S. Low, Son & Marston.

Maybury-Lewis, David and James Howe. 1980. *The Indian peoples of Paraguay: their plight and their prospects*. Cambridge, MA: Cultural Survival, Special report no. 2.

Métraux, Alfred. 1946. 'Myths of the Toba and Pilagá Indians of the Gran Chaco.' *Memoirs of the American Folklore Society*. Philadelphia: American Folklore Society, vol 40.

Münzel, Mark. 1973. *The Aché Indians: genocide in Paraguay*. Copenhagen: IWGIA. Document no. 11.

Reed, Richard. 1997. *Forest Dwellers, Forest Protectors: Indigenous Models for International Development*. The Cultural Survival Studies in Ethnicity and Change. D. Maybury-Lewis and T. McDonald (eds), Boston: Allyn & Bacon.

Stahl, W. 1993. 'Antropología de accion entre indigenas chaquenos. Una evaluación.' *Suplemento Antropologica* 28(1–2): 25–42.

Chapter 9

Jon Abbink

■ **DOING JUSTICE TO CLASTRES**, LETTERS,
Anthropology Today, 15.4, August 1999, p. 21

T HE ASSESSMENT OF PIERRE CLASTRES by Bartholomew Dean
(A.T., April 1999) is marred by inconsistency and anachronism and does not
put this French ethnologist's contribution in a proper perspective.

The article opens with a paragraph of praises for the work of Clastres on the
Aché Guayaki Indians of Paraguay (published in French in 1972, in English in 1998),
which is indeed justified. But it then goes on to retrospectively debunk Clastres'
whole approach, thereby virtually reducing his contribution to Amerindian studies
to a primitivist gloss in the history of anthropology. Dean suggests that Clastres'
work is marred by his 'exoticist/primitivist' perception, and his 'unabashed pristinism'. He states further that Clastres' book is, 'in design and content, [. . .] an
old-fashioned monograph detailing heroic encounters with the exotic Other', and
goes on to say that it shows a 'profoundly self-assured empiricism', 'can be read as
a response to our discontent with western modernity', and that the author shows
'ahistoricism, rhetorical romanticism, and museumification'. And so on.

We all know what Dean means, but this is too much invective for a book which
did nothing else but draw attention to the plight of the Aché, a marginal and
exploited group, describe in depth their way of life and culture, and evoke their
common humanity with us, the Others. As such the book has had its impact. Based
on his image of anthropological practice of the late 1990s, Dean perhaps expected
a contribution to a full-fledged emancipatory project and to the struggle of indigenous peoples. But in 1972 these concerns had to take a different shape, partly
because of the great differences in intellectual and political space for anthropology
and for action research then and now, and especially in the South America of the
late 1960s and early 1970s. In France, however, Clastres was one of the engaged,
'anti-imperialist' scholars in post-1968 ethnology.

One can also see the so-called 'romantically positive light' in which Clastres
allegedly portrayed the Guayaki as a rhetorical device of social criticism, meant to
ultimately retrieve their way of life and continued existence. Clastres' emphasis on

the disturbing effects of 'our civilization' on the 'hardly touched' Aché should be read as a fundamental critique against the arrogant idea — still widely present in Western and other powerful societies; see development aid and international politics — that they should be reformed in our image and respond to our models of social and economic life. Thus, apart from the fact that Dean's remarks cannot in themselves disqualify any of the book's information on Aché Guayaki society in the 1950s and 1960s, one cannot deny its having a critical message. Only its clear prediction that this people would 'disappear' soon was proved wrong. Clastres' ethnography has depicted the Guayaki in a certain light, but in presenting them as 'indigenes' with specific cultural values and identity, he has also tried to ground their presence and their historical rights within Paraguayan society, in whatever problematic way these were and will be implemented.

Clastres' studies on the Guayaki still stand as invaluable reference works (see also his *Society against the State*, Oxford 1977) which in places offer some theoretical challenge as well. We should obviously take his work as an account of the Guayaki at one point in time — it cannot be otherwise. Dean's insistence on the 'primitive perspective' and the 'cultural essentializing' of Clastres tends to yield too much to the emerging stereotype in 'globalization studies' that all non-western/ non-industrial peoples have been connected always and in virtually equal measure to the outside world and have been decisively shaped by the emerging world political economy — as if nothing existed before that. Thus Dean's retrospective criticism of Clastres's ethnography has a point, but as a whole strikes one as too facile and exaggerated. Some more historical understanding of the evolution of ethnology and the choices its practitioners realistically had would be useful in evaluating monographs of the past.

A New Occult Science

■ *RAINews*, 47, December 1981, pp. 5–6

EAROLOGY IS THE STUDY of the external ear as developed by Shri J.K. Karmakar, a former headmaster of Calcutta, and now director of the Research Institute of Earology. He claims our attention because his recent book *Earology (Volume One)*, published at Rs. 30 by Mondal and Sons, Calcutta, contains tributes not only from the Chief Justice of the Calcutta High Court, who has presided over an earological seminar, but also from some Indian anthropologists including Professor L.P. Vidyarthi, former President of the International Union of Anthropological and Ethnological Sciences and now Chairman of its Commission on Development and its Task Force on the Future of Anthropology.

Mr Karmakar's science is a unique blend of anthropometry and astrology, having little in common with modern scientific research on the external ear as it has developed since a chapter on it in *Human Genetics* (1946) by R. Ruggles Gates. Mr Stephen Lewis of the human biology department, University of Surrey, who has written a dissertation (available at his university) on bilateral asymmetry of the external ear, has kindly sent us a list of some two dozen publications on the ear in genetic and medical journals. Scientific attention now focuses on the relationship of abnormal ear morphology to Down's syndrome and other conditions, including some forms of hereditary deafness. One particular diagonal crease in the lobe is believed to develop after birth and to be correlated with a predisposition to coronary heart disease. Anthropometric techniques are also used in plastic surgery research, for instance at the Hospital for Sick Children, Toronto.

The flavour of Mr Karmakar's method, by contrast, may be sampled from the following section on the Thief in his chapter on the interpretation of ear morphology:

> Such person cannot do any good work in life. I myself have conducted enquiry in Sealdah and Alipore Police Court in this regard, and have found their ears highly deformed. None of the parts are simple and

natural. Their ears are either unnaturally coiled or their helix, unnaturally deformed, have suppressed their anti-helix for good. Such people can never be made to lead a good and honest life by any medicine . . . Medicine can tone up the matted nerves, but it cannot redress the deformed ear. No amount of talisman or precious stone prescribed by the learned astrologers will make him follow a correct path of life . . . Ordinary men as we are, we run after hope, but fate cannot be dispensed with, we cannot make it move according to our will — were it so, the poor and the destitute would have passed their days happy in air-conditioned rooms.

Those fortunate enough to be born with a large and pointed anti-helix are, however:

generally famous persons, not only at home but also abroad . . . Such persons are generally gentle and sensitive, ambitious, determined and self-confident . . . They do not like to work under any person. They must be the departmental heads or likewise. Such persons were good people in their previous birth.

Since the external ear changes but little in form during a human life, earology offers a totally deterministic reading of fate, more so than palmistry, and certain ideological assumptions appear to underlie it. Ruggles Gates, though he wrote many scientific papers on the genetics of hairy ears, was entirely dismissive of Lombrosian theories of connections between criminality and hairy ear-rims, and he similarly exonerated the adherent lobe. Mr Karmakar inherits the criminological ambition of Lombroso but chooses different indicators, based on the location of planets in different parts of the ear.

Philosophical support for earology must be found within Indian culture rather than in what we call science, and it would be typical of European arrogance to approach the question of its validity with anything other than a completely open mind. As Professor Vidyarthi notes in his foreword: 'much intensive work needs to be done for providing Earology a sound base. And, I hope, at a future date we will have calibrated the rarity and preciousness of what many of us take so much for granted.'

Jonathan Benthall

PART THREE

Fieldwork as Intervention

■   JONATHAN BENTHALL

I N 1997, AS EXPLAINED in the Introduction, *AT* initiated a series of articles on 'gift relationships between ethnographers and their hosts', with special reference to poorer countries (13.6, December 1997).

Though the **Glynn Flood–A.F. Robertson** exchange in 1975 could have been included equally well in the sections on 'indigenes' rights' or 'war and civil strife', it seemed right to include it here because Glynn Flood's fieldwork resulted in the loss of his life. For various reasons I have contextualized the exchange with some prefatory remarks and also by commissioning some concluding up-to-date comments by an expert on Ethiopia.

John Knight tackles one of cultural anthropology's *causes célèbres*, the late Colin Turnbull's *The Mountain People*. It seems now in retrospect that Turnbull's negative account of the Ik of northern Uganda, first published in 1972, was ethnographically flawed and that if he had written it twenty years later the Ik might have succeeded in taking legal action against him, even if he could find an academically respectable publisher (so that this article might also have been placed in the section on indigenous rights). Turnbull's morality tale of the Ik was taken up by the leading avant-garde theatrical director of the 1970s, Peter Brook – which might have justified my placing Knight's article here in the section on mass media, since the name of the Ik quickly became familiar to the public of Paris and London because of Peter Brook's fame.

As correspondents pointed out in the issue of *AT* succeeding Knight's article (and as was pointed out by others in the 1970s), there should be nothing to surprise us in a suspension of cultural norms, such as giving priority to child care, when the survival of an entire breeding group is under threat.

Sarah Pink's was the most original of the articles on fieldwork that *AT* stimulated in 1997. We had drawn particular attention to the exchange relationship inherent in fieldwork. The researcher gains 'material' which s/he can use: for the publication of research, for teaching and education and journalism, for deposit in archives. What is the pay-off for the 'hosts'? Sometimes the issue has been neglected and the fieldworker simply disappears back home, but nowadays it is normal to reflect on various possible benefits for the hosts: such as enhancing their capital of cultural heritage, defending their political rights, or contributing to some form of community development. Personal friendship with individuals or families, preferably over a long period, is another form of reciprocity. Cash transfers, such as a share of publishing or film royalties, are also not uncommon. Appropriate return of information, and respect for informants' privacy, are among the ethical issues related to this exchange relationship.

Bygone anthropologists sometimes exaggerated the uniqueness of their professional fieldwork relationship with informants and host communities – and, in particular, there was a kind of long-running 'sibling rivalry' with missionaries. The colonial context also tended to be understated. Pink sets us in an up-to-date Third World context where an anthropologist is most likely to be locally conflated with the ubiquitous aid workers. She also points out that what is intended as a gift may not be accepted as such. For instance, in the eyes of the local people of Guinea Bissau in west Africa, 'so-called "development" projects appeared to bring no noticeable improvement to their lives'. If such people welcome the intervention of Euro-American fieldworkers, with their relative wealth and their freedom to travel, it is in order to gain economic resources and/or benefit from social networking. Anthropologists have to recognize this fact – well-known to experienced aid workers too – and avoid the trap of sentimentalizing personal relationships.

Pink illustrates this kind of dilemma with a wealth of vivid anecdote. For instance, a local woman left with a daughter by a white, married aid worker, and subsequently deserted, does not see herself as a tragic Madame Butterfly. Having a 'white' child is like being dealt a winning card; she may indeed eventually make it to Europe and bring her mother prosperity.

Pink's article describes a period in Guinea Bissau before the breaking out of armed conflict, and there is no reference to the white fieldworkers being in personal danger. If her fieldwork had been done a couple of years later, the tone of her account would have been very different. Western aid agencies are now increasingly concerned about the safety of their field officers, and ethnographic fieldwork in many countries is also becoming more hazardous.

Editorial note on Flood–Robertson exchange

The Afar since 1975

This exchange was published in 1975, not long after the deposition by armed forces in September 1974 of the last Emperor of Ethiopia, Haile Selassie (whose rule is here called the Old Regime). At the time, the armed campaign for the independence of Eritrea – bordering the area discussed by Flood and Robertson to the north, and annexed by Ethiopia since 1962 – was intensifying.

The Afar live in Ethiopia, Eritrea and Djibouti. The Afar population in Ethiopia is estimated to be somewhere between half a million and 1 million. The Issa or Ise, mentioned by Flood, are a Somali clan who dominate Djibouti (to the north-east of the area), compete for grazing and water with the Afar, and are traditional enemies. Sporadic fighting between the Afar and the Issa has continued over the past quarter century.

Coincidentally, the Afar Liberation Front began armed operations just after publication of Flood's article, in March 1975, and it continues its campaign today sporadically. One of its factions, in which kinship and politics intertwine, was later known as the Afar People's Democratic Organization, but this was abolished in 2000 in favour of a single party that rules the Afar Regional National State. Another faction was led by the Sultan Ali Mirah, mentioned in Flood's article, who lived in exile in Saudi Arabia for some years but has now returned to Addis Ababa.

Recent external evaluations of the record of development aid and government policies over the past few decades in what is now the Afar National Regional State have been largely negative. While a few Afar have benefited from sedentarization projects, the vast majority have seen no improvement in their living standards, health care or educational provision. Perhaps Flood was over-pessimistic in his prediction that 'a huge area once frequented by about 150,000 people during the wet season will become a total desert'; but his article understates the exploitation of the labour force in the 1970s by tax-exempt companies such as Handels Vereniging Amsterdam (HVA), and the pollution of the Awash River by industrial waste from cotton plantations and sugar factories.

Glynn Flood's research and his death

Tragically, Glynn Flood was murdered by Ethiopian soldiers on or about 7 June 1975 in Aseita (see London *Guardian* and *The Times*, 8 October). He was 26 years of age, a history graduate from Oxford, and carrying out field research for a doctorate in social anthropology at the London School of Economics. He had returned to the field early in the year despite having temporarily exhausted his research funds, and while still convalescing from a severe attack of brucellosis. He and a number of other non-combatants were killed during a savage governmental suppression of Afar militancy. It is believed that he was captured with a number of people of different nationalities (Eritreans, Arabs and Afars), having taken photographs. After being held in prison for a time, he was finally killed with others.

His supervisor, Ioan Lewis, wrote in *RAINews* 11 (November/December 1975) that Flood was one of the most outstandingly gifted young anthropologists he had supervised. A group of seven fellow-students in the same issue of *RAINews* wrote that they had long agreed that he was 'the best and most imaginative thinker' among them. There is no doubt that a potentially fine Africanist and university teacher was lost to anthropology.

The justification for reprinting the exchange between Glynn Flood and Sandy Robertson — who was at the time Assistant Director of Development Studies, and Director of the African Studies Centre, at Cambridge University — is partly summed up in Lewis's obituary. He wrote that 'the corrosive conflict between tyrannical regimes, whether of the left or right, and dissident minority groups – which is now such a widespread phenomenon in our world' exposes 'all the ambiguities which are inherent in the anthropologist's role, and questions our fundamental principles'. The argument between Flood and Robertson about the contradictions inherent in 'development' is no less urgent today. Professor Christopher Clapham, of the Department of Politics and International Relations, University of Leicester, has contributed a brief comment on the exchange.

Caution, however, must be exercised in interpreting the personal tragedy. One of Robertson's criticisms was that Flood became, according to him, too involved with a particular group, the Afar, at the expense of a wider and more balanced understanding of all the various interest groups in the Awash Valley. If this was a weakness in Flood's position, it is one which many anthropologists who have lived with and studied minorities will readily sympathize with, especially when these minorities have little influence on the media and 'world opinion'. It is quite common for an anthropologist to act deliberately as an advocate for a disadvantaged indigenous group, but fortunately rare for them to be murdered. Likewise, a fieldworker with a completely different analytical position to Flood's – for instance, with more interest in Ethiopia's political economy – might have been caught up in civil conflict, and met with a similar fate, by accident.

Even during the relative peace of colonial times in north-east Africa, clan conflicts were endemic. It is now fairly common for anthropologists to undertake research in contexts of war and civil strife – to which a section of this anthology is devoted, including an article by Anatoly Khazanov which discusses some of the ethical and professional issues.

Note

Special thanks are due to Glynn's parents, Mr and Mrs Harry Flood, and his widow Michèle Flood, for permission to reprint the exchange from *RAINews* and to use a family photograph for the cover of the paperback edition of this book.

Chapter 10

Glynn Flood

■ NOMADISM AND ITS FUTURE: THE AFAR,
RAINews, 6, January/February 1975, pp. 5–9

THE DANAKIL, OR AFAR as they prefer to be called, inhabit the lowlands of north-east Ethiopia within the triangle formed by joining the towns of Awash Station, Massawa and Djibouti (TFAI)[1]. Traditionally they subsist as pastoralists, depending almost totally on milk from their herds of cows, camels, goats and sheep.

The Afar area is one of the hottest in the world. As a whole the region is extremely inhospitable, but is able to support a population of transhumant pastoralists thanks to the presence of a large and permanent water-course, which traverses the desert and semi-desert landscape for a distance of nearly 800 km before evaporating in the string of saline lakes on the border of Ethiopia with TFAI. This river, the Awash, is the life-source for some 150,000 Afar pastoralists and their animals in the southern two-thirds of Afar territory.

Rain-fed pastures exist in the north, and in higher areas towards the Ethiopian Highlands, but these are by no means sufficient either in extent or in duration. The long rainy season in Afar, as in the Highlands, is from June to September. The short rains are less reliable coming within the period from March to mid-May.

The most important pastures are those fed by flood-waters from the Awash and its two main tributaries, the Mille and the Kesem. Normally the heavy rains in the Highlands lead to extensive flooding in the flat plain of the Awash, some time in late August or early September. The flooded areas dry out progressively during the dry season, providing adequate grazing during a period of perhaps eight months without rain. This reliance on flooded pastures should be borne in mind when we come to deal with explanations of famine in a later section.

The Awash Valley contains the most fertile soils in Ethiopia, but these were not used for crop growing, except in a very limited way, until quite recently. Under the Old Regime land ownership was defined in terms of the State Domains concept whereby land traditionally used by pastoralists was deemed to belong to the State, whilst 'rist' rights of traditional *cultivators* in other parts of Ethiopia were recognised. (This discriminatory attitude is likely to be abolished under the new regime.)

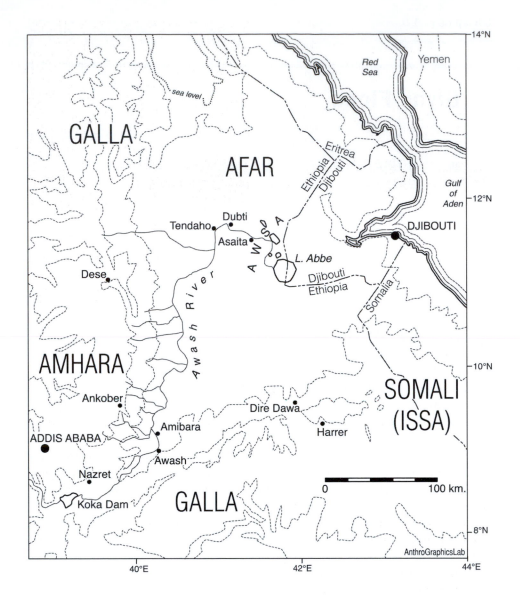

Figure 10.1　Map of the Awash Valley.

Until recently, however, the Afar were in little danger of losing their lands: the Government in the Highlands might claim that the land was State Domain, and even award concessions in the area, but there were few Highlanders who dared venture into the land of the fearsome Afar, an area which has been out of bounds to Highland Christians since at least the times of Ahamad gura (early 16th Century) and was only nominally reconquered in the period 1905–35.

The relative autonomy of the Afar pastoralists has been severely threatened since the early 1960s by a double process of economic expansion made possible by massive investments of foreign capital (USAID, World Bank, etc.). This has enabled the

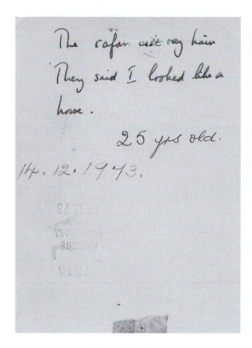

Figure 10.2   Glynn Flood.

Highlanders of Ethiopia to continue the policy of internal colonization begun under Menelik II (died 1913), and to establish capital-intensive, highly profitable agricultural units in the Awash Valley. At the same time, because the capital and know-how has come from abroad (Britain, Israel, USA, Holland and Italy) many of the holdings in the Valley are typical neo-colonialist enterprises which do little to help either the Afar or the people of Ethiopia as a whole. In the Ethiopia of the Old Regime, government posts were highly profitable sinecures and planning decisions were more often influenced by personal than by national interest.

In 1962 the Awash Valley Authority (AVA) was created as an autonomous public authority of the Ethiopian Government, charged with the following functions:

(a) to conduct surveys of the Valley's resources;
(b) to prepare plans and programmes for the utilization and development of these resources;
(c) to co-ordinate the activities of the various Ministries and Authorities connected with this development;
(d) to authorize third parties to construct, manage and administer the necessary infrastructures;
(e) to promote or organize agricultural and industrial enterprises;
(f) to administer and control the waters of the Awash River and its affluents;
(g) in general, to do all such things as may be necessary to ensure the best use and development of the Awash Valley.

Surveys were made concerning all aspects of the Awash Basin except its people. No master plan for development exists. An FAO expert was hired in 1968 to survey

Table 10.1

	Area in hectares	% of total	Value ($ Eth.)	% of total
Cotton	29,000	60	25 m	27
Sugar	10,000	22	58.5 m	63
Cereals	6,000	12	c. 4 m	5
Fruit and vegetables	3,100	6	c. 4 m	5
Total	48,000		92 m	

NB Although the totals are correct, figures in column 1 (area in ha) have been rounded off to the nearest 1,000 ha, in most cases.

Table 10.2

	Area in hectares	Value of product ($ Eth.)	% foreign owned	Admin. and control of product
AWSA	14,200	7 m	—	Alimirah (Afar)
HVA Wonji & Shoa	6,840	40.8 m	80	Dutch
HVA Metahara	4,000	17.7 m	51	Dutch
TPSC (Mitchell Cotts)	8,200	9 m	30	British
Abadir	2,800	c. 2.5 m	no inf.	Israeli
Nura Era	2,000	c. 2 m	no inf.	Italian
Total	38,040	79 m		

social conditions in the Valley, and in his report stated that the present direction of development held inherent dangers. In 1970 the Ministry of Land Reform employed an FAO expert to study 'The Problem of Nomads' in Ethiopia, with special reference to the people of the Awash Valley. This report urged that a much longer study be made; but nothing was done until 1973 when AVA began to employ an Ethiopian sociologist on a permanent basis in connection with a settlement scheme in the Middle Valley.

In the whole of the Awash Valley there are perhaps 200,000 irrigable hectares, of which about 50,000 were farmed in 1970/1. 113,000 ha. are projected for cultivation before 1980. The quickest and cheapest expansion of agriculture here is possible by the method of gravity irrigation. Consequently, the areas where the

Awash flows through flat plains susceptible to flooding were the most attractive to the developers. That these are precisely the most important grazing areas for the pastoralists was of little import to the farmers: they had their legal title to the land from the AVA and they paid their taxes. And, as the developers are quick to point out, the land taken so far represents less than 1% of the total area exploited by the Afar.

The areas involved, the crops cultivated and their value for the year 1970 can be seen in Table 10.1.

The area, production and ownership of the larger units in existence in 1970 is seen in Table 10.2.

Farming in the Awash Valley is highly profitable and investments are recovered after 3–4 years in most cases. Ethiopian individuals and foreign companies are rushing to get concessions in the Valley from AVA. At the moment more than half the developed land in the Valley is controlled by foreign companies.

The major exception to this pattern of foreign-owned enterprises which pay little or no attention to the needs of the indigenous peoples of the Valley, is the huge co-operative cotton plantation administered by Amoyti Alimirah, the political and religious chief of the Afar of the Awash Delta in the Lower Plains.

After the formation of AVA in 1962 it was obvious to the Afar that their territories were in danger, hence this spontaneous development of cotton agriculture by a people whose traditional economy is pastoral. The only realistic way in which the Afar leaders could combat the farming invaders of their territories was and is by using the land for farming themselves. This is not to say that the pastoralists could not and did not make life very difficult for the farmers in the beginning – there are still many armed conflicts between farmers and herdsmen in the Valley – but that in the long run the farmers, supported by the Ethiopian Government and international capital, were bound to win.

Alimirah saw that cotton plantations could best be fought with cotton plantations, and was wealthy and influential enough to provide the initiative for the setting-up of a huge plantation in his own area. On the Afar-owned plantation productivity per hectare is not the be-all and end-all of farming. Profit-making is never far from the minds of the farming Afar: but a factor of major importance in their development is their desire to get as much land as possible under the plough so that outsiders cannot take it. Yields per hectare are lower on the Afar plantation than elsewhere, because many hectares are only nominally farmed. A more significant figure by which to judge Afar development is the rate of expansion of their enterprise: they began in 1964/5 from practically nothing, had 14,200 hectares by 1970, and in 1974 included 22,500 hectares. Whilst expanding rapidly themselves they have been most careful to prevent or hamper any similar moves on the part of outsiders: thus the TPSC (Mitchell Cotts) holding at Dubti in the Lower plains is now almost totally surrounded by Afar holdings registered as farmland and therefore not susceptible to allocation to outsiders as State Domain.

The situation in the Valley is thus extremely complex, with several types of economy operating, and with all the elements of a land war at hand. Alongside and in direct competition with the farmers, whose techniques range from the most to the least sophisticated, are the original inhabitants of the Valley, the Afar pastoralists. Only where the Afar themselves have taken to farming has mixed pastoral and agricultural life evolved, and even then to a very limited extent. In general, throughout the Valley, the differences between farmers and pastoralists are as clear cut as the fences which surround most of the plantations.

In all the controversy which surrounded the beginning of development, and which continues, no-one in authority has thought to ask the pastoralists their opinion, or to discover what will be the exact effects on Afar traditional society. Initial reports for the AVA are couched in terms of helping the pastoralists 'to lead a normal life'. One such report states most clearly that 'The Afar are not gypsies' (in one sentence), and then goes on to explain at great length that they resemble gypsies in many ways.

In the absence of specific studies dealing with the effect of development on the pastoralists, we can only look to their reaction if we are to understand their attitude to what has happened.

Early development was frequently upset by the destruction of surveyors' marking posts and the burning of machinery. Mitchell Cotts, a British company, have resorted to surrounding their large plantation at Dubti with barbed-wire fences, but are still unable to prevent large herds of camels from enjoying the cotton. The Israeli-managed concern at Abadir is said to have resorted to machine-guns in order to defend its crops against encroaching herds.

The effect of development on the pastoral economy has been belittled by those concerned in the development, but there is no doubt that the Great Famine of 1972/3 owed much to it. If Government Agencies denied this it was not always through wanton neglect, although in some cases this was so. Quite simply, there was a lack of knowledge, in the quarters concerned, about the Afar pastoralists' way of life. Any information possessed by those in positions of authority was readily assimilated to a central kernel of ideas about cultural supremacy, so that the very reasons why any form of rapid development amongst the pastoralists would be most difficult became construed as valid reasons for ignoring the people completely. With the notable exception of the Afar spontaneous development in Awsa, farming interests know and care little about the pastoralists. Under the Old Regime anything which made life difficult for the pastoralists was more or less encouraged by the central Government, even to the extent of giving both Afar and Issa weapons and sending police trucks to help the two sides get at each other.

In the pastoral economy, flooded grazing was absolutely essential during the dry season. This is obvious to anyone who bothers to go and look. What is less obvious is that each group of pastoralists and their animals needs access to several types of flooded grazing. When land is totally under water it cannot be grazed; and when it has dried, the new grass is rapidly burnt off by the sun. When land is too marshy the abundance of mosquitoes makes occupation undesirable: the Afar know that mosquitoes bring fever. Furthermore, certain areas, which have all the appearance of good grazing, carry disease for the livestock and are best left alone. Above all, each group needs access both to land which drains quickly after flooding and to land which drains slowly, if it is to survive a dry season which can last from mid-September to late June.

The land which has been taken for early development is mostly land close to the river in areas which flooded easily and took a long time to drain. Consequently the pastoralists have lost the land which is of greatest importance to them — that land which gave good grazing during the hottest and driest part of the year from February to June.

It would be wrong to blame the farmers entirely for the disaster of 1973. The Afar themselves say that from about 1965 onwards the short rains (April–May) have failed often, and there is some evidence that up until c. 1968 Afar herds had increased above the carrying capacity of the land. Nevertheless, charges of over-grazing, which those in development are so quick to make, can never be proven, since those in positions to make the necessary studies *before* development began, failed to do so. It goes almost without saying that those who neglected to make the required studies and those who now state glibly that the Famine of 1973 was due to the Afar overgrazing are often one and the same. Overgrazing is a relative concept and, since at least 1962, the pastoralists have been losing land to the farmers.

Since much of the land taken had been good grassland, cattle in particular have been hit by the development. Consequently many pastoralists have devoted all their time and interest to their goat herds, and as the situation worsened from 1968 to 1972 goats and camels came to dominate the pastoral economy, with resultant destruction of tree cover and topsoil in forest areas close to the river.

Lacking grass, the pastoralists were obliged to cut the top branches from trees to provide leaves for their animals. The boomtowns which have sprung up near the plantations all use vast amounts of wood, both for building and for cooking. There are now huge areas of dead forest in the Awash Valley.

Apart from these developments, the regime of the Awash River itself has been drastically altered. Koka Dam, to the south of Addis Ababa, has reduced the peak flow of water from 700m^3/second to 300m^3/second, and increased the minimum flow from 200 litres/second to 30m^3/second. The Awash has been tamed and regu-larized for the farmers, but the effects of this reduction in the river's potential to flood has an obvious effect throughout the Valley. The irrigation process, too, takes much water from the river and allows it to drain away or evaporate in the fields, where it is lost to the herdsmen. Less water reaches the inland delta of the Awash nowadays, so that vegetation balances have been disturbed and the desert is allowed to encroach.

Although the actual area of land taken for farming purposes represents a tiny proportion of the total land inhabited by Afar, the effect of this loss has already proved disastrous, and will soon result in the complete destruction of the pastoral culture with an accompanying loss of life which will be considerable.

Huge areas used by the Afar during the wet season have no permanent water supply. The great plains which support no human habitation during the dry season are capable of providing grazing for several million animals during the wet. But if they are to be able to exploit the vast areas into which they move during the west season, Afar pastoralists must have access to adequate dry-season grazing near the river. In the dry season, with most people clustered around the river, density of population is high; whilst in the wet season the people are very sparsely scattered on the land. When a small area close to the river is made unavailable for dry season grazing, a much larger area away from the river is rendered useless.

Traditionally, institutionalized activities such as secondary funeral rites and marriage-making are carried on in the dry season when population density is high.

These have been disrupted locally by the existence of plantations, forcing whole groups to find new dry season grazing. Thus new groups lacking amity have been thrust together, and conflict is high; whilst groups which before had many ritual links have sometimes been separated.

But the greater disruption is in the wet-season activities. Before the Great Famine of 1973 the wet season migrations and patterns of group placement were already breaking down: some people, having lost many of their cattle, found it pointless to make the long journey when the big rains came. Since the Famine, with animal and human populations so drastically reduced, the distribution of wet-season encampments has often been such that social interaction became minimal. Since co-operation with other groups is necessary (if only for reasons of safety), life in the wet season has become more hazardous than before, with the result that fewer and fewer people are likely to move out in future. Increasingly, the pastoral economy is dominated by goats, which in the short term give the best chances of survival. But in the long term, as Afar herdsmen are well aware, goats destroy their own grazing. Many herdsmen with whom I have spoken see the Famine in traditional terms and expect gradually to shift from goats to cattle as the situation improves: very few are able to see that there will be no improvement, that they have been caught in a downward spiral. The growing concentration of people and goats in a steadily diminishing area close to the river leads to conditions in which the arguments of the cultural supremacists in charge of development appear all too correct: and the destruction of tree cover by the goats of pastoralists under pressure to survive becomes but the first step in the process of clearing and levelling the land to make it suitable for irrigated agriculture.

It is important to recognize that in an economy such as that of the traditional Afar, simple measurement by hectares is no way of judging the impact of taking away land for other uses. No-one knows better than an Afar pastoralist that the potential and actual resources available in a given region have little to do with its surface area: but when the developers came, they neglected to ask. More often than not, those whose judgement was regarded as the most valuable flew over the heads of those who knew, and made their estimations without ever putting their feet on the ground!

When the inevitable disaster came in 1972/3, a herd of cattle estimated in number at between 500,000 and 1,000,000 moved into the Lower Plains and ate the only grazing available – the cotton. This despite the fact that the pastoralists know that the insecticides used on the cotton, often Eldrin or DDT compounds, are highly toxic to mammals (man included).

The Afar co-operative in Awsa was not spared in this onslaught which took place early in 1973, but it is significant that the cotton on the British-managed plantations in Dubti and Dat Bahari was the first to be invaded. Alimirah's cotton in Awsa was spared until last. Whilst it would be wrong to assert that there is no conflict of interests between Afar pastoralists and Afar farmers, there is far greater tolerance between them than between pastoralists and outside interests. Afar unity owes much to the presence of outsiders, for pastoralists are aware that without their own cotton people, they themselves could not exist as cattle people.

The Great Famine of 1972/3, which killed an inestimable number of people in Wallo Province, including the Awash Valley, was noticeably less in evidence in Awsa than elsewhere – although population density is higher than in the rest of the Valley, and although many thousands of Afar from other regions flooded into Awsa to seek help. This is because the leader of the Afar of Awsa, Alimirah, used the profits from farming accumulated in earlier years to save the people. In this he was almost alone amongst the great local leaders of the Old Regime – a fact that has been recognized by the new Provisional Military Government, which has spared him in the recent round-up of wrongdoers and political opponents.

Nevertheless Alimirah is in a morally difficult position, for if he continues to support the pastoralists in these times of need he diminishes the Afar's capability of expanding their farming interests, and thus risks losing much Afar land to outsiders. The answer to the problem is to settle the pastoralists quickly: and the Afar leaders are exerting great efforts to this end. Livestock raising schemes, with irrigated pastures away from the river, are also under consideration.

With a new progressive Government in power in Addis Ababa, it is to be hoped that the story of development in the Awash Valley will end well, and that the Afar enterprise in self-development will receive due praise. But there are several obstacles to any move for a re-appraisal of the role of Awsa in the region. It is diffi-cult for any Government – even a revolutionary one – to admit that something remarkable and good has occurred outside the realm of its own influence. AVA still exists much as before: but the Afar farming enterprises, which are now spreading throughout the Valley, have grown up independently of AVA and sometimes in open opposition to it. If the Government is a little wary of recognising the Afar contribution in the Valley, it is also quite understandable that the Afar, both farmers and pastoralists, should remain suspicious of any outside interest in 'their' land. These problems are very much the heritage of Haile Selassie's often rather crude policy of divide and rule. It remains to be seen whether the age-old suspicion and conflict between the Highlanders and the Afar can be forgotten in the common interest of developing the Awash Valley efficiently and for the benefit of its peoples.

Development is, we all know, A Good Thing. It is one of the almost universal and unquestionable myths of our age that the productive capacities of land (in terms of quintals of cotton or tons of wheat) must be maximized. We all know that there are 'shortages' of many products in the world – mainly of foodstuffs, though to watch the developers in action one might be excused for thinking that it was of dollars! Land, we know, must not be 'wasted' (for who and by whom?) by 'inef-ficient usages'. We measure something called Progress in terms of 'per capita income', but are hardly concerned about the realities of life for most of the 'capita' whose (often imaginary) income is being measured. And all is justified in terms of the 'standard of living' of peoples whose way of living we despise and intend to change anyway, whether it be for the better or not.

Behind a hypocritical mask of seeking to do good, the developers make their fortunes and cleverly omit the huge debit of human suffering from their balance sheets. There are always a few willing examples from the indigenous culture to be displayed like prize cattle at an auction: and the many more who find their own way of life infinitely preferable to any other are powerless and mute at the begin-ning of the process, only to find themselves becoming ridiculous as time goes on. I do not wish to attack all development here. Change is inevitable, and change for the better is to be hoped for – though in whose terms it will be better is a difficult question for most developers to answer. When development of the type normally encouraged by the industrial nations occurs outside Western Europe or North America, highly paid experts descend armed with a certainty of the superiority of their own culture and a set of unquestionable assumptions based on the tenets of imperialist growth economics: for example, that Progress equals growth and that growth can be measured in terms of gross figures for exports, imports and average per capita incomes for a given state.

Government officials of the state in which the miracle of development is to take place usually fall over themselves in their haste to agree with the foreign experts, in whose country, likely as not, they have been educated in the same basic tenets of the ideology of development. In fact, so powerful and widespread has the common acceptance of neo-classical economic ideology become, that usually the only people who are unable to agree are those whose daily lives will be thoroughly disrupted by 'inevitable' and 'necessary' changes, the meaning of which will escape them.

The arguments for development of the Awash Valley are many. Some of them are valid. Ethiopia is an extremely poor country, though by no means as poor as figures published by the various agencies of the United Nations suggest. In the sense that a vast majority of Ethiopians are self-sufficient in their daily needs, Ethiopia might be termed very rich. The bulk of the nation's imports are luxury goods, motor vehicles and machinery. Paradoxically, the result of development is the creation of a large dependent rural proletariat. And even if figures for per capita income increased over the years, it is probable that this reflects the growing accumulation of capital in a few hands rather than any general increase in prosperity. However, development is necessary, if only to make Ethiopia economically powerful enough to withstand the economic imperialism of other nations, and to provide food for her own peoples and for others in the world. But unless development is planned carefully with clear objectives other than crude profit-making in view, the net results are positively harmful. The use of capital and expertise from abroad to develop capital-intensive agriculture can easily result in a demonstrable loss to the host country even in purely neo-classical economic terms. The absolute loss, as I have tried to show, is considerably greater.

The Famine of 1973 was caused in great part by development allowed and encouraged by a Government elite working in corrupt liaison with international capitalists. If the present type of development continues unchecked, the full utilization of the 200,000 irrigable hectares in the Awash Valley will leave many millions of hectares of desert and semi-desert totally under-utilized – for the only people or culture capable of exploiting such land will no longer exist. Until now no cattle-raising scheme has come to fruition – for the simple reason that no-one has really tried: profits come quicker with cotton, sugar and fruit.

What happened in the Awash Valley is perhaps untypical, but I suspect not. At the beginning, appropriate noises were made and appropriate statements put on paper about settling the people of the Valley and improving their living conditions. This is laudable if questionable. But no studies were made to help achieve this end and the existing settlement schemes and re-education schemes have the obvious appearance of mere appendages to a massive development of capitalist agriculture. Unless we count settlement by burial, many more Europeans and Ethiopian Highlanders have been settled in the Valley than Afar, whose land it is by traditional usage.

In terms of national interest a net loss is being incurred, quite apart from the moral questions involved. One culture, of great interest to would-be tourists, is in the process of being destroyed. A huge area once exploited by about 150,000 people during the wet season will become a total desert. On the 200,000 ha which will be developed, employment will be found for perhaps 50,000 permanent workers; and seasonal employment for about 250,000. If the present situation continues, most of the capital amassed in these enterprises will leave Ethiopia, and the ordinary workers on the farms will maintain a 'standard of living' slightly higher than most Ethiopians at the expense of becoming dependent seasonal labourers migrating from the Highlands for harvest times. The original 'nomads' will have been replaced by modern wage-labourer nomads. Then shall we see who most closely resembles gypsies.

Note

1   TFAI = French Territory of the Afar and Issas, formerly French Somaliland.

Chapter 11

A.F. Robertson

■   ANTHROPOLOGY AND THE NOMAD:
ANOTHER VIEW OF THE AFAR,
RAINews, 8, May/June 1975, pp. 7–9

BECAUSE SOCIAL ANTHROPOLOGY has become accustomed to dealing with different systems of values in methodical and objective ways, it can be of considerable value in the study of development. However, development in its various forms frequently brings two different systems of values into confrontation, presenting the anthropologist with new problems and responsibilities. His study becomes political, and as such it demands particular care in the treatment of social values. Constructive comment on the situation depends on methodical and balanced study of all the interests, issues and activities involved. If he throws in his lot with one party the anthropologist puts the credibility of his analysis at stake. To be convincing, a partisan account of a political situation must be very thoroughly researched.

Some anthropologists have been showing increasing concern about the plight of hunter-gatherers, nomads and other people affected by drastic changes in the world about them. Through such bodies as Survival International they have sprung to the defence of Amazonian Indians or tribal peoples in the Philippines, bringing their anthropological knowledge and experience to bear on what are undoubtedly political arguments. Without questioning their good intentions, we may justly feel concerned about their qualifications for entering some of these debates. There is a real risk that clumsy intrusion will ultimately do more harm than good.

However thoroughly he may know a particular tribe, the anthropologist may lack the knowledge and experience to argue effectively about its involvement in a wider national or international context. Far from making a cool, critical appraisal of the relations of a peripheral community in the development of a particular country, he may give a one-sided, emotionally committed account which stresses the integrity and viability of tribal life. This is not only bad tactics, it is bad anthropology. Those of us who are professionally concerned with development have learned the need to take the widest possible perspective, and to step out of the village, the region and the country in order to make more balanced judgements about what is happening to primitive man.

I found much of Glynn Flood's article on the Ethiopian government's development of the Awash Valley (*RAINews*, Jan.–Feb. 1975) instructive and well argued. He has gone far to try to understand the external forces bearing down on the Afar people but his account remains biased in favour of one of the interests currently involved in the political arena of the Awash, the 'sultanate' at Awsa. The interests of the other Afar, the Issa people, or the highlanders, are given little or no attention. The account of the Awash Valley Authority is certainly unsympathetic, and it is mainly in an attempt to redress the balance a little in *their* favour that I am writing now. I clearly lack Mr Flood's detailed knowledge of the Afar, and my view is based on just a few weeks' work with the AVA (as a neutral, unpaid observer) in the summer of 1974. I hope that what I have to say, taken in conjunction with Mr Flood's view, will present a rather broader picture of what is happening in the valley and why. Although I too am critical of the current development, I hope that my account will also make it apparent that the fate of the Afar necessarily involves some understanding 'from within' of the AVA, its experience and the alternatives which confront it, as well as the sympathetic view of the Afar which Mr Flood has given us.

The AVA probably has a larger measure of autonomy than any other development body in Ethiopia and is undoubtedly very powerful. The Awash Valley, extending from the narrow upper reaches of the river about 40 miles south of Addis Ababa out into the Danakil Desert in the north and to the mountains of Harrer to the east, has been identified as an area of great potential for irrigated agriculture. The AVA was set up in 1962 to plan, control and co-ordinate the development of the valley, and there are now some 50,000 hectares of irrigated land, farmed by the AVA and by foreign and Ethiopian concessionnaires. The Authority is jointly managed by the Ethiopian Government and FAO, and a condition of World Bank finance for the AVA's projects is that the indigenous peoples of the valley, predominantly the Afar or Danakil pastoral nomads, should not be victimised. Since the expansion of agricultural enterprise along the river amounts to dispossessing the Afar of their dry-season grazing, the AVA has decided to promote their settlement in communities based on irrigated agriculture. The Authority also intends to assist the pastoral life of the nomads by providing wells in selected areas, controlling water to regulate the available grazing. Two settlements have been established for the Afar, one at Amibara in the Middle Valley, and one at Dubti in the Lower Plains. There is a tendency to speak of these settlements as if they were very new, whereas Dubti was set up in 1966 and Amibara in 1967. Each has an instruction farm, and at Melka Warer near Amibara the AVA runs an impressive experimental station. The technical success of AVA is very striking; long staple cotton is produced expertly and profitably, and experiments with citrus fruits, tobacco and other crops have been very promising. Pasture trials have indicated that irrigation may transform livestock rearing, indeed the concessionaire company at Melka Sadi now imports cattle from the highlands, fattens them in the valley and exports the carcasses to Saudi Arabia. The banana plantations of this company, the extensive sugar estates at Metehara, and the cotton plantations of three Ethiopian concessionnaires all testify to the productivity of the valley.

The AVA has less cause for satisfaction with its efforts to extend these technical achievements to the social development of the Afar. The Amibara 'settlement' presents an intriguing picture; it consists of the AVA headquarters and a township of shacks built by immigrant highland labourers and those providing services for this transient population. The Afar 'settlers' continue to live very much as they always have, in small encampments around the cotton plantations. Each settler family is allocated a 2.5 hectare plot of the irrigated cotton which has been developed and is maintained by the AVA. Already 214 families have been 'settled' and there are plans to provide plots for up to 600 more. It seems that the Afar's enthusiasm for settlement depends solely on the fact that a family is assured, at the moment, a very large cash income from its 2½ hectares. Persuading the Afar to maintain their plots is a perplexing problem for the scheme management. Highland labourers paid at the rate of E$1.50 per day must be drafted in to work the cotton, but even after this has been debited to him the Afar plot holder can collect as much as E$3,000 a year. The difference between this and the highland labourer's income raises very sharply the moral and political questions about who should be allowed to benefit from the development of the Awash Valley. There can be no doubt that the highlanders would transform Amibara into a stable and prosperous community very much more rapidly and with very much less formal planning than could the Afar. There can also be no doubt that if this were allowed to happen the Afar would be provoked to drastic political and physical reaction. They have the nomad's scorn for sedentary agricultural peoples, and an ostentatiously paraded firepower to back up their reputation for dealing brutally with intrusions on their rights.

The AVA acknowledges that the Dubti settlement (which I did not visit) has stagnated, and is uncomfortably aware of the shortcomings of Amibara. In both physical and social terms the settlement cannot yet be said to exist, although in economic and legal terms it undoubtedly does. Here is a classic case of the need for what we are pleased to call an 'integrated' approach to rural development. The lack of adequate health, educational and other facilities testifies to the weakness of governmental co-operation and demonstrates that even an autonomous body like the AVA is limited in its capacity to provide an adequate community infrastructure. There is clearly nothing more than a crude financial incentive for the Afar to remain at Amibara. In this vacuum they will find their own organisational solutions to their changed circumstances, solutions which will almost certainly be displeasing to the AVA. They will acquire political aptitudes which will outstrip the Authority's very limited capacity to manipulate them, and they will be blamed for making trouble and for squandering the economic opportunities which have been put their way. To that extent the Afar are being harshly and unfairly treated.

It is encouraging that some AVA officials have perceived and are attempting to cover these risks. The Authority has been making efforts, so far fruitless, to design suitable dwellings for a permanent Afar settlement, and has lately been attempting to initiate a co-operative society. The social organisation of the Afar at Amibara remains firmly Afar tribal organisation. Faced with the well-known resilience of nomadic culture and unable as yet to offer any constructive alternative, the AVA has been obliged to accept and transact its business with the local descent groups. It has identified the *balabbats*, or clan heads as 'chiefs', as the persons through whom transactions with the Afar should be made. This appears to have authorised the *balabbats* in ways which are unconventional in Afar terms; responsibility in such societies is rarely focused on individuals but is diffused quite widely through a mobile and oddly 'egalitarian' population. The AVA hopes that responsibility for selecting settlers and managing their affairs can be vested in the clans but I think it is probable that this will be frustrated by their continued dependence on the *balabbats*. Such transactions will only be possible if the AVA has a more authentic perception of the Afar authority structure. Now keenly aware of the pressing need for social development, the AVA has engaged two sociologists, one American and one Ethiopian, to assist in planning. The Authority has also expressed a preference for regional planning techniques and personnel training with a wider disciplinary frame of reference than is customary. There is some impatience among the technocrats of AVA with the recalcitrance of the Afar and the lack of some clear-cut 'social engineering' from the sociologists engaged by the Authority. It was somewhat depressing to rediscover in AVA the tendency to compartmentalise responsibility. It was, however, gratifying to discover a critical self-awareness among senior AVA officials, and a realistic appraisal of its political problems in dealing with such varied interests as the Ethiopian government, the foreign and international agencies, the commercial concerns established in the valley, the powerful sultanate at Awsa in the Lower Plains, and the increasing political awareness of the Afar people.

As is so often the case, communication is a fundamental problem for the AVA. It is strung out between headquarters at Addis Ababa and field stations in the valley, and there is the concomitant alienation from higher authority of individuals and groups working in the field. The AVA sociologist Dr Tekeste Zergaber is building up a valuable picture of the Authority's relations with the Afar, facilitated by his increasing proficiency in the Afar language. As a highlander, he has come to appreciate the profound gap between the foreign and Amharic-speaking officers of the Authority and the Afar, and the need to bridge this. A single '*evolué*'[1] Afar liaison officer has served as the principal link, building up for himself a turbulent but powerful status. The Amibara 'Field Committee' of the Afar is clearly a feeble affair, and the AVA still depends on communication, very much by remote control, through the liaison officer and the *balabbats*. To a short-term visitor like myself it seems that progress could be made by improving the linguistic competence of the AVA officials; most are content to assume that Amharicisation of the Afar will make this unnecessary, but current attitudes in Ethiopia and in the valley suggest that this may be an unsound assumption politically. In terms of social research and planning, it seems important to understand the strategic value of careful study of Afar political organisation. I would rank this as of more immediate importance than research addressed to the Afar individual — attitude surveys, censuses, and so on. At some point in the very near future the AVA will need to meet the Afar in some kind of joint decision-making body, and for this a knowledge of how the Afar govern themselves will be essential. The AVA has the material inducements for Afar co-operation, but at the moment it has no structure whereby it can transact effectively with the Afar and consolidate this co-operation. The exotic and over-worked co-operative society model has appeared in Amibara, but it must be clear to AVA officials that its long-term value will be minimal.

The intellectual and practical problems of settling the Afar are absorbing, and certainly much more complex than these few trite observations would suggest. Time is short, and the AVA must be commended for the determined way in which it is now setting about the tasks of social development.

As I do not in fact know how well Mr Flood knows the AVA, I must be lenient in my assessment of his account. I find quite sensible his points that Afar know as well, if not better, than outsiders how to make a living out of the valley; and I would agree very much with his views about the (non-) communication with government agencies. However I find his prognoses on development less adequate. I am sure he is over-sanguine in his praise for the 'sultan' Alimirah of Awsa; this man leads a very particular segment of the Afar, others of whom are not at all appreciative of his interests and methods. One could debate whether the 'colonial zeal' of Alimirah is necessarily more virtuous than that of the Ethiopian government. Mr Flood and I might agree that 'Awash for the Afar' is a plausibly just cry, but I for one would need to know much more about the situation before I could assess the relative merits of 'Awash for the Issa' or 'Awash for all Ethiopians', or even 'Awash for Mitchell Cotts & Co.'

Finally, the ambivalence of Mr Flood's sentiments shows through in two apparently contradictory statements which I find typical of anthropological writing in this genre: (a) 'there are always a few willing examples from the indigenous culture to be displayed like prize cattle at an auction'; (b) 'one culture of great interest to would-be tourists is in the process of being destroyed'. *Why* is Afar culture to be preserved and *for what*? The cultural integrity and viability of the Afar is of great importance to the anthropologist, but it is neither pleasant nor practicable to think of the Afar making a living out of their culture *per se* in a changing world. They are not going to become museum stock, they are going to change and be changed. Alimirah may help to show them how to make a more profitable adjustment of their way of life to a changed environment and a new kind of involvement with Ethiopia and the world, but whether we like it or not their fate is more specifically in the hands of the Ethiopian government and the AVA.

It is to the organisation and operation of the Ethiopian government and its agencies that our anthropological studies must turn if we are going to be anything more useful than impassioned commentators on the plight of such peoples as the Afar. Are anthropologists up to the task?

Note

1   *Evolué* was a colonial-era term for educated Africans already going out of use in 1975. *Editor.*

Chapter 12

Glynn Flood

■ **DEVELOPMENT IN ETHIOPIA**,
RAINews, 9, July/August 1975, pp. 18–19

A. F. ROBERTSON'S REPLY (*RAINews* 8) to my piece in *RAINews* 6 on development and the Afar raises both theoretical and practical questions.

In his last paragraph Dr Robertson suggests that anthropologists must turn to the 'organisation and operation' of government agencies if they are to be 'anything more than impassioned commentators on the plight of [primitive] peoples'. I could not agree more, and see no reason why a total anthropology should not be 'up to the task' of studying the relationship between primitive peoples and development agencies – in academic terms at least. The differences between primitive peoples and development agencies are not such as would render the usual anthropological approach worthless. The only problem I envisage is one well-known to field workers: certain types of data are always more difficult to obtain than others. Particularly where deeply felt economic or political interests are at stake, opposition is encountered. I must admit that my knowledge of the workings of the Awash Valley Authority is not as extensive as my knowledge of Afar, but this is not entirely my fault. Government agencies can be more inaccessible than the densest jungle or most forbidding wilderness. One almost suspects that they have something to hide.

An adequate 'knowledge of how the Afar govern themselves' would be a necessary prerequisite of any plans for the better functioning of AVA, suggests Dr Robertson. Such knowledge has been available for over one year now, in the form of a reasonably well-researched study of the political structure of Awsa and of its role in the Awash Valley. This report was suppressed shortly after its completion and has recently surfaced in an abridged form. It is said (for few have actually laid hands on the original) that in its uncensored form this report hinted that development in the Valley might proceed more smoothly if AVA left it to the Awsa Afar. Attitudes towards the Afar enterprise in self-development have changed considerably in the last few months, and AVA's change manifests itself in a tacit acceptance of the value and accuracy of this document. Attempts are now being made to pull as many Afar as possible into AVA, to use their recognised abilities to develop the Valley.

Dr Robertson reports that World Bank conditions for financing AVA schemes say that the indigenous inhabitants of the Valley should not be victimised. This is all very well, but when did World Bank officials last go to see if the inhabitants of the Valley were being victimised? The people of the Valley – Afar, Karrayyu Galla and Ittu Galla – have lost land, cattle and lives because of development: is this not victimisation? Has *any* project in the Valley ever been abandoned for fear of harmful effects on the original inhabitants?

In attempting to defend the role of AVA, Dr Robertson devotes much of his article to the settlement scheme at Amibara in the Middle Valley. I emphasise my previous statement that the existing settlement schemes in the Valley have the obvious appearance of mere appendages to a massive development of capitalist agriculture. What else is a settlement scheme involving 214 families each on 2.5 hectare plots, in comparison with 50,000 hectares of 'developed' land?

When I wrote that 'there are always a few willing examples from the indigenous culture to be displayed like cattle at an auction' it was Amibara that I had in mind. In the political battle between AVA and the Afar leadership, the Amibara settlers were just pawns. This, and AVA's need to make a success of the scheme *on paper*, explains why the 'settlers' were given ridiculously high wages for practically no work on 'their' farms. A report commissioned by AVA (Asmarom Legesse *et al.* April 1974) severely criticises AVA for its paternalism in the Amibara scheme. When people put forward the Amibara scheme as evidence of AVA's success or good intentions, they are simply taking the role of auctioneer in the auction game.

My other remark, that 'one culture of great interest to would-be tourists is in the process of being destroyed', does not mean that I advocate the preservation of Afar as a museum-piece, but it does require clarification. Most of my argument was intended to convey a criticism of a certain type of development: but here my point would be that *even within the terms of reference of that type of development*, the eradication of Afar culture is possibly undesirable. At the moment, Ethiopia's tourist industry is underdeveloped. But tourism is one of the world's largest industries and *if* Ethiopia wished to follow the pattern of development pushed by the capitalist world, then presumably the development of a tourist industry would follow. Inasmuch as tourism is based on geographical and cultural diversity, the destruction of Afar culture would hamper any projected development of an Ethiopian tourist industry. Surely, even from a neo-classical view of development, there are at least two alternatives: one would be capitalist agricultural development; the other, the development of a tourist industry based on Ethiopia's cultural diversity. My remark about tourism should be understood to mean that the preservation of Afar culture was perhaps desirable even in neo-classical terms: *not* that the neo-classical type of development (and hence guided tours of Afar) was desirable.

Why should Afar culture be preserved? Because cultural diversity is of intrinsic value to mankind as a species. For what should it be preserved? For the Afar, by the Afar – they like their culture. The preservation of Afar culture does not preclude social change: in Awsa in the last 15 years there has been massive social change, but the people are still Afar. In the Amibara settlement one element of success noted by Asmarom Legesse *et al.* involved the working of the 'field committee' of the settlers: this is an institution straight from the traditional culture, known to Afar as *fi'ima*, perfectly adapted to the needs of the settlement and formed spontaneously by the settlers. Legesse also noted that land distribution by the traditional leaders was working fairly and efficiently. In Awsa there is a core of Afar farmers which has been in existence for hundreds of years. You do not have to stop being an Afar to become a farmer, or to enter the 'modern world'.

I must make it clear that my criticisms of AVA should be understood to apply to the pre-revolutionary period, since rapid, and one hopes profound, changes are now taking place. Since the nationalisation of rural land, Afar have a legal right to own land for the first time in Ethiopian history. This alters the relationship between the Afar and AVA considerably. Inasmuch as Ava was hampered by and subordinate to individuals and other government agencies in the old regime, I must also temper my criticism. In the last few months there have been signs that the development of the Awash Valley will now proceed in a much fairer and more humane way. AVA is to get closer links with the Afar, and the role of Awsa in the development of the Valley is now recognised. With this comes a greater readiness from the Afar themselves to work within the various government agencies concerned.

A few last rejoinders to Dr Robertson's reply. In *RAINews* 6 I did not 'stress the integrity or viability' of Afar society. The whole point of the piece was that, owing largely to a particular kind of development, Afar is threatened with disintegration. Of course, in a sense, the 'cultural integrity and viability of [primitive peoples] is of great importance to the anthropologist': presumably just as important as the integrity and viability of development is to those engaged in development studies. But one thing is clear: there is no justification for members of the respective disciplines to rest entrenched behind their own lines with their own subject-matters as company. The division between what are commonly regarded as separate disciplines is quite arbitrary, and in a situation where primitive peoples are almost invariably in some kind of relationship with external forces (central government) it is incumbent upon the anthropologist to understand those forces. It is nonetheless important for the development studies people to make an effort to see development from the point of view of those who are being developed. Development can have some very nasty consequences for the ordinary people in whose name development is undertaken. If development studies people are not prepared to recognise this, then they cease to be students of development and become apologists for it.

Chapter 13

Christopher Clapham

■ THE FLOOD–ROBERTSON EXCHANGE:
A BRIEF COMMENT, September 2001

T HE EXCHANGE BETWEEN GLYNN FLOOD and Sandy Robertson resonates as sharply now as when it was written over twenty-five years ago. At issue is not merely an anthropologist's concern for 'his people', and the desire to preserve a vanishing lifestyle for some open-air museum of human cultures; nor even a controversy about the impact of capitalist development on the Awash Valley area of Ethiopia. It is much more basically about the idea of 'development' itself, about whether it has anything to offer the indigenous peoples of the areas in which it takes place, and about the sustainability of pastoralism within the modern world economy.

In this clash, Robertson finds himself – incongruously, given the tenor of much of his other writing[1] – cast as the spokesman for the top-down conception of planned development that in imperial Ethiopia was represented by the Awash Valley Authority (AVA), and by the *mise en valeur* of fertile and well-watered land along the valley floor that appeared to have far more productive uses than just as dry-season grazing for a relatively small group of pastoralists. From this viewpoint, sugar cane, cotton and fruit trees not only provided profits for a group of largely expatriate investors, but also created useful goods that would not otherwise have been available. Flood occupies a more sympathetic position as the defender not only of the Afar way of life as something worth preserving in its own right, but also of the social and ecological structures through which indigenous peoples have adapted to life in a peculiarly harsh environment, and as spokesman for a form of development that sought to build up from those structures, rather than down from the state and the global market. The intervening years have generally favoured Flood's stance rather than Robertson's.

This particular exchange formed part of a wider debate at that time, about the impact of mechanized agriculture in the Awash Valley, and in late imperial Ethiopia as a whole. Writing at the same time as Flood – the two papers must have been in press simultaneously, for neither refers to the other – Lars Bondestam criticized

HVA and TPSC in classic dependency theory terms as part of a process of global capitalist exploitation that necessarily operated to impoverish indigenous peoples.[2] John Markakis and Nega Ayele took up the case as part of their broader Marxist critique of the imperial regime, and the contradictions of the revolutionary military government that followed it.[3] On the other side of the argument, Dessalegn Rahmato – himself a noteworthy critic both of the imperial regime and of its successor – came to the defence of commercial agriculture, certainly as compared with the state-run systems that followed it.[4]

Flood differed from his fellow critics largely in the benevolent view that he took of the involvement in commercial agriculture of Sultan Alimirah, whom he regarded as taking pre-emptive action to preserve as much of his people's land as possible from alien encroachment. Others viewed the Sultan as an exploiter much on a par with foreign capitalists, and as part of an incipient process of class formation within Afar society. And though Flood for the most part undoubtedly gets the better of the exchange recorded here, Robertson is right to question his implicit association of the Sultan with the interests of the Afar as a whole. John Harbeson probably provides the most balanced assessment of the Sultan's position: 'From a strictly economic perspective, Ali Mira earned the designation "self-interested capitalist", but he was also a religious and political leader of his people and defender of their interests against the intrusions of greater Ethiopia.'[5]

There is nothing more tragic in Flood's assessment than his belief that, following the Ethiopian revolution of 1974, 'rapid, and one hopes profound, changes are now taking place'. Those hopes took him back to Ethiopia, and led directly to his death. Profound changes did indeed take place, but in a direction quite opposite to that which he had wanted and expected. Behind the shattered expectations that Flood – like many others – had placed in the revolution lay the belief that *capitalism* lay at the root of the exploitation that he observed, and that an alternative system – call it socialism – would therefore reverse it. Given the very visible role of foreign multi-nationals, notably HVA and TPSC, in the Awash Valley, that was understandable enough; but behind the spectre of capitalism, whether expatriate or domestic, lay two other forces which, so far from being removed by the revolution, were instead immeasurably strengthened by it.

The first was a sense of manifest destiny on the part of Ethiopia's rulers, which was converted by revolution into a Jacobin quest for control. The Ethiopian state has since its foundation been based in the heavily populated highlands, and has been closely associated both with Orthodox Christianity and with the Amharic language; its rulers have looked on the surrounding lowlanders, most of them Muslim, with a mixture of suspicion and disdain. 'Nomads' such as the Afar were in themselves regarded with contempt, and their sedentarization was viewed as an essential prelude to civilization. But while the imperial government was conscious of its limitations, and for the most part willing to leave the Afar to their own devices, its revolutionary successor had a boundless confidence in its quest for social transformation, and in its ability to achieve it.

The second, which was so effortlessly adopted from the Soviet Union because it was perfectly in keeping with the new regime's underlying attitudes, was a belief in 'development', as something that could be achieved by planned, determined, and if need be coercive direction from above. Never was there a clearer example of 'seeing like a state'.[6] Though the immediate precipitant of the breach between the Afar and the Derg may well have been a misunderstanding – Alimirah refused to go to Addis Ababa, from a fear that he might be imprisoned or executed by the government – ultimately a Marxist military regime was something from which the Afar had nothing to hope and much to fear. The ruthless suppression of the resulting Afar uprising, in which Flood died, was followed by the conversion of the capitalist enterprises which he attacked into state farms that were far more coercive, and far less productive, than their predecessors.

Since then, the wheel has not turned full circle, but it has turned a long way. The Derg's vision of a centralized and socialist Ethiopian nation-state proved to be entirely unsustainable, and collapsed after much bloodshed in 1991. Its successor proclaimed a federal system, in which each 'nationality' – the Afar included – would have the right to internal self-government and even, if it wished, secession. How far that promise has been honoured is another matter: the Afar have in practice a right to self-government, only so long as they vote for the party – the Afar National Liberation Party – approved by the government in Addis Ababa.

More important for our present purposes, however, is that the basic points made in Flood's analysis are both right, and are now much more clearly recognized than when he made them, not just in Ethiopia but in the development literature as a whole: that 'development' is not something that can be imposed from outside, even by regimes far more benevolent than those from which the Afar have had the misfortune to suffer; that it is instead vital, as Flood concludes, 'to see development from the point of view of those who are being developed'; and that pastoralist societies, which as in the case of the Afar have adapted to the demands of some of the most inhospitable terrain in the world, are both peculiarly difficult to incorporate within conceptions of development that have been devised in much more favourable environments, and have much to contribute to the understanding of humanity.

Notes

1   See A.F. Robertson, *People and the State: An Anthropology of Planned Development*, Cambridge University Press, 1984.

2   Lars Bondestam, 'People and Capitalism in the north-eastern lowlands of Ethiopia', *Journal of Modern African Studies* 12, 3, 1974, pp. 423–39.

3   John Markakis and Nega Ayele, *Class and Revolution in Ethiopia*, Nottingham: Spokesman, 1978, pp. 55–7, 137–8.

4   Dessalegn Rahmato, 'Moral crusaders and incipient capitalists: mechanized agriculture and its critics in Ethiopia', *Proceedings of the Third Annual Seminar of the Department of History*, Addis Ababa: Addis Ababa University, 1986, pp. 69–90.

5   John Harbeson, 'Territorial and development politics in the Horn of Africa: the Afar of the Awash Valley,' *African Affairs*, 77, 309, 1978, pp. 479–98.

6   J.S. Scott, *Seeing like a State: How Certain Schemes to Improve the Human Condition have Failed*, New Haven, CT: Yale University Press, 1998.

Chapter 14

John Knight

■   'THE MOUNTAIN PEOPLE' AS TRIBAL MIRROR,
Anthropology Today, 10.6, December 1994, pp. 1–3

> In some ways this book was difficult to write, and in some ways it was
> easy. The actual writing only took a few weeks, but I had been brooding
> over the whole harrowing experience for some three years. Then, when
> I was back in the Ituri Forest with a people who lived in a near paradise,
> I saw the same thing happening to them that had happened to the Ik;
> and out came the book.

WITH THE RECENT DEATH OF COLIN TURNBULL (see obit-
uary, *AT*, October 1994), anthropology lost one of its most committed
popularizers. *The Forest People*, Turnbull's well-known and much-read book on the
Mbuti Pygmies, remains a favourite among anthropology undergraduates. *The Mountain People* (1972), his account of a mountain-dwelling people in northern Uganda
at a time of drought and starvation, has also been widely read, and was even put
on stage by Peter Brook. The two books have often been taken together by critics
as complementary accounts of human society, the good Mbuti whom Turnbull loved
as against the 'selfish, uncaring and unloving' Ik who, in their degeneracy, corrupted
their ethnographer in the process. However, as the above excerpt from his new
introduction to the 1994 Pimlico edition of *The Mountain People* indicates, Turnbull's
love for the Mbuti even underlies his study of the Ik.

Written for a popular rather than professional audience, *The Mountain People* has
also proved to be one of the most controversial pieces of anthropological writing.
Soon after publication, the book was condemned by one anthropologist as 'poor
anthropology in method, in data, and in reasoning . . . [as] emotionally dishonest
or superficial . . . [as] deeply misleading to the public it sets out to inform . . . [and
as] grossly irresponsible and harmful to its unwitting objects of study' (Barth 1974:
100). The book exhibited 'a number of anthropological difficulties and failings
in such a crass form that it deserves both to be sanctioned and to be held up as
a warning to us all' (*ibid.* 99–100). So extreme were the shortcomings of this

book deemed to be that, in a perverse way, it could become useful in inducing much-needed reflection within the discipline, a deeply regrettable professional transgression that might nonetheless serve to indicate the limits of acceptable anthropological practice.

Twenty years on, another anthropologist, on re-reading *The Mountain People*, offers a rather more benign assessment. In a letter to *The Times*, Roland Littlewood, President of the RAI, defends Turnbull's practice of drawing moral conclusions from his study of the Ik from the trend of 'cultural relativism' which would proscribe it, and goes on to lend support to the conclusions themselves. Reacting to an obituary of Turnbull in which the book was characterized as a record of the 'sadistic customs' of 'a vicious people', Littlewood suggests that '[f]ar from depicting them as some sort of savage civilization, Turnbull speculated that the Ik were merely a little way ahead of the rest of us in disregarding our obligations to our fellows and to our environment, and that aggressive economic individualism in a world of diminished resources is incompatible with social morality' (Littlewood 1994).

Much of the controversy caused by *The Mountain People* has had to do with the injustice it was deemed to have done to the Ik. This injustice involves ethnographic competence as well as anthropological ethics. First, Turnbull was accused of misrepresenting the Ik. The accuracy of his study has been seriously challenged, with questions raised about his linguistic competence, the quality of his ethnography, and his basic understanding of Ik culture and social structure. Even the basic premise of *The Mountain People* – that the Ik were a fallen hunter-gatherer society – has been directly challenged. For Turnbull, the Ik were nomadic hunter-gatherers who, on being displaced from their traditional lands, were forced to become farmers; this crucial discontinuity in the Ik way of life underpins the tragic structure of the book. But Bernd Heine, a linguist who worked with the Ik in the early 1980s, argues that in fact the Ik had long been farmers, and that this agricultural identity is readily evident from their major cultural institutions (Heine 1985: 5–8). From the beginning, Turnbull saw the Ik as a group of hunter-gatherers who, with their different environment, could be profitably compared with Mbuti Pygmies. This is the background, Heine suggests, to understanding why Turnbull, when faced with an actual farming people, 'invented a history of an earlier [Ik] hunter culture'.

Second, Turnbull's book would seem to have disturbed the Ik themselves. On hearing of its content from the Catholic mission, Ik felt that Turnbull had 'spoilt' their name. Henceforth the Ik would be reluctant to share information with white researchers, and warned of serious retribution were Turnbull ever to return to Ik country (Heine 1985: 3). Heine reports that at a meeting with Ik elders in 1983 he was asked if it was possible to take legal action against Turnbull; a more recent commentator has even suggested that the Ik would indeed have had a strong legal case against Turnbull, and that, at the very least, they could have stopped sales of the book through a court injunction (de Waal 1993: 5).

Turnbull was also heavily criticized for disregarding the welfare of the Ik, even to the point of physically endangering them. Barth denounces *The Mountain People* for the cavalier way it publicizes illegal activities, names people accused of cattle theft, and even provides photographs of named persons engaged in illegal activities such as forging spears or poaching (Barth 1974: 100).

Most notorious of all was Turnbull's advice to the Ugandan government that, on the basis of his research findings, the Ik should be disbanded. As they would never go voluntarily, '[t]hey would have to be rounded up in something approaching a military operation . . . [and] taken to parts of Uganda sufficiently remote for them not to be able to return . . .' (Turnbull 1994: 283).[1] To be most effective 'men, women and children could be rounded up at random . . . [to be] dispersed through-out the country, its mountainous regions, in small units of around ten' (*ibid.*). For an anthropologist to advocate the ethnocide (or 'culturecide') of the people s/he studies seems scarcely less shocking than a doctor calling for the death of a patient s/he was expected to heal. Turnbull's perception seems to have been precisely that the Ik were suffering from a chronic sickness that demanded an extreme response; that he was like a doctor who endorses the euthanasia of a terminal patient. Later, in a response to critics of the book, Turnbull defended his advocacy of dispersal by arguing, first, that, given the moral degeneration of the Ik, 'there was no culture to kill'; second, that at least the programme would contribute to 'the survival of individual lives'; and third, that by facilitating assimilation into other societies the programme would, in a sense, rescue the Ik, helping them to 'become resocialized and restored to a richer, more truly social life, making use of a potential for humanity' among them (Turnbull 1975: 355). If such a drastic measure would erase what was left of Ik *society*, at least Ik *people* would be saved, their humanity recovered. From this perspective, far from being an act of malice, physical dispersion appears an act of compassion, a kindness intended to put the Ik out of their social misery.

Reflecting on *The Mountain People* and the prescribed disbandment, Alex de Waal has suggested that, while Turnbull might have got away with such comments in the 1970s, he could not do so today in the light of the ethnographies of disaster now available. Descriptions such as Turnbull gives of the Ik 'tell us more about the disturbed psyche of their author than the social realities of disaster' (de Waal 1993: 5; cf. Heine 1985: 14). From this point of view, *The Mountain People* stands as a stark example of the sheer liberty that anthropologists could once take with those they study, a monument to the anthropological insensitivity of another, albeit uncomfortably recent, era.

While undoubtedly a widely read book, *The Mountain People* has also been questioned as an example of 'responsible popularization' (Sallnow 1976: 1). What seems to be at issue here is the degree to which an anthropologist is obliged, even in an avowedly popular work, to gave a full and fair account of the people who are the ostensible subjects. If most anthropologists would agree that their first task is to represent the lives of those they have actually studied, it is also the case that they are often making larger statements *through* their subjects; ethnographic subjects are often made to bear the weight of anthropological generalization (informants to village, village to peasants, peasants to nationals etc.) up to and including humanity itself. These two aims are not necessarily inconsistent. A widespread criticism of *The Mountain People*, however, is that the Ik are, as it were, grossly overloaded by the universal narrative that Turnbull attempts to tell through them. The book is a statement – a judgment – about humanity. Through the Ik we are invited to glimpse ourselves. Hence the readiness with which Turnbull's story lent itself

Figure 14.1   From Peter Brook's production at the Round House, London, 1976, of *The Ik*, dramatized by Denis Cannan and Colin Higgins from Colin Turnbull's *The Mountain People*. The actor playing Turnbull is driving an imaginary jeep with an Ik informant.

to dramatization in the theatres of Western cities. For the director Peter Brook, 'the story of a tiny, remote, unknown African tribe in what seems to be very special circumstances is actually about the cities of the West in decline' (Brook 1988: 136). In a similar vein, McCall suggested that 'the Ik themselves were not important to Turnbull's work', and that the book is really 'a morality tale for North American and, perhaps, other European suburbanites' (McCall 1975: 345).

'The Ik teach us that our much vaunted human values are not inherent in humanity at all, but are associated only with a particular form of survival called society, and that all, even society itself, are luxuries that can be dispensed with' (Turnbull 1994: 294). The Ik are a reminder of the fragility of society, of the potential within all of us to dispense with society, to degenerate, to morally disintegrate. 'The Ik have relinquished all luxury in the name of individual survival, and the result is that they live on as a people without life, without passion, beyond humanity' (*ibid.* 295). We too, like the Ik, are not guaranteed our humanity, for the message of *The Mountain People* is that humanity, society, far from being a given, is something that has to be actively maintained. In the Ik, Turnbull discovered the finitude of humanity; ahead he saw the sort of circumstances – environmental pollution, over-population, widespread famine – which would threaten humanity as a whole with an Ik-like fate, as well as signs – increasing individualism – that this degeneration had already begun.

The Mountain People is a striking example of the sort of tribal didacticism that often seems to mark attempts to popularize anthropology. More recently, in his television series (and accompanying book, see Maybury-Lewis 1992) *Millennium: Tribal Wisdom and the Modern World*, David Maybury-Lewis has held up another 'tribal mirror'. Like Turnbull, Maybury-Lewis foresees a bleak future for the modern capitalist world; both writers regret what they see as the unrelenting trend towards individualism and the breakdown of family structures. However, for Maybury-Lewis, as our modern capitalist societies, despite all their technological proficiency and material abundance, lose the confidence in the future that they once had, there exists the possibility that they will come to appreciate the wisdom retained by those other, tribal societies. If modern life deprives us of the basic moral principles that make us fully human, help is at hand in the margins of the modern world. These principles can still be found – if only we are prepared to peer into the tribal mirror, held up by anthropologists, to see what we should really look like.

If Maybury-Lewis shows us what we have lost, Turnbull announces that we stand to lose much more. Maybury-Lewis *instructs* his readers using so many tribal exemplars, Turnbull *warns* his readers by unleashing a tribal monster. As *The Forest People* makes clear, for Turnbull too the modern world could benefit from tribal wisdom. But the lasting message of *The Mountain People*, in many ways itself an outcome of the earlier study, is that the modern world can also learn where tribal wisdom fails.

When Turnbull wrote *The Mountain People*, it was generally assumed that the sentimentalization of traditional societies and their depreciation were contradictory processes. We now see them more as reciprocal inversions. Ethnography has become more reflexive and hence more responsible. De Waal is right to say that *The Mountain People* would be turned down by publishers today. Yet it is likely to remain as much of a *cause célèbre* in the history of anthropology as *Coming of Age in Samoa*.

Note

1   In 1987 Turnbull suppressed these controversial passages from the French translation, writing 'The Ik still live near their sacred mountain. That is an objective fact. I regret that violent solution which I proposed fifteen years ago, and which was the expression of my despair in the face of a deadlock' (Turnbull 1987: 248). In the Introduction to the 1994 edition, Turnbull seems to have reverted to his earlier opinion; not only is no mention made of a change of mind, but the 'more "humane" approach' actually pursued by the Ugandan government is condemned (Turnbull 1994: 11). The suppressed passages are reprinted without comment.

References

Barth, Fredrik. 1974. On Responsibility and Humanity: Calling a Colleague to Account. *Current Anthropology* 15(1): 99–102.

Brook, Peter, 1988. *The Shifting Point*. London: Methuen.

De Waal, Alex. 1993. In the Disaster Zone. *Times Literary Supplement* 16 July.

Heine, Bernd. 1985. *The Mountain People*: Some Notes on the Ik of North-Eastern Uganda. *Africa* 5(1): 3–16.

Littlewood, Roland. 1994. 'Lessons for Society.' *The Times* 3 August.

McCall, Grant. 1975. Comment. *Current Anthropology* 16(3): 344–8.

Maybury-Lewis, David. 1992. *Millennium: Tribal Wisdom and the Modern World*. London: Viking.

Sallnow, Michael. 1976. 'The Loveless People'. *Royal Anthrop. Inst. News* 13, March/April.

Turnbull, Colin. 1975 [1972]. *The Mountain People*. London: Cape.

—— 1987. *Les Iks*. Paris: Plon.

—— 1994. *The Mountain People*. London: Pimlico.

Editorial note

Correspondence by Don Moody and Harry A. Powell was published in the following issue (11.1, February 1995, p. 27), also a note by Roland Littlewood clarifying that, while he defended Turnbull's drawing moral conclusions from his fieldwork, he certainly did not endorse his quite unacceptable proposals for dispersal of the Ik.

As well as the article by Michael Sallnow in *RAINews* in 1976 cited by John Knight, it also published articles by Jean-Marie Benoist (no. 14, May/June 1976) and Colin Turnbull (no. 16, October 1976).

Chapter 15

Sarah Pink

■ THE WHITE 'HELPERS': ANTHROPOLOGISTS,
DEVELOPMENT WORKERS AND LOCAL
IMAGINATIONS, *Anthropology Today*, 14.6,
December 1998, pp. 9–14

'CAN I HAVE YOUR BED WHEN YOU GO?': our neighbour
Jacqueline greeted my partner Alberto on the first day that he arrived in his
house in Canchungo, Guinea Bissau, West Africa. She was keen to put herself in
line for the spoils from the *brancu*'s (white person's) house on his inevitable departure. In the past other people in the neighbourhood had done well, collecting various
electrical and gas appliances, cameras, saucepans, televisions, clothing and other
items from the *brancus* who had preceded us. Who would harvest the fruits of
'friendship' with the rich *brancu* development worker this time?

This article is intended as a response to the question recently launched in *AT*
of how anthropologists may help their informants and the types of exchange this
may entail. I will address this through two critical strands. First, I seek to prob-
lematize the idea of 'helping'; 'helping' is not a universal, shared and fixed category
understood on the same terms or solicited with the same intentionalities between
different cultures and different individuals. Second, I argue that if in an 'ethical'
ethnographic narrative anthropologists ought not expect to extract and take home
some concrete thing from people 'different' from them in far off exotic places, they
therefore should not feel morally obliged to 'give something back' in return. The
discussion is related specifically to one example: my experience of fieldwork in
Guinea Bissau from which I generalize to suggest that it is important to situate our
understandings of 'helping' informants in terms of local people's understandings of
the roles that (in this case *brancus*) rich foreigners play in local culture and society
– whether they are anthropologists or development workers – and how local people
attempt to gain 'help' from this category of foreigner. In connection with this, I
reflect on the role I played as an anthropologist and 'helper' of local people. I situate
my involvement with local lives in relation to how the actions of development
workers affected the biographies of, and were incorporated in the discourses of,
local people. This discussion also has implications for, but does not directly address,
the question of what 'anthropology' may constitute in contemporary 'developing'

countries that are swarming with salaried development workers, volunteers and anthropologists, each of whom has his/her own personal agenda and meeting points with local culture.

The discussion is based on fieldwork in the Cacheu region of North West Guinea Bissau in 1996–7. I spent 8 months living in a town called Canchungo with Alberto, my partner who was working as a VSO [Voluntary Service Overseas] mathematics teacher at the time. My intention was to explore transnational themes by focusing broadly on topics such as media, performance, textiles, migration and trading. This 'fieldwork' involved much 'sitting around' chatting with my neighbours and other friends and informants, visiting, photographing, video recording and field diary writing; I wanted to develop the ethnography as a multi-stranded process of learning about aspects of local experience. I later undertook a consultancy commissioned by the Cacheu Department of Health for the Ministry of Health and UNICEF, a more structured and formal research project that produced a report and a set of policy recommendations. As is probably the case for most anthropologists working in 'developing' countries, I was working in a post-colonial context that included a diversity of European and North American development workers, volunteers and business people. I was implicated as part of this group, and local people predicted and interpreted my tastes and actions in terms of their own experience-based knowledge of these *brancus*. My discussion of local people's treatment of *brancus* is based on the idea that individuals develop their own personalized strategies for moving through social, material and imagined landscapes. I focus on how local people construct transnational landscapes, agendas and strategies in relation to their experiences of white foreigners and their understandings of the opportunities these *brancus* may offer them. I understand this local knowledge as existing in terms of its dynamic relationship to how development workers interpret and treat local culture and individuals. The implications of such discourses and knowledge were significant for me not solely as subject matter for anthropological study in themselves but also because they were key to how I was situated and how I attempted to situate myself in 'the field'. As a white woman anthropologist in Guinea Bissau I was (as may be expected) usually presumed to be a *cooperante* – the Portuguese term for development worker used in Guinea Bissau (or at least the wife of a *cooperante*).

The *brancus*: anthropologists and development workers

Whilst it is always problematic to categorize people, I tended to divide the overseas development workers whom I met in Guinea Bissau into three 'types'. Those who work for International Organizations earning high salaries (*cooperantes*); people working for the same organizations but earning 'local' salaries; and VSO and Peace Corps volunteers who are also paid at 'local' rates. 'Local' wages are considerably higher than the earnings of most Guinea Bissauan families. Therefore volunteers' housing, amenities and health care facilities are more comfortable and superior to those of their Guinea Bissauan neighbours. However, in comparison with *cooperantes*, volunteers' resources are extremely limited and they rely on public transport and electricity supplies. Some more educated Guinea Bissauans and those who had

had contact with development organizations had a sense of 'what anthropologists do'. However, much as I would insist that I was not a *cooperante*, locals tended not to separate me from one broad category of 'white *cooperante*'. To them anthropologists are highly paid *brancus* who do projects and write reports for international organizations. I arrived in Guinea Bissau to carry out unfunded fieldwork during my sabbatical leave. I lived with my partner who was already working in Canchungo, in the house VSO supplied him with, depending on his 'local' salary. Previously the house had been occupied by European *cooperantes* and it was difficult to persuade local people that we were not similarly 'rich'; that unlike the *cooperantes*, we did not have a generator to power the fridge and provide a constant supply of chilled water.

We developed reciprocal relationships of 'help', 'trust' and 'friendship' with some people in our neighbourhood. Women neighbours asked to work for us, cleaning the house and carrying water. One man occasionally borrowed (and repaid) money to advance his business interests. One of his enterprises was money lending; we lent him money interest free whilst he earned on his own lending. It had been he who helped out when our cesspit overflowed into the bathroom, invited us to parties, and offered his friendship and conversation. In short we became intertwined with people's strategies for earning money. We were also instrumental in the wider projects of those who received international calls on our telephone or for whom we wrote letters dictated in *kriolo*, translating them into English and other European languages. These letters were sent off to the migrant relatives of our neighbours, usually asking for money, goods and 'help' with obtaining an invitation to Europe and the appropriate emigration documents. As informants told us stories of the other development workers who had preceded us in the neighbourhood, or in other parts of Canchungo, we began to understand the models by which we were being categorized and the expectations people had of us.

Brancus themselves of course also produce discourses and knowledge about the 'help' they are asked for and are able to give to local people. One of the first times I socialized with VSO volunteers, the conversation turned to the question of how different individuals dealt with Guinea Bissauans' constant requests for money and other items. Each person drew their own criteria to determine whether or not to give, and how to respond in ways that they found culturally and personally comfortable. *Patin* translates as 'give me' and precedes requests for money or goods. It is of course not always used in the same sense or with the same intention or expectation. Children and teenagers (and less often adults) may approach *brancus* in the street – 'give me 5.000 *pesos*' – and friends and strangers frequently asked for my clothes. Often '*patin . . .*' became a form of greeting. As Alberto taught at school one day, our teenage neighbour stuck her head through the classroom window; 'Alberto!', she called, '. . . *patin* 5 *kontos*' (one *konto* is 1,000 *pesos*). In other contexts it becomes a filler of silence. During a two-hour wait in a village compound I pulled out my diary to check the project schedule, 'Sarah, haven't you got a diary to give me?' asked the driver who sat opposite me. Another way to ask for things was '*tisin*' – 'bring me'. On the two occasions that I returned to Europe, friends and informants asked me to bring specific items. Anyone who lives in Europe or in other parts of West Africa, like the Gambia, where a greater range of consumer goods is available, will be asked to bring or send cash and goods. For migrants these requests are embedded in social relations and obligations. For *brancus* this is not the case, unless a *brancu* becomes implicated in the personal relationships that bring such obligations (see below). I would suggest that the requests Guinea Bissauans make of white people are framed by different expectations and are perceived as entailing different social relationships to those requests they make of Guinea Bissauan friends and family. However, white people's experiences of Guinea Bissau are often lived out in contexts which allow them to be incorporated into (and sometimes exasperated by) individual Guinea Bissauans' strategies for obtaining goods and cash.

Maybe the 'guilt' of the anthropologist, who through his/her experiences of a 'poor' country will be able to enhance his/her CV and publications record, situates him/her differently from the position of a volunteer who feels that he or she has already, by the very nature of volunteering, given something and may him/herself stand to 'get something back'. However, as I have suggested above, the notion of an exchange between ethnographer and informant, whereby the ethnographer feels morally obliged to 'give something back', is in itself problematic. This principle depends on a 'conventional' modern ethnographic narrative by which the notion of 'giving something back' implies that the ethnographer, having extracted something (usually 'the data') from somewhere else (usually a far-off exotic place), then makes a gift of something else to those supposedly passive people from whom he/she has got it. Such practices do not eliminate the exploitative nature of research, but attempt to compensate for it morally by 'giving something back'. In an ironic scenario, the anthropologist may feel ethically virtuous whilst the informants are left wondering why they have been given whatever it was they 'got back', and what precisely they got it in return for. By focusing instead on collaboration and the idea of anthropologist and informant 'creating something together', or at least both actively seeking to gain from their relationship, agency may be attributed to both researcher and informant, rather than solely to the researcher. In collaborative research anthropologist and informants may participate using negotiated practices towards specific goals, although it would be idealistic to assume that these were 'shared'.

Experience, knowledge and constructing the Others

Questions concerning the importance of individual experience and creativity to the production of knowledge (see Okely and Callaway 1992, Cohen 1994), and representation (most recently reviewed by James, Hockey and Dawson 1997) are now common currency in anthropology. Fieldwork is a very personal experience and its results represent the ethnographer's best attempts to communicate his/her subjectivity to particular audiences. The personal and professional selves, identities and agendas of development workers, like anthropologists, are inextricably interwoven and cannot be divorced from their creativity in producing texts, practices and polices. This is shown most explicitly in the reflexive anthropological writing of those who have carried out participatory and action research (e.g. Huizer 1991, Schrijvers 1991). However, whilst anthropologists have been placed at the centre of their own texts (e.g. arising from Clifford and Marcus 1986 and the 'writing culture' debate), less attention has been given to the question of to what extent development workers who are not anthropologists are cultural producers who create aspects of the worlds that they act on. The role of anthropologists in development has been attended to; for instance Gardner and Lewis (1996) discuss the question of the relationship between the individual and the institution (in this case development agencies) in development work. Whilst the 'success' of development projects is often evaluated, the 'informal' impact of 'development' is less frequently reflexively explored. Nevertheless it is not only the wells dug, seeds sown, classes taught and systems implemented that are appropriated in better or worse ways by 'local cultures'; the personal relations and intersubjectivities of development workers and local people also become interwoven into local discourses. Below I shall reflect on some local Canchungo narratives on *brancus* to explore the implications of personal relationships for anthropologists, local people and 'development' agendas.

Representation is a central issue, defined here, following James *et al.*, as a term with 'multiple meanings . . .: interpretation; communication; visualisation; translation and advocacy' (1997: 2). These are all aspects of the practices of anthropologists and development workers – 'us' representing 'them' and in doing so building a stock of 'knowledge' upon which to base theory and practice on a day-to-day basis as projects progress. But at the same time local people engage in similar processes of evaluating 'us' and using us as case studies for their own warehouses of examples and generalizations about white people and how 'we' can be used to advance *their* careers. Existing academic work has paid attention to the local impacts of individual colonial administrators and the influence of national intellectual and bureaucratic traditions on the behaviour of colonial officials (Chabal 1992:41). Colonial characters constructed in feature films and TV series (e.g. the BBC series *Rhodes*) tend to be heroic men, the powerful agents of change and progress. That contemporary development workers, living in less dangerous, luxurious, glamorous circumstances and without the operatic soundtrack of a feature film, have not become the heroes of popular culture, does not mean that their personal lives are any less interwoven in local development histories and power relations. Gardner and Lewis recognize the presence of power relationships, suggesting that 'Power is hierarchical in development projects: between expatriate and local staff, external consultants and local personnel, project staff and local people or "clients"' (1996: 140). However, the simplicity of this power structure is deceiving. Power dynamics are inevitably uneven as the 'formal' power of the 'development process' interfaces with the 'informal' power that is integral to connections between the project and local community or town leaders, technical assistants, donors, and the lovers, friends, and families of all of these people. Here I shall reflect on how white development workers figure in some of the local 'stories' told by Guinea Bissauans and become central to local knowledge about where power and access to resources and privilege is situated. This involves a discussion of how the 'help' *brancus* can offer is constructed and understood by local people. Such narratives constituted important representations for me as an anthropologist attempting to do 'fieldwork' in Guinea Bissau, since they were crucial to my understanding of how I was situated by local people. There are many different aspects which could be explored, one of which is local people's exploitation of the material resources available for 'development'. But here I focus on some of the ways that local people exploit the 'human resources' of development, the *brancus* themselves. I concentrate on narratives that developed around sexual relationships and the different moral perspectives that surround them.

'Development' is often criticized as a corrupt and ugly business characterized by ministerial kickbacks and a series of misguided. economically driven international 'development agendas'. As such, the personal gain of those at the top is cited as an obstacle to the success of 'development'. Here I suggest that personal gain is also part of the projects of both development workers and of the local people who collaborate in 'development' projects, clean the floors of development workers' luxurious homes, and have sex or make friends with them. I do not argue that individualism is at the core of society (see Cohen's critique of such perspectives 1994: 168–92). Rather I suggest paying close attention to how experience of and knowledge about development is partially constructed through the interface between the self-conscious strategies of locals, migrants and development workers. Thus I am concerned with how their intentionalities intersect, and how this 'inter-intentionality' (see Pink 1998) becomes part of both 'development' processes and knowledge about them. In short, how do development workers 'help' and how do they become part of local people's 'self-help' strategies?

White 'husbands', 'white' babies

I have met none of the Europeans implicated in the tales related below. Therefore my discussion is of the stories told and representations offered by my Guinea Bissauan informants: I have no basis upon which to suggest they are 'true', but would assume that they relate to real events that my informants had experienced and that are not particularly unusual. My account is intended as an analysis of the discourses and practices that were developed by local people in relation to these cultural narratives and models. However, such work raises ethical issues. First because the judgments that I discuss below are inextricably linked to an academic critique of (post) colonialism that cannot avoid having a moral perspective. Second, although no confidentiality was offered (and in fact other *cooperantes* often told me that 'these things should be discussed publicly'), the stories told and the situations in which I was asked to 'help' were concerned with other people's private lives. My personal dilemma concerned whether I ought to be implicated in the arrangements of these individuals' strategies for gain, or involved in their personal lives. It forced me to ask myself to what extent I felt comfortable 'helping', and if writing about it was justified. Eventually, as I shall describe below, my decision, about whether a private affair should be revealed to those from whom it had been hidden, was made for me by others. Nevertheless, I maintain that, as far as I know, the story could be untrue. At the very least, like any ethnographic account, it is based only on my own patchwork of a series of narratives, documents and images.

My informants tended to refer to lighter-skinned Guinea Bissauans (of one white parent) as *brancu*; 'white'. 'White' Guinea Bissauans are usually thought to have privileged access to Europeans and their resources. Some informants believed Europeans were more likely to 'help' 'white' Guinea Bissauans. These advantages were extended further if the 'white' Guinea Bissauan maintained links or had been able to contact their white relative. In such cases access to Portuguese residency documents and European resources could be easier. It is in this context that I consider the enthusiasm of Guinea Bissauan women to have 'white' children.

Antonieta, aged 15, lived in a house directly behind ours with her mother and younger brothers and sisters. Antonieta had presented herself to Alberto before my arrival in Guinea Bissau, asking him for work. He contracted her to carry water, starting the week of my arrival. However, Alberto soon dismissed her after he discovered she had told us numerous lies to avoid working at the appointed times. One afternoon whilst I sat talking with my two neighbours, Jacqueline who was pregnant and Chamba who had two young children, we began to discuss the number of children I would have. Antonieta stopped to greet us on her way to fetch water for her family, and we began to joke about how many children she would have. 'But Sarah, you know, Antonieta wants to have Alberto's baby', provoked Chamba. The blatancy of her statement disturbed me. I laughed it off, trying to divert my uncertainty over whether she had spoken in jest. I joked, pretending to lament for Antonieta that she had very little possibility of becoming pregnant by my husband. Antonieta herself remained silent, smiling bashfully up at us and the verandah.

I never knew if Antonieta had wanted Alberto's baby or if she thought the opportunity would arise. However, as I learnt more about the stories that were interwoven with local women's knowledge about 'white' babies, I became quite certain that her behaviour could easily have been interpreted as a strategy for becoming pregnant by a *brancu*. Moreover her project would not have been regarded as utterly inappropriate. Such women were sometimes criticized by those who were allegedly jealous of the good fortune that a 'white' child brings. However, women who secured economic stability in this way were also admired role models with privileged access to outside wealth. According to one informant, local women always 'walk by the houses of male *brancus*' at night, but chasing a *brancu* is not always considered the best strategy. Courting the attention of a *brancu* is not universally approved, nevertheless rather than being essentially 'right' or 'wrong' it was judged depending on what the speaker intended to say about the woman in question. One informant, Miranda, had argued with her friend after hearing that she had criticized her for having a 'white' child. The row had escalated; Miranda accused the other woman of calling by the house of another white development worker who had lived in the *barrio* and trying to attract his attention whilst her own husband was away. The two women did not speak for over two years.

In Canchungo the stories of two women stood out as exemplary of the fortunes that a white child may bring. The father of the first woman's child was a European who returned to his country. When their son was two years old his mother allowed him to go and live with his father in Europe. She lived very comfortably in Canchungo and the father financed her travel to visit her son. A child in Europe also represents a foothold in Europe, access to European money and a guarantee of security for the future. Miranda (whose story is also discussed in another context elsewhere – see Pink 1998), my second informant, was desperate to send her 'white' daughter to Europe. She held this woman's story as a model to pursue, although in her own scheme she too wanted to live in Europe. The fortunes of Miranda were more varied. Her *brancu*, who, in his fifties, had been considerably older than her sixteen years, was married but unaccompanied by his wife. When Miranda became pregnant, to the envy of the neighbourhood women, she moved into the big *brancu* house with him. There she lived until the following year when his contract ended, surrounded by electrical appliances and cared for by a man who on her terms behaved impeccably towards her. As far as local people were concerned Miranda was *casadu* with her *brancu*. In *kriolo*, as in Portuguese and Spanish, *casado/a* translates as 'married': in this case meaning having set up a *casa* – a house or home. Whilst the term has a Latin root it is given further meaning in the local context of polygamous marriages: the fact that her husband had another wife in Europe was not considered problematic and was consistent with the practices of Manjaco migrants. Of importance was that he behaved properly to Miranda in Guinea Bissau by providing her with food, clothing and prestige items. When his European wife visited him for a holiday, Miranda behaved according to local norms, acting as if she did not known him. Thus she allowed him to behave in a way that women informants identified as 'respectful' to his first wife, by not letting her become aware of Miranda's existence. According to women informants, most African men have affairs with other women, and there would be little they could do to prevent this. Of more importance was how one's husband went about his affairs: he should be discreet, only meeting with his lover in private and not making a public scene out of his affair; the affair should remain a secret from his wife or formal girlfriend whom he should continue to take out and buy gifts for; and he should return home to sleep in his house at night. Another woman whose husband was openly having affairs told me that if he took another wife it would be less problematic than his current unacceptable behaviour: he was a *bandido*. She was angry that he was always out, drinking and spending his money on other women rather than on her and their children. A *bandido* was a man who did not 'respect' his wife and family.

Once his contract ended Miranda's European 'husband' went home, leaving her with some money and a wealth of electrical appliances, furniture, a collection of photographs and a small 'white' child. When I met her, no money had arrived for over two years, she was living from hand to mouth, was heavily in debt, had not paid the rent for her house for several months and sent her two children begging food from neighbours. Once her 'husband' had left, two newly arrived development workers, a couple, had taken care of her and her child, giving her work and showering gifts on her daughter. Two years later they departed for their next posting, again leaving her with some money to keep her going and the furniture and electrical appliances that were left over. When I first met Miranda she told me this story, the next day she brought me her collection of photographs, contained in a small plastic album. I had a sense of the bizarre as I found myself being introduced to images of her white 'husband', and his wife and children who knew nothing of Miranda's existence. 'Look how white Ana was when she was born', Miranda pointed out proudly; 'Everyone thought she was the daughter of my white friends.'

Given that Miranda and her daughter were now living in poverty, with no local family support networks or help from local people who argued that Ana's rich father should be sending money, I was surprised that she still had a good word for him. He was a *bandido*, I concluded. 'No!', she insisted, 'he treated us very well and he wants to send money, but it is difficult. I speak to him on the phone sometimes and he wants to come if he can this summer.' On her terms, it was the father of her second child who was the *bandido*. Once she had fallen pregnant he, a relatively affluent local man to whom she had never been *casadu*, had started to have affairs with other women. Whilst he visited his daughter and occasionally gave them some fish or meat to cook, he did not fulfil his obligations by providing an appropriate supply of food or cash for his daughter.

Although by the time we met Miranda her situation had deteriorated greatly, her 'white' child helped her again. It was *because* she had a 'white' child and had apparently been deserted by a European man with whom she had had a relationship of massive inequalities that, in our terms, she had been wronged. Her story seemed a direct analogy to narratives of colonialism and exploitation. However, from her perspective she had not been wronged, she had reaped the fruit and benefits of her links with *brancus*. Until we came to understand how, this was exactly why we were useful to her: we 'helped'. The series of *brancus* who pitied and helped Miranda, by giving her work and feeding her children, served to confirm local notions that a 'white' child will bring further fortune; white people will help a 'white' child. As in the case of the son of her contemporary, the *brancu* may even take the child 'home', providing the mother with a direct kinship link to the resources and riches of Europe. More stories supported this idea. Miranda described to me how one night, when Ana was two years old, a European who she did not know, but had been staying for a week with another development worker in Canchungo, had called at the house where at the time she was living with her grandmother and cousin. The man had told her to wake Ana and dress her because he was going to take her to a children's party. Since it was 2 a.m. she thought it strange that there should be a children's party, but the man had insisted. She was on the point of giving Ana to him when her grandmother warned 'If you let her go with him you know you will never see her again.' The man left empty-handed. When she found that he had indeed left Guinea Bissau for Senegal and a flight to Europe during the early hours of that morning, Miranda was convinced that he had intended to steal Ana. But, she told me, 'if he had just asked, allowed me to prepare some clothes for her and to give her a photo of me and let her know how to contact me, I would have let him take her'. She saw this as another lost opportunity of getting her daughter to Europe and guaranteeing financial security for both of them. However, before I left Guinea Bissau, Ana brought more luck: Miranda's mother's 'white' half-sister from Paris was trying to arrange to take her to France; and her *cooperante* friend had visited delivering some new gifts and cash. He also set up a bank account for her in Canchungo and her white 'husband' was in the process of transferring a considerable amount of money. We had 'helped' as our telephone had been used for most of the negotiations, we had taken messages and we had called Miranda over from her house when there was a call for her. But we refused to become implicated any further in her deals. I was uncomfortable with the agendas and intentions of Miranda, her 'husband' and her friends, and there my involvement and 'help' ended. Meanwhile Miranda walked proud in the neighbourhood, wearing her new clothes and boasting of her new-found wealth to the women who had watched her fall into increasing poverty. Restored to her former glory, I could see why she would be the envy of the teenagers who had stalked my husband at night.

At the time of writing, Guinea Bissau is embroiled in an armed conflict. I doubt Miranda's transnational connections will serve her in this horrific situation. I would assume that she is still in Guinea Bissau, for in the latest episode that I received from Alberto by e-mail when he returned to Guinea Bissau in October 1997, Miranda was still waiting for her money: the international bank transfer had not worked. By this time we had almost no contact with her, but I fear that the gifts I made to her during fieldwork had a greater impact than I anticipated. For me the most shocking news of all was that Miranda had told Alberto that someone had sent a photograph of Ana to her father in Europe, leading to his wife's discovery of Ana's existence. I suspect that one of Miranda's *cooperante* friends who had been supporting her economically had made a moral judgement on the situation and had decided to intervene. I had photographed Miranda's daughter on several occasions, and maybe I *did* naïvely feel that by giving her photographs I was able to give her something in return for the help she gave me locally. But I did not give her photographs so that she could pass them on to other white people, who would send these images to the elderly and unsuspecting wife of the man with whom Miranda had had an affair several years before (if this is indeed what happened). I didn't feel morally virtuous, but I felt utterly sick when I came to suspect how my contribution may have been used.

As powerful individuals on a local stage, where the majority of people have considerably limited access to resources and self-consciously define themselves as 'powerless', the significance of the subjectivity of anthropologists and development workers should not be underestimated. Moreover, anthropologists and develop-ment workers themselves become instrumental in the elaboration of transnational imaginations, and in the construction of transnational connections and flows. They may, as in the case of Miranda's 'husband' and friends, maintain enduring links after they have left and by sending a photograph create other transnational connections and knowledge.

How do we 'help'

How can anthropologists help? Do we 'help' on the terms that local people demand – by bringing material goods, giving out our cash and fulfilling the obligations that a migrant relative would be morally bound by? Do we help by morally gratifying ourselves through 'giving something back' to our informants that we know they will be grateful for? Do we become resources to which local people may 'help them-selves', or is it our brief to paternalistically devise ways that will allow local people to develop ways of helping themselves that are independent of our cash? On whose terms should 'help' be defined? In Guinea Bissau the *kriolo* word that best translated as 'help' was *juda* (like Portuguese or Spanish *ajuda*). When my infor-mants asked for 'help' this often meant cash or privileged access to development worker social networks that may bring speedier access to health care or educational resources. Since for many local people so-called 'development' projects appeared to bring no noticeable improvement to their lives, the *brancus* who worked on them were not necessarily seen to offer European expertise, but social networks and economic resources – the stuff of personal relations and individual agendas. Returning to the question: how *do* we help? I am confident that my contribution to the narratives of the lives of some of my informants in Guinea Bissau could be inter-preted as any one of the types of 'help' I have suggested above. But before we can say we have helped, we need to recognize that 'help' does not have a universal meaning and the gifts of help we give or think we are 'giving back' may never be received because they become invested with new meanings as they are appropriated by their recipients.

References

Chabal, P. 1992. 'The African Crisis: context and interpretation', in R. Werbner and T. Ranger (eds) *Postcolonial Identities in Africa*. London: Zed.

Clifford, J. and Marcus, G. 1986. *Writing Culture: the Poetics and Politics of Ethnography*. Berkeley: U. of California P.

Cohen, A. 1994. *Self Consciousness: an Alternative Anthropology of Identity*. London: Routledge.

Gardner, K. and Lewis, D. 1996. *Anthropology, Development and the Post-Modern Challenge*. London: Pluto.

Huizer, G. 1991. 'Participatory research and healing witchcraft: an essay in the anthropology of crisis', in L. Nencel and P. Pels (eds) *Constructing Knowledge: Authority and Critique in Social Science*. London: Sage.

James, W., Hockey, J. and Dawson, A. 1997. 'Introduction: the road from Santa Fe', in W. James et al. (eds) *After Writing Culture: Epistemology and Praxis in Contemporary Anthropology*. London: Routledge.

Okely, J. and Callaway, H. 1992. *Anthropology and Autobiography*. London: Routledge.

Pink, S. 1998. 'Sunglasses, Suitcases and Other "Symbols": intentionality, creativity and "indirect" communication in festive and everyday performances' paper presented at the ASA Conference, University of Kent.

Schrijvers, J. 1991. 'Dialectics of a Dialogical Ideal: Studying Down, Studying Sideways, and Studying Up', in L. Nencel and P. Pels (eds) *Constructing Knowledge: Authority and Critique in Social Science*. London: Sage.

February 1988

■   *Anthropology Today*, 4.1, February 1988, pp. 2–3

A T CHRISTMASTIDE IN ENGLAND, the zone of kinship is hyper-trophic. Psychological balance is threatened by either much too much kinship, or much too little. On New Year's Eve at midnight, the television provides us with a jolly party on screen, then cuts to a dear old lady sitting alone with her dog, singing along to Auld Lang Syne on *her* television. In either of these extremes, curling up with a book can be unusually restorative, and books read over Christmas can be specially memorable, which is why we should regard the annual pre-Christmas recommendations by literary journalists as an integral part of the calendrical ritual.

I was fortunate this Christmas to have two outstanding new books to read, both published by Cambridge and both important enough to deserve special treatment in *AT*, which they will duly get from suitably qualified hands. First, Michael Herzfeld's *Anthropology Through the Looking-Glass: Critical Ethnography in the Margins of Europe* (£24.50), which is an ambitious and exciting attempt to shift the ethnography of modern Greece from the periphery to the centre of social anthropology as a comparative and reflexive discipline. Opportunistic, for an ethnographer of modern Greece? I don't think so, because Herzfeld is able to show that the ideological heritage associated with ancient Greece had a great deal to do both with the formation of anthropology and with the formation of the modern Greek state, so Greece is indeed a very special case.

There is one odd omission in the book. It is heavily indebted to neo-Marxist *Ideologiekritik*, yet the author makes only the scantiest reference to the fact that nearly all the other Balkan states are now officially Marxist; nor can I find any reference at all to the Yalta conference of 1945. It is commonly believed that romantic Hellenism on the part of the leading Western statesmen resulted in Greece being kept outside the Soviet sphere of influence, despite the prominence of the Greek communist movement. Why is a fact so germane to Herzfeld's theme, so central to everyday life in Greece today, ignored? Perhaps the omission merely exemplifies a truth which he states at length in his book: that academics, however heavyweight,

Figure PP3   Sir James and Lady Frazer.

can be as ethnocentric as everyone else. But this is a small point against a book which may be one of those few which change a landscape.

My other Christmas fare – a classic feast compared to Herzfeld's *nouvelle cuisine* – was Robert Ackerman's new biography of J.G. Frazer (£35). This must be easily the best biography yet written of an anthropologist, and the author is masterly in making such an outwardly uneventful life so absorbing. Here I will merely note that he is far fairer to Lady Frazer (Lilly Grove) than anyone else has been, since Sir James's colleagues seem to have unanimously hated her, and she was posthumously the victim of memoirs by secretaries whom she employed in their old age when she was deaf and he blind. She was by common consent hard-working, intelligent and forceful, and totally devoted to Frazer. Ackerman does conclude, however, that his unfolding of her many unpleasant traits – rudeness, deviousness, self-aggrandise-ment, etc. – 'does not list her main faults', which he sees as having been her tendency to manage and mother her husband, so that he came to know fewer and fewer people and became more and more wrapped up in his own speculations, to the detriment of his scholarship. Should Lilly Frazer really be blamed for her husband's well-attested imperviousness to the most friendly criticism? We must recall that Frazer was a retiring, benign, in his prime highly creative man who also became an international celebrity, with all the business dealings and exposure to the public which that involves. There are numerous examples in the creative arts of men who have maintained a private stronghold of impregnable serenity by using a devoted wife as their defensive 'dragon' against publishers, agents, reviewers and the like. Lilly, who kept herself alive till Frazer's death as late as 1941, and died later the same day, deserves our kindest thoughts.

1987 was the centenary of one of the Anthropological Institute's better-known members of the nineteenth century. He was a great frequenter of the British Museum Library where he studied such ethnological subjects as voodoo and sacri-fice, but he actually published two monographs for the *Anthropological Journal* on the morphology of the human ear – knowledge which he was able to put to the public benefit, for unlike many anthropologists today he was fond of saying 'You know my methods: apply them.' These methods were based, he claimed, on the observation of trifles and the discarding of all prejudices; some saw method in his madness, others madness in his method, so he was not unlike many of our colleagues today. He has been seriously characterized by Professor Thomas A. Sebeok as the nineteenth century's consulting semiotician.

I refer of course to Mr Sherlock Holmes,[1] and those who know 56 Queen Anne Street, W.1 (which the RAI now leaves, after leasing premises for ten years from the Royal Asiatic Society), will not be surprised to hear that during these last ten years I have often seen him in the building, especially when the fog swirls in from the street. His friend Dr Watson, who is of course an old hand from India and Afghanistan, is often to be seen at the Royal Asiatic Society tea-meetings; and frequently Mrs Hudson the housekeeper drops by in a state of agitation from nearby Baker Street to say that one of the pair is urgently needed by a client or patient. I suspect that Mr Holmes comes not only to replenish his memory on thuggee or Chinese tattooing, but also to check out the basement, because it is likely that the traces of the most dastardly crimes would remain undiscovered there for many months. Now the Institute moves down the road to 50 Fitzroy Street, and must accumulate its own ghosts.

Note

1   See *Wisteria Lodge* and *The Cardboard Box*.

Jonathan Benthall

PART FOUR

Markets of Desire

■   JONATHAN BENTHALL

THESE TWO ARTICLES, by leading American anthropologists, explore what one might loosely call the irrational element in economic activity, and thus relate to the later section on 'the technology of enchantment'.

Jane Schneider writes in the tradition of the major American anthropologist Sidney Mintz, author of a classic historical study of the sugar industry. She represents the interaction of consumption and production as much more concerned with taste and values – and their manipulation – than is accounted for in conventional economics; and she draws thoughtful analogies between changes in the textile industry and changing perceptions of science, the environment and architecture. She recalls how the miracle fibres, nylon and rayon, once epitomized the dazzle of a liberating and egalitarian technology, the promise of an open future. She examines different explanations of how it came to be that in the 1970s synthetic fibres were rejected by the fashionable West in favour of wool, cotton and silk – kinder to the breathing and sweating body, which thus reasserted its autonomy against mass production. The rejection of synthetic fibres is part of a process of 'gentrification', taken advantage of by international cotton and wool marketing boards and paradoxically empowering Third World producers. Synthetic textile companies have hit back by designing new forms of blended fibre which are increasingly hard to distinguish from the 'real thing'. Among her other insights, Schneider goes some way to explaining the strange way in which the values of fashionable 'chic' become internalized.

'Something for nothing' is the essence of magic. **Katherine Verdery**'s article is a specimen of the 'transitology' of the former Eastern bloc referred to in the Introduction. What, she asks, do the institutions and practices of financial capitalism mean to societies that have been dominated for decades by top-down central planning? 'Caritas' (no relation of the extremely respectable Catholic aid agency of the same name) was a notorious pyramid scheme which flourished in Romania for two years in the early 1990s, tying up billions of dollars of citizens' money until its inevitable collapse. Verdery contends that whereas under Communism, 'socialist plans generated the illusion that everything is under social control', the exact opposite obtains in advanced market economies: 'their secret lies in their being invisible, taken for granted, abstracted from the actions of concrete agents'. During the transition to capitalism, then, the economy has to become like a force of nature beyond human responsibility. Depositors in Romania, ruined by hyper-inflation, were persuaded to sink their savings in a simulacrum of a capitalist investment vehicle.

Chapter 16

Jane Schneider

■ IN AND OUT OF POLYESTER: DESIRE,
DISDAIN AND GLOBAL FIBRE COMPETITIONS,
Anthropology Today, 10.4, August 1994, pp. 2–10

MANY PEOPLE BELIEVE that clothes made from natural fibres – wool, cotton, linen, silk – are superior to clothes made from synthetics. Scores of college-educated American women and men with whom I have spoken on the subject of polyester – the most versatile and emblematic of the synthetics – are convinced that it does not 'breathe'; that it 'feels' inferior; that it comes in garish or less than subtle colours. Polyester, I have been told, feels like Saran Wrap on a hot day; provokes uncontrollable itching and sweating; is a 'yucky' plastic (see Melinkoff 1984: 178). My casual probing has also elicited numerous references to class stigma: the word polyester conjures up the image of a lower middle-class tour group filing off a bus at Disneyland in pastel leisure suits. To one of my informants, a self-described cotton person, 'polyester is K-Mart'. On a more analytical note, I have been told that, like other plastics, polyester violates certain rules of integrity, such as the rule that when cloth is set on fire, it should reduce to ashes, not melt and then solidify into a sticky mass.

As readers might imagine, or already know from personal experience, synthetic fabrics come close to being taboo for some people. In such cases, one voids pollution by carefully reading labels before buying, thus avoiding what is ever more likely in the 1990s – that the 'man-made' fibres will escape detection or sneak through in blends. Serious fabric buyers conduct burn tests on samples that are otherwise hard to identify or, to test for real silk, they run samples through their teeth, knowing that the authentic version is abrasive whereas the counterfeits are slippery. One can also protect oneself by shopping exclusively through certain catalogues or in certain boutiques and stores. In a recent J. Crew catalogue, about the only compromised item was the 'heather jacket' for men which contains an unspecified dash of nylon, undoubtedly to strengthen its very soft alpaca-laced woollen yarns. Of course, like all taboos, there are degrees of vigilance in practice. Older advocates of the naturals, if their jobs involve travelling, welcome wrinkle-free clothing, even if this means lowering their standards. And a younger would-be purist told me that she will 'tolerate up to 20 per cent polyester if it feels good'.

Among those who stigmatize synthetic fabrics is a subset of people like myself who are old enough to remember when it was otherwise – when nylons and orlons and dacrons were thought of as minor miracles, first for their quick drying, no-iron, permanent press qualities; subsequently for possessing a new range of brilliant, near-neon colours. Such reversals in taste provoke a nagging question: do consumers' changing values motivate what gets produced or do producers, in possession of capital, promotional know-how, and political influence, mould what consumers want?

Grant McCracken (1988: 61), theorist of culture and consumption, offers one model for avoiding this polarized set of alternatives: clothing not only reflects 'changing historical circumstances but also [serves] as a device which creates and constitutes this change in cultural terms'. Clothing, in this sense, is 'an agent of history, giving cultural form and order to innovative, dynamic moments'. Because clothing is made of cloth, however, and because cloth industries are often key players in great trans-regional and transnational systems of political and economic power, manufacturers' concerns with market share should also attract our attention. The approach of Sidney Mintz in *Sweetness and Power* (1985), which pays simultaneous attention to social upheavals in production and consumption, seems helpful. For the commodity, sugar, Mintz demonstrates how innovative producers (English captains of the tropical plantation system) interacted with emergent social groups (the working class in England) in order to generate a new consumption style.

In this article, I begin by historicizing the American middle-class revolt against polyester, noting its coincidence with the broader cultural movement that many would label 'post-modernism'. I then present this revolt from the point of view of the manufacturers of synthetics. My purpose, here, is twofold: first, to dispel their image as an 'external force', manipulating the situation from 'outside'; and, second, to consider their relationship not only to consumers, but to their most fierce competitors, the manufacturers of other fibres. A final section discusses the transformation of American capitalism since the 1970s, a transformation which, I believe, constitutes a unified context for a wide range of developments, among them the stylistic overthrow of modernism and the intensification of the 'fibre wars' between the 'naturals' and the 'synthetics'. By asking what new social groupings and classes emerged from this transformation, I attempt to show, in the tradition of Mintz, the interaction of consumption and production – of socially changing, value-creating consumers with competing, predatory industries, organized at ever higher levels the better to lure their prey.

Polyester's moment

America's middle-class households had already gone a considerable distance towards the mechanical displacement of the live-in, full-time servant before World War II. Powered since the 1920s by electricity and running water, most such homes were blessed with several appliances, among them the washing machine (Katzman 1978;

Figure 16.1   Advertisement for Courtaulds rayon underwear, 1932.

Matthews 1987: 177–81). Yet the upkeep of clothes still required setting aside most of Monday for washing. On Monday evening, clothes that had dried on the line were generously sprinkled, rolled and (since we are still before the steam iron) placed in the vegetable bin of another machine, the refrigerator. Here they remained moist without mildewing until the housewife, her daughters, or a day-worker got around to starching and ironing them (Melinkoff 1984: 39). As the Los Angeles writer Ellen Melinkoff recalls, in her 'offbeat' social history of women's fashion in the postwar decades, when Dacron-ruffled blouses first appeared in 1956, they attracted instant converts.

Repelling water, Dacron dried fast and required so little ironing that women defined it as liberating – not as a fabric beset with a breathability problem. In Melinkoff's words, 'we were so charmed by synthetics that we turned up our noses at cotton . . . weeded it out of our wardrobes as quickly as possible' (*ibid.*: 57–8). I remember that the weeding extended to linen sheets and the scary mangles on which they were laboriously ironed. Especially remarkable, in retrospect, was our tolerance for Orlon sweaters that discharged electricity in one inch sparks when we pulled them over our heads. More than 70 million Orlon sweaters were sold in the United States between 1952 and 1956, the first four years of their existence (*ibid.*: 57).

New and luminescent colours followed the breakthrough to wash-and-wear, and expressed the yearnings of a youth culture that had been developing luxuriantly since the end of the war. (By the second half of the 1960s, nearly a half of all outerwear purchased in America was bought by shoppers 15 to 19 years of age, notorious for having leisure time and small, disposable incomes (Wilson 1985: 82; Powell and Peel 1988: 32–3, 37–46, 74–8, 100–1). Consonant with the appearance of the birth control pill, which the Food and Drug Administration approved in 1960, participants in this culture wanted clothes that were at once sexy and rebellious. The designers who responded were not, initially, in the fashion capital, Paris, where the power to structure Euro-American trends had been concentrated for more than a century. Rather, innovators in New York, California, Milan, the Riviera and, above all, London, rose to the occasion, encouraged in no small degree by manufacturers of synthetic fibres and fabrics. Amidst experiments that tested the boundaries of nylon, plastic, even paper clothes (Powell and Peel 1988: 100–1), 'the most obvious field for new young talent' was the man-made fibres. In the words of English fashion writer Janey Ironside, 'this is a thing of now, of how to use them and exploit them' (1973: 128).

Among the features to be exploited, colour was as important as easy care. Because of the way a non-absorbent synthetic interacts with synthetic dyestuffs, it has the potential to give off near-fluorescent tones. Lime green, lemon yellow, hot pink, are among the vivid colours that lent adventure to clothes (see Powell and Peel 1988: 22, 60–61, 64, 100–1). Unusual combinations of such 'out of sight' shades in uninhibited, kaleidoscopic swirls gave both men's and women's apparel the image of, to quote Melinkoff, a 'visual candy store' (1984: 121). 'We felt so young, so free', she writes. 'We weren't a bit bothered by the plasticity of it all' (*ibid.*).

Nor were doubleknit suits and pants despised then. Those garments owed their existence to an industry effort to address the breathability problem, which is magnified in woven, but ameliorated in knitted, cloth. By 1960, manufacturers had upgraded knitting technology so as to turn out flat knits, heavy enough to hold their shape in a new range of garments. No longer confined to jersey dresses and Italian striped tops, polyester knits took over both men's and women's pants and suits (Melinkoff 1984: 115). If weaves in this fibre were acceptable for easy-care shirts and mod mini-skirts – if they were coveted for their convenience and riveting chromatic display – why would anyone attend, really, to the sensation of knitted Dacron against their skin? The eventual rejection of polyester was, then, a reversal in public taste – an upheaval that engaged a vast segment of the middle class whose attitudes towards the fibre, and very perception of how it feels, shifted from 'treasure to trash'. Precisely when did the revolt occur?

The timing of the revolt against polyester

The transformation of polyester from a fabric of esteem to one of contempt seems to have unfolded through several stages over the 1970s. In the preceding decade, hippies rose up against fashion, their 'anti-plastic' longings for a simpler, more natural world finding expression in native-American beads, worker-American blue jeans, cotton T-shirts and cottons acquired on journeys to India and other heart-lands of peasant and artisan production. Resisting Paris-based designers' attempts to supplant the mini with the 'midi' skirt around the turn of the decade, the carriers of this tradition also experimented with long dresses in the mode of Edwardian grannies. From this it was not a big step to Laura Ashley and macramé, according to Melinkoff's history. Quoting her again, 'about 1973, the freakiness settled down and a [new] style emerged: conservatism with a choice' (1984: 170).

Choice exploded in the 1970s. This was the decade when Jonathan Robbin, sociologist and statistician, developed the computer-powered marketing strategy known as 'geodemographics'. Analysing each American zip code area according to hundreds of characteristics grouped around five criteria – social rank, mobility, ethnicity, family life cycle and housing – he and his collaborators assigned neigh-bourhoods to one of forty 'life-style segments' or clusters. Given descriptive names like Urban Gold Coast, Pools and Patios, Shotguns and Pickups, Mines and Mills, the clusters were also ranked according to affluence. The resulting 'cluster system', presented to marketing specialists in 1974, was a welcome advance over 'standard demographic surveys that classified consumers by age, sex, and income'; in these specialists' eyes, the mass market of the postwar era had already come unglued (Weiss 1989: 10). Armed with disaggregated forms of knowledge, merchandisers now had the power to customize their products and sales for specialized audiences whose tastes might be quite varied and unstable (*ibid.*: 14).

Contemporary fashion is much remarked for its variation and instability, against which attempts at standardization seem irrelevant. Rather, incongruity and paradox prevail as identities fragment and tolerance expands. The evanescent features of contemporary shapes and colours, historical and ethnic referents, imaginative new departures, underscore fashion writer Kennedy Fraser's observation that once rebel youths had opened the floodgates in the 1960s, 'everything and nothing' could qualify as being 'in style' (1981: 241). All the more remarkable, then, to discover that towards the upper end of the rank order of forty American 'clusters', the natural fibres constitute an underlying common thread. For, what are the building blocks of 'conservatism with a choice' if not a grammar of mix and match compo-nents: blouses of pure silk, designer jeans of indigo denim, one hundred per cent cotton shirts – and all manner of pants, shirts, vests, and suits of cotton, linen, silk and wool?

This is not to argue that synthetics have been banished. On the contrary – and in conformity with the principles of fibre competition outlined in this paper – they

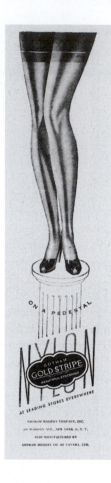

Figure 16.2   American advertisement for hosiery selected to illustrate the title essay in Marshall McLuhan's classic *The Mechanical Bride* (1951).

are presently attempting a comeback. Witness the new 'microfibres', advertised as 'lustrous', 'mobile', 'nervous', 'fluid and forgiving' improvements on silk. According to DuPont representatives, 'micro' is the fashion message of the 1990s, with the company's own 'micromattique' poised to take the lead. This trade-marked fibre has a 'denier' or filament diameter that is half as thick as silk, three times less thick than cotton, and four times less thick than wool, making it twice as fine as its polyester forerunner. More than this, the promoters tout a chameleon-like ability to imitate not only silk, but also cotton and wool, depending upon the choice of processing and blending techniques. The microfibres are, however, the wave of the future. Throughout the 1980s, synthetic materials (excepting rayon) were pushed toward the low-market end of the consumer spectrum. In the middle to high-market end, their place was reduced to a small percentage in blends. The retro-dressing of theatrically inclined thrift-shop buyers, ironically commenting on industrial society's 'man-made' wonders, dramatizes how far the 1980s fibre wheel turned. Flaunting the now tacky splendour of the 1960s, they achieve what Kaja Silverman refers to as a 'tarnished and stagey elegance' (1986: 149–55).

Having located the revolt against polyester as a movement with 1960s roots that gathered momentum during the following decade, it is interesting to note its resonance with a wider cultural context where, it appears, similar rhythms of displacement have occurred. Most broadly, this sartorial reversal shares a space with related challenges to 'modernism'. Certainly, disenchantment with science, especially science as exaggerated by the competitive processes of the free market and the arms race, has encouraged the vestimentary upheaval we are tracing. Synthetic fibres are miracles of science whose very nickname, the 'man-mades', draws attention to a kind of scientific power that is now widely questioned. When the questioning began, moreover, it was easy to overlook the extent to which the so-called natural fibres are also operated upon by scientists, calling into question the very category 'natural'.

As we will see, below, the synthetics emanate from giant petrochemical firms like DuPont, Dow, Union Carbide and Celanese in the United States; and Rhone Poulenc, Courtaulds, Montedison and I.G. Farben in Europe (and yet others in Japan). All are notorious despoilers of the environment. In the context of antimodernism, the miracle of permanent press and the excitement of exploding new colours are easily portrayed as outcomes of a Faustian bargain, enjoyed in ignorance of the pollution that their manufacture enjoined. Again, this interpretation gathered

Figure 16.3 A wedding gown made of white parachute nylon – part of the Norma Kamali spring 1998 fashion show at her retail store in New York, November 1997. In the background are three other outfits made of the same material.

steam at a time of minimal public awareness that cotton and linen, at least, deplete soils, and are grown and processed in noxious, polluting, ways.

The rejection of polyester also parallels the assault of post-modern architects on standardized constructions serving an abstractly conceptualized 'mass society'. What Charles Jencks calls 'the social failure of Modern architecture' – grey, slab-block housing, alienating prefabs, lack of personal space – corresponds to the sartorial uniformity of the leisure-suited 'polyester crowd' (Jencks 1986: 15–16). As with the polyester suits, the early 1970s marked a high point in the dissemination of mass-produced abominations, and the middle of that decade the moment when impassioned critics gathered the necessary momentum to protest. Literary theory, and theory in the social sciences, seem also to have taken their turns against the 'grand narratives' of progress, proletarian emancipation, science and Western destiny, with the same pace and rhythm that has defined the spreading rejection of mass produced polyester clothes. All of these movements, together with the new buildings, books and wardrobes that are their material expression, point to radically creative social action – to the contemplation, initiation and promotion of new cultural principles, values and ideas (see McCracken 1988: 59–60).

The political economy of fibre competition

Significantly, the history of the American fibre and fabric industry is consonant with this rhythm, too. One can point, in fact, to 1973 – the year, says Melinkoff, when the 'freakiness' settled down – as the peak year for synthetics. Up to that time, its market share had steadily expanded; afterwards, it declined. The voices of the petro-chemical industry, recorded in the trade magazine *American Fibers and Fabrics*, minimize what might seem an obvious reason for this boom-and-bust profile: the OPEC-initiated rise of oil prices in, precisely, 1973. More significantly, they attribute consumers' rejection of plastics to manipulation rather than creativity.

To appreciate this perspective, it is important to know how closely intertwined the development of synthetics has been with attempts on the part of industrialized nations to lessen their dependence for textile products on the tropics and semi-tropics. Western Europe, Japan and the United States have this trajectory in common. Among them, only the American South and Southwest, and selected regions in Italy, France, and Japan, are well suited to the cultivation of cotton or silk; to grow these fibres, and wool, on a scale appropriate to the demands of a mass society, is difficult. Put another way, the natural fibres are land and labour intensive and have specific climate requirements, whereas the synthetics thrive, above all, on large concentrations of capital (see Wilson 1985: 71).

In fact, 'the man-made fibre industry was founded on the observation of the silk worm' which exudes a viscous substance through its glands (Ironside 1968: 208). The underlying concept is one of forcing a hot liquid through the tiny holes of a 'spinneret' – a perforated object resembling a showerhead. The molten threads solidify, upon cooling, into continuous filaments which can be wound at very high speeds, then woven into luminescent taffetas and satins. Alternatively, manufacturers cut the filaments into 'staples' for combing, spinning and weaving or knitting into matt-finished fabrics that mimic cotton or wool. Either way, a high tensile strength facilitates rapid operations, and with this, economies of scale. Other labour-saving aspects of synthetics manufacture include the elimination of twisting, cleaning, sorting and grading (Grilli 1975; Tisdell and McDonald 1979).

The first synthetic was rayon, patented in France in 1885 at a time when the silk industry was beset by a worm disease. Nicknamed 'artificial silk', rayon is made from wood pulp, obtained from fast growing trees like eucalyptus, balsam and poplar. (Its enthusiastic acceptance by consumers who have rejected polyester is in a way 'sartorially correct', as its cellulose base makes it an anomaly among the 'man-mades'.) The greatest expansion in rayon manufacturing occurred between the wars and during World War II, when the fascist governments of Germany, Italy and Japan alike defined it as the cornerstone of a sought-after textile autarky. Germany taxed its textile mills to build rayon plants, while in 1938 Japan decreed the substitution of rayon for cotton in civilian clothes. In Italy, regime-supported fashion magazines touted rayon for its drape and feel (Jeffrey Schnapp, personal communication). Overall, global rayon output, contributed by other countries as well, grew by 200 per cent in this period – so much so that Finland and Sweden became specialized wood pulp exporters. (Meanwhile attempts were made to develop a protein fibre from milk, soybeans, peanuts and cornstarch; Grilli 1975: 158–9).

Nylon, synthesized from coal, air, water and ammonia, was an invention of DuPont scientists between 1929 and 1935 – the same years in which rayon was established as a viable substitute for cotton as well as silk. Welcome for its ability to imitate silk in costly stockings, it too was called 'artificial silk'. Requiring twice the capital investment of rayon, however, its full development was associated with military applications during World War II (1975: 161). Following the War, scientists at DuPont, together with colleagues in the Calico Printers Association and at the Imperial Chemical Industries (ICI) in England, began work on acrylics and polyesters, synthesized from natural gas or coal, air, water, and petroleum products.

Most manufacturers of polyesters and acrylics are huge, multinational petro-chemical firms located in Europe, Japan and the United States. The degree of concentration is impressive. In 1972, 32 of the 500 largest companies in the world were synthetics fibre manufacturers, while 13 giant firms supplied three-fifths of the world supply. Companies of the scale of DuPont, Monsanto, Celanese and Akzona, which accounted for three-quarters of US sales, generate their own capital, which they invest in research, and in marketing, promotional and information campaigns directed not only at consumers, but at textile and apparel manufacturers as well. In the 1960s, such companies spent $70 million on promotion – compared with $4 million spent by the cotton fibre industry. In addition they advanced credit to retailers, subsidized their advertising, and financed the installation of faster knitting and weaving machines by up-stream fabric manufacturers (Clairmonte and Cavanagh 1980; Tisdell and McDonald 1979).

In this oligopolistic set-up, science and discovery, product differentiation and patenting, are everything. DuPont, in fact, went into polyester as its nylon patent ran out. US synthetics manufacturers poured $135 million into research in 1965, against $26.5 million put up by cotton manufacturers. By 1969, DuPont had invented not one, but 31 dacrons and 70 nylons. (The figure for dacrons was 71 by 1985; AFF 1985: 5.) Qiana, a DuPont polyester that mimics silk, had gone from the test tube to a hotel in Europe where the continent's ten leading 'silk men' had gathered. Only three of the ten were able to distinguish it from the real thing (*AFF* 1969: 62).

The year 1969 was the eve of the maximum synthetics expansion, and that year's Spring issue of *American Fibers and Fabrics* describes a 'bullish attitude' in the industry, whose polymer chemists were said to be poised, like visionaries, to engineer a 'third generation' of fibres. The main task was to answer what was already perceived as a growing consumer demand for prettier fabrics with a more 'natural' feel. The commercial edge, the magazine editors pointed out, would go to custom-tailored fibres, engineered for specific markets and 'branded' like prize bulls. Fibres that took on a mass commodity aspect with no particular identity would, alas, undergo a downward drift in price and profit. The warning was timely given that, in the late 1960s, the US fibre market was expected to absorb 17 million pounds of production per day! If manufacturers failed to pursue additional aesthetic and comfort advances, this vast poundage would, said the editors, 'pile up around their ears' (1969: 49–50) – and it did.

During the decades of the 1950s and 1960s, synthetics producers saw themselves responding heroically to a dramatic increase in textile demand as natural fibres succumbed to 'severe price fluctuations' (see Grilli 1975). Between 1950 and 1966, the world production of all textile fibres increased from 9.4 million tons to 17.7 million tons, an increase of 4 per cent per year compared to an annual rate of population growth of 1.7 per cent. The synthetics' share of the market doubled. Silk had already lost ground to rayon and nylon. Cotton production increased, but its share of world fibres fell from 75 per cent in 1940–41 to 49 per cent in 1976–7. Similarly wool, whose output remained stable in terms of quantity, saw its market share decline from 12.4 per cent to 5.7 per cent in the same period. (As world per capita textile fibre consumption climbed from 5.1 kilograms in 1961 to 6.7 kilograms in 1974, cotton supplied 24 per cent of the increase as against 76 per cent supplied by the synthetics – there was an eight-fold rise in the production of man-mades between 1966 and 1976; Tisdell and McDonald 1979).

Demand soared in the United States. By 1966, world per capita consumption of fibres was 11.5 pounds per year, but the American market, released from its war-time sacrifices, had grown to a staggering 47.9 pounds per capita (*AFF* 1969: 49–50). To the scientists and planners at DuPont and related companies, it was foolish to think that cotton, the closest competitor, could reliably supply this colossal level of use. Third World and southern US cotton producers were inextricably caught up in the political upheavals of independence from a former colonial or subaltern status and were, in addition, anticipating the growth of their own textile industries, helped by World Bank and US bank investment. Unstable cotton pricing led the United States government to discontinue the cotton crop subsidies that had been in place since the Depression, even paying landowners, after 1965, to take land out of cultivation. Meanwhile, cotton picking had been mechanized, sending thousands of African-American sharecropper families to the North.

Unlike the cotton industry, chemical corporate power demonstrated itself eager to perpetuate the war-time national policy of becoming more self-sufficient in textiles. Given state guarantees of a legal framework protecting patents, this sector was also committed to maintain a competitive advantage, even as textile production spread abroad. Oil prices were then low and supplies abundant, thanks in part to national policy. But compared with the cost of research and development, that of raw materials is relatively unimportant in synthetic fibre manufacturing (Tisdell and McDonald 1979). Indeed, this is why the OPEC price hike of 1973 is not considered pivotal to the industry's loss of altitude.

Which brings us back to what the industry thinks the reasons were. In 1985, over a decade into the fibre 'counter-revolution', the *American Fiber and Fabrics* editors dedicated an entire issue to polyester. 'When selecting the contents for this issue', they wrote, 'we were surprised by the inflexible attitudes held by so many we talked to who should know better. The perception of polyester as inextricably linked to the doubleknit suit, an image which has nothing to do with the performance and hand of the fibre today, is shocking'.

The editors admit to an earlier time – around 1970 – when an oversaturated market led producers to compete on price, alone. The result was 'fashion indigestion', in which stores were flooded with similar colours and textures and a massive homogenization of styling. This was when doubleknit became a by-word for bad taste, tarnishing polyester's name. But to dwell on this moment, they argue, is unfair. In the interim, fibre engineers had been hard at work 'naturalizing' the synthetics to meet objections to their 'hand' or feel and creating new varieties. Demonstrating that solutions are in sight for even the breathability problem, the issue on polyester includes a section called 'Touch and Tell', with 15 unidentified fabric swatches and an answer key several pages later, enabling readers to test their ability to discriminate between natural, synthetic and blended cloth. (I missed on seven of the 15 samples, Peter Schneider on nine.)

Introducing the special issue on polyester, the publisher, Didier Raven, makes a further point: 'We were also disturbed to find a kind of "class warfare," fueled by the elitist and pretentious advertising of designers such as Ralph Lauren and Calvin Klein, harkening back to a natural way of life that never existed. I am sure that most customers who followed Mr Klein's view of "back to nature" would be surprised that the tiny Mexican village serving as the backdrop for his recent ad campaign is today still mired in abject poverty, with hardly any indoor plumbing . . . Additionally, we were dismayed by so-called consumer research, which led Cotton Incorporated to tell this publisher that wearing polyester may be "socially risky". From every point of view such attitudes are distressing' (*AFF* 1985: 3).

The reference to Cotton Incorporated is not accidental. Provoked by the expansion of synthetic fibres in the 1950s and 1960s, both cotton and wool manufacturers, historically far less cohesive than their counterparts in synthetics, had formed themselves into world trade boards, each with a distinctive logo: the 'pure cotton' flower and the 'woolmark' of spiralled yarns. Pooling resources, these boards also began promoting capital investment in research and development that would give to the natural fibres some of the wash and wear qualities of the synthetics (Tisdell and McDonald 1979: 59). After 1980, a cotton revival took off in the American South, with acreage expanding in ten states from 2.2 million in 1983 to 4.6 million in 1990 – close to the 1937 peak. Whereas in 1937, cotton was picked by sharecroppers, however, now expensive machines, supplemented by migrant Latino fieldhands, do most of the work (*NYT* 6 July 1991). In other words, from the point of view of the synthetics industry, the problem is not just that the consumers changed their image of polyester, undermining its share of the market since the mid-1970s, but that Ralph Lauren and company, together with the Wool and Cotton Boards, had managed that change.

Nor are these the only problems identified by spokespersons for the synthetics. The Cotton and Wool Boards are international, and it is the globalization of textile manufacturing over the last two decades that, from their point of view, has created the most compelling context for the synthetics' decline. The 1984 issue of *American Fibers and Fabrics* is devoted to what the editors call 'the important crisis'. On the magazine's cover are two dozen cartoon figures representing different nationalities seated around a pie in the shape of the USA; holding knives and forks, they appear about to dig in. Didier Raven's letter, on the inside cover, declares that no single issue has been more important in 38 years of publication. Textile and clothing imports put at risk not only the American textile industry but the future standard of living of the nation (*AFF* 1984: 5).

One of the issue's contributors argues that American 'PRODUCTION' has given way to 'knowledge industries', with the nation now seeking international advantage through the export of food, weapons and corporate knowhow, rather than manufactures (*AFF* 1984: 44–6). As marvellously sketched by the magazine's managing editor, Martha De Llosa, this conversion is a betrayal of American textile history. She begins with the Englishman, Lord Cornbury, who, in 1705, warned of rebellion once the colonists saw they could 'cloathe themselves, not only comfortably, but handsomely too, without the help of England'. No wonder that 'the very roots of the American Revolution were nourished by resistance to oppressive English laws like the Wool Act . . .'. Appropriately, in 1789, George Washington declared that it should be 'unfashionable for a gentleman to appear in any other dress except homespun'.

De Llosa then moves to the War of 1812, when Eleuthere Irenee DuPont formed a committee representing 27 cotton manufacturers and 14 wool makers from Delaware. Their goal was to convince Congress of their commitment to 'our national safety and independence, our Army and Navy clothed by our own industry'. In exchange, this 'DuPont group' sought 'interference and protection of our own Government to nurse and foster their infant manufactories [against] superior advantages, public and private capital, ill-founded prejudices on the part of their own fellow citizens, and a powerful foreign government'. Ms De Llosa also catalogues the mid-century contributions of Elias Howe and Isaac Singer, inventor and promoter of the sewing machine, and Levi Strauss, who transformed canvas tents and wagon covers into miners' overalls during the California gold rush. Three succeeding wars are cited as crucibles of further development: the Civil War for nurturing Milliken and Westpoint Pepperil, and the two world wars for giving us the synthetics. During the second of these wars, DuPont nylon not only went into combat: in 1941 it was the material of choice for football pants when Army played Notre Dame (*AFF* 1984: 7–12).

The foregoing interpretation of American textile history presents the synthetics manufacturers as inheriting the mantle of promoting the national interest that, in earlier centuries, was worn by the makers of wool and cotton. Hence the special (1984) issue of *American Fibers and Fabrics* on 'the import crisis'. With 35 per cent of the apparel sector already in importers' hands, the editors declared, for every 100 yards of cloth and clothing made at home, 53 yards were imported – equivalent to 10 billion square yards. Fifteen per cent of America's mounting trade deficit was attributable to these goods. In addition, there was the loss of jobs. In 1970, 210,000 people were employed in New York City's garment sector but this figure had declined to 126,000 by 1981. The entire industry, the third largest in the country, generating 45 billion of GNP in 1983 compared with 40 billion for auto-mobiles (also see Powell and Peel 1988: 60–61), was in jeopardy, its 2.3 million workers in the fibre, textile and apparel sectors vulnerable to lay-offs. Fifty-one per cent of the workers were women, 24 per cent minorities, thus foretelling social dislocations greater than the actual numbers (see Wilson 1985: 82–3 for an English parallel).

With a few exceptions, the chemical manufacture of synthetic fibres has been concentrated in the already industrialized First World. Third World industrializing countries are more likely to be aggressive, competitive exporters of silk and partic-ularly cotton than of the 'man-mades'. In 1968, US companies manufactured 32.2 per cent of all man-made fibres in the world (43.3 per cent if one excludes the cellulosic man-mades like rayon). The American percentage of world production in other fibres was, by comparison, minor: 18.4 for cotton, 10.3 for wool, 8.6 for silk. Only 17.4 per cent of all the world's natural fibre production was located in the United States (*JAF* 1969: 69). This is not to overlook either the 'Polyester Rows' in Korea and Indonesia or the recent increase of cotton garment output in America – usually at the hands of immigrant women in newly reconstituted sweatshops (Waldinger 1986). It does, however, point to the fact that middle-class consumers overthrew polyester in favour of natural fibres during a historical conjuncture in which these fibres were presented to them laden with foreign labour.

Synthetics manufacturers draw attention to the low cost of this labour. In 1982, the average hourly wage in the formal, American textile sector was $5.83, as against $1.65 in Hong Kong, and $1.00 in Taiwan. In apparel, the figures were $6.52 in the United States, $1.46 in Hong Kong, $1.43 in Taiwan, and 79 cents in Korea. Designers, however, counter that lower-cost labour enables them to enhance the quality of tailoring and complexity of ornamentation, adding to their products' appeal. Liz Claiborne is reported to have been especially impressed that the 2 million immigrants who flooded into Hong Kong after the Chinese Revolution included hundreds of thousands of women with background and skills in knitting and sewing. For this reason, too, quality could be upgraded (Lardner 1988).

In 1961, the American government negotiated the first of a series of agreements with other countries aimed at protecting domestic apparel from undue disruption by imports, but the pressure from imports was not then as serious as it would become. 1974 marks the first year of a new approach, the 'multifibre' textile agree-ment, according to which bilateral quotas are set for the amounts, in weight, of particular fibres that the US will admit, whether in yarn, cloth or clothes. The voices represented in *American Fibers and Fabrics* are sceptical of MFAs, which the negotia-tors must renew every few years. In 1961, they point out, imported cottons supplied only 5.2 per cent of US cotton textile consumption. In 1982, 28.8 per cent of cottons and 33.9 per cent of wools were manufactured abroad, as against 10.8 per cent of synthetics.

Hong Kong, South Korea, Singapore and Taiwan were the first major offenders, but a score of countries – India, Pakistan, Indonesia, the Philippines, Thailand,

China, Bangladesh, Colombia – also look to textile exports as the most strategic way to employ their people and cancel foreign debt. So much is this the case that in 1980, the International Trade Commission reported that 30 per cent of manufacturing employment in developing countries, but only 14 per cent in developed countries, was in textile and apparel fields (Aggarwal 1985: 9). At the same time, the Reagan administration, advocating free trade and a strong dollar, became notably lax in MFA enforcement. According to James Lardner's *New Yorker* essay on Liz Claiborne, the Hong Kong government took advantage of this laxity, playing the 'cat and mouse game of quota evasion' with aplomb. Out of this dynamic came ramie, a variety of hemp. Twice the cost of cotton, and possessed of a crinkled if not wrinkled look (thereby addressing concerns about upkeep), ramie became both fashionable and quota free.

Along with Ralph Lauren – also well grounded in Hong Kong – and Cotton International is a third villain in the *American Fibers and Fabrics* version of why polyester had declined: the 'Retail Industry Trade Action Coalition' whose representative, William Andres, is cited for making 'virulent attacks' on import restrictions. In an Open Letter to Andres, Seth M. Broder, Executive Director of the National Knitwear and Sportswear Association, asks, 'Who decided that customers were demanding blends of ramie and linen with their customary cotton? Are there crowds in the street chanting RAMIE! RAMIE!? Can one really expect American consumers to believe that the retail community is fighting on behalf of its customers? "Fighting over them" would be more like it.'

According to Broder, domestic apparel has a 100 per cent mark-up, but the mark-up on imports is 300 to 400 per cent. Rhetorically, he asks, why not pass on to the customers:

> what you gain now by exploiting sixteen cent per hour Chinese, Sri Lankan, Haitian and other labor? Mr. Andres, why not come right out and indicate the basic motive and indicate that you believe that unlimited access to lower cost products will increase your profits? . . . Remember, Mr. Andres, it doesn't take as long to get from Manhattan to Brooklyn as it does to get to Hong Kong. Transportation is cheaper and passports are not yet needed. Customers are not choosing these goods. They are reacting to a situation in which you give them no choice (*AFF* 1985: 43–6).

Capitalism in transformation

As a cultural movement, the rejection of polyester would seem to be an autonomous development, motivated by thinking and acting human beings whose disdain for plastic, and for the mass industrial society that was its crucible, developed in response to observation and experience. The history of synthetic fibres and fabrics is objectively part of a morally troubling pollution of the environment and aesthetically offensive massing or sameness. In contrast to this innocence are the synthetics industry voices that belittle consumer autonomy, and attribute the collapse of polyester's hegemony to a different cause: the advertising campaigns, organization and investment, and pressures on government policy fostered by powerful competitors associated with cotton and wool. Before assessing this contradiction, a third perspective is necessary, one that places both producers and consumers in the context of the 1970s transformation of American capitalism, and the associated restratification of American society.

Like Melinkoff historicizing the fashion shift to 'conservatism with a choice', and like *American Fibers and Fabrics* tracing the decline in market share for synthetic fabrics, English economic geographer David Harvey treats 1973 as a watershed year. 'There has been some kind of transformation in the political economy of late twentieth century capitalism', he writes '. . . and we need some way . . . to represent all the shifting and churning that has gone on since the first major post-war recession of 1973.' In language that many others have appropriated, Harvey goes on to characterize the 'long postwar boom, from 1945 to 1973 [as] built upon a certain set of labor control practices, technological mixes, consumption habits, and configurations of political-economic power . . . that . . . can reasonably be called Fordist-Keynesian'. The successor he labels a 'flexible regime of accumulation', drawing attention to the breakup of unionized aggregates of factory labour and mass markets, accompanied by intensified geographical mobility and peripatetic consumption practices (Harvey 1989: 121–4).

A monumental economic 'restructuring' and computer-driven technological revolution are associated with these trends. In the United States, investments have flowed toward the production and export of financial services, management and control functions, at the expense of manufacturing. These are the 'knowledge industries' that the advocates of synthetics complain about. At the same time, corporations that had been at the core of the main growth and export sectors during the postwar era – most especially automobiles and apparel – moved many of their manufacturing operations overseas. Most significant, when American industries moved off-shore, information-processing technology and fibre-optic communications cancelled out the increased distance, facilitating ever faster and more flexible responses to fashion change (Lardner 1988). For industries that stayed put, workers saw important operations transferred from shop floor to computer, with an attendant growth in technical and professional staff.

Sociologists of the American economy like Saskia Sassen have amply documented the impact of restructuring on social stratification. The massive expansion of the middle class that had defined the postwar era came to an end, as 35 per cent of manufacturing jobs and 41 per cent of manufacturing-headquarters office jobs disappeared between 1970 and 1980. Instead there began a bifurcated growth of marginal, low-wage earners on the one hand and, on the other hand, a new American gentry of young professionals and technicians with annual incomes of $40,000 or more. Filling niches from near-top to near-bottom of the new social 'order' was an immigrant population, 4.5 million of whom entered during the 1970s – the largest number in any single decade in US history.

At each level of the emergent new society, household incomes had to be maintained by women's as well as men's earnings. Whereas in the 1950s, more than half of all households conformed to the wife as homemaker model, by the 1980s, over half of all American women worked outside the home. One in two marriages ended in divorce, while every fourth household had a single parent as head. In the 15 years after 1973, the number of persons living alone grew by 90 per cent to more than 20 million. Not to belabour a familiar litany (and I am skipping over its baby boom-generated demographic dimensions), it is worth noting how poor a predictor the 1959 survey was that found three out of four American couples wanting to establish and live in 'traditional' families (Sassen-Koob 1984; see also Weiss 1989: 39, 43–4, 103, 170–3, 185, 244–5).

Part of the shift from polyesters to naturals is, clearly, an aspect of the process of gentrification, which carries with it the development of new cultural principles and ideals. Attracted to 'old money status, professional success, "refined" taste, and body cultivation', gentrifiers choose clothes that, as McCracken points out (1988: 145), 'best [give] voice to these principles'. Ornamentation and tailoring – value added by intensive labour – are high on the list of qualities sought while the passion for fitness translates into a heightened awareness of how different fabrics respond to perspiration and touch. Fitness centres are among the arenas where women and men 'talk clothes', contrasting, for example, the feel of spandex during exercise with cotton after a shower.

For cultural historian Deborah Silverman another, powerful arena was the nexus of Bloomingdales and the Metropolitan Museum of Art in the early 1980s. Bringing together the worlds of the department store, the museum, the media, the White House, and fashion, this nexus fostered 'aristocratic invocation'. Among the diagnostic framing events studied by Silverman were the early 1980s marketing extravaganzas at Bloomingdales, in which first the 'exotic riches' of the Chinese emperors, then the 'aristocratic crafts' of Old Regime France, imbued the store with luxury. According to Silverman, these sales campaigns were but a translation into commerce of shows curated by the Costume Institute of the Museum at about the same time: Chinese Imperial Robes in 1980, followed by Francophile displays of The Eighteenth-Century Woman, La Belle Epoque, and Yves Saint Laurent in retrospect. In 1984, the Institute 'glorified English gentry and equestrian apparel and ownership in "Man and the Horse", presented by Polo/Ralph Lauren' (Silverman 1986: 9). In a similar vein, J. Crew sells the image of the WASP New England boating set.

Aristocratic invocation carries with it an aristocratic price tag, the natural fabrics out-pacing the synthetics by a wide margin, especially when they are beautifully decorated and stitched with care. In addition, these fabrics require expensive cleaning and laundering if they are to be kept up. This is in direct contrast to polyester whose 1950s and 1960s history was that of an an equalizing fabric – not, at first, cheaper than its competitors, but nevertheless intended as a 'quality good for the masses'. As we noted above, polyester's easy care raised the possibility that middle-class households might dispense with domestic service altogether (see Powell and Peel 1988: 32–3). Significantly, perhaps, its dissemination as a wash-and-wear alternative to cotton coincided with the Civil Rights movement, whose goals included overcoming servile relations between blacks and whites. In this respect, it is worth noting that the retreat of the synthetics has coincided with 'gentry' working women turning to immigrant working women for household help.

The gentrifying aspects of the return to natural fibres are highlighted by the realization that polyester took hold under strikingly different social conditions. Even in its second, 'mod' incarnation, this fabric was democratic, or at least that is how the flamboyant designers of the 1960s employed it. Fashion journalist Ironside describes a postwar social revolution in Britain that, through government grants, enabled 'otherwise miners or domestic servants or whoever' to acquire training as artists and fashion designers (1973: 113). And Kennedy Fraser, looking back on the 1960s in America, remembers a time when 'fashion spoke in a kind of common voice. Women of different ages, social backgrounds, political opinions very often chose a single, distinctive silhouette – namely skirts well above the knees'. If Jackie Kennedy embraced this shape, so did nurses in uniform (Fraser 1981: 241; Melinkoff 1984: 123–30).

In a 1967 essay celebrating Twiggy's 'concave droop like a punctured marionette', Cecil Beaton, fashion photographer and artist, concluded: 'Today's models do not try to simulate the grand ladies. They do not want to look rich, for dressing is no longer a matter of one-upmanship. Class distinction has gone from the model scene . . .' (Ross 1986: 158–60; Powell and Peel 1988: 72). No wonder that Mary Quant, whose mini-skirt innovations at the King's Road Bazaar in Chelsea helped break the hold of Parisian couturiers on European and American designs, wrote as follows in her autobiography, *Quant by Quant*: 'Once only the Rich, the Establishment, set fashion. Now it is the inexpensive little dress seen on girls on High Street . . . They may be dukes' daughters, doctors' daughters, dockers' daughters. They are not interested in status symbols. They don't worry about their accents or class . . . They represent a whole new spirit . . . a classless spirit that has grown up out of the second world war . . . they are mods' (quoted in Wilson 1985: 175).

When the social dimension of fabric choice is brought into focus, it becomes more difficult to treat those who changed their minds about polyester as either fully autonomous or blown by the winds of powerful political and economic forces. Their growing disdain would seem, rather, to be a reflective reworking of priorities, conditioned by the formation of new social groups. That the producers of natural fibres and fabrics, and of apparel in these materials, took advantage of the moment should not surprise us. Their role, however, was one of intensification, not definition. Moreover, as I hope I have demonstrated, we need not view them as an external element: synthetics manufacturers and natural fibres manufacturers are important participants in the very re-alignments that bring new groups to the fore.

Note

A condensed version of this article was presented at the American Anthropological Association meeting in the fall of 1992, at a session honouring Sidney W. Mintz. That same fall, I presented a longer version to the Society for the Humanities at Cornell University, where I was a fellow, and where the integrative theme concerned material culture, both 'trash and treasure'. Members of the Society and others from the Cornell community contributed both encouragement and criticism. The university's widely known 'home economics' collections were, as well, indispensable for uncovering the point of view of the manufacturers of synthetics. With more time, I would also have pursued the cotton industry's perspective. This must await a future project.

Among the Cornell scholars, I wish to acknowledge, in particular, Roald Hoffmann who, after hearing my lecture, challenged my conception of the boundary between 'naturals' and 'synthetics'. A charming and insightful article by Hoffmann (1990) is included in the bibliography for readers who wish to probe a chemist's understanding of the impossibility of disentangling the two. Hoffmann asks, for example, whether ores that have been operated upon by geo-chemical forces are really natural, and why nylon should be opposed to silk when both are strikingly similar on the molecular level. He also addresses the consumer revolt against synthetics. Associating the synthetics with a democratizing process, he interprets the revolt in terms of an inevitable search for 'cachet' or difference, for less alienating products, and as a reaction to the 'man-made' horrors of Chernobyl and Bhopal – reminding us, though, that nature is capable of generating horrors too.

References

AFF, Editors. 1984. *American Fabrics and Fashions* 131.
—— 1985. *American Fabrics and Fashions* 132.
Aggarwal, Vinod K. 1985. *Liberal Protectionism: The International Politics of Organized Textile Trade*. Berkeley and Los Angeles: U. of California P.
Clairmonte, Frederick F. and John Cavanagh. 1980. World Chemicals: the Anatomy of Corporate Power. *Journal of Contemporary Asia* 10: 444–53.
Fraser, Kennedy. 1981. *The Fashionable Mind: Reflections on Fashion*. New York: Alfred A. Knopf.
Grilli, Enzo. 1975. *The Future for Hard Fibers and Competition from Synthetics*. World Bank Staff Occasional Papers. No. 19. Baltimore, Maryland: Johns Hopkins U. P.
Harvey, David. 1989. *The Post-Modern Condition*. Baltimore: Johns Hopkins U. P.
Hoffmann, Roald. 1990. 'Natural/Unnatural', *NER/BLQ (New England Review and Bread Loaf Quarterly)* 12: 522–5.
Ironside, Janey. 1968. *A Fashion Alphabet*. London: Michael Joseph.
—— 1973. *Janey, an Autobiography*. London: Michael Joseph.
JAF, Editors. 1969. *Journal of American Fabrics* 82.
Jencks, Charles. 1986. *What is Post-modernism?* New York: St Martin's P.
Jernigan, Marian H. and Cynthia R. Easterling. 1990. *Fashion Merchandising and Marketing*. New York: Macmillan.
Katzman, David M. 1978. *Seven Days a Week: Women and Domestic Servants in Industrializing America*. Oxford: Oxford U. P.
Lardner, James. 1988. Annals of Business: the Sweater Trade I. *The New Yorker* 11 January, 1988: 39–73.
—— 1988. Annals of Business: the Sweater Trade II. *The New Yorker* 18 January, 1988: 57–73.
Matthews, Glenna. 1987. *'Just a Housewife': The Rise and Fall of Domesticity in America*. Oxford: Oxford U. P.
McCracken, Grant. 1988. *Culture and Consumption: New Approaches to the Symbolic Character of Consumer Goods and Activities*. Bloomington: Indiana U. P.
Melinkoff, Ellen. 1984. *What We Wore: An Offbeat Social History of Women's Clothing, 1950–1980*. New York: Quill.
Mintz, Sidney W. 1985. *Sweetness and Power: The Place of Sugar in Modern History*. New York: Viking.
Morawetz, David. 1981. *Why the Emperor's New Clothes Are Not Made in Colombia*. Oxford: Oxford U. P.

Powell, Polly and Lucy Peel. 1988. *50's and 60's Style*. London: The Apple P.

Quant, Mary. 1966. *Quant by Quant*. Portway, Bath: Cedric Chivers.

Ross, Josephine. 1986. *Beaton in Vogue*. New York: Clarkson N. Potter, Inc.

Sassen-Koob, Saskia. 1984. 'The New Labor Demand in Global Cities', in *Cities in Transformation: Class, Capital, and the State*. M. P. Smith, ed. pp. 139–73. Beverly Hills, London, New Delhi: Sage.

Silverman, Deborah. 1986. *Selling Culture: Bloomingdales, Diana Vreeland, and the New Aristocracy of Taste in Reagan's America*. New York: Pantheon Books.

Silverman, Kaja. 1986. 'Fragments of a Fashionable Discourse', in *Studies in Entertainment: Critical Approaches to Mass Culture*. M. Tania, ed. Bloomington, Indiana: Indiana U. P.

Tisdell, C. A. and P. W. McDonald, 1979. *Economics of Fibre Markets: Interdependence Between Man-Made Fibres, Wool and Cotton*. Oxford: Pergamon P.

Waldinger, Roger, 1986. *Through the Eyes of the Needle: Immigrants and Enterprise in New York's Garment Trades*. New York: New York U. P.

Weiss, Michael J. 1989. *The Clustering of America: A Vivid Portrait of the Nation's 40 Neighborhood Types – Their Values, Lifestyles and Eccentricities*. New York: Tilden P. (Harper and Row).

Wilson, Elizabeth. 1985. *Adorned in Dreams: Fashion and Modernity*. Berkeley and Los Angeles: U. of California P.

Chapter 17

Katherine Verdery

■   'CARITAS' AND THE RECONCEPTUALIZATION
OF MONEY IN ROMANIA, *Anthropology Today*,
11.1, February 1995, pp. 3–7

AMONG THE MOST FASCINATING new sites for anthropological
investigation are the transforming societies of the former socialist bloc.[1] They
are veritable laboratories for all manner of subjects, including the nature of states
and their relationship to nationalism, the redefinition of property rights, the decom-
position of 'latifundia' or large agricultural estates as in post-colonial Latin America
and post-feudal Europe, and the transformation of class structures. In addition, they
are host to a new variant of something anthropologists have been studying in other
parts of the globe for decades: changed cultural conceptions that accompany the
increasing presence of capitalism and markets in formerly non-capitalist, non-market
contexts. These changed conceptions affect everything from people's ideas about
time, self and work to their understandings of money and commodities.

The present essay deals with one way in which people in formerly socialist
Romania began learning to think differently about money and 'the economy'. It is
a pyramid scheme called 'Caritas', a scheme that achieved astonishing proportions
between its inauguration in Transylvania in April 1992 and its collapse two years
later. One of a large number of such schemes that appeared not just in Romania
but in Russia, Slovakia, Bulgaria, and many other countries in the region after 1989,[2]
Caritas surpassed these in magnitude, partly because of its special connections with
the nationalist Party of Romanian National Unity (PRNU), headed by Gheorghe
Funar. As mayor of the Transylvanian city of Cluj, where Caritas set up its headquarters soon after its founding,[3] Funar openly welcomed its 'patron', Ioan Stoica,
and rented him space right in city hall. This location helped build credibility, as
many depositors assured me. Among Funar's motives in supporting Caritas were
his attempt to gain greater visibility and more financial resources for his party, which
was at the time seeking greater leverage within Romania's governing coalition.[4]

Caritas drew its appeal from its promise to repay depositors their investment
eightfold within three months. This possibility attracted numerous depositors
because with inflation then running at 250–300%, people's savings were becoming

worthless while their salaries fell ever further behind the increased cost of living. For these reasons, Caritas grew to encompass people from all across Romania; for a time, its owner Stoica was better known and more popular than any other figure in Romanian public life.

It is difficult to get an adequate sense of the scheme's amplitude. Estimates vary greatly with respect to both the number of people involved in it (from 2 million to 8 million, and from 10% of the population to as many as 50% of Romanian households), and the amount of money tied up in it (which, according to the president of the Romanian National Bank, may have been as high as one-third of the country's liquid reserves but was in any case of the order of billions of dollars).[5] Even if we accept conservative estimates, however – 20% of all Romanian households, and about 2 million depositors – it was a major phenomenon.

Anything of such magnitude is evidently entangled in many different aspects of the process of transforming socialist societies. Elsewhere I have suggested that Caritas and similar schemes are a vehicle through which the old elite and its newer political allies concentrate the dispersed capital of the Romanian population into their own hands, thus furthering their entrenchment as a new 'bourgeoisie'. (In recognition of the ongoing political connections of these groups, I call them 'entrepratchiks' in a post-socialist 'bourgeoiscracy'.)[6] Here I will concentrate on a different aspect: the role of Caritas in forming new conceptions about money, the economy, and people's relation to them. My data come from conversations with Romanians in villages and cities, primarily in Transylvania, and from some publications by groups both pro- and anti-Caritas.

Rethinking money

To the extent that a once-socialist economy moves toward a market system, people's conceptions of the economy and the place of money in their lives must undergo a radical change. Market-based systems regulate the flow of wealth in a very different way from the planned economy of socialism. This is not because socialist plans unfolded as planned, but because they obstructed the flow of money and goods in certain characteristic ways, different from the obstructions characteristic of market systems. For one thing, in socialism most prices were determined not by 'supply and demand' but politically. Adjustments might come from bribery, gifts, shadow production and barter, but these occurred within constraints set visibly by the party. In my experience, any Romanian asked to explain some aspect of the workings of 'the economy' could readily generate an answer based on something the party was up to, usually some nasty plot against common folk. It was presumed that economic events had an agent: the political system and those who ran it.

Markets in advanced economies, however, work differently. Their secret lies in their being invisible, taken for granted, abstracted from the actions of concrete agents. Precisely here is the ongoing usefulness of Marx's insights about commodity fetishism: market exchange obscures the social relations surrounding production and distribution. Socialist systems too had a form of fetishism: plan fetishism, which produced the illusion of agency and obscured the anarchy and chaos that actually took place behind the scenes.[7] That is, socialist plans generated the illusion that

Figure 17.1 Cartoon by Jeremy Panufnik.

everything is under social control; the illusion of market exchange, however, is exactly the opposite. As markets achieve greater significance in post-socialist society, then, we must look for social visibility to be transformed: the proverbial invisible hand must replace the all-too-visible one of the party.[8] Things that were personal must become impersonal; the economy must become a force of nature for which no one in particular is responsible. Caritas was a critical locus for the recoding of money and the economy that such a shift might entail.

At the simplest level, by participating in Caritas people began to think differently about money. It enabled them to manipulate in their minds sums of which they had never dreamed, to think about what they might do with such sums – to *plan* their expenditures – and to grow accustomed to thinking about larger and larger amounts in a gradual way. First they would have amounts that could go toward consumer items, then the amounts would get so large that more ambitious possibilities suggested themselves: buying a tractor or a combine, opening a restaurant, founding a newspaper or publishing house. But the change to a market

Figure 17.2 An emblem of American capitalism entices Romania. Romanians cross the street in downtown Bucharest, 1999, by an unfinished apartment building draped with a poster of American actor Larry Hagman posing as J.R. Ewing, the character from the *Dallas* television series. The poster is part of an advertising campaign for the Russian oil giant Lukoil. *Dallas* was one of the few American series which the late communist dictator Ceaucescu allowed to be shown on Romanian television.

economy also involves shifts that are more subtle. Socialist propaganda had taught people that the only acceptable source of money and gain was work in the productive process; money from 'commerce' and from 'speculation' was tainted with capitalist traces. Now, however, with increased trade of all kinds and major efforts to increase the circulation of money through the financial system, these habits of mind are being challenged. Caritas has been a prime site for challenging them.

One form of this challenge is a distinction between 'my money' and 'their money', a distinction made by nearly everyone I spoke with. 'My money' was the amount people first deposited. Most who received a pay-out withdrew that amount before turning over the rest: at this point, they would say, they were not playing with their own money but with Stoica's money, and it was no longer possible to lose. A woman I spoke with on a train put it this way: 'You put in 100,000, get 800,000 back, take 500,000 of it to buy things you need, and keep playing the game with 300,000 – *their* money. Am I playing with *my* money then? No. If it gets lost, have I lost *my* money? No. YOU CAN'T LOSE in this game.'

Here is how another woman from whom I heard this distinction elaborated it:

> I got all my money back, so if it falls I can't complain. [K.V.: *Isn't the pay-out money also yours?*] No, it's not quite the same, though I'm not sure why – I never really thought about it. When they pay it to me in cash, it's my money, but when it's not in my hand, it's not like my money. If the thing collapsed, I wouldn't feel I'd lost my money. Even when you get it in hand you spend it differently from other money – you spend it more easily. I had *three million lei* in my hands and I took it right over to the next window to deposit it. [*Didn't that bother you?*] No!

Another couple who also made the distinction talked about it as follows:

> You should take out *your* money and play further with *theirs*. [*If I put in 100,000 and get back 800,000, bring it home, and put it here on the table, is this my money?*] No! [*Why not? I'm not talking about money I rolled over but money I've brought home with me.*] We have no idea. [*But why did you say it isn't my money?*] Well . . . Because it's been in there only three months. It can't be yours. In a savings account, you leave money for a whole year and get 50% interest. Then it's more like your money. But eight-fold in only three months . . .

Almost no one gave me the answer I got from one peasant woman who told me that she had a lot of money in Caritas. [*But it's not your money, is it? You've rolled it over.*] 'It's still my money. If I'd taken it out, it would have been my money.' This woman was rare in not separating 'their money' from 'mine'.

These ruminations on 'my money' and 'their money' intersect with another feature of Caritas to illuminate some of what it was accomplishing. I asked many people to explain to me how it worked: how could you possibly get eight times your deposit in only three months? Many did not find this a meaningful question: they had seen people on TV taking out huge piles of bills, or they knew of someone who had done so, and this was all the explanation they needed. Caritas *works*, for whatever reason. They had faith in it and needed no further account. When I asked how they could entrust such large sums to something they didn't understand, they shrugged. The whole thing was incomprehensible, but it worked. From this I conclude that one of Caritas's most important hidden effects was that it was working to produce an abstract sphere in which money might circulate and multiply *without clear agency*. Through it, the economy was beginning to become an impersonal, unregulated social fact, something to be taken for granted because it worked. A young sociologist expressed this nicely, in explaining what he thought were the effects of his own participation in Caritas: 'I noticed that it made money seem more distant, as if it were happening elsewhere, to someone else. It had become an abstraction, rather than *my money*.' Effects this man could articulate may also have been at work less consciously with others.

Caritas was thus a 'technology', in Foucault's sense, that fostered the process of transforming people's ideas about the economy toward a market sensibility. It was not the only such instrument, but it was an especially widespread one. Although the scheme's collapse in May 1994 may alter or abort its contribution to that process, the experience it afforded its participants was something new. Particularly for those who received and made use of a pay-out, the experience was significant – and, I believe, likely to be durable.[9]

Questioning the moral order

'My money' versus 'their money' was more than just a question of whether or not the economy is impersonal, however: it led directly into questions perhaps even more basic, about a changing economic morality and a new moral order.[10] As I pursued 'my money' and 'their money' further, asking people if the money they won at Caritas was the same as the money they put in, it became clear that for the large majority what defined 'their money' was that it was *unearned* [*nemuncit* – from *munci*, to work], whereas 'my money' is *earned*. For these people 'my money' embodies my work and is its concrete representation, whereas 'their money' has none of me in it. 'If you lose money you earned, you feel bad about it', said one woman, 'but if you lose after that – money you didn't work for – you don't feel bad.' Another: 'In any case, money you've sweated for is different from this money.' A Bucharest cab driver who had not yet received anything greeted my news that Caritas had stopped paying with these words: 'If we don't get anything, I'll string him up! I'll run a stake through him! That's *my hard-earned money!*'

More than simply descriptive, the distinction between earned and unearned money was a question of morality. 'We aren't used to living off unearned money. It seems somehow dishonest to us.' 'I'm not used to having money gotten for nothing; it seems *unnatural*.' 'Something's wrong with it, it can't be honest, someone's going to lose.' 'I was raised to think that you never get anything except by hard work, you can't get something for nothing. There must be some trickery at the bottom of it. I won't put my money in something like that, I've worked too hard for it.' Some people moralized the relationship of Caritas to work even more explicitly. 'With Caritas, people lose interest in working.' 'People won't work any more, they'll just sit around and live off interest.' 'Earnings should come from productive investments, not from some crazy miraculous scheme.' 'Caritas is dreadful! It encourages a beggar's mentality, it undermines people's interest in work. I've heard of people who simply quit their jobs and went home, expecting that it will go on forever. It's based on greed.' These views show strong moral reservations about Caritas earnings, censured because they rest on *greed*, do not come from *production*, and make people *lazy*. It is striking that in a time of privatization-induced unemployment and concerns about Romanians' productivity, what we see people fearing is unemployment and laziness that are *voluntary*, brought on by Caritas.

Not everyone, however, is critical of Caritas money. Here are two agronomists who have bought a tractor with Caritas money and are embarked on an 'entrepreneurial' trajectory:

> Some people say it's [bad because it's] unearned money. This is an idea left over from before, that earned money is money you actually earn by producing something. Unearned money was from speculation, and it was condemned, along with anything that didn't have to do with producing. People who complain about its being unearned money are those who like to sit around, who have no enterprising spirit to risk something.

This couple's opinion was informed by their success with Caritas – something that, I found, seemed to predispose one to a more positive assessment. They and others like them engaged in vigorous argument with other people concerning the morality of earnings from Caritas. Indeed, even those who were critical were likely to have mixed feelings; they too had money in Caritas, and perhaps their minds would change once the earnings started to roll in. And so, as they waited for that to happen, people were *debating* the morality of Caritas money. That is, Caritas focused their genuine ambivalence about money's morality and became a space in which they sought to convince themselves and others that their old ideas about money were or were not outmoded, by arguing about just why Caritas money might not be immoral after all.

Here are some examples. The first two see Caritas as a kind of moral compensation. To a friend in Cluj, I say that a lot of people seem upset that Caritas money is unearned and comes from greed. She replies:

> Well, but I've heard people saying, 'Isn't the West stealing from us with all this cheap labour?' And I know some pensioners who object to those criticisms of Caritas. They say, 'We pensioners worked our whole life, we put our money in savings, and now the money in those accounts is worth absolutely nothing. Who stole it from us? Is *that* moral? Stoica offers me a chance to eat better, have a TV – is this morally bad? Is it morally worse than the fact that the Communist Party reduced us to paupers? No!'

Second, a woman has been telling me how she plans to use her Caritas money. Then she volunteers, 'Lots of people say it's immoral to live on unearned money, but I say, for all these years people worked unpaid, now we get a kind of compensation, don't you think?'

Others puzzle over how much enrichment is acceptable, natural or otherwise justifiable. Many people talked uncomfortably about the greed that motivates people to roll their money over. As one fellow said to me of his stint in line:

> People are so greedy! The guy right in front of me took out 120 million lei, went over to the next register, and deposited 100 million of it. I asked him, 'Why are you doing it *again*? Isn't what you already have enough?' And he replied, 'I can do what I want with it. It's my money.' But I said to him, 'It's *not* your money. It's mine and the other people's who've just deposited it. Leave some for the rest of us!'

This comment epitomizes the very common negative judgment of those who want to get rich, as well as genuine puzzlement as to whose resource Caritas money really is. A similar concern shows in a friend's comment, 'If Caritas money is immoral, it's because Stoica lets [some] people get so incredibly rich with it and others can't get in at all.' She added, however, 'But we can't make ends meet with our work, so it's good to have Caritas money.' Thus, she finds enrichment acceptable after all because everyone is so needy.

It seems, then, that people are deeply divided as to whether it is acceptable to have money for which one has not worked. After years of hearing that commerce, high-interest loans, interest from capital, and the other forms of gain in the capitalist system were evil, Romanians are having to revalorize those forms as they struggle to make do in inflationary and uncertain times. Many (but far from all) use words like 'greed' with clear disapproval – yet they too are getting or awaiting money from Caritas. Some use words like 'crookery' to describe Caritas, see it as 'unnatural', as a form of theft. The notion of theft recurs often: what *is* theft, after all? Who is stealing from whom? In other words, which forms of gain are licit, socially acceptable, and which are not? Under socialism certain forms of theft were acceptable, but how about now? If Caritas *is* a form of theft, can we justify it by our need? Does or doesn't money have something to do with work? If money comes from non-work, is that natural? Is greed natural? How should we feel about people who want to get rich? How should we feel about *ourselves* if we want to get rich? Romania's supposed transition to a form of capitalist market economy occasions such questioning for all its citizens.

There were other forms of questioning the morality of Caritas money besides the distinction between earned and unearned money, though this was the most common. Another was a distinction between 'dirty' money and 'clean'. That Caritas money might be dirty underlay most of the public criticisms of the scheme. Any of several sources might soil it: arms smuggling, the Italian mafia, prostitution, drug trafficking, roots in the Secret Police, etc. – anything illegal. All these would require 'cleaning' for which Caritas was an instrument, and all would make Caritas morally reprehensible for laundering money of this kind. In my experience, the concern with 'dirty money' was a preoccupation of intellectuals, journalists and politicians rather than of average folks, who (in keeping with a personalized attitude toward money) did not seem to care about the *wider* social provenance of Caritas funds.

As one village friend said, when asked if she would take her money out if she found out it was from illegal sources:

> No. If Stoica is doing something wrong, it's between him and God. It doesn't affect us. Besides, we're too poor. We need every possible source of income these days, never mind where it comes from. For so long we had no possibilities, we have to try to make ends meet with so little, prices keep going up, people lose their jobs. . . . We're just too needy to worry about whether it's dirty money.

Questions of morality are central for her too, but (as with the woman above) they have to do with the immorality of want, rather than of illicit gain.

There was a third, perhaps unexpected, form of arguing the morality of Caritas money, a form that links Caritas with Romanian nationalist political parties. Its most energetic manifestation appears in a booklet called *The Caritas Phenomenon or the Salvation of Romanians Through Themselves*, written by two defenders of Stoica who are both closely associated with Romanian nationalist politics. Their argument has two central 'moral' points: that Caritas is moral because it is the product of *social solidarity* (rather than of individualized gain-seeking), and that the beneficiary of this solidarity is *the Romanian nation*. Caritas, they proclaim, is good because it is the revolt of the united Romanian nation against the dictatorship of foreign money and foreign plans for 'reform'. It is 'a response, a solution, a reaction, a manifestation of national energy in the face of a fantastically well organized process of demolishing Romania and bringing the Romanian people to its knees through poverty and demoralization'; the authors decry 'so-called "reform" and "shock therapy" that are in essence only a vast project of economic, spiritual and biological *extermination* of an entire people . . .'[11]. They go on to describe in detail the international plot involving privatization and market competition through which foreigners will conquer all key positions in the economy. Why, they ask, do so many people accuse Caritas of being a swindle and ignore the *real* swindle, which is: 'the actual collapse of Romania beneath the burden of a program of "reform" that has proved everywhere an economic catastrophe for the countries obliged to accept it and a political one for the West itself'.[12] To be sure they have made their point, they declare in large letters, 'THE BATTLE FOR OR AGAINST CARITAS HAS BECOME PART OF THE BATTLE FOR OR AGAINST THE ROMANIAN PEOPLE'S RIGHT TO EXIST'.[13]

Here, then, is a third kind of immoral money: not unearned money or dirty money but *foreign* money. Against this kind of immorality, Caritas becomes a patriotic institution that will produce an *indigenous* middle class, bearing *good*, moral money rather than the immoral money of foreigners. It is moral because, unlike many other things going on in Romania (including, of course, criticism of Stoica and Caritas), it is *pro-Romanian*. It is more than this: it is a crusade by Romanians for their own salvation, 'the salvation of Romanians, by the will and the grace of God, through themselves'.[14]

Caritas, God and the Devil

What these Romanian nationalist authors offer us is a new, Caritas-based morality that unifies religious faith and nationalism. They quote with admiration the Romanian Orthodox Vicar in the United States, as he asks who will buy the industries bankrupted by government policy:

> Foreigners will. But Caritas has come as a divine phenomenon not only so that people can have money and be happy; it is the salvation of the Romanian people. Now true Romanians will have millions, maybe billions, so as to buy this economy and not have it in foreign hands.[15]

Thus, these authors have made Caritas and Stoica into something akin to a millenarian movement. Its nationalism makes it very different, however, from those of Oceania or other places where such movements have accompanied the penetration of capitalism.

In millenarizing Caritas, the authors tap widespread popular imagery of Stoica as divine. For his hopeful depositors, Stoica was 'a saint', 'the Pope', 'a messiah', 'the prophet'.[16] The folklore surrounding Caritas was full of 'good Stoica' stories, such as one I heard in which an elderly man went to headquarters and asked to see 'Mr Caritas', offering a deposit of 2,000 lei so he could have a decent burial. Stoica took him to the cash register and gave him 20,000 lei on the spot. My informant concluded, 'I don't know why but I have faith in what he says', and her cousin chimed in, 'It's said that God sent him to take care of us.' I heard others say that he's not in this to make money for himself but gets satisfaction from seeing *other* people win, that he's very religious and gives lots to churches, that he has the morality of a saint. Stoica's repeated references to his faith and his use of religious expressions doubtless fed such beliefs. Reflecting the widespread reverence for Stoica, publications presented him as 'the saviour of the people' and 'a god of the Romanians', his supporters as prophets and apostles, Caritas as 'the miracle of Cluj', 'a divine phenomenon', and depositors' journeys to Cluj as like pilgrimages.[17] (Critics, for their part, viewed it as the 'swindle of Cluj', 'a demonic game', and 'a perilous disease'; they dismissed the salvational and moral imagery and refused to see in Stoica a new sacred leader.)[18]

Thus saturated with divine symbolism, Stoica and Caritas became matters of *faith*, of *trust* – in Romanian, *încredere*. More than any other word, this was the one people used in speaking of them. Over and over, those I met described to me like this their decision to put money in Caritas: 'I didn't have faith [*n-am avut încredere*] in it at first, but when I saw everyone else getting money, I decided to trust it too.' As with other millenarian movements, 'faith' came partly through the social effects of others' behaviour, a kind of conversion accompanying knowledge that others were in it too, and winning. Participants also proselytized actively: one woman told me she was fed up with how many friends and people in her workplace kept trying to get her into Caritas, and I heard several stories about people who had gotten in because someone else deposited some money for them as a starter. (I myself was proselytized into depositing $350, which I lost.) Faith was what enabled people to accept for months all manner of excuses as to why pay-outs were stagnating or stopped, and it was what Stoica banked on when, during an October 1993 interview, he urged people not to lose faith despite all the negative press.

With faith came also hope. People referred to Caritas money as their 'hope money' [*bani de nadejde*], without which they would have absolutely nothing, and declared that their only hope was Caritas, one of the few things to look forward to in otherwise disheartening times. A new train added to bring people to Cluj from the south was named the 'train of hope'. 'Faith', 'trust' and 'hope': these words and the associated moral and religious imagery were crucial to the process of making the circulation of money impersonal. Anyone who could not (or did not feel the need to) explain how it worked could assign it to the sphere of the divine.

The discourse of sacrality invited, however, its opposite and brought into play a very specific, malevolent agent: the devil. Did Caritas give out money from heaven or money from hell? Some people unsure of the moral ground explored it in these cosmic terms. In research among a group of Transylvanian shepherds, Michael Stewart found a lively sense of the devil's intervention in Caritas. He reports that a family who had used their Caritas money to buy furniture later had it carted away, for the rattling of the devil in it had caused them too many sleepless nights.[19] Newspapers told comparable stories:

> The Antichrist is acting through Caritas. Lately, people returning from Cluj tell of extraordinary things. It is said that a woman by the name of Maria Badiu from Maramures, who had deposited a certain sum of money in Caritas, had a dream in which an angel told her 'Do not touch this money, for it comes from the Antichrist! Go and tell them that you renounce it.' . . .
>
> Another happening concerns Maria Pantea from Panticeu. She seems to have bought with Caritas money a new house, new furniture, and chandeliers for each room. The first night all the chandeliers in all the rooms fell, shattered into a thousand pieces, the furniture moved from its places, and the foundations of the house cracked.[20]

Among my own more urbanized village informants such views were rare, but even there a retired bus driver gave me this account of why his family had a new tractor but no plough. They had taken money out of Caritas to buy the plough, he said, but before they could do so their son-in-law wrecked the car in an accident and they had to spend all the money repairing it. 'The money was no good', he said, 'it came too easily. We thought Caritas was OK, but look what happened.' More concisely, a woman warned me, 'Caritas is the work of the devil: money can't give birth!'[21]

Reminiscent of Taussig's (1977) Colombian peasants and other groups being drawn into a capitalist economy, these stories reveal yet other ways in which Romanians were struggling to moralize money and Caritas and to understand money's capacity to multiply without effort. They were deeply suspicious of this capacity but at the same time desirous of it. In looking for divine or diabolical intervention, they were giving the economy agents, yet these were nonetheless more abstract than the party cadres who had controlled it before. And in embedding their revalorization of money in a divine context, they were helping to construct a new post-communist moral cosmology.

Conclusion

Communist parties sought to install in the societies they ruled a specific moral order. Their fall entails a disorganization of that order and efforts to define new ones. In Romania, some of the work of creating a new morality – especially a new *economic* morality – was being done through Caritas, just as people elsewhere have used millenarian movements to construct new moralities as their worlds fall apart.[22] As with those movements, the present confrontation between capitalist and non-capitalist systems is being played out as a cosmic struggle between Good and Evil, God and the Devil; its warriors include journalists, politicians and ordinary folk. The often apocalyptic imagery they use testifies to the urgent matters being addressed. What is money? Where does it come from? How should we use it? Is it acceptable to have money we haven't earned? What is the place of money in a moral universe? Answers to these questions are of the essence for legitimating a post-Ceausescu economy and state.

Notes

1   See, for example, Anderson 1994, Hann 1993, Holy 1992, Humphrey 1991.

2   There were reportedly over 100 such games in Romania (I believe it was probably closer to 200) after 1989. In August 1994 a huge pyramid, the MMM scheme, collapsed in Russia; the government was considering action against others as well (for details, see the *Financial Times* for July–September 1994). In Bulgaria and Slovakia, schemes sprang up right after 1989 but were banned by the respective governments. (The Romanian 'Caritas' has of course no connection with the long established and entirely respectable Catholic aid organization of the same name.)

3   Caritas was licensed in April 1992 in the city of Brasov but moved to Cluj two months later. The warm welcome accorded by the nationalist party, in contrast to the scepticism of Brasoveni with their democratic-opposition mayor, may have disposed Stoica to move to Cluj.

4   For more detail, see Verdery 1995.

5   See, among western papers, for example, *The Times* (London), 19 November 1993, p. 11; *The Economist* 328, 18–24 September 1993, p. 87; *Washington Post*, 17 October 1993, p. A25; *New York Times*, 13 November 1993, pp. 1, 47. I have the estimate of the Romanian National Bank president from member of parliament Stelian Tanase.

6   See Verdery 1995.

7   See Verdery 1991: 422–3.

8   Czech Finance Minister Vaclav Klaus put it in almost exactly these terms in 1990: 'The aim is to let the invisible hand of the market act and to replace the hand of the central planner' (cited in Holy 1992: 236).

9   Only future research can assess how durable the changes in people's conceptions might prove to be. Stoica was arrested in August 1994 for fraudulent bankruptcy and later provisionally released; that he will in fact be convicted is, in my view, doubtful (see Verdery 1995). [In fact, he was convicted but served only a small part of a long sentence. *Editor.*]

10   That money and market exchange require 'moralizing' far beyond the East European context is an anthropological truism. See, e.g., Parry and Bloch 1989 and Dilley 1992.

11   Zamfirescu and Cerna 1993: 17. Emphasis in original.

12   *Ibid.*, p. 23.

13   *Ibid.*, p. 17.

14   *Ibid.*, p. 17.

15   Cited on the back of the brochure by Zamfirescu and Cerna 1993.

16   Smeoreanu *et al.* 1993: 31, 36, 103.

17   See *ibid.*, pp. 31, 89, 93, 103; and Magyari-Vincze and Feischmidt 1994: 36.

18   These quotations are all from Magyari-Vincze and Feischmidt, *op. cit.*

19   Michael Stewart, pers. comm.

20   Smeoreanu *et al.* 1993: 14–15.

21   More common, however, was the expression, 'leave your money in so it will hatch chicks'.

22   See, e.g., Burridge 1960, Worsley 1968.

References

Anderson, David G. 1994. The Novosibirsk stock-market boom of 1993. *Anthropology Today* 10 (August 1994): 10–14.

Burridge, K.O.L. 1960. *Mambu: A Melanesian Millennium*. London: Methuen.

Dilley, Roy, ed. 1992. *Contesting Markets: Analyses of Ideology, Discourse and Practice*. Edinburgh: Edinburgh U. P.

Hann, Christopher 1993. From production to property: Decollectivization and the family–land relationship in contemporary Hungary. *Man* 28: 299–320.

Holy, Ladislav 1992. 'Culture, market ideology and economic reform in Czechoslovakia.' In Dilley, ed., pp. 231–43.

Humphrey, Caroline 1991. 'Icebergs', barter, and the Mafia in provincial Russia. *Anthropology Today* 7 (April 1991): 8–13.

Magyari-Vincze, Enikö, and Margit Feischmidt 1994. The Caritas and the Romanian Transition. MS.

Parry, Jonathan, and Maurice Bloch, eds. 1989. *Money and the Morality of Exchange*. Cambridge: C.U.P.

Smeoreanu, Gheorghe, *et al.* 1993. *Caritas: radiografia unui miracol*. Rîmnicul Vîlcea: Ed. Antim Ivireanul.

Taussig, Michael 1977. The genesis of capitalism amongst a South American peasantry: Devil's labour and the baptism of money. *Comparative Studies in Society and History* 19: 130–55.

Verdery, Katherine 1991. Theorizing socialism: A prologue to the 'transition'. *American Ethnologist* 18: 419–39.

——— 1995. Faith, hope, and *Caritas* in the land of the pyramids, Romania 1991–1994. *Comparative Studies in Society and History*, 37: 625–9.

Worsley, Peter 1968. *The Trumpet Shall Sound: A Study of 'Cargo' Cults in Melanesia*. New York: Schocken (second edn).

Zamfirescu, Dan and Dumitru Cerna 1993. *Fenomenul Caritas sau mântuirea românilor prin ei însisi*. Bucharest: Ed. Roza Vânturilor.

A Snack With Wittfogel

■ *Anthropology Today*, 4.4, August 1988, pp. 18–19

Karl Wittfogel (1897–1988) was a well-known German sinologist and political theorist, remembered chiefly because of his concept of 'oriental despotism', an adaptation of Marx's concept of the Asiatic mode of production. In subsequent correspondence, Ernest Gellner wrote that Wittfogel's work 'continues to exercise strong attraction and repulsion' (4.5, October 1988, p. 22), and T.O. Beidelman that Wittfogel's career should be remembered 'as an illustration of how the far left can easily become sympathetic to the far right' (4.6, December 1988, p. 24).

I MET KARL WITTFOGEL, whose death is recorded in this issue, in the late 1970s in a hamburger bar in Houston. Familiar with the gist of his Marxist revisionism, I had however formed the erroneous impression that he had died about the time of Rosa Luxemburg. I told him it felt like meeting Vico, and he was not offended.

He said he had once been in an American hospital and had been asked to state his religion on the admission form. He had written 'Judaeo-Christian'. After the operation, as he came to, he heard a nurse confide to her colleague, 'He must be one of those Jews who make out to be Christian'.

At the time I thought the anecdote very funny, no doubt because it raised the conversation for a moment to Wittfogel's level of grand historical movements and made one feel reassuringly superior to the nurse who was portrayed as ignorant and probably prejudiced. Later I reflected that his anecdote had mordant overtones, since he had come to America as a refugee from the Nazis, though on account of his communist affiliations, not for reasons of ethnic origin; and he must have known perfectly well the difference between anti-Semitic prejudice in the USA and mass murder of Jews in Europe.

Only after Wittfogel's death did I learn that, having been an active Communist Party member in his youth in Germany, he testified in 1951, to the U.S. Senate's

McCarran sub-committee on internal security, that Owen Lattimore had followed a line favourable to the Communists. His anecdote now seems laden not only with the history that Wittfogel lived through, but also with the uneasiness in his own position as a German Marxist who as a naturalized American citizen was ready to lend his name to the McCarthyite purging of Un-American Activities.

Jonathan Benthall

PART FIVE

Anthropology in the Mass Media

■   JONATHAN BENTHALL

AS ANTHROPOLOGY HAS BECOME more sophisticated in dealing with issues of representation arising from its subject-matter, so it has devoted some thought to its own image in the mass media.

There is a serious problem with what marketing experts would call brand identity. This is nicely explored by **Mark Allen Peterson**, an anthropologist with extensive experience of professional journalism in the USA. The image of anthropology in the American tabloids – a category of newspaper quite distinct from the British tabloids – turns out to be a ghastly distorting mirror. The price which anthropology pays for its marginality – hailed in my Introduction above as an asset – is that it is associated with the bizarre and the freakish. The few anthropologists in the USA who have op-ed articles published in serious newspapers are more likely to be labelled as 'experts' in order to assert their credentials.

Cris Shore takes up the problem from a British perspective. All anthropologists are familiar with the difficulty at cocktail parties of explaining what they do. Shore rightly notes that the split between biological/physical and social/cultural anthropology – mentioned above in the Introduction – is one of the sources of confusion. I would go further and say that this is perhaps the single most serious problem which anthropology as a whole faces as a discipline and profession. I cannot claim that *Anthropology Today* has done much to resolve the issue (but see Pot-pourri eight).

Shore, like Peterson, notes the danger to anthropology of being the preserve of 'eccentric boffins', and has some practical proposals for sharpening up the discipline's image. Since this article was published in 1996, the British anthropological associations, like the American ones, have devoted some collective attention to the problem.

Pat Caplan's appreciation of the documentary television programme *We are All Neighbours*, from the *Disappearing World* series, must represent here the contribution made by ethnographic film to modernizing the image of anthropology and making a large public aware of its potential. As Caplan writes, this film by Debbie Christie and Tone Bringa does record a world disappearing before our eyes under 'ethnic cleansing'; but the world is that of a mixed Catholic-Muslim village in the Bosnian war zone in 1993. The series title was originally intended by Granada Television to allude to the supposedly vanishing tribes of South America and similar settler societies.

The film poignantly records the breakdown of community relations under the pressure of civil war. What distinguishes it from the most accomplished piece of war journalism is that the anthropologist, Tone Bringa, knew the villagers well and had built up a relationship of trust. Like David Turton and Leslie Woodhead's series of films about the Mursi of Ethiopia, also in the *Disappearing World* series, *We are All Neighbours* will be carefully studied one day when, and if, serious ethnographic film comes back into fashion among television programme controllers.

As a regretful coda, **Marcus Banks** comments on the sad decline of British television. However, he also notes the flaws in the early *Disappearing World* programmes of the 1970s and early 1980s: some of them were superficial and suffered from a 'prurient exoticism'. To the extent that anthropologists collaborated with these films (which were always the subject of sharp debate) they actually helped to consolidate the 'whacky' image which is now seen as such a problem.

Chapter 18

Mark Allen Peterson

■ ALIENS, APE MEN AND WHACKY SAVAGES:
THE ANTHROPOLOGIST IN THE TABLOIDS,
Anthropology Today, 7.5, October 1991, pp. 4–7

T HE ANTHROPOLOGICAL LITERATURE is full of stories about how
the 'natives' understand what an anthropologist is and what he or she requires
of them. Relatively scarce are accounts of how the anthropologist is conceived in
the public discourse of the Western cultures that produced anthropology. As anthropologists turn once more to the study of Western cultures, we must begin to explore
the disjunctions between what we believe we are doing and what the rest of the
natives think we're up to.

Literature about how informants view anthropologists falls roughly into two
categories. The first consists of accounts by anthropologists of how informants clas-
sify outsiders in general and ethnographers in particular (see, for example, Stoller
1987). The second category consists of accounts of informant reactions to what the
ethnographer has written about them (a superb example being Feld, 1982). What
I would like to present here are some preliminary observations on discourse about
anthropologists in American public culture, observations that fall into the first category rather than the second.

A complete cultural analysis of representations of anthropologists in public
culture (films, advertisements, fiction, newspapers, and so forth) would make fascinating reading, at least for anthropologists. I have chosen here the easier preliminary
task of examining one genre of public discourse in which anthropologists play a
significant role: the American tabloid press.[1]

Tales of the margins

Among printers, the word 'tabloid' refers to the size of a newspaper: about eleven
by fifteen inches. The size is common among school newspapers and the alternative
press, but the term itself has become synonymous with 'yellow' journalism, sensa-
tionalistic reporting of events ranging from the dramatic to the absurd.

Media analysis has generally overlooked the tabloids in favour of the 'prestige press'.[2] This may be an error. The circulation of the *National Enquirer* is the highest of any newspaper in the United States. Although we cannot assume influence and significance on the basis of readership alone, we should not ignore it completely. There is something culturally significant about newspapers that are bought in millions, read aloud over morning radio shows, commented on by stand-up comics in clubs and on television, and whose headlines are read and laughed over in checkout lines by millions of shoppers who would never dream of purchasing one (or at least admitting to it).

The United States has six major tabloids with circulations in the millions, at least a few of which seem to be available at every grocery store, supermarket and news-stand: *The National Enquirer, Weekly World News*, the *Sun*, the *Star*, the *National Examiner* and the *Globe*. The best known tabloid is certainly *The National Enquirer*. At one time the *Enquirer* ran stories about UFOs and Bigfoot sightings, but in the late 1970s, it changed its approach. Today it focuses on celebrity lifestyles and scandals. A typical headline was 'X [a fundamentalist preacher] rips off own daughter for $50,000 – now she's living in poverty and can't afford milk for her baby'. The wild stories *Enquirer* used to run can be found in a sister paper, *Weekly World News*. The *News* offers us such fare as 'UFO Expert Says Aliens to Land at Monday Night Football Game on October 2'. The *Star* fills the remaining niche as the mirror image of the *Enquirer*. Where the *Enquirer* focuses on scandals and 'bad' news, the *Star* focuses on positive, 'upbeat' articles about celebrities, as well as self-help and diet advice. This triadic structure is repeated in the three tabloids owned by Globe International (*Examiner, Sun, Globe*).

The common denominator among these stories is that they are all tales of the marginal. Tabloids tell stories about people set apart by their wealth, fame or strange behaviour and about normal people beset by abnormal circumstances. Tabloids resemble professional wrestling in that, because their primary function is to entertain, and to act out social categories, the truth or falsehood of their assertions is a secondary matter (Barthes, 1972: 15–25; Lincoln, 1989: 148–59).

A parody of the press

The language of the tabloids is parodic, an exaggeration of the structure and style of the mainstream press. The prose is a hyperbolic version of standard news prose and the photos, nearly always retouched, are often patchwork quilts of spliced images brought together to create a new graphic text. Were there the faintest hint of self-consciousness, the effect would be ironic, but the articles are strictly deadpan.[3]

This parody plays on a number of the rhetorical strategies used by mainstream newspapers. The most revealing for this argument is the centrist stance adopted by the press. Because one of the roles of the American press is to provide 'objective' coverage of events from which a community of voters may form their own political opinions, most mainstream newspapers present themselves as centrist, both in political stance and in the subject matter they cover. This is expressed not only as a rhetorical strategy but as a moral obligation of the press as 'the Fourth Estate'.

The mainstream press attempts to cover issues which journalists and editors perceive as having potential affect or interest for most of their readers, relegating other news to special sections or failing to cover it altogether. Their stock-in-trade is the collective representations of American culture, the taken-for-granted assumptions of everyday life.[4]

Defining news is thus a figure–ground problem. The problem is to frame certain events as standing out from the ordinary run-of-the-mill of human experience. Walter Lippmann long ago defined 'news', as 'that which protrudes from the ordinary' (Lippmann 1922). The ordinary, in such a case, is exactly these collective representations. That is why things that don't happen can be news – because these are stories that speak to expectations. So the mainstream press selects its material in a large part by framing stories which in some way stand out as figures against the ground of common culture as defined by the press. Political news thus makes up a predominant part of mainstream news stories, while celebrity news and unusual event stories are placed in special sections marked 'Style' or 'Reviews' etc.

Tabloids, on the other hand, specialize in the marginal. Celebrity and unusual event news comprises most of their material. If regular news is a frame, then tabloid news is a frame of a frame: the 'figure' of the mainstream news becomes the 'ground' for the tabloid press. For example, when a mainstream newspaper publishes a story like, 'Bush Compares Saddam Hussein to Hitler', a tabloid may run as a story, 'Saddam Hussein is Reincarnation of Hitler Claims Leading Psychic'. In reframing thus, tabloids operate like mainstream newspapers to define the centre in a heterogeneous, complex society. But whereas the mainstream press does this by focusing on (what it perceives to be) the centre, the tabloids define the centre by focusing on what it is not.

Tabloids, then, parody the mainstream press by taking what the mainstream press considers out-of-the-ordinary and treating it as the everyday. The function of this is not to reflect ironically upon the mainstream press, like a newspaper or magazine parody in *National Lampoon* or *Spy*. Although many readers can and do choose to read them this way, it is not clear to what extent readers recognize the tabloids as parodic. Rather, the focus on the margins allows the tabloids to fulfil their functions of entertaining readers, drawing them to the advertisements whose sale supports the newspapers. At the same time, these newspapers provide readers with a sense of orientation. In the increasingly fragmented and heteroglot culture(s) of the West, a 'centre', a shared domain, is increasingly difficult to find. Tabloids aid their readers in finding a centre not by defining one (as the mainstream press does) but by defining what the centre is not: it is not the domain of the strange, the absurd and the bizarre that fills the pages of *Weekly World News* and the *Sun*; it is not the world of the super-rich, publicly displayed protagonists of the *National Enquirer* and its ilk.

Anthropologists in the tabloids

This being the case, it is instructive to compare the place of cultural anthropologists in the tabloids and the mainstream press. During a random one-month period, 1–31 October 1989, eleven stories appeared in the six tabloids described above in which cultural anthropologists were the central figures, either as subjects or as sources.[5] Of these stories, six appeared in either the *Sun* or *Weekly World News*, the papers specializing in the bizarre and absurd rather than in the celebrated.

During the same 31-day period, no stories featuring cultural anthropologists appeared in five newspapers of the mainstream 'prestige' press: *New York Times*, *Los Angeles Times*, *Washington Post*, *Wall Street Journal* or *Christian Science Monitor*. A review of the indexes of these periodicals showed that during the course of the year 1 January to 31 December 1989, only eleven stories about cultural anthropologists appeared in all five of these daily newspapers combined. This disparity is even more marked when one realizes that the combined wordage of the prestige press is thousands of times the weekly wordage of the tabloids. Why this discrepancy? Why is the popularity of anthropologists so much greater in the tabloids? The answer, I think, becomes clear when we examine the nature of the texts. Anthropologists are perceived as dealing with the bizarre, the unusual and the marginal; their subject-matter and the 'news' of the tabloids coincide in content if not in form and rhetoric.

Stories about anthropologists in the tabloids fall into four rough categories: (1) aliens and ape men stories, (2) whacky savage stories, (3) whacky anthropologist stories and (4) silly studies stories.

Aliens and ape men

Cannibals Ate Six Space Aliens – Savage Tribe Tried to Keep Feast a Secret Since 1936. South American cannibals murdered and ate six space aliens who came to earth on a mission of peace in 1936. That's the word from Swiss anthropologist Fritz Greder, who actually spoke to an elderly savage who dined on one of the extraterrestrials 53 years ago this spring.

'It's a fantastic story but one that I am convinced is true', Dr. Greder told reporters in Switzerland. 'The cannibal chief I spoke with is almost 100 years old but his mind and memory are sharp.'

. . . 'He said that the extraterrestrials tasted like frogs' legs or fish. But humans, he told me, taste like pork.' Dr. Greder claims to have met the cannibal chief while studying tribal life in the jungles of Brazil last year . . .

The expert plans to publish a full scientific report on the close encounter later this year.

'I'm sure that the cannibal chief's story is accurate', he said. 'And it really is a shame. These savages felt guilty about what they had done – that's why they kept it a secret all these years.'

This story contains the standard features of such tales. The anthropologist studies the totally other, 'savages' and 'cannibals' who live to be abnormally old. The anthropologist goes among them, wins their friendship, discovers their secrets, then reveals them to the 'normal' world. Other stories in this genre include:

Blue Devil Man Roams Voodoo Jungle. Frightened inhabitants of voodoo island Haiti seldom venture from their homes at night – in fear of ghoulish blue devil men that still roam the dark hills.

Figure 18.1   'Cannibals ate 6 space aliens!'

Known as the 'ju-ju', the mysterious half-man, half-devil creature was long thought to exist only in the minds of superstitious natives. But now modern science is backing up legend, after top anthropologist Dr. Francois Dubois found the body of a ju-ju in a cave . . .

Hitler Is Alive! 100-Year Old Dictator Found in Mountains of Chile. A respected anthropologist has found dramatic evidence to prove Adolf Hitler fled Germany in 1945 and has been living in Chile ever since.

'Hitler is alive', Dr. Reiff, the Swiss anthropologist told newsmen in Santiago, Chile. 'He is in the mountains with Indians who revere him as a living god.' . . .

The features of stories in this category should be clear from these examples. Anthropologists go into the field and discover extraordinary and earth-shattering things. The anthropologists are scientists, the experts of the everyday world, whose voice authorizes as authentic the extraordinary objects and events described. The authors do not report on the academic credentials of the anthropologists but vouch for them through the use of adjectives like 'famed', 'noted' and 'respected'. The fields these famed, noted and respected anthropologists enter are the non-Western worlds imagined by the collective representations of the West. The secrets they bring back concern not problems of modernization, kinship descriptions, or health and nutrition studies, but things of concern for the West: former world leaders living as gods among 'natives', extraterrestrial legacies and so forth.

Whacky savages

The second category is disturbingly close to what anthropologists actually do: describe the Other to those here at Home. Here the focus is not on the fantastic, merely the bizarre – that is, the bizarre practices of the inferior other. For example:

> *Girls Marries Four Brothers at the Same Time.* Lots of women complain that it's hard to find a nice guy from a good family, but some lucky women get to marry all the brothers in the family when they meet and fall in love. The Nyinba people and other groups in Nepal, Sri Lanka, and India think its natural for a woman to have several husbands, says UCLA social anthropologist Nancy Levine . . . The polyandrous life has several advantages for them, says Levine. 'They have a better ratio of adults to children and they're much better off economically than their neighbors.'

> *Bizarre Tribesmen Use Dreams to Find Wives . . . And Make All Other Decisions in Their Lives!* Bizarre tribesmen are so completely controlled by their dreams that they even use their nightime visions to find wives.
> Incredibly, the Teminar of Malaysia won't make a move when awake unless it has already been approved by a dream, says Bulgarian anthropologist Yvegan Blatu. Anthropologist Rene Verdu, of the University of Antwerp, Belgium, also studied the Teminar and noted that they have managed to survive in their dangerous jungle environment thousands of years by following their dreams.
> 'It may seem silly to us – but it works for them', said Verdu.

> *Meet the Bizarre Topsy-Turvy Tribe of Brazil – Baffled Scientists Discover Remote Village Where Natives Always Walk on Their Hands.* An anthropologist has discovered a bizarre tribe of topsy-turvy Amazon savages who spend every minute of their lives standing on their hands.
> Portuguese anthropologist Antonio Picarra said he was the first contact the savages ever had with the civilized world.

In this genre, the focus has moved from the totally outré to the merely abnormal. In these tales, flabbergasted, stunned and amazed scientists discover 'whacky savages' (*Weekly World News*) and 'bizarre tribesmen' (*Star*) and mediate between them and the 'civilized' world of tabloid readers. In these stories, anthropologists no longer need to be vouched for by the writer with such adjectives as 'famed' or 'respected'. Instead they are identified by place of origin or even academic affiliation.

Whacky anthropologists

The third category turns to the behaviour of anthropologists themselves as marginal figures, worthy of attention for their own abnormal behaviour. Whacky anthropologist stories include:

> *Blood, Sweat & Beers — Real-Life Indiana Jones Braves Snakes, Crocs and Headhunters in Search of Perfect Suds.* Alan Eames is the Indiana Jones of beer. His 20-year search for exotic brews has driven him to the far corners of the earth — and into some hair-raising experiences that would chill the blood of a swashbuckling movie hero . . .
>
> To ferret out a rare beer brewed by South American Indians, Eames had to confront a tribe of headhunters living in the Amazon jungle . . .
>
> . . . The 42-year old anthropologist from Chesterfield, NH has tasted and graded more than 2,000 varieties of beer.

> *Mom Survives Weeks of Hell in Remote, Snake-Infested Jungle.* An adventurous Mom found herself trapped in remote snake-infested jungles for two terrifying weeks and ate nothing at all for five days — but she chopped down trees with her machete and crossed more than 30 rivers on home-made rafts to find her way back to civilization.
>
> Anthropology student Lorri Evans, 41, had planned to spend 8 days on a jungle expedition when . . .

Ah, the hazards of fieldwork; what we'll go through to bring back those shrunken alien heads! Stories of this type appear primarily in the 'upbeat' celebrity papers, the *Star* and the *Globe*. They emphasize the anthropologist's position as dealer in the (potentially dangerous) world outside the boundaries of Home. Anthropologists are clearly positioned as part of the 'normal' world – they have families and come from small towns – but their lives are a continuous series of adventures as they leave home to explore the distant and exotic.

Silly studies

The final category consists of critiques of anthropologists. These are relatively rare, but do appear from time to time in the 'critical' celebrity press (the *Enquirer* or the *Examiner*). A typical example is:

> *Why Do Pygmies Hunt With Nets? You're Paying 70G To Find Out.* America's harried and hounded taxpayers have been speared again – this time to the tune of $69,863 to finance a ridiculous study of hunting techniques used by African Pygmies!
>
> The money is being spent by the National Science Foundation to check out the different food gathering methods of tiny Bambuti tribesmen in Zaire's Ituri Forest . . . NSF contends that the study 'will

increase our knowledge of the importance of hunting, so that models which reconstruct early human band subsistence can be based on improved understanding'.

But Rep. Caroll Hubbard (D-Ky.) snapped: 'I find it appalling that the federal government would provide almost $70,000 to this study when there are people in our nation starving each and every day.'

'Obviously, this money could have been better spent.'

Certain common representations of anthropologists can be extracted from these four genres of news:

1. Anthropologists are liminal figures. They mediate between the bizarre and the normal, the savage and the civilized.

2. The bizarre and savage subjects studied by anthropologists are not intrinsically important. They are interesting, as a freak show is interesting, but we have little to learn from them. Savages have bizarre and amusing lifestyles. They destroy or conceal the important things that do come their way (alien visitors, disappearing dictators) and the only valuable service provided by anthropologists is to salvage these.

3. Anthropologists are featured in the tabloids with greater frequency than the mainstream press because their activities fit in well with the tabloid focus on the marginal, while such activities are inconsistent with the centrist approach of the mainstream press.

4. Because anthropologists deal with the marginal, their work is not really very important, and spending federal money on them is an insult to the taxpayers.

Conclusions

The tabloids are parodies of the mainstream press; anthropologists are powerful sources of authority for their stories. Does this make anthropologists parodies of 'mainstream' social scientists? If tabloids function, as I have argued, to suggest the centre by illustrating the margins, the boundaries and beyond, does it not follow that, as represented in this public discourse, anthropologists function to reveal our own society by presenting to it images of the alien Other?

This argument is an inversion of recent debates about the role of anthropological knowledge in developing social and cultural criticism, and a parody of older debates on how anthropologists could understand similarity and difference in human experience around the world. In the tabloids, the anthropologist is still the adventurous explorer of the unknown bringing the Other back to the real world of the West. And what Others we find in the tabloids! Ape-men, aliens and whacky savages: these are the objects of study we bring home to the readers of the tabloids.

The examples I've recounted here are ridiculous, it's true. But they are read by millions of Americans every week. The social categories that can be identified in these tales of the bizarre, I am arguing, represent general assumptions about anthropology in Western mass culture. We are as ill-represented in the mainstream press as we are overrepresented in the tabloids, and for the same reasons. The mainstream press is centrist and chooses scientists who are viewed as experts on 'central' issues of crime, war and peace, public policy. Anthropologists are the scientists of the marginal, the strange and unimportant.

William O. Beeman, anthropological linguist and author of *Language, Status and Power in Iran* has published several hundred newspaper articles. In 1981 he was nominated for a Pulitzer Prize, America's highest honour for a journalist. Yet throughout the recent Gulf War, many newspapers running his articles preferred to identify him as 'an expert on the Middle East' rather than as a cultural anthropologist. The vague title 'expert', it appears, carries far more weight with the prestige press than the title 'anthropologist' when talking about something as 'central' as American foreign policy in the Middle East.

A sobering thought to those who follow Richard Handler's (1988) call for commitment to the analysis and critique of the American 'centre': if you aren't studying the margins, you may not really be an anthropologist at all – just an 'expert'.

Notes

1   For another preliminary approach, starting from English-language fiction, see Firth (1984).

2   'Prestige Press' is a term which came into general use among communication scholars in the 1960s to refer to those fifteen or twenty newspapers which consistently appear in 'Best Newspaper' polls. Two studies which focus on the tabloids, from a content analysis and reader segmentation position respectively, are Hinkle and Elliot (1989) and Lehnert and Perpich (1982).

3   This is not to say that either the authors or the readers are unaware of the absurdity they deal in. One of my informants, a former production manager for one of the tabloids, claimed that most of the writers came from good journalism schools, often British, enticed by the high salaries, pleasant environments and low-stress working conditions. Most treated their work at the tabloids with considerable humour, he said.

Readers, even the most dedicated, seem to derive a great deal of their enjoyment from the absurdity of the papers. Readers I have spoken with often laugh derisively at one article, savouring its ridiculous premise, while pointing out that the next article might possibly be true.

4   The fact that these collective representations may not really be reflective of what all, or even many, of the public experience, or that they may reflect class, gender and ethnic agendas has been much discussed and need not distract us here.

5   In focusing here upon cultural anthropologists, I excluded stories featuring archaeologists or physical anthropologists, which are commonly covered by both the tabloids and the mainstream press but which fall into a different set of narrative schemes. I also exclude coverage of museum exhibits.

References

Barthes, Roland. 1972. *Mythologies*. trans. Annette Lavers. New York: Noonday P.
Feld, Stephen. 1982. *Sound and Sentiment*. Philadelphia: U. of Pennsylvania P.

Firth, Rosemary. 1984. Anthropology in fiction: an image of fieldwork. *RAINews* 64, October 1984.

Handler, Richard. 1988. The center in American culture: analysis and critique. *Anthropological Quarterly* 61(1): 1–2.

Hinkle, Gerald and William R. Elliott. 1989. Science coverage in three newspapers and three supermarket tabloids. *Journalism Quarterly* 66: 353–8.

Lehnert, Eileen and Mary J. Perpich. 1982. An attitude segmentation study of supermarket tabloid readers. *Journalism Quarterly* 59: 104–11.

Lincoln, Bruce. 1989. *Discourse and the Construction of Society*. Oxford: Oxford U. P.

Lippmann, Walter. 1922. *Public Opinion*. New York: Harcourt, Brace.

Stoller, Paul. 1987. Son of Rouch: Portrait of the ethnographer by the Songhay. *Anthropological Quarterly* 60(3): 114–23.

Chapter 19

Cris Shore

■ ANTHROPOLOGY'S IDENTITY CRISIS:
THE POLITICS OF PUBLIC IMAGE,
Anthropology Today, 12.2, April 1996, pp. 2–5

To see ourselves as others see us is a most salutary gift. Hardly less important is the capacity to see others as they see themselves. (Aldous Huxley, *The Doors of Perception*)

SOCIAL ANTHROPOLOGISTS ARE VERY SKILLED in representing and analysing the identity of others, but when it comes to defining and projecting their own identity as professionals and practitioners they are often deeply troubled and confused. To put it simply, anthropology as a discipline in Britain suffers from acute problems of public image and visibility. That, at least, is one of several findings contained in the Report on the Teaching and Learning of Social Anthropology in the UK, published in October 1995.[1] The Report highlights a number of interesting facets about the way anthropology is perceived by the general public, many of which are causes for alarm. Indeed, it reveals that the discipline's poor public image is leading most anthropology graduates to abandon the 'anthropologist' label altogether when working in the non-academic sector. At least twenty alternative labels were reported to be in use by those who nonetheless consider themselves to be anthropologists. These alternative identity-markers ranged from 'social analyst' and 'regional specialist' to 'development planner', 'community development worker', 'urban change researcher' and 'business strategy and organisation consultant'. Even 'sociologist' and 'public health nurse' were apparently preferable badges of professional identity to 'anthropologist'.

Why are most anthropology alumni rejecting their title and disguising their credentials once they leave the academy? This question raises a host of issues about anthropology's corporate image that I wish to explore, if only to initiate a deeper debate about how we present ourselves to the world. The report cites two clear reasons above all others for this evident lack of enthusiasm in embracing the 'anthropologist' mantle: first, the term 'anthropologist' is simply not recognized outside of the discipline and, second, most employers still have little or no idea about what anthropology actually means, either as a university subject or as a discipline. As the report observes phlegmatically, this has important implications for the employment opportunities available to graduate and postgraduate students. Indeed, a review of the job advertisements in a range of quality newspapers indicates that 'the discipline is predominantly associated with academic posts' and that with the exception of overseas voluntary agencies 'it is rare to find jobs outside academia which specifically mention a degree in anthropology as essential or desirable'.[2]

Much of the problem is that, in terms of its popular image, British anthropology is still very much a prisoner of its past, indelibly tainted (however unfairly) with the idea of colonialism and 'primitive' societies. The antiquated image of anthropology as a kind of 'managerial science' of tribal peoples, popularized in Malinowski's day, continues to shape perceptions of the discipline. My own experience certainly corroborates this. When responding to the inevitable question 'What job do you do?' (inevitable in Britain, at least, where pigeon-holing others by occupational status and class position is still *de rigueur* in encounters between strangers), the answer 'I'm a social anthropologist' typically provokes responses of the kind 'Is that something to do with bones?' or, 'Do you study African tribes?', or 'Does that involve monkeys?' Only rarely are these said with irony. Alternatively, the response is embarrassed silence or a puzzled frown followed by 'What's "anthropology?"'. The conversation usually falters terminally at this point as both parties struggle not to appear either stupid, patronizing or from another planet.

Much of the confusion arguably stems from the split between biological and social anthropology. However, it is not the *split* so much as the failure to acknowledge this distinction that causes confusion. In Britain, as in America, both biological and social (or cultural) anthropologists habitually use the generic term 'anthropology' when referring to their own particular sub-disciplines. Equally confusing is the tendency of practitioners from other disciplines to appropriate the term 'anthropological' when describing their own approach or perspective – however tenuously anthropological these may be.[3] Unlike commercial products and brand names, anthropology is not covered by any copyright law or Trade Descriptions Act.

The problems of explaining what exactly the anthropologist is or does was highlighted at a recent conference on the Teaching and Learning of Social Anthropology.[4] During one of the plenary sessions on the character of anthropological teaching attended by over 80 people – most of them anthropologists from university departments throughout the country – a delegate from the Department for Education and Employment asked the audience provocatively 'What does an anthropological education actually achieve?' (or, as he put it, 'What is your *product?*'). This produced a stunned silence followed by some ritualistic claims about the uniqueness and value of anthropological insights compared with other disciplines, and finally an attack on the notion of an anthropological 'training' deemed to be implicit in the question. The questioner had apparently hit a raw nerve. None of the responses felt comfortable or gave good answers to the question. The only comfort for the audience was the thought that their timely conference was at least raising questions of this kind.

That social anthropology needs to rethink its public image is also a point highlighted by Jonathan Benthall in one of the Report's appendices.[5] Among the problems he cites is the familiar complaint about inscrutable academic prose: the fact that most academics write for one another rather than for the public beyond the academy. Yet recent changes in higher education policy only seem to have exacerbated this tendency. The current system of academic weighting undermines attempts to bring anthropological writing to a wider audience by fetishizing competitive and hierarchical league tables for research and publications and the policy of giving priority to articles in refereed journals and learned tomes over and above all other forms of mass communication. Within the current system of accounting, an arcane monograph read by fourteen people carries far more status and value than an article published in one of the serious newspapers and read by 140,000 non-academics – however important their role as the nation's intellectuals and opinion multipliers might be.

Another problem is that there is a chronic lack of effective communicators who speak for the discipline in public debates, as Frazer, Malinowski, Mead and Leach in their heyday. The problem here is not so much the calibre of today's generation of anthropologists as the status of their discipline.[6] As Benthall says, anthropologists may be called upon 'to pronounce on such enticing topics as cannibalism or infibulation' but they are seldom consulted 'as general-purpose media pundits to the same extent as, say, economists or political scientists'.[7] Or, as another colleague complained: 'I often get asked to speak on radio programmes, but only on subjects that are considered bizarre, exotic or frivolous'. Once again, the culprit is anthropology's outdated public image – the 'bones, monkeys and tribes' identity that the discipline seems unable to shrug off despite the efforts of organizations like the Royal Anthropological Institute, Anthropology in Action and the American Anthropological Association to 'popularize' anthropological knowledge and engage with the media.

But does this antiquated public image really matter? Benthall suggests that, in marketing terms, social anthropology in Britain and the USA has maintained quite a distinct profile which has 'generally worked to our advantage'.[8] Unlike, say, sociology or psychology, which experienced a massive expansion throughout the 1960s and 1970s, entering into most universities and developing as pre-university A-level subjects, the growth of anthropology was tightly controlled and attempts to introduce it as an integral subject into the school curriculum were opposed most forcefully from within the discipline itself. However, it is often argued (by tenured anthropologists if by no one else) that the reputation and identity of sociology and psychology have become more of a liability than an asset to practitioners of these disciplines. Whether this is accurate or simply academic chauvinism is an interesting question, but not one I propose to answer, although one might ask who is this 'we' for whom anthropology's profile is advantageous?

Anthropology's image and identity *are* important if only because they have direct consequences for research funding and for the employment opportunities of anthropology graduates. They are also important for those who wish to make anthropology's voice heard in public arenas – or simply to see anthropologists invited to speak in such arenas – and on debates that go beyond such exotica as cannibalism and infibulation. In terms of its public credibility, anthropology has little to be smug about – unless there is merit in being stereotyped as eccentric boffins who specialize in 'bongo-bongoism'.

Stereotyping anthropologists: who is responsible?

Who is responsible for these negative stereotypes and what can be done to challenge or change them? These questions also go to the heart of the problem of rethinking how we teach and learn about anthropology outlined in the Report. Two candidates immediately present themselves for investigation: anthropologists *themselves* and the popular media. Turning to the latter first, Hollywood films and television have much to answer for. Among the most popular media images of the anthropologist in America, according to Spitulnik,[9] are 'the archaeologist Indiana Jones from the *Raiders of the Lost Ark* trilogy and the transgalactic ethnographers of the *Star Trek* television series and films'. Both representations echo the nineteenth-century caricature of the anthropologist as a gazing explorer-hero adventuring amidst the 'gazed upon'. By contrast, the anthropologist depicted in Roger Donaldson's recent film *Species* is anything but heroic. The storyline follows a familiar alien-on-the-loose genre. A top-secret laboratory succeeds in creating a hybrid from human and alien DNA. The experiment completed, the scientists find they have created a fast-growing predatory monster (slimy tentacles and sticky tendrils à la Ridley Scott) perfectly disguised in the body of a young woman, and driven by an insatiable desire to procreate. A team of 'experts' is assembled to track down and destroy the alien before it can reproduce. The team includes an 'empath', a biologist, a professional killer, the hard-nosed scientist who led the experiment and a Harvard anthropologist – the logic being that the latter's expert knowledge of alien cultures will help the team predict the behaviour of this particular (a-cultured) alien. Unfortunately, the anthropologist is an amiable buffoon whose knowledge amounts to a few derisory platitudes about sexual competition. Worse, he ends up being seduced by the alien and precipitating the very disaster the team was created to prevent. Needless to say, it is the professional killer not the anthropologist who rescues mankind from the abyss. The film's plot may be weak, but its derision of the academic anthropologist comes across clearly: useless knowledge, large ego, dangerously incompetent, but good as a figure of fun.

Similar stereotypes prevail in popular fiction. For example, Frank Parkin's novel *Krippendorf's Tribe*[10] tells the story of an anthropologist who, having spent his doctoral research grant on household expenses, decides to invent an imaginary Amazonian tribe which he claims to have discovered. Using his children and neighbours as models, his lurid descriptions and near-pornographic photographs rapidly elevate him to international fame and fortune. In David Lodge's novel, *Paradise News*,[11] the anthropologist is Dr Roger Sheldrake, an eccentric specialist in tourism from South-West London Polytechnic. Sheldrake wears a 'beige safari suit', has terrible dandruff, and has come to Hawaii to advance his theory that tourism has become the new world religion. We also learn that his supervisor had wanted him to study an obscure African tribe called the 'Oof' whose only interesting feature is that 'they have no future tense, apparently, and only wash at the summer and winter solstices'. Like Krippendorf, Sheldrake is a figure of fun. But he is also a fraud.

No doubt one can find other allusions to anthropologists in contemporary fiction. As Rosemary Firth concluded in her 1984 literature survey of anthropology in novels, most representations of anthropologists in action reinforce negative and derogatory stereotypes.[12] Of the twenty-one novels she analyses, ranging from work by Iris Murdoch and Anthony Burgess to Barbara Pym, Penelope Lively and Paul Theroux, most trivialize anthropologists, using them merely as lay figures 'on which to build a romance, a thriller or a satire, against a highly exotic background'. Indeed, the commonest topics associated with fieldwork in these books are 'sexual practices seen as bizarre, such as "incest", clitoridectomy, castration, and polygamy', closely followed by practices of 'infanticide, cannibalism, ritual killing and violence' and 'witchcraft, magic, myth and taboo'. There is something ironical about this, given how committed the discipline has been in countering cultural stereotypes and prejudices in other spheres of life. Perhaps one could write an interesting thesis entitled 'Anthropologists: Ethnography of a Stigmatised Group'. The other irony, as Firth herself notes, is that 'we, the professional observers of others, have now to accept ourselves the cool observation of another profession, the novelist, because of the increased use of literacy in our own society'.[13] In other words, our literary 'persona' has today become a social fact.

Admittedly, these are only fictional representations and, as Salman Rushdie would have it, the novel is by nature a 'privileged arena' for the imagination and for the voice of irreverence and satire.[14] However, the problem is that there are very few positive models to counter these popular misrepresentations. Indeed, anthropologists themselves often seem to reproduce some of the worst caricatures, in particular those for whom ethnography is itself a kind of creative fiction. For example, Geertz's caricature of himself in 'Notes on the Balinese Cockfight'[15] follows what has now become a hackneyed genre of ethnography: a humorous tale of entry in which the naïve (male) adventurer-hero and awkward simpleton, arriving as a stranger in a strange land, is unsure of his own identity, and – thanks to good fortune – wins the confidence and trust of the natives.[16] The same kind of trope recurs in Nigel Barley's *Innocent Anthropologist* and *Plague of Caterpillars*.[17] Even where the anthropologist becomes a kind of picaresque hero, like Krippendorf and Sheldrake, he (sic) is still depicted as a figure of fun; nice but a bit dim and cranky.

Anthropology and 'autobiography': the politics of self-representation

With these kinds of representation perhaps it is little wonder that anthropology alumni chose to shun or hide their anthropological background: it is hardly flattering to be identified as a crank. Of course we should be able to laugh at ourselves, but there is a price to pay for this (notably in terms of jobs and credibility), and it becomes problematic when others do most of the laughing.

It would be wrong, however, to attribute anthropology's poor public image to the media or novelists. The key agents in this drama are usually anthropologists themselves. The 'culprits' can be divided into two (ideal) types. On the one hand are those who insist on preserving a putative 'purity' in anthropology's scope and methodology: those for whom 'real' anthropology is an honorary title bestowed only upon the deserving few who have carried out fieldwork in 'remote', Third World (and preferably hostile) places like the tropical rainforests or the Arctic Circle,[18] and those in tenured university positions who pursue 'pure' anthropology (i.e. theoretical) as opposed to 'applied' anthropology – which has traditionally held a greatly inferior status in Britain.[19] These are the anthropologists who collude most in maintaining the traditional, elitist images of the discipline as one that specializes only in arcane knowledge and whose leading practitioners are rather disdainful of the idea of addressing the 'vulgar' concerns of the wider non-academic public.

On the other hand, equally insidious are those anthropologists who have un-critically taken to heart the discourses of French post-structuralist theory and post-colonial criticism and enthuse lyrically about the death of the author, modernity and the grand narrative. James Clifford's warning that extreme self-consciousness carries dangers of 'elitism, of solipsism, of putting the whole world in quotation marks' ought be heeded more seriously.[20] As Fleming notes[21] textualist critiques of ethnographic representation not only have a paralysing effect on the discipline ('What can anthropology hope to accomplish if it cannot represent its subject?'), they also leave anthropology 'vulnerable to accusations that the discipline has lost its relevance'. Ironically, those who try to distance themselves from anthropology's 'sterile scientism' and colonial encounter by continually attacking the discipline for its sins of realism, Orientalism and Eurocentrism often end up confirming and strengthening the very stereotypes they seek to challenge by giving them so much status. As Sahlins points out, anti-ethnocentrism inspired by post-colonial guilt sometimes turns into 'a symmetrical and inverse ethnocentrism'.[22] This was brought home vividly in the comment of a recently graduated student from London University: 'The main thing I got from my degree was a sense of guilt for being an anthropologist and a feeling that you couldn't comment positively on anything in the world as an anthropologist; all you can do is "deconstruct" things.'

To improve anthropology's public image I suggest four things should be done, many of which came up in discussions at the conference. First, anthropologists should speak to (and write for) a wider audience – including other disciplines. Second, it is time to consider ways of introducing more anthropology into the class-room and pre-university curriculum, perhaps as an A-level subject, or through the International Baccalaureate and Access courses; the demand for anthropology courses is certainly there. Third, anthropologists should stop hawking their consciences about colonialism – or, if they really do still feel guilty for the sins of their fathers, they should reflect more critically and honestly about themselves and the kind of anthropology they practise. At the same time, it would be no bad thing if instead of pandering to the tired old stereotypes of anthropology, they started to emphasize some of the discipline's achievements and applications (or remind them-selves why they became anthropologists). Finally, more efforts are needed to popularize anthropology. I do not mean by this 'vulgarize' or 'trivialize' anthro-pology, but rather, in the older political sense highlighted by Raymond Williams, to democratize the discipline by making its knowledge more accessible to a larger and lay audience.[23]

As to the question 'what is your product?', the answer contained in the Report is that anthropology has a highly marketable 'product' to offer, one that involves important kinds of knowledge as well as a host of transferable skills. Public rela-tions and marketing firms usually ask their clients to carry out an assessment of their strengths, weaknesses, assets and threats (the 'SWAT' analysis). Anthropologists, it seems, are rather more adept at listing their weaknesses than their strengths.[24] To pursue the marketing metaphor, these assets include an understanding of other cultures and value systems and how they work; critical awareness of the importance of social context in shaping thought and action; a recognition of one's own ethnocentricity and the limits and boundaries of one's own culture; insights into problems of intercultural communication (including racism, nationalism, xenophobia and ethnic conflict); an understanding of how societies are organized and what that means to people. In a word, a grasp of what it means to be human, to have culture and to live in different kinds of society.

The Grillo Report of 1984[25] drew interesting conclusions about the dangers of the academic direction in which anthropology was heading in the 1980s. The problem then was not only the massive increase in PhD students – who were growing at a rate that would have enabled the discipline to renew itself entirely every three years – but the fact that the doctoral degree was still conceived primarily as a trade-union membership into the (by now saturated) academy and not as a gateway to employment *outside* the university. That was a reflection of the way anthropology as a profession saw itself then. A decade later British anthropology is still grappling with much the same problems. The time for serious debate on the nature and purpose of anthropological teaching and learning is long overdue. My contention is that this cannot be adequately addressed without a radical re-appraisal of anthropology's identity and self-image as well. As Spitulnik suggests, greater attention to popular representations and appropriations of anthropology outside the discipline may also reveal much about our own culture and the politics of mass media more generally.[26] To follow Aldous Huxley's maxim cited earlier, to be professional observers of others we need to understand not only how others see themselves, but also how we appear to others. Or as an old Scottish prayer puts it:

Lord, Lord the wisdom gi'us,
To see ourselves as others see us.

Notes

1 Stella Mascarenhas-Keyes and Susan Wright *et al.*, *Report on teaching and learning social anthropology in the United Kingdom*. London: Anthropology in Action, 1995.
2 *Ibid.* p. 67.
3 For example, the latest book by neurologist Oliver Sacks carries the alluring title *An anthropologist on Mars: seven paradoxical tales*, London: Picador, 1995.
4 The conference, entitled 'How do we teach and how do we learn social anthropology?', was organized by the Social Anthropology Teaching and Learning Network at Middlesex University, 3–4 November 1995. For reports on the event see *Anthropology Today*, 11(6) (December), 1995.
5 Jonathan Benthall, 'Improving the public image of anthropology: the RAI's experience', in S. Mascarenhas-Keyes *et al. op. cit.*, pp. 139–43.
6 For an interesting view on this see Anthony Giddens, 'Epilogue: notes on the future of anthropology', in A. Ahmed and C. Shore (eds) *The future of anthropology: its relevance to the contemporary world*, London: Athlone Press, 1995, pp. 272–7.
7 J. Benthall, 'Improving the public image of anthropology', in S. Mascarenhas-Keyes *et al.* 1995, p. 141.

8   *Ibid.* p. 141.

9   Deborah Spitulnik, 'Anthropology and mass media', *Annual Review of Anthropology* 22, 1993, p. 301.

10   Frank Parkin, *Krippendorf's tribe*, London: Collins, 1981.

11   David Lodge, *Paradise News*, Harmondsworth: Penguin, 1991.

12   Rosemary Firth 'Anthropology in fiction: an image of fieldwork', *RAINews*, 64 (October), 1984, pp. 7–9.

13   *Ibid.*, p. 7.

14   Salman Rushdie, 'Is nothing sacred?', in *Imaginary homelands: essays in criticism 1981–1991*, London: Granta, 1995, pp. 415–29.

15   Clifford Geertz, 'Deep play: notes on the Balinese cockfight', in *Interpretation of cultures*, New York: Basic Books, 1973, pp. 412–54.

16   These points are taken from Vincent Crapanzano's penetrating critique, 'Hermes' dilemma: the masking of subversion in ethnographic description', in James Clifford and George Marcus (eds) *Writing culture: the poetics and politics of ethnography*, Berkeley: U. of California P. 1986, pp. 51–76.

17   Nigel Barley, *The innocent anthropologist*, Harmondsworth: Penguin, 1986 and *A plague of caterpillars: a return to the African bush*, Harmondsworth: Penguin, 1986.

18   This criticism was made long ago by John Davis in *People of the Mediterranean*, London: Routledge and Kegan Paul, 1977.

19   For discussion of this point see Susan Wright 'Anthropology: still the uncomfortable discipline?', in A. Ahmed and C. Shore (eds) *The future of anthropology*, London: The Athlone Press, 1995, pp. 65–93.

20   James Clifford, 'Introduction: partial truths', in Clifford and Marcus (eds), *op. cit.*, p. 25.

21   Vanessa Fleming, 'Representation and anthropology', *Anthropology in Action* 2(3), 1995, p. 31.

22   Marshall Sahlins, 'How "natives" think', *Times Literary Supplement*, No. 4809, p. 13. Similar criticisms have been levelled against the multiculturalism agenda in the United States. For an interesting critique see Terence Turner, 'Anthropology and multiculturalism: what is anthropology that multiculturalists should be mindful of it?', *Cultural Anthropology* 8(4), 1993, pp. 411–29.

23   Raymond Williams, *Keywords*, London: Fontana, 1976, pp. 236–8.

24   For a good assessment of this destructive tendency, toward excessive autocritique, see Jonathan Benthall's chapter 'From self-applause through self-criticism to self-confidence', in A. Ahmed and C. Shore (eds) *The future of anthropology*, 1995, pp. 1–11.

25   ASA *Working Party report on training for applied anthropologists*, London: Association of Social Anthropologists, 1984.

26   Spitulnik, *op. cit.*, p. 300.

Chapter 20

Pat Caplan

■ 'WE ARE ALL NEIGHBOURS': REVIEW,
Anthropology Today, 9.6, December 1993, pp. 20–2

THE SERIES TITLE *Disappearing World* has sometimes aroused unfavourable comment from anthropologists for being inappropriate, but during the course of this one-hour film (producer/director: Debbie Christie, anthropologist: Tone Bringa, first screened on ITV, 11 May), we watch a world literally disappear before our eyes.

Norwegian anthropologist Tone Bringa first worked in Bosnia in a mixed Catholic-Muslim village – 'a small village in Europe' – five years ago. This village now lies in the Bosnian war zone. The film was shot mainly over a three-week period in January 1993, but eight weeks later, with the film almost ready for screening, the team heard reports of violence in the area. They made a return visit to obtain the material which forms the film's epilogue.

During the first part of the film the front line, fifteen miles away, can be almost ignored most of the time; village life remains relatively normal and relations between Catholics and Muslims are still good. We are introduced to two women and their families, those of Nusreta, a Muslim, and Slavka, a Catholic. In an early scene, Nusreta makes pastry while she talks to Tone: 'It's the same as before, we must get along. Because we have to live together – Serbs, Croats, Muslims. That's how it's always been. And yes, definitely in the future.'

Even so, Nusreta and her husband Nurija have sent their 11-year-old son away for safety to their married daughter's house in a village across the mountains. Nurija meanwhile chops wood to keep himself occupied, since he hasn't been to work for ten months – sufficient time, he says, to chop enough wood to last them for two years. He also kills time by helping his wife with washing up on the terrace. He is unaccustomed to such domestic chores and embarrassed to be filmed doing this, but in a jokey scene, she tells him 'Let them [the viewers] see how up-to-date Bosnian men are.'

Slavka, the Catholic woman, is shown feeding the animals: 'A house stands up because women are its three cornerstones, men only one. The men go to war and

Figure 20.1   Anthropologist Tone Bringa and Nusreta, a Bosnian Muslim from *We Are All Neighbours*.

the women have to struggle for the land and the livestock. We do 100 things, they only do one – and they get paid for it!'

We then meet two elderly women who are close friends as well as neighbours – Muslim Remzija and Catholic Anda. They are shown embracing and sharing their worries about their families. Remzija's son had come home recently to find an empty house, but his Catholic neighbour Anda had fed him. Remzija thanks Anda, who replies that she told the boy to come to her if he needed anything. 'We'll divide [the last] kilo of flour [between us]' and 'Whatever happens we'll drink coffee together.'

At this point, then, we have an impression of people resisting what is happening, trying to adjust to the real problems caused by the war, but social relationships across the religious divide remain intact. The second part of the film shows the way in which such relationships are changed.

Nusreta is seen going to visit some new refugees to ask about the area where her son is staying. An old woman tells how her daughter and other relatives have been killed in Sarajevo and how in the area she comes from, 28 people were massacred, everything burned, and people not allowed to bury their dead.

The commentary explains that the shelling has moved closer to the village and it is now Croat versus Muslim. Nusreta still maintains 'We're all neighbours and we'll have to live together afterwards.' But she is worried about the future and especially about her children: 'Will I ever see them again? Let my house go and my head too, but we'd be really sorry about our kids.' Nusreta and Nurija decide to go and visit their son and daughter to reassure them of their safety; their son wants to return home, and we see his delight as he chases the chickens, hugs his mother, and says 'It's best to be home!'

Meanwhile, Slavka's sister has been made a refugee by Muslims and her tale loses nothing in the telling: 'You just wait for them to come to your door, slit your throat, set fire to your house, kidnap you.' This is the turning point, and the next scene in the village is of women looking out of the window of their house. The anthropologist asks them what they are looking at: it is men digging gun emplacements. 'They're out to get us – *our* Croats. Neighbours, Tone, this is what they're like. Dad went to the shop and those who used to greet him turned their heads away.' Tone asks how things changed: 'It changed . . . we can't understand.'

The third part of the film shows the effect of these changes. Nurija and his Muslim neighbours, convinced an attack is imminent, form their own patrol each night while the women gather together for company. The try to sing, but, as one of the women comments, it is hard to do so now. They joke and laugh, but the slightly hysterical quality of their laughter is all too apparent. Nusreta takes a piece of cake and pretends it is Bosnia. She cuts it up and eats it, while the others protest.

The commentator notes that the pressures to declare themselves Muslim or Croat are now acute. Tone asks Nusreta if she could visit Slavka now. 'No definitely not, I am offended. The Chetniks yes, but we never expected it from our neighbours.' Tone also interviews Slavka: 'We're barely saying good-day – previously we shared everything . . . Suddenly people can change their face . . . For me the change happened in a day – it's on our doorstep.'

The effects of this change are seen most poignantly in an encounter between the two old women, Remzija and Anda. Remzija catches sight of her old friend working in a field, and calls her to come down, but the latter ignores her. It is the end of a 40-year friendship.

By this time, denial of what is happening is impossible. Nusreta and Nurija decide to send their son away again. Tone asks why. The normally articulate Nusreta cannot speak, so Nurija replies: 'We're expecting the worst.' So why don't they leave? Neither of them wants to do so as everything they possess is in the village. 'As long as the child is out of here . . . our children will remain.' But he admits that 'Waiting is very difficult – I never sleep.' His wife weeps silently and he removes a tear from her cheek.

The final few minutes of the film were shot eight weeks later when the film crew were only able to get into the area with the UN. They find Nusreta, Nurija and their children at the married daughter's house; all of them rush out to greet Tone, to embrace her and weep with her, to tell their tale of five days of violence, several of which Nusreta spent in hiding.

The camera shows us the village in which all the Catholic houses are still intact but almost every Muslim house has been shelled, burned or vandalized. Tone seeks an explanation from Slavka – 'Why?' Slavka shrugs: '*I* don't know.' Tone is angry: 'What have you done to them?' Slavka: '*We* didn't do it.'

Tone talks to refugees from the village including Remzija, who laments that her former friend and neighbour Anda did not warn her. 'If only I had been able to take my own clothes.' She also talks to the people who used to live in the house from where she had first seen the gun emplacements being dug, and which is now totally destroyed. She asks them 'Do you know who did it?' 'We know exactly. My brother was killed by his next door neighbour.'

So what of the future? Nurija is clear: 'I don't want to return – to live with them.' Tone asks Nusreta whether she could live with them again. 'Impossible!'

The final few moments of the film have no commentary, are silent, although at each of the three screenings of this film I have attended, the sound comes from the audience, most of whom are deeply moved as they see a series of flashbacks from earlier parts of the film, each one coupled with a scene from the present: we see Nusreta making pastry, then her destroyed kitchen; we see Nurija helping to wash up on the terrace, then its now desolate remains; their son shoos chickens from the door of the house, then we see the same doorway, but now without a door; finally the scene in which Nusreta hugs her son in their living room is followed by views of the same room, but now open to the outside as the wall has been blasted away.

In the last few months, we have seen many films about the war in Bosnia on our TV screens – so what makes this one different?

It is an example of what can be done with the participation of an anthropologist who, knowing an area and its people well, is able to elicit the latter's own words. Like a good novel, it enables us, through a series of conversations and everyday scenes, to feel that we know the main characters, and understand their thoughts and emotions. They come across as 'ordinary people' wanting to get on with their lives, concerned about their children, wondering why things cannot continue as before, especially their relations with neighbours of a different faith. The film clearly establishes a momentum in its narrative; we get a sense of what life was like before, of the war coming ever closer, the inevitable consequences for the villagers and the final dénouement.

The film manages to explain a very complex situation in ways which are comprehensible to a wide audience, through a combination of sympathetic commentary (by Debbie Christie) and conversations between the anthropologist and people who are allowed to tell their stories. Such techniques are standard today in ethnographic films. Less so is the inclusion of the anthropologist herself in the film. Tone's role shifts from that of interpreter at the beginning as she explains the situation, to that of witness as she listens to people's horrific stories, finally to that of protagonist, as she expresses her outrage at what has happened to her Muslim friends.

I discussed this film with a Croatian friend who commented that newsreel and documentaries do not usually show what life is like for ordinary people caught up in such extraordinary circumstances. He could relate to the film in a very personal way because his own family had gone through similar experiences to those of the villagers in the film: it was very typical of what had happened.

People had wanted to live together, but the pressures to declare who and what they were became irresistible. Initially, people had refused to move, having built their own houses, room by room, over long periods, and still having vivid memories of the period during and after the second world war when they suffered grinding poverty. But finally, the desire to stay alive forced many of them to become refugees.

When I asked Tone Bringa herself why she wanted to make the film, she replied that in all the media coverage, she had not recognized the voices of the people she knew. She wanted to allow ordinary people to speak for themselves.

It is precisely at this level that the film succeeds so brilliantly in capturing the horror of civil war and 'ethnic cleansing'.

Note

We Are All Neighbours has been awarded an EMMY international television award, tying for first place in the documentary category. The award was made in New York on 23 November before an audience of 1,000 television executives.

Chapter 21

Marcus Banks

■ ANCIENT MYSTERIES AND THE MODERN
WORLD, *Anthropology Today*, 15.5, October 1999,
p. 20

N O ONE, OR AT LEAST NO ANTHROPOLOGIST in Britain, can have
failed to have noticed that as the 1990s come to an end, the ethnographic film
genre has largely disappeared from British terrestrial television broadcasting, probably for good. For a few, this may actually be cause to celebrate: finally, the screens
have been rid of those functionalist and superficial one-tribe-per-film representations typified by Granada's 'Disappearing World' programmes of the 1970s and
early 1980s. But celebrations of any victory of academic rigour over prurient exoticism may be hollow and premature. By and large, any interest in the non-European
world has vanished from our screens completely. Away from occasional current
affairs programmes investigating political issues in the non-European world, the area
of British television documentary has shrunk to the narrow focus of the docu-soap
– the inside of a driving school car, the fly on the wall of a hotel kitchen, the cult
of the celebrity mediocrity. But there is one significant exception, one which
frequently invokes the legitimization of anthropology and archaeology.

Discussing the decline of broadcast ethnographic film a year or so back with a
practising ethnographic film-maker, I asked him what kinds of films are currently
getting commissioned: 'Ancient mysteries' he replied without hesitation. 'Ancient
mysteries', for those unfamiliar with the genre, are now showing on British
small screens with a vengeance, albeit not as ubiquitous as docu-soaps. These are
programmes that reveal for the first time the true secrets of Stonehenge, or the
Pyramids, that allow often flamboyant amateur (and occasionally professional)
anthropologists and archaeologists to air their pet theories before millions, free of
the scrutiny of peer review. Their protagonists' views are frequently described as
'controversial', yet – as the voice-over invariably continues – 'scientists have been
reluctantly forced to accept the truth of their claims' and so on. These programmes
often cultivate an atmosphere of delicious unease through a combination of spooky
electronic music, dramatic camera shots, swirling mists and ghostly re-enactment

that would be the envy of any B-movie horror director. They are also anthropologically fascinating.

A prime example was screened in Channel Four's 'Secrets of the Dead' series this summer. For a series that has largely concentrated on respectable (and therefore dull, from an Ancient Mysteries point of view) archaeological investigation, *Cannibals of the Canyon*, by its very title alone, conjured up the required Ancient Mysteries frisson of morbid excitement. The first two-thirds of the film told an enthralling story, spiced with gruesome detail and more than a whiff of controversy. As Christy Turner, a physical anthropologist at Arizona State University and the film's main protagonist put it: 'People have a big problem . . . watching our evidence say that someone was being eaten.' Turner stirred together a heady brew of political correctness cast down ('being politically correct is not doing science; science finds the truth and it takes the community then to deal with the truth'), the mysterious disappearance of the Anasasi of the American South-West, and the gory technicalities of stripping human flesh from human bones for consumption. In short, it was suggested that the peaceful Anasasi farmers we knew and revered, might have been a bunch of brutal murderous cannibals.

Just in case the viewers might be unclear as to what was actually involved in the disarticulation of the human body for consumption, Turner hacked away at some spare ribs with a stone hammer. Later, an archaeologist gorily butchered a sheep carcass with stone flakes, trimming the joints down to fit an Anasasi-style cooking pot, and then boiling up a greasy stew. 'Look,' confided Turner in an aside, 'that's all game food there [in the pot], and they're eating it. If I turn my back and tell you that this [holding up fragments of raw meat and bone] is human, why are you going to reject it as having been eaten when you just accepted the same bones as having been eaten as game animals?'

But was there actually any evidence that the flesh was in fact eaten, rather than being prepared for some elaborate funerary ritual? Luckily, forensic analysis of a human coprolite, conveniently left at the site of an apparent cannibalistic orgy, revealed the presence of human myoglobin – proof that one person's flesh had passed through another's gut. This, of course, was not particularly welcome news to modern Zuni and Hopi of the South-West, who consider themselves to be the descendants of the Anasasi. As an archaeologist for the Hopi Tribe put it: 'There's a long tradition in the United States of science trying to dehumanize Native Americans . . . I think that when the idea of cannibalism gets picked up by the media it takes on a life of its own, it becomes fact.'

But the audience was being set up. In the final third of the film, fresh evidence was uncovered (teeth filed into points, no less) to reveal that the true villains were in fact . . . Mexicans! This was actually quite a startling claim, until the narrator made it clear in a passing reference that the 'Mexicans' referred to were actually 'Meso-Americans – Toltecs and ancient peoples'. It may in fact be standard practice in Meso-American archaeology to refer to 'Mexico' and 'Mexicans' as general category labels for the region and its groups in the pre-Hispanic period, and thus legitimate to speak of 'Mexicans' coming up from the south after the decline of the southern empires and falling upon the peaceful Anasasi like wolves upon a flock of sheep. Certainly Turner seems to do so: 'I've got a Mexican over here someplace with chipped teeth,' he said, waving his arm around an Anasasi site, 'I got canni-balism . . . I see Mexico!'

But there may be another reason too. The film in fact demonstrates a well-known ethnographic truism – that unlike us, the people over the hill, or across the river, or in the next valley are cannibals and/or incestuous. We are civilized, they are barbarians. This was not an Ancient Mystery at all, but a modern morality tale. At the end of the film the Anasasi had been restored to virtue, victims of the 'Mexicans'' gastro-terror. Their modern descendants had thus been redeemed by white man's science from the slur of breaching the ultimate taboo, and Native American and white American could stand arm in arm in brotherhood, looking south over the border with pity and horror at the cannibals beyond.

Note

Cannibals of the Canyon (dir. Larry Engel) was broadcast as part of Channel Four's 'Secrets of the Dead' series on 20 July 1999.

The Great Anteater's Attractions

■ *Anthropology Today*, 8.5, October 1992, pp. 1–2

FRENCH-SPEAKING ANTHROPOLOGISTS seem to preserve a characteristic style – it might be called the structural-existentialist, if that is not a paradox – during some recent forays into social criticism of the West. It's not everyone's cup of tea, but anthropology would be a weaker mixture without it.

One of France's leading anthropologists, Marc Augé, reported for last August's issue of *Le Monde Diplomatique* on a visit to Euro Disneyland, the controversial American entertainment park to the north of Paris which has been massively subsidized by the French state but is damned by many intellectuals and visited by fewer tourists than hoped for. Augé notes that the visitors include far more adults than children, who seem to serve mainly as a pretext for a visit, and an optional one at that. He concludes that Disneyland represents the quintessence of tourism: 'what we come to see does not exist; we discover there only the memory of our dreams. We live the experience there of a pure liberty without object, without reason, without a stake. We find there not America, nor our childhood, but the absolute freedom of a play of images in which everyone who rubs shoulders with us can inject what they want, and we shall never see them again'.

The terms of Augé's interpretation recall those of a dashing book recently published by a French-Canadian colleague, Bernard Arcand, about another form of popular pastime based on the excitation of fantasy, annulment of social space and linear time, provision of high-tech services for the 'lonely crowd' – but Arcand's book is about pornography,[1] which at first sight is a different thing altogether from the Disneyparks (and nothing in the following should be taken as implying that any emanations of the Walt Disney Co. are less than 100% clean and decent). Both Augé and Arcand, however, have recourse to the idea that ours is the 'era of emptiness' – the title of a book on contemporary individualism (*L'Ère du Vide*) by Gilles Lipovetsky, who writes that 'God is dead, the great finalities are extinct, but *no-one gives a damn*, there is the joyful news, that is the limit of Nietzsche's diagnosis.' This might seem too commonplace a reflection on which to build an argument, but

Arcand also gives an older quotation from Edgar Morin's *L'Homme et la Mort* which sums up the darker mood of 1940s existentialism, once so dominant in French intellectual life and so widely influential: 'There is nothing left of the universal, nor of the cultural. The individual is left alone in irrationality . . . The breaking-up of participation leads to the fear of death, and the fear of death reinforces the breaking-up of participation. Solitude brings on the obsessive fear of death, and that fear closes in on the solitude.'

Arcand argues that though the iconography of Western porn has much in common with that of, for instance, the erotic reliefs sculpted in medieval Indian temples (and many tourists now read these reliefs as pornographic) there is the big difference that porn is marginal, a result of the specialization of roles and discourses, whereas in medieval India religion, art and sex were to a great extent integrated. Porn relates to sexuality as the Disneyparks relate to our sense of legend, myth and fiction, in so far as these are relegated to the marginal sphere of leisure. In fact, though both pornography and the Disneyparks are big businesses, many Euro-Americans find both of them tedious.

For Arcand, a well-known ethnographer of South American Indians, the spirit of porn is represented by the great anteater as it appears in the rituals of the Sherente Indians of central Brazil. The anteater has a long muzzle with minimal mouth, and its anus is completely hidden by lips, so that it is thought of as blocked-up and self-sufficient. Its sexual organs are tiny and also concealed; it is generally seen alone, and its grey-black coat and lack of teeth make it a symbol of old age; it eats what is normally regarded as putrefied, and its own meat is extremely tough. The anteater 'offers the image of a small quiet life where it has no appetite except for a few ants, an undemanding life where it asks nothing of others and would do no harm to anyone'. Yet it is a fierce, strong beast whose forepaws can lacerate not only tree-trunks and termite-nests but also a human skull.

The Sherente hold an occasional ceremony in which men dressed as anteaters are symbolically killed by men dressed as jaguars. The jaguar is agile, powerful, all-seeing, sociable, highly sexed – standing for all the qualities which a Sherente woman would like to see in her husband and which a shaman needs in order to perform miracles. In effect, the Sherente recognize the anteater's attainment of a kind of tranquil immortality – which they reject in favour of risk, excitement, sociability and predation. They do so because societal reproduction matters more than individual survival.

The question Arcand poses is, are the Sherente's priorities the same as ours, for the dangers of any community's dying out now seem outweighed by those of over-population? Possibly masturbation, generally despised in most cultures, is becoming the Western paradigm of sexuality, the partner being reduced to a catalyst.

To bring together the findings of Augé and Arcand, it may be that porn in the special sector of sex, the Disneyparks in the special sector of leisure, represent a triumph of individualism, a denial of death. For this model to work, the nuclear family must be taken as an individualist unit. Cameras are important to both experiences but they are used to make what T.S. Eliot called a 'wilderness of mirrors', not to make images which strengthen personal relations over time and space through awareness of mutual knowledge. It would seem that the worthy aims of ecological equilibrium, control of sexually transmitted diseases, and political equality may all be actually favoured by the anteater's practice of spiritual constipation.

Such attempts to defy mortality are likely by and large, Arcand argues, to be profitable to investors, but ultimately limited by the inability of our technology to cheat death or, as yet, to create children. Traditional commitments to face-to-face reciprocal relationships as the primary source of meaning are not, then, quite obsolete, even though such commitments are heavy laden with the risks and asymmetries which the Sherente accept as the price of an exciting and worthwhile life.

Perhaps we may sum up Arcand's insight (originally the Sherente's) as an acceptance that the borderlines between relationships of symbiosis, parasitism and predation are always porous. Pornography and the Disneyparks are projects to escape this fact of life, projects which will enjoy increasing support but which will also continue to be vigorously opposed. As for those who profess expertise in the 'social', thinking about the extent of fantasy in human relations should foster some humility among them when they use that adjective.

Note

1   *Le Jaguar et le Tamanoir: Vers le degré zéro de la pornographie*, Boréal, Montreal, 1991, C$29.95. The Brazilian ethnography referred to later in this article derives from Curt Nimuendaju as interpreted by Thomas F. Portante, a student of Arcand's, under the inspiration of Lévi-Strauss. An English translation by Wayne Grady will be published in September 1993 by Verso.

Bernard Arcand also gives more conventional attention to various ethical aspects of pornography relating to gender, violence, censorship etc. – in a book originally designed to show the dean of his social science faculty that anthropology was relevant to the 'modern world'.

Jonathan Benthall

PART SIX

New Social Movements

■   JONATHAN BENTHALL

To REPRESENT THE MANY NEW SOCIAL MOVEMENTS which have arisen over the past quarter-century and have been studied by anthropologists, I have chosen one pair of articles on environmentalism, and one pair of articles on North and West Africans in France and their relations with the native French.

Michael Thompson's 1980 article on the pro- and anti-nuclear movement in the USA was one of the more controversial published in *RAINews*, and two letters attacking it are republished too, by Lionel Caplan and Charles Leslie. What Thompson did was to take up the approach to environmentalism initiated in Mary Douglas's lecture 'Environments at risk', which I had had the privilege of hosting in a lecture series on ecology at the ICA in 1970. While it is true that some of Thompson's arguments are frivolous, and would probably not have survived the more rigorous peer review introduced when *RAINews* graduated into *Anthropology Today*, it would seem that his real crime was to challenge what later came to be called political correctness. Thompson's position was that if anthropologists decide to apply their skills to advocacy, it must not always be on the same, *bien pensant* side of the debate – or they will be seen by the public as merely rationalizing their own political bias. Thompson's article is an early application of ethnographic methods to studying the pressure groups and Non-Governmental Organizations whose importance as constituents in our 'civil society' is now increasingly recognized.

Arne Kalland was also inspired by Mary Douglas, in pointing out that whales more easily become the object of myths and taboo because they elude the simple categories of mammals and fish. In the anti-whaling movement, environmentalism and animal rights overlap, and the whale serves as a totem for goodness and respect for nature. Kalland supports the environmental movement in general, but believes that its naivety is often taken advantage of by corporate and political interests. 'Green' lapel-badges become a means of fund-raising and an excuse for not making hard political decisions. Kalland appends a brief update on whale politics over the eight years since the article was first published.

Liliane Kuczynski describes a successful economic niche that has been found in Paris by North and West African marabouts. A marabout (Arabic *marâbiT*) is a holy man in Moroccan Islam, though some of the practitioners studied by Kuczynski appear to have no connection with Islam. She sensibly took as her starting-point the French clients who provide a market. For one victim of unrequited love, 'Marie' – an affluent Parisian who has some personal links with Africa – the acceptable alternatives to an African marabout are clairvoyants, psychics or 'gentle' therapists; she wants to hear echoes of her own thoughts, not challenges. Marie has no conception of, or interest in, the theology that underpins the rituals and amulets.

Sketchy though Kuczynski's short article published in 1988 was, it identified a recognizable social pattern which has parallels in other cities and other belief contexts. For instance, Caroline Humphrey wrote in 1999 of the Buryat shamans who in the late 1980s began to appear in Siberian cities, where 'it is now normal for anyone with a misfortune or a quandary to visit a shaman' (*AT* 15.3, June 1999, 'Shamans in the city').

An equally original article by **Anne-Marie Brisebarre**: 'The sacrifice of 'Id al-kabir: Islam in the French suburbs', was published in 1993. Brisebarre's starting-point for her research was her interest in French shepherds, for whom the sale of sheep to North African Muslims is a steady market (live sheep are also an Australian export to the Middle East). French public policy has dictated that, rather than allow minority ghettoes to become established as in Britain, suburban housing estates should be ethnically and religiously diversified. The annual blood-sacrifice of sheep is important to North African and many other Muslims but can give offence to Christians, in whose religion, as in Judaism, the primordial myth of Abraham's near-sacrifice of his beloved son has been sublimated into theological symbolism. The French government, sensing a potential ethnic flashpoint, has sponsored research into the practice of the ritual since 1990, and Brisebarre and her co-workers have since published two books.[1]

Note

1   *La Fête du mouton* (A.-M. Brisebarre and others, Paris: CNRS Editions, 1998) and *Le Sacrifice en islam* (ed. P. Bonte, A.-M. Brisebarre and A. Gokalp, Paris: CNRS Editions, 1999).

Chapter 22

Michael Thompson

■   FISSION AND FUSION IN NUCLEAR SOCIETY,
RAINews, 41, December 1980, pp. 1–5

In November 1979 Dr Michael Thompson presented a paper to an American pro-nuclear group SE$_2$ (Scientists and Engineers for Secure Energy) at a meeting concerned mainly with the safe disposal of nuclear waste and with the Three Mile Island accident. Thompson, as a freelance social anthropologist, is not committed to either the pro- or the anti-nuclear camp and points out that his advice has in fact not been heeded by SE$_2$. He considers that the problem of America's indecision over peaceful nuclear energy must be addressed wholly in social and political, rather than technical, terms and that it is basically due to different perceptions of risks and their acceptability. More recently, he has studied the anti-smoking movement in both Britain and the USA.

In this article, Thompson offers some general inferences from his researches and distinguishes two kinds or organization which he characterizes as sectist *and* caste-ist.

To use the word 'caste' for groups in Western society such as SE$_2$ is, perhaps, to stretch its precise meaning beyond the limits of anthropological tolerance. Yet (Dr Thompson argues) these groups do display many caste-like characteristics, just as secular 'sects' display many of the characteristics of the religious groups to which this term is usually restricted. Unlike their anthropological equivalents, these groups do not usually dominate every aspect of their members' lives and, in consequence, they are not so much castes and sects as groups that are biased in the direction of castes and sects respectively; they are groups that display a tendency towards caste-ism *and* sectism.

Also the 'real castes' of the anthropologist are always part of a caste system, *while these Western castes form part of some social whole which (whatever else it might be) is certainly not a caste system. The author prefers not to define castes so tightly that the study of castes and caste-like groups outside of caste systems would be excluded. His extension of the term, inspired by a reading of Louis Dumont's* Homo hierarchicus, *is not yet recommended to examinees.*

Sectist and caste-ist groups

A SECT ERECTS A WALL OF VIRTUE between itself and the nasty outside world from which it wishes to set itself apart. The members collectively reject the outside world; they do not negotiate any sort of relationship with it. The result is that, though the collectivity may in some cases exercise almost total control over its members, it can do nothing to the rest of the society.

A *caste* separates itself off, not with a wall of virtue, but by means of clearly defined distinctions between it and those other groupings that exist outside it. The result, as each caste defines itself by its distinction from (yet clearly specified inter-relation with) other castes, is a complex hierarchical framework of status distinctions, prescriptions, restrictive practices, correct channels and proper procedures. The members of a caste, therefore, do not reject the outside world; they collectively take up a clearly specified position *within* it. A caste, as a result, can come to exercise a high level of control over its own members *and* over those outside its boundary.

Though this fundamental distinction between sects and castes originates in anthropology, it has now been developed to the point where it connects with similar distinctions that are drawn in other fields of contemporary enquiry. Table 22.1 lists some of the operationalizable criteria that can be used to determine whether a group is a sect or a caste.

One interesting prediction from this model is that, though individuals can (by letting their sect loyalty lapse and then developing a more caste-ist account of themselves, or *vice versa*) move between these two contexts, whole groups cannot.

Such a prediction is directly counter to the evolutionary sequences sometimes advanced in the sociology of religion in which tiny persecuted face-to-face sects are depicted as the acorns from which the mighty oak trees of hierarchically organized established churches grow. Instead, it suggests that each is a separate species that grows or withers according to the nature of the social context soil. Where both appropriate contexts are found in the same society, then massive churches and tiny sects are likely to co-exist, the latter providing a continual critical commentary on the former.

The reason why whole groups, be they sects or castes, cannot move is that each is stabilized by the collective pursuit of a distinct strategy. The members of a caste end up manipulating others; the members of a sect end up manipulated by others. Because of this divergence between their stabilizing strategies, castes and sects always remain clearly separate. A sect is an egalitarian and externally impotent collectivity; a caste is a status-conscious and externally potent collectivity.

Now before someone else says it, let me say that a group like Friends of the Earth,[1] though it is clearly a sect in terms of this definition, is *not* impotent; if it were, there would probably be no need for an organisation such as SE_2. The difference between FoE and a *life sect* (like the Amish or the Jonestown Commune) is that the members look to their group for only a part of their life support, not for it all. The same sort of thing is true for most of the caste-like groups we will be looking at: the collectivity has relevance for only a part of the lives of each of its members. It is in order to maintain this distinction between the *total commitment* of the members of life sects and life castes and the tendency or bias of the group members we will be looking at that we choose the terms *sectist* and *caste-ist*.

Table 22.1

CASTES	SECTS
Dominant Criterion	
Multi-issue aim	Single-issue aim
Secondary Criteria	
1. **Membership:** quality	quantity
2. **Internal organization:** differentiated and hierarchical	homogeneous and egalitarian
3. **Relation to outside:** negotiated and clearly-specified relationships	opposition and rejection (unnegotiated)
4. **Power:** manipulates others (collectively)	is manipulated
5. **Stability:** follows collectivist manipulative strategy that tends to maintain its position on 'peak of power'; mature castes inherently stable	follows collectivist survival strategy consistent with its situation; adopts hit-and-run tactics; cannot mature and is inherently unstable; cannot abide compromise
6. **Leadership:** many different levels, each highly specialized, provide clear multi-stepped career structures; leaders tend to be mobile within these structures	problematical – leaders contradict egalitarian ideal; maintain themselves by maintaining the wall of virtue – by constantly reaffirming group values, attacking those on the outside, spotting outsiders who have crept in undetected; no career structure, so leaders are immobile.
7. **Order:** the basis of morality, hence rejection of disorderly bodies, e.g. sects; formal and elaborate structures; high level of prescription and elaborate rules	rejection of outside the basis of morality, inside the wall of virtue all is unstructured and informal; no prescription or rules except those that emphasize boundary between inside and outside
8. **Commitment:** expressed in ritual and in adherence to correct procedures and proper channels	expressed in collective moral fervour, ad hoc-ism, and spontaneous affirmations of shared opposition to the enemy outside
9. **Scope:** national or global; if there are local chapters, organization remains strongly centralized	tends to be local; if there is a central head-quarters this creates problems with hierarchy and may render the organization unstable
10. **Recruitment:** not particularly joinable; operates by invitation to those who have taken the trouble to make themselves acceptable	joinable; open to all who clearly subscribe to the single aim and who reject the outside world
11. **Concern:** may well be for the welfare of all (though all may not accept that this is so)	restricted to a minority – those inside the wall of virtue
12. **Use of scientific knowledge:** science respected (especially scientific method) but new insights that threaten to confuse existing paradigms are resisted. The social context of 'normal science'	scientific knowledge valued only if it supports 'us' in fight against 'them' and is accessible to all. Emphasis on egalitarian ideal renders specialist and inaccessible knowledge suspect. Scientific method subordinated to requirements of boundary maintenance. The social context of 'scientism'

Note: The sectist use of scientific knowledge, though it contrasts so strongly with that of the caste-ist groups, is certainly not the source of breakthroughs and paradigm change. These are initiated by those prickly (but brilliant) individualists who, respecting neither persons nor disciplinary boundaries and conventions, occupy yet another social context – that of the entrepreneur – and operate the high-risk/high-reward strategy of the manipulative individualist.

In a life sect, leaders and followers are in daily face-to-face contact; they are united in their impotence. If impotence goes with unity, perhaps power goes with separation? Perhaps it is not the sect but just the sect leadership that can acquire power? Surprising though this suggestion may seem, it turns out to have some substance; the reason sects such as FoE have managed to acquire power lies largely in the separation between leaders and followers.

Many American sects have a Washington-based leadership and a provincial mail-order membership. On top of this, the sect leaders (unlike their followers) have impressive media skills. At the SE_2 meeting there were many moans about the anti-nuclear bias of the media and frequent laments about the devil having all the best tunes. Nor does it stop there. The devil, it seems, has all the pretty faces too; the antis have Jane Fonda, Paul Newman and Linda Ronstadt, to name but three, whilst the pros have only the bushy-browed Edward Teller. The sect leaders are thus able to do two things at once in two different places: they can put pressure on government in Washington at the same time as they feed suitably sectist exhortations back to the provinces to maintain the unity of their fissure-prone followers.

For instance, the FoE book *Frozen Fire*[2] opens with the following quote:

> An official of one of the country's largest gas companies said yesterday 'absolute safety' for liquified natural gas is impossible and 'inconsistent with national goals and public interest'.

Only those of a sectist disposition would see this statement as anything other than a truism; those in other social contexts (be they caste-ists, entrepreneurs, hermits or down-trodden proletariat)[3] would all agree that no technology can be absolutely safe and that, in consequence, a commitment to absolute safety would be infinitely expensive and so could never be consistent with natural goals or public interest. The various non-sectists only begin to disagree when they get to the next question which is 'granted that no technology can be absolutely safe, how safe is safe enough?' Since the remaining 298 pages of *Frozen Fire* are devoted to a detailed and meticulously argued discussion of this second question, culminating in a long list of suggestions as to how these inevitable risks might be better reduced and more carefully and equitably handled,[4] one can only assume that this opening appeal to the uncompromising rejection of risk (especially risk imposed by big business) is a sectist sop thrown to the faithful followers to keep them happy while the author hob-nobs on what are really rather caste-ist terms, with those who tread the corridors of power.

A powerful sect is a colossal contradiction, and this two-places-at-once feat by its leaders must inevitably result in a lot of skilfully disguised hypocrisy. The greater the power of the sect leadership, the greater its separation from its followers; and the greater this separation become, the harder the leadership will have to work to create the illusion that it does not exist. This contradiction, without doubt, is the Achilles' heel of power-wielding sect leaders (the 'Porsche populists' as they have been dubbed) and without doubt it is the weak spot on which a caste-ist group such as SE_2 should concentrate its attack.[5]

The third factor that has enabled these sect leaders to wield so much power (the first two being their separation from their followers and their media skills) has

Figure 22.1 Preparations in 1998 for removal of 2,300 tons of highly radioactive waste from leak-prone basins in the Hanford nuclear reservation near Richland, Washington, USA. Openings in the floor are tubes where the fuel and glassified radioactive liquid wastes will be inserted into containers and inserted into huge underground vaults.

been the eagerness of government to listen to them. Instead of performing its proper (from a caste-ist point of view) role of referee, government has failed time and time again to blow the whistle while the sects went on and on inventing their own rules. It is here that the American experience with the anti-nuclear movement (and other movements, like the anti-smoking movement) differs so markedly from those in Europe.)[6] In the hope of finding out why this should be so, I turned to a political scientist.

> In American history, the Radical, although the founder of party is also its most persistent critic. Forever disillusioned with the actual tones in which party speaks, he seeks to eliminate interference by bosses, corruption and special interests and to tune in the authentic voice of the people by regulating party processes, by setting up a direct primary, by instituting the initiative and the referendum. The strength of the Radical ideal in America is one major reason for the weakness of our parties.[7]

America currently seems to be suffering from an excess of this Radical ideal. By contrast, some European countries (France, Sweden, Britain, Austria, for instance), though of course they have their strenuous internal disagreements about nuclear power, do seem to be able to make *some* progress[8] and this is because, in their various ways, their governments do blow the whistle – they do not allow the sects to go on and on changing the rules. They are not wholly convinced that, when the sect leaders speak, they speak with 'the authentic voice of the people'.

From analysis to prescription

If this *is* the current predicament, what can SE_2 do about it? How can it induce American government to exercise some of this healthy scepticism?

(1)   SE2 can probably do very little directly to lever government away from the sects but it can, in its lobbying, point out that, since sects are uncompromising in their demands and are not prepared to enter into negotiation whilst politicians are in the business of compromise and negotiation, too close an association with sects may not be in a politician's long-term interest.

(2) SE_2 can probably do quite a lot to reveal to both government and to the populace that the voice of the sect leader is not 'the authentic voice of the people'. Since the sect leaders make much of their moral righteousness, their hypocrisy (if it can be revealed) could well prove to be their political undoing. Much more thought would be needed to develop the appropriate tactics for applying this strategy but here are a few suggestions.

   (a) SE_2 should not, in frustration, try to adopt the tactics of the other side. Their tactics are suited to their strategy and would not work well in the cause of a different strategy.

   (b)   Healthy scepticism is a very effective weapon in the journalist's armoury and several good examples of its application to the New Class already exist. Ridicule is a most effective medium and a well-chosen epithet, like 'Porsche populist', is worth a hundred pages of analysis.

(c)   The two great unifying themes of a sect secure inside its wall of virtue are: 'Small is beautiful' and 'natural is good'. The sectist component of the anti-nuclear movement is vulnerable on both these scores. First, its own organization at the leadership end is massive and only the media skills of the Washington-based leaders prevent the followers from perceiving that this is so. Second, I was most impressed at the meeting to learn that so much of what is involved in nuclear power is so technologically simple (in principle, anyway) and so natural. The sun is a huge reactor (but well sited, admittedly); there have been natural reactors on earth millions of years ago in Gabon, radiation is natural and there has always been background radiation – sometimes higher, sometimes lower than at present; radiation in the proper medical hands is *good* for you. In particular, the Swedish waste disposal system, with its absence of moving parts, the way it fits itself into natural processes that extend through aeons of time, and its imitation of nature as, for instance, in using copper containers because native copper has been present in the granite *from the time it was created*, has great spiritual appeal thanks to its simplicity and its respect for nature and for creation. It contains a powerful theme that would have inspired Wordsworth. So, other things being equal, always go for the option that is simplest and that *imitates*, rather than masters, nature.

(3)   Implicit in 1) and 2) above is a major shift in strategy: a redefinition of who SE_2's enemies are. At present, SE_2 tends to see itself opposed by a monolithic enemy: the anti-nuclear movement. But my anthropological analysis reveals that the anti-nuclear groups are not all the same and, equipped with it, SE_2 can now discriminate between the castes and the sects. Castes and sects are not natural allies. Castes negotiate, compromise, value scientific knowledge, and respect expertise. Sects refuse to negotiate, will not compromise, value scientific knowledge *only* when it upholds their position, and, being committed to egalitarianism, suspect expertise. Sects go for quantity, castes for quality.[9] So, by these criteria, SE_2 is itself a caste and therefore has much more in common with an anti-nuclear caste such as the Sierra Club than the Sierra Club has with a sect within its own movement – the Friends of the Earth for instance. Let me give an example.

There is in Britain (and I suspect in the USA too) a group of lawyers opposed to nuclear power because they believe that the security measures that will have to be taken to minimize the threat posed by the non-state aggressor will result in Britain moving towards a police state. Now lawyers, in Britain anyhow, are not very sectist people: they are professionals, their arguments stand or fall according to whether the evidence is (by the caste-ist rules of evidence) sound or false; they wear sober suits and old school ties. Such a group becomes aligned with the hairy anti-nuclear sects largely because of the reaction of the pro-nuclear people. But these lawyers are not opposed to nuclear power *per se* (as, for instance, is the FoE leader Amory Lovins). They are opposed to certain types of reactor which they believe bring with them an unacceptably high security risk. They do not want the end of nuclear power – just a rearrangement of the present reactor preferences. They, for their part, could benefit from SE$_2$'s technical expertise in arriving at a more accurate assessment of the security risks posed by different reactors (and other techniques such as reprocessing and waste disposal) whilst SE$_2$ could, in return, concede the validity of the lawyers' legal and social concerns and add them to the technical criteria that they already apply in their considered evaluations of the various reactors and techniques.

What I am suggesting is that SE$_2$ should identify these caste-ist (or potentially caste-ist) anti-nuclear groups and begin to make friends with them (on the basis of what they already have in common). In so doing, SE$_2$ would move them further towards the caste pole, would derive a wedge between them and the sects, and would itself become a much less isolated target for anti-nuclear attack. As such links were forged, government would begin to see the advantages of listening to the considered, orderly and coherent counsels of the cautious but progressive castes rather than to the increasingly fractured, strident and hysterical demands of the uncompromising and regressive sects. America would begin to recover from its institutional paralysis.

Finally, I should point out that, though these prescriptions are all based on the assumption that it would be a good thing if America were to recover from that paralysis, such an assumption is not built into the analysis. The analysis just tells you what you can have; it is up to you to decide what you would like. If you are of the more revolutionary opinion that such tinkering is a waste of time and that the only solution is to hasten the inevitable and total collapse of the whole wretched system, then you will be interested in a rather different set of prescriptions and, if you feed in these contrary assumptions as to what is good and what is bad, the analysis will generate that appropriate set of prescriptions for you. A cynic might object that there is no need to go to all this trouble to find out what these prescriptions might be: we only have to look at current United States policy!

Notes

1   Friends of the Earth was founded in the USA; the British and 23 other national groups are affiliated to it.

2   Lee Niedringhaus Davis, 1979. *Frozen Fire: Where Will It Happen Next?* (Friends of the Earth, San Francisco).

3   Lest it appear that social contexts be starting to multiply towards infinity, I should perhaps explain that, according to social context theory, their number cannot go beyond five. Four of these are the social contexts originally described by Mary Douglas in her essay *Cultural Bias* (RAI Occasional Paper No. 35, 1978). The fifth – the hermit – corresponds to the 'autonomous individual' that she elected to take 'off the social map'. For a discussion of how he can be included on the social map see: Michael Thompson, 'A three-dimensional model' and 'The problem of the centre', both in M. Douglas and D. Ostrander (eds) *Essays in the Sociology of Perception*. (Routledge, London, and Basic Books, New York, to be published January 1981).

4   One of the options considered is not to have the technology, but the author is careful to point out that this is not a risk-free option.

5   Were I making helpful suggestions to a sect, I would point out that their pursuit of power will inevitably give rise to this dangerous contradiction and that they will become increasingly vulnerable to any attack that is directed at it. Beyond a certain point (the position of which will vary with their media skills, government sympathy and caste-ist opposition) their pursuit of power will become counter-productive and the leadership will have to choose between two alternatives: to increase the loyalty of their followers by abandoning their pursuit of power, or to increase their power by abandoning their followers. (In this latter case, the individual leaders move into the caste-ist context).

6   There is, for instance, much admiration in the USA for the Windscale Inquiry in Britain at which all parties were able to air their views at length, but on oath and within an impartial framework of rules firmly imposed by Mr Justice Parker.

7   S. H. Beer, *Modern British Politics* (Faber, 1965, p. 43).

8   Progress, that is, with making acceptable decisions, not necessarily progress with nuclear power.

9   For instance, only those SE_2 members who happened to be Nobel laureates were mentioned by name in the telegram that the meeting sent to the President of the United States – a hierarchical distinction that no sect would tolerate.

Chapter 23

Lionel Caplan, Michael Thompson and Charles Leslie

■ CORRESPONDENCE,
RAINews, 43 April 1981, pp. 18–20

Nuclear reactions

THE ISSUE CARRYING Brian Morris's letter, cautioning social scientists against pretensions to neutrality, contains an apt illustration of the very point he is making. The lead article in *RAINews* 41 (December 1980) is devoted to a report on a paper presented by Michael Thompson to a meeting of the pro-nuclear Scientists and Engineers for Secure Energy (SE_2) group. His brief seems to have been to instruct them in how best to combat what they and, apparently, Thompson perceive as the anti-nuclear bias of the American media and the inability of the US government to decide a nuclear policy. Groups like Friends of the Earth who vigorously oppose the nuclear option are defined as 'hairy', 'uncompromising and regressive sects', making 'strident and hysterical demands', while the pros, like SE_2, are more reasonable 'castes', who 'negotiate, compromise, value scientific knowledge and respect expertise'. Thompson's advice to the latter is to expose the 'hypocrisy' of the sect leaders ('Porsche populists'), so that the American public and government can finally come to appreciate, like the author, that radiation 'can be *good* for you'. While he is entitled to his opinion, are your readers really expected to believe the claim made (by the Editor?) in the Preface to the article that Thompson 'is not committed to either the pro- or the anti-nuclear camp'? Is this *RAINews*'s idea of unbiased action anthropology at work?

Lionel Caplan
London N.12

Michael Thompson writes:
As no great lover of 'negotiation' and 'compromise', as someone who retains a healthy (I hope) scepticism about 'scientific knowledge', and as something of a disrespecter of 'expertise', I intended these compliments to SE_2 to be a mite backhanded. Certainly, the (American) Friends of the Earth would not regard negotiation

and compromise as admirable when what is at stake, they firmly believe, is the very survival of mankind. 'We cannot be dilettante and lily-white in our work. Nice Nelly will never make it' (David R. Brower, Farewell Address to the Sierra Club, *New York Times*, 4 May 1969, p. 30). 'We plan to be extremely aggressive and uncompromising in our activities' (David R. Brower, 'Naturalists get a political arm', *New York Times*, 17 September 1969, p. 21). (David Brower founded Friends of the Earth on 11 July 1969, 69 days after being ousted from the Sierra Club.)

My idea of action anthropology is that it should strive to reveal (sympathetically) all the cultural biases in any debate. Since the debaters themselves seldom wish to acknowledge their biases, I find the following rule of thumb quite helpful: if it doesn't give equal offence to each party there must be something wrong with it! I see the role of the anthropologist as rather akin to that of the barrister (with his tongue in his cheek much of the time) but I do not share Lionel Caplan's perception of my brief. The SE_2 meeting was called to discuss how the current US stalemate concerning nuclear power might be moved off 'dead centre' and I began by suggesting that SE_2 themselves were, in a very real sense, actually the cause of the problem they were trying to resolve. All the prescriptions I put forward (which, incidentally, were not aimed at getting the US government to decide a nuclear policy but simply at getting it to decide a policy) followed directly from this opening position – a position which I expected would give some offence to my hosts and which, as it turned out, did.

Of course, anyone who does work for pro-nuclear organizations, for the Rockefeller Foundation or for the tobacco companies (and also, be it said, for government departments, for public interest groups or for the good of the discipline) should be keenly aware of the moral dangers that he faces and I would not wish to suggest that I have developed a method that guarantees me immunity. Such methods as I have evolved tend to be rather intuitive and I am grateful to Lionel Caplan for encouraging me to examine them and make them a little more explicit. Some kind of neutrality – an even-handed offensiveness akin, perhaps, to Austria's 'positive neutrality' – is, I think, possible for the action anthropologist and, rather than damning him for not getting it perfectly right first time, would it not be better to open up the discussion of what that neutrality might be and of how it might be possible to draw nearer to it?

One step in that direction, I cannot help thinking, is to inject just a little humour into a debate that is often over-inflated with serious self-importance. As Oscar Wilde once said, 'Some things are far too important to be taken seriously.' Nuclear power is one such thing and anyone who has immersed himself in the current debate (especially in the United States) cannot fail to be struck by its often farcical nature. Whether to accept or reject nuclear power is, perhaps, the ultimate tragic choice and it seems to me that an anthropological approach capable of handling the farcical aspects of this debate *as farce* may well help us in making that choice.

*   *   *

The sycophantic, ignorant, self-deceptive and incompetent advice Dr. Michael Thompson gave the Scientists and Engineers for Secure Energy (SE$_2$) was a disservice to anthropology. Nevertheless, *RAINews* has printed it as the lead article in its December 1980 issue (No. 41), with a plug for Thompson's book, *Rubbish Theory*, and for a forthcoming volume with an even catchier title. The editor's arch disclaimer that Thompson's primary concept, an ill-used distinction between 'caste' and 'sect', 'is not yet recommended to examinees' was perhaps a forewarning to readers that they should be amused rather than outraged by Thompson's reactionary politics and misrepresentation of issues.

The sycophancy is evident in the way Thompson made a distinction between 'caste' and 'sect' to flatter his sponsors by assigning the good 'caste' label to them and the bad 'sect' label to their opponents. As a 'caste' he asserted that SE$_2$ was composed of 'quality' members who 'may well be for the welfare of all (though all may not accept that this is so)', and who respected science, 'especially scientific method'. He assigned the pejorative label to Friends of the Earth and other undesignated critics of nuclear energy programs. In contrast to the quality-folks of SE$_2$, they were 'quantity' – read 'masses', as in *Revolt of the Masses*, for Thompson's kitsch anthropology shows a similar snobbish contempt, and lack of comprehension for popular democratic institutions. These 'quantity' people were nevertheless a social minority, and in Thompson's view they were unconcerned for the general welfare because they only care about people who were 'inside the wall of virtue' they claimed for themselves. They valued scientific knowledge 'only if it supports "us" in fight against "them" and is accessible to all' (meaning, I suppose, that they did not defer to experts who were incapable of explaining themselves to 'quantity' people). Also, they lacked respect for scientific method, and subordinated it 'to the requirements of boundary maintenance'.

Since the quality folks and their sectarian opponents were both minorities, Thompson might have completed his description of American society with 'the silent majority' of President Nixon's day, or President Reagan's 'moral majority'. This would have appealed to his conservative sponsors, who are accustomed to it as a goad to win elections. Instead, Thompson tried to tell them what they wanted to hear by criticizing radicals. Ordinarily this would have worked, but his ignorance of American politics and insensitivity to American rhetoric caused his sycophancy to go awry. He quoted a political scientist who described a 'Radical' tradition, with capital R, that in America 'seeks to eliminate interference by bosses, corruption and special interests and to tune in the authentic voice of the people by regulating party processes, by setting up a direct primary, by instituting the initiative and the referendum'. Thompson then asserted that America is now 'suffering from an excess of this Radical ideal'. He came to America with the message that we are too much opposed to 'bosses, corruption and special interests'. He did not know that reactionary interest groups like SE$_2$ claim to represent 'the authentic voice of the people', and in recent years they have gotten a lot of mileage from instituting the initiative and the referendum to oppose abortion, the Equal Rights Amendment, property taxes, environmental laws, and so on.

Thus, Thompson criticized the democratic institutions that all mainstream Americans agree in praising, and that right-wing groups as well as liberals use to their advantage. In the same paragraph he compounded his gaffe by misusing the whistle-blower metaphor. The American understanding is that individual citizens blow the whistle on government, not the other way around, yet the image Thompson presented for admiration was of European governments blowing the whistle on their citizens!

Thompson's ignorance is compounded with self-deception so that it is impossible to tell where one stops and the other begins. He said that sects are unstable, egalitarian, anti-scientific, single-interest, local groups that close themselves off from the rest of society. The only 'sect' he named was Friends of the Earth, but it does not fit his criteria. Its local, national and international levels of organization are concerned with a broad range of environmental interests, and its leaders have considerable influence in the larger society. Compared to the formality of his initial definition of 'caste' and 'sect', Thompson casually distinguished 'life sects' that might satisfy his criteria from the kind of sect that Friends of the Earth supposedly represents. Since he failed to define this other kind of sect his elaborate opening definition was hocus-pocus. Apparently he needed it to persuade himself that he was being rational and analytic.

Thompson asserted that Friends of the Earth is a powerful organization, but that 'a powerful sect is a colossal contradiction'. Instead of reasoning that his definition or facts were faulty he explained the contradiction by saying that the leaders used their 'impressive media skills' and practised 'a lot of skilfully disguised hypocrisy'. Also, for some unstated reason they are powerful because governments are eager to listen to them. The only 'sect' leaders Thompson mentioned were Jane Fonda, Paul Newman and Linda Ronstadt. I imagine that they would be astonished to learn that the Royal Anthropological Institute has published an 'anthropological analysis' exposing their hypocrisy and dread influence on American government. He advised SE$_2$ not 'to adopt the tactics of the other side' (publishing books like *Frozen Fire*, which he cites, or, Amory Lovins' *Soft Energy: Paths toward a durable peace*, to give a British example). Instead, Thompson recommends that 'Ridicule is a most effective medium and a well-chosen epithet, like "Porsche populist", is worth a hundred pages of analysis.'

Thompson's advice was incompetent: he assumed that his sponsors did not know that the critics of nuclear energy programs are often distinguished scientists, lawyers, physicians, bankers, artists, publishers, and so on. He advises ridiculing leaders of Friends of the Earth, without bothering to find out that this would include the Stanford University ecologist, Paul Ehrlich and the Nobel laureates, Konrad Lorenz and George Wald. In Thompson's terms they would be the kind of people that SE$_2$ members might dine with since they would share a 'caste-ist' point of view. Apparently knowing absolutely nothing about the membership of Friends of the Earth, or of other organizations like the Union of Concerned Scientists, the Scientists' Institute for Public Information, the groups Ralph Nader has initiated, and so on, Thompson assumed that his sponsors were equally uninformed and would appreciate the news that his 'anthropological analysis reveals that the anti-nuclear groups are not all the same'. Of course, 'anti-nuclear' is his label for such groups. They would say that they are for a scientifically informed, critical, responsible and democratic nuclear policy, along with other environmental and humanistic concerns. Thompson speculated, 'There is in Britain (and I suspect in the US, too) a group of lawyers opposed to nuclear power . . .', showing that he knew nothing at all about the Natural Resources Defense Council, the Environmental Defense Fund, and other law firms, or about the cases, legislative issues, and the arguments concerned with environmental policies. Perhaps he is too young to remember anthropologists who joined with other scientists to oppose the atmospheric tests of nuclear bombs in Micronesia, or Margaret Mead's work with Barry Commoner and others in the Scientists' Institute for Public Information. Anthropology is an historical and contextual discipline. Anyone who presumes to work in this field should be responsible to its traditions, and to the facts. By publishing his talk the Royal Anthropological Institute has validated his claim to having made an 'anthropological analysis'. This seems to me an action to be regretted.

Charles Leslie
Professor of Anthropology and the Humanities,
University of Delaware, Newark, Delaware

We do not regret having published Michael Thompson's provocative article. An anthropological tradition of examining conservation issues was set by Mary Douglas in her lecture ten years ago 'Environments at risk' though she did not adopt a 'brief' for any school of opinion. If Dr Thompson's facts are wrong, Professor Leslie should correct them. RAINews, has, of course, no commitment to either side of the nuclear energy debate. Editor.

Chapter 24

Arne Kalland

■ WHALE POLITICS AND GREEN LEGITIMACY:
A CRITIQUE OF THE ANTI-WHALING
CAMPAIGN, *Anthropology Today*, 9.6, December
1993, pp. 3–7

NORWAY RESUMED COMMERCIAL CATCHES of minke whales
in June 1993, in spite of angry protests and threats of boycott from environmental and animal welfare/rights groups as well as from politicians and governments. In this short paper I will ask why whales and whaling receive this attention,
by analysing, first, how whales have been turned into a totem for many people in
the western world, and, second, why some governments have found anti-whaling
campaigns good issues to support. I will undoubtedly provoke some 'whale-lovers',
but time is overdue to take a critical approach to the environmentalist movement. It will be argued that anti-whaling campaigns do more harm than good to the
environment.

From ecology to whale rights

When the International Whaling Commission (IWC) voted in 1982 to halt all
commercial whaling, it was claimed that a moratorium was necessary until uncer-
tainties regarding the conditions of whale stocks had been removed and a new
management scheme had been adopted.

Since then, research has shown that stocks of minke whale can sustain controlled
harvests both in the North Atlantic and in the Antarctic. At the same time, scientists from many countries have worked together in IWC's Scientific Committee in
order to develop a 'revised management procedure' (RMP), the most sophisticated
ever devised for any marine exploitation. There is now consensus in the committee
that the RMP can be implemented. Despite the progress made during the last
decade, however, IWC is unwilling to adopt the RMP or to lift the moratorium,
which prompted the chairman of the committee to resign in protest after the last
IWC meeting in Kyoto in May 1993. After having pointed out how IWC had missed
a unique opportunity to 'put in place a mechanism for the safe management of

commercial whaling', Dr Philip Hammond, of the Sea Mammal Research Unit at Cambridge, continues in his letter of resignation:

> What is the point of having a Scientific Committee if its unanimous recommendations on matters of primary importance are treated with such contempt? . . .
>   I have come to the conclusion that I can no longer justify to myself being the organizer of and spokesman for a Committee whose work is held in such disregard by the body to which it is responsible.

Environmental groups have reacted to higher population estimates and the RMP in various ways. All the main Norwegian environmental organizations have left the anti-whaling bandwagon and turned to what they consider more urgent matters, such as acid rain, global heating and thinning of the ozone layer. The main international organizations, however, continue their anti-whaling campaigns, and in so doing they have used two main strategies.[1] Realizing that the 'terms of the [whaling] convention have required that this debate be conducted in a scientific guise' (Butterworth 1992: 532), some whale protectionists stubbornly stick to the ecological discourse denying the validity of new scientific evidence. There has nevertheless been a clear shift from an ecological discourse to animal welfare or rights discourses in recent years, not only in organizations like Greenpeace and WWF but in governmental rhetoric, particularly in English-speaking countries.

Leading UK and US politicians, for example, continue to support the anti-whaling crusade but claim that it is now necessary to argue against whaling on ethical and moral grounds. To many people in whaling countries, however, it is incomprehensible why the British government regards whaling as 'uncivilized' while fox-hunting is a 'basic human freedom'.[2] It is equally incomprehensible why it is more ethically right to eat meat from animals that have been kept captive, have never seen the sky and end their days in slaughter-houses, in some instances after long and painful transportation across Europe, than to eat the meat of whales which have been killed in a couple of minutes, on the average. Many whalers do not understand why the IWC ignores the recommendations of its own scientists and why the IWC allows Alaskan Inuits to hunt the endangered bowhead,[3] while the Japanese are not allowed to harvest the Antarctic stocks of minke whales estimated to be about 750,000. Or why whales among all animals have been singled out as special and have become such powerful symbols. Questions such as these ought to be of great interest not only to affected whalers and their few friends, but to anthropologists as well, not least those of us who are interested in people's perceptions of nature, in political rhetorics and in power relations.

The 'super-whale' – our marine relative?

Whales do not easily fit into our simple categories of mammals and fish, and hence form an anomalous category of animals which easily become the object of myths and taboos (Douglas 1966). Moreover, we know relatively little about what is going on in the oceans, which opens this realm to mystery, manipulation and myth creation

(Pálsson 1991: 95; Kalland and Moeran 1992: 7–8). Finally, the ocean – consisting largely of salt and water – becomes *the* symbol of purity, and thus stands in sharp contrast to the polluted soil on which we land mammals tread. Cetaceans are animals to which symbolic significance can easily be ascribed.

Environmental and animal rights groups have skilfully played on our susceptibility towards whales and created an image of a 'super-whale' by lumping together traits found in a number of species (Kalland 1993), thereby masking the great variety that exists in size, behaviour and abundance among the 75 or so species of cetaceans. We are told that 'the whale' is the largest animal on earth (this applies to the blue whale); that it has the largest brain on earth (the sperm whale); that it has a large brain-to-body-weight ratio (the bottlenose dolphin); that it sings nicely (the humpback whale); that it has nurseries (some dolphins); that it is friendly (the gray whale); that it is endangered (the blue and right whales) and so on. By talking about *the* whale, an image of a single whale possessing *all* these traits emerges.

Whales are often anthropomorphized by being given human traits as well. They are depicted as living in societies similar to our own. The super-whale is endowed with all the qualities we would like to see in our fellow humans: kindness, caring, playfulness. While commercialization has penetrated most contemporary human relationships, leaving many people with a nagging conscience for not taking care of ageing parents and for not giving the children the attention they need, whales are depicted as the guardians of old values now lost. The super-whale cares for the sick and dying, baby-sits and runs nurseries, without charging anything for these services.

In further attempts at mystifying whales, emphasis is also given to the fact that whales have existed for millions of years. It is claimed that their long history gives them special rights to the sea (e.g. Barstow 1991) – a kind of 'aboriginal' of the oceans, apparently – and that whales have had more time to develop their intellectual capacity. Whales are said to have been highly intelligent when humans were still 'insignificant nocturnal insectivores' (Watson 1985: 48). The age of whales places them above humans; they become our teachers and might be capable of telling us stories 25 million years old if we only manage to learn their language (Lilly, quoted in Linehan 1979: 539).

In short, whales 'represent the closest approach to civilization, not as defined in terms of machine or technology, but as realized among all intelligent beings, cetacean or human, where communication and social bonds transcended the mere exigencies of life' (Abbey 1990: 80). What *Homo sapiens* is on land, cetaceans are in the sea (Barstow 1991: 7). They are our brethren. In Lévi-Straussian terms, whale society has become a metaphor for the lost human paradise or utopian world, and caring for whales has become a metaphor for kindness, for being 'good'.

An urban totem

Environmental issues are complex and beyond the comprehension of most of us. To mentally organize a bewildering array of conflicting messages, simplifications are called for, and totemism is one powerful symbol system which brings order by creating distinctions where none previously existed. Parts of the environmental and animal rights movements make use of totemic systems of thought, by which mankind is divided into two opposing categories: those who care for the earth and the future *versus* those who seek short-term profit. In this world-view, whales serve as totem for 'nature-loving' people and money as a totem for 'greedy' capitalists, represented by the whalers, who are depicted as evil, blood-thirsty barbarians (Kalland 1993).

Claims that whalers are evil are even presented in scientific journals. In an article in *The American Journal of International Law*, for example, D'Amato and Chopra (1991: 27) suggest that whalers are more likely 'to accept genocide of "inferior" human beings'. Saying 'no' to whaling is, on the other hand, synonymous with being civilized. 'Caring for whales is a sign of personal and social maturity' preaches Victor Scheffer (1991: 19), former member of the US Marine Mammal Commission. And a UK minister of agriculture John Gummer, promised before the Parliament 'to do my best to ensure that Iceland does not leave the IWC . . . I want to keep Iceland within the fold of civilized nations' (3 June 1991).

The IWC has authorized aboriginal peoples to catch whales, but if the hunt is for commercial purposes it creates disorder in this binary conception of the world. Hence, aboriginal peoples can hunt whales only as long as this is done to meet subsistence needs, keeping them shielded from commercial activities.[4] At the annual IWC meetings Greenlanders and Alaskans therefore have to stand trial before the IWC judges testifying to their own 'primitiveness'. The protectionists thus seek to 'freeze' their cultures by appropriating aboriginal people's obvious rights to self-determination and to partake in the world economy on their own terms and not be dictated to by outsiders. The concept 'aboriginal subsistence whaling' has turned into a powerful concept in the hands of imperialism (Kalland 1992a).

Moreover, the concept is flawed in several ways. Empirically because there are no qualitative differences between, for example, minke whaling in Greenland (allowed by IWC) and in Iceland, Japan and Norway (ISGSTW 1992). Logically it is flawed, as Brian Moeran has shown (1992), because 'subsistence' and 'commercial' are a false opposition. Both are forms of exchange and the end-products constitute commodities, whether whaling is done for 'subsistence' or 'commercial' purposes. The concept 'aboriginal' is also fraught with difficulties. The Greenlanders and the Faroese, for example, both enjoy home rule under the Danish realm, yet the former are classified by the IWC as 'aboriginals' while the latter are not.[5] Hence, minke whaling in Greenland is endorsed by the international community although half the meat might enter the commercial market, while boycotts have been launched against the Faroese for their pilot whaling, although much less meat enters the market.

Tournaments of value

With the focus on commercial activities, it is not surprising that the whale protectionists have tried to destroy the markets for whale products, i.e. to remove whale products from the 'commodity state' (Appadurai 1986) by imposing trade restrictions, by placing whales on 'endangered species' lists, and by imposing sanctions on

Figure 24.1 Anti-whaling demonstration, 1992, outside the hotel in Glasgow where the 44th Annual IWC Meeting was held.

whaling nations. At the ideological level it has become barbaric – bordering on cannibalism – to eat whale meat. Today more people feel aversion to eating whale meat than most other kinds of meat (Freeman and Kellert 1992: 29).

At the same time, the super-whale has been commoditized. What has turned this image into a commodity is the emergence of a new demand among individuals, enterprises and governments to appear 'green'. This demand has been created by the growing environmental awareness among people, fuelled by the crisis-maximizing strategies of many environmental groups. In the ecological discourse, whales have come to play the role of a metonym for nature, and whaling has become a symbol for the environmental and animal welfare movements because this issue provides them with an easily identifiable *enemy* (a few whalers living in marginal areas of the world) and a sense of *urgency* (whales allegedly being endangered), two factors a consultant to Greenpeace identified as the requirements for raising money (Spencer *et al.* 1991: 179).

We are then faced with two simultaneous processes in changing the 'commodity path': one seeks to remove the whalers' products from the commodity state; the other turns whale symbols into new commodities. Both processes are highlighted at the annual IWC meetings and other 'tournaments of value', where 'central tokens of value in the society' are contested (Appadurai 1986: 21). Tournaments of value provide the arena, and ecological and animal welfare discourses provide the cultural framework that protects transactions between companies, governments and environmental/animal welfare groups from being classified as bribes or blackmailing.

Figure 24.2 *Daily Star*, 11 May 1991, front page.

The annual IWC meetings, where the world is totemically divided into the so-called 'like-minded group' (i.e. those opposed to whaling) and the 'whaling nations', are the most spectacular of these tournaments,[6] with three actors competing for status, rank, fame and reputation.

The national delegations are led by diplomats or high-ranking bureaucrats, and may also include environmentalists and animal rights advocates (in the case of anti-whaling nations), whalers (in the case of whaling nations) and scientists. Their task is to contest opposing values pertaining to whales and their exploitation (Moeran 1992) and to give scientific legitimacy to their positions.

A large number of non-governmental organizations (NGOs), the majority of which are anti-whaling, play important roles during the meetings. First, they lobby the delegates and try to convince the general public that their world view is the right one. Second, they report directly back to their followers without going through the whims of mass media, thus enabling them to control the distribution of information regarding their own activities. Finally, the NGOs monitor the proceedings and report their interpretations and evaluations of the delegates' performances to the mass media, the third actor in the drama without whose participation the meeting would have been a much less attractive arena for contesting the commodity path.

The press is severely restricted in their work as it has no access to the conference room. Instead, coffee breaks have been turned into intense press-briefing sessions where the media rely heavily on the services of the NGOs and some of the delegates. NGOs from both sides are thereby put in a unique position to manipulate the flow of information, to put pressure on national governments and politicians, to endorse their opinions and statements thus enhancing their prospects of being re-elected, and to create a 'ranking list' of the most 'progressive' delegations and nations. With anti-whaling NGOs in a majority and with most of the media coming from anti-whaling nations, it should come as no surprise that anti-whaling sentiments dominate the newspaper columns and news broadcasts. In short, the IWC meetings provide environmental and animal rights groups with a rare opportunity to get their message out to millions of people.

Whales as symbols – good or bad?

A Norwegian colleague of mine has argued against whaling because whales have become symbols to many people, and we ought to respect this symbol. Moreover, he claims that this symbol has contributed positively to the higher environmental awareness among large groups of people worldwide. Similar sentiments are held by many whale protectionists (e.g. WWF).

Of course, there is a widely held notion that we ought to respect one another's symbols. Defilements of national symbols, such as burning flags, are therefore powerful expressions of anger and protest. Similarly, eating whale meat, i.e. eating the totem animal of environmental and animal rights groups, has for some people become a means to express their indignation against what they conceive of as outsiders' infringement on their customary rights to harvest not only whales but marine resources in general. Norwegian fishermen-cum-whalers, for example, feel they have lost influence over local resources to the national bureaucracy and increasingly to international bodies. To them, whaling has become a symbol of their rights to harvest local resources in a sustainable way. To governments of whaling nations, whaling has become a symbol of national sovereignty. Thus whales and whaling have taken on new symbolic meanings to the whalers and the whaling nations as well.

This does not mean that whales and whaling were not loaded with symbolic meanings before the anti-whaling campaigns were launched. On the contrary, whales and whaling have long been powerful symbols to whalers in Alaska (Alaska

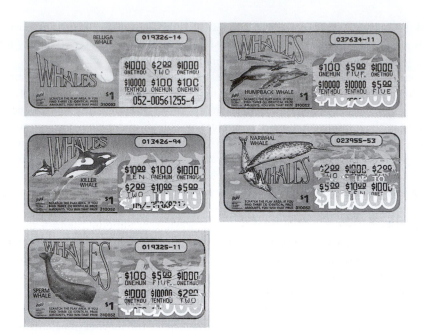

Figure 24.3   Scratchcards – British Columbia Lottery Corporation.

Figure 24.4   Whale motif on a fire-station in Ayukawa, Japan.

Consultants, Inc. 1984), Canada (Freeman *et al.*, 1992), the Faroe Islands (Wylie and Margolin 1981), Greenland (Caulfield 1991), Japan (Kalland and Moeran 1992), and Norway (ISG 1992). In all whaling societies there exist rules as to how the animal shall be shared or the profit used in order to reproduce the social and cosmic order (Moeran 1992). More generally, whaling is a way of life and must be seen 'as a process whereby hunters mutually create and recreate *one another*, through the medium of their encounter with prey' (Ingold 1986: 111). Whales typically constitute multi-vocal symbols in that they convey several meanings simultaneously, and no 'meaning' deserves *a priori* more respect than the others.

The super-whale might have contributed to a higher environmental awareness among people, but we have to ask a what cost. The campaigns against whaling have triggered nationalistic sentiments in Iceland (Brydon 1991) and Japan (Kalland and Moeran 1992), have turned coastal people against environmental organizations and have turned whale eating into ritual consumptions of the enemies' totem animal. Worse, the campaigns distract attention from issues of greater importance to the global environment and have produced a symbol which individuals and corporations can afford to buy. The totem is for sale and one can buy a place in the sun, as well as green legitimacy, by joining the flock of 'converts'.

Many people are in need of a green alibi. Some buy totem emblems to stick on their jackets or windscreens to display their green state of mind. Others buy the logo of environmental organizations in order to give their products a green image.[7] Such connections are deliberately made in fund-raising campaigns, as when WWF Denmark wrote to business leaders:

> Sponsorship [of a whale] will link your activities in a positive manner to the WWF . . . A sponsorship will provide your business with the opportunity of showing associates that it takes the environment and the 'green wave' seriously . . . I am sure you will appreciate the opportunities a whale sponsorship will provide for your business.

One leading Danish chemical company bought a sperm whale and has got its name and green legitimacy linked to WWF, but whether this has contributed to the welfare of the global environment is rather doubtful.

The anti-whaling campaign is an ideal issue for national governments and polluting industries to support. Being of only marginal economic importance – and in most countries of no importance at all – whaling is a 'safe' issue and there is hardly anything to lose by joining the crowd. The rewards in terms of 'green images' are, on the other hand, substantial. The anti-whaling campaigns, therefore, offer governments and industries an opportunity to show their consideration for the environment, while at the same time they have proved excellent fund-raisers for the environmental and animal rights movements. By giving support to the super-whale myth, companies and governments have acquired 'green' legitimacy (and partial immunity) while the movements have got political legitimacy in return. It is, perhaps, not coincidental that some of the nations most vehemently opposed to whaling (and sealing and elephant hunting for that matter) are among the nations with the poorest records when it comes to international cooperation to combat acid rain, global heating and destruction of the ozone layer.

Notes

1   There are good economic reasons to continue the anti-whaling campaigns because they have proved extremely efficient fund-raisers for many of these organizations, some of which have been labelled 'money-making machines' (cf. Schwarz 1991, see also Spencer *et al.* 1991).

2   No longer in 2001. *Editor.*

3   The bowhead stock was estimated by the Scientific Committee to be only 2,000 animals or less in 1981, when IWC went against the recommendations of its Scientific Committee and endorsed this hunt under the concept 'aboriginal subsistence whaling'. Fortunately, later estimates have set the figure at about 7,000 animals.

4   Commercialism in itself seems to be considered bad by the protectionists as well as by the majority of the contracting members to the IWC, and it is ironic that this view is expressed by governments that are usually strong advocates of free trade and movement of capital.

5   Concepts like 'aboriginal', 'indigenous' and 'native', which are used interchangeably by IWC, all imply a state of domination. This means that the Greenlanders should no longer be classified as 'aboriginals' after they obtained home rule (Dahl 1992). The Faroese have never been regarded as aboriginals, probably because of their 'Nordic' classification, i.e. blond hair and blue eyes.

6   Other important tournaments are national parliaments, the EC Parliament, whale strandings, whale safaris and anti-whaling demonstrations.

7   The Norwegian state oil company, for example, paid about £100,000 for the use of the WWF logo when the company launched an advertisement drive in order to increase its sale or oil-products in Denmark.

References

Abbey, Lloyd. 1990. *The Last Whales*. London: Doubleday.

Alaska Consultants, Inc. with Stephen Braund & Associates. 1984. *Subsistence Study of Alaska Whaling Villages*. Report to the US Department of Interior, Washington, DC.

Appadurai, Arjun. 1986. 'Introduction: Commodities and the politics of value'. In A. Appadurai (ed.) *The Social Life of Things – Commodities in Cultural Perspective*. Cambridge: Cambridge U.P., pp. 3–63.

Barstow, Robbins. 1991. 'Whales are uniquely special'. In *Why Whales* (eds N. Davies, A.M. Smith, S.R. Whyte and V. Williams). Bath, UK: Whale and Dolphin Conservation Soc., pp. 5–7.

Brydon, Anne. 1991. *The Eye of the Guest: Icelandic Nationalist Discourse and the Whaling Issue*. PhD thesis, Department of Anthropology, McGill U.

Butterworth, D.C. 1992. Science and sentimentality. *Nature*, Vol. 357 (June 18), 532–4.

Caulfield, Richard A. 1991. *Qeqertarsuarmi arfanniarneq. Greenlandic Inuit Whaling in Qeqertarsuaq Kommune, West Greenland*. Cambridge: IWC/TC/43/AS4.

Dahl, Jens. 1992. *Indfødte folk* [Indigenous Peoples]. Copenhagen: IWGIA.

D'Amato, Anthony and Sudhir K. Chopra. 1991. Whales: Their emerging right to life. *Am. J. of Int. Law* 85(1): 21–62.

Douglas, Mary, 1966. *Purity and Danger: An Analysis of the Concepts of Pollution and Taboo*. London: Routledge and Kegan Paul.

Freeman, Milton M.R. and Stephen R. Kellert. 1992. *Public Attitudes to Whales: Results of a Six-Country Survey*. Edmonton: U. of Alberta, Canadian Circumpolar Inst./New Haven: Yale U., School of Forestry and Environmental Studies.

Freeman, Milton M.R., Eleanor E. Wein and Darren E. Keith. 1992. *Recovering Rights: Bowhead Whales and Inuvialuit Subsistence in Western Canadian Arctic*. Edmonton: Canadian Circumpolar Inst.

Ingold, Tim, 1986. *The Appropriation of Nature*. Manchester: Manchester U.P.

ISG (International Study Group on Norwegian Small-Type Whaling) 1992. *Norwegian Small-Type Whaling in Cultural Perspectives*. Tromsø: Norwegian Coll. of Fisheries Science.

ISGSTW (International Study Group for Small-Type Whaling) 1992. 'Similarities and diversity in coastal whaling operations: A comparison of small-scale whaling activities in Greenland, Iceland, Japan and Norway. Report of the Symposium on Utilization of Marine Living Resources for Subsistence (Vol. II) held at Taiji, Japan. Tokyo: Inst. of Cetacean Research.

Kalland, Arne 1992a. Whose whale is that? Diverting the commodity path. *Maritime Anthropological Studies* 5(2): 16–45.

—— 1992b. 'Aboriginal subsistence whaling: A concept in the service of imperialism?' In G. Blichfeldt (ed.) *Bigger than Whales*. Reine, Norway: High North Alliance.

—— 1993. Management by totemization: Whale symbolism and the anti-whaling campaign. *Arctic* 46(2): 124–33.

Kalland, Arne and Brian Moeran. 1992. *Japanese Whaling – End of an Era?* London: Curzon P.

Linehan, E.J. 1979. The trouble with dolphins. *National Geographic* 15(5): 506–40.

Moeran, Brian. 1992. The cultural construction of value. 'Subsistence', 'commercial' and other terms in the debate about whaling. *Maritime Anthropological Studies*, 5(2): 1–15.

Pálsson, Gísli. 1991. *Coastal Economies, Cultural Accounts. Human Ecology and Icelandic Discourse*. Manchester: Manchester U.P.

Scheffer, Victor. 1991. 'Why should we care about whales?' In *Why Whales?* (eds N. Davies, A.M. Smith, S.R. Whyte and V. Williams). Bath: Whale and Dolphin Conservation Soc.

Schwarz, Ulrich. 1991. Umweltkonzern im Zwielicht. Geldmachine Greenpeace. *Der Spiegel* C 45(38) (16 September): 84–105.

Spencer, Leslie with Jan Bollwerk and Richard C. Morais. 1991. The not too peaceful world of Greenpeace. *Forbes Magazine*, November 11, pp. 174–180.

Watson, Lyall. 1985. *Whales of the World*. London: Hutchinson.

Wylie, Jonathan and Margolin, David. 1981. *The Ring of Dancers: Images of Faroese Culture*. Philadelphia: U. of Pennsylvania P.

Update by Arne Kalland, 2001

Since this article was written in 1993, the whaling controversy has, if anything, become even more deadlocked. The IWC has still not implemented the RMP; on the contrary the IWC voted in 1994 in favour of a whale sanctuary covering much of the southern hemisphere. Norway continues her commercial catches of about 500 minke whales annually, lifting her self-imposed ban on exports in 2001, whereas Japan has enlarged her scientific whaling programme to include the North Pacific in addition to the Antarctic. Canadian Inuit have taken a handful of bowheads under threats of trade sanctions from the United States, and Russian whaling in Chukotka has been replaced by re-invented indigenous whaling regimes.

The resumption of whaling in 1999 by the Makah of the north-west coast of America has undoubtedly been the most dramatic event since 1993. Forced to stop in the 1920s due to decimation of stocks, this north-west coast nation wanted to resume whaling to revitalize its culture. Stocks having recovered, environmentalists have reacted to the Makah request in different ways. Greenpeace has recognized this as aboriginal subsistence whaling. Paul Watson and his Sea Shepherd Conservation Society, on the other hand, has led militant protests claiming the 70-year hunting interruption proves that the Makah have no cultural needs to whale and that what they really want is to get rich on exports to Japan. To justify whaling by claims to tradition made one protester 'anxious to know where I may apply for a license to kill Indians' because 'it was [my forefathers'] tradition to kill every Redskin they saw' (quoted in Ellingson 2001: 370).

Others want to resume whaling, and in 1997 the World Council of Whalers was established to unite actual and potential whalers around the world. The Council unites groups from more than 20 countries: from Iñupiat and Makah in the west to the Japanese and Chukchi in the east, and from the Greenlanders and Norwegians in the north to the Maori and Tongan in the south. Led by a Nuu-chah-nulth hereditary whaling chief from Vancouver Island, the Council has also become an important voice within the indigenous peoples' movement.

Reference

Ellingson, Ter. 2001. *The myth of the noble savage*. Berkeley: University of California Press.

Other recent publications on whaling

Caulfield, Richard A. 1997. *Greenlanders, whales, and whaling: Sustainability and self-determination in the Arctic*. Hanover, NH: University Press of New England.

Freeman, Milton M.R., Lyudmila Bogoslovskaya, Richard A. Caulfield, Ingmar Egede, Igor I. Krupnik and Marc G. Stevenson. 1998. *Inuit, whaling, and sustainability*. Walnut Creek, CA: AltaMira Press.

Freeman, Milton M.R. and Urs P. Kreuter (eds). 1994. *Elephants and whales: Resources for whom?* Basel: Gordon and Breach Publishers.

Friedheim, Robert (ed.). 2001. *Towards a sustainable whaling regime*. Edmonton: Canadian Circumpolar Institute Press.

Jenkins, L. and C. Romanzo. 1998. 'Makah whaling: aboriginal subsistence or a stepping stone to undermining the commercial whaling moratorium?' *Colorado Journal of International Law and Policy* 9: 71–114.

Kalland, Arne and Frank Sejersen (forthcoming). *Marine mammals in northern cultures*.

Nuttall, Mark. 1998. *Protecting the Arctic: Indigenous peoples and cultural survival*. Amsterdam: Harwood Academic Publishers.

Nuttall, Mark (forthcoming). *North Atlantic whaling: Politics, ethics, culture*. New York: Mellen Press.

Stoett, Peter J. 1997. *The international politics of whaling*. Vancouver: UBC Press.

Chapter 25

Liliane Kuczynski

■ RETURN OF LOVE: EVERYDAY LIFE
AND AFRICAN DIVINATION IN PARIS,[1]
Anthropology Today, 4.3, June 1988, pp. 6–9

A FRICAN MARABOUTS IN PARIS are increasingly present in the media. Increasingly, too, French people are coming to consult them to settle various problems of daily life. What I put forward here, starting from the case of a young woman, Marie, which I followed for more than a year, are some preliminary thoughts on why French people are going to see marabouts, what they are seeking to put right in these encounters.

Marie is under 30; she is cultivated, from an affluent social background, a Parisian. She follows a liberal profession. Over more than one year, she has consulted a dozen marabouts,[2] contacted through different intermediaries: three through newspapers, seven through the recommendation of African friends or acquaintances. The remaining two introduced themselves or were introduced as replacements for colleagues already consulted who had gone back to Africa. The aim of her venture is to make a man come back to her whom she has loved unrequitedly.

This case study was conducted over a period of time with many incidents and it allows me to suggest that Marie's actions are a sort of paradigm of different attitudes towards the marabout. Moreover, research carried out with other French people as subjects shows that those attitudes, far from being specific to Marie, can be identified as constants.[3]

How the intervention of marabouts is justified

It was first of all for practical reasons that Marie decided to consult marabouts. Starting from a precise problem put by the client or brought to light by divination, they propose concrete solutions. 'They take action' she says. This makes them different from clairvoyants, whom she also consults but who for the most part do only diagnostic and prognostic work. As for those clairvoyants who do intervene,

Figure 25.1   A marabout's publicity card, Paris, 2001.

it is their ideology ('religious frippery') which Marie has a horror of. So it is to other cultural references that Marie directs herself; some aspects of her groping search can be discerned in the personality of the marabout as she describes him.

'Psychics' are no more suited to her wishes than clairvoyants. There is no question for her of gradually giving up, coming to terms with a reality that is hostile to her. Clairvoyants and psychics have in common their inability to resolve a situation about which she will stand no discussion. Little by little, though, marabouts stand for a 'taking charge' of her; though this psychological requirement is surely there in her – and vastly more important to her than she admits – her *explicit* search is for a magical solution. Marie thinks she has used all means at her disposal in a situation such as hers. It is necessary, then, to get away from the 'brick wall' she is up against, to pass to a different mode of knowledge accessible only to a particular category of individuals.

We must underline here how Marie's commitment is constructed and argued. Justifying, for example, her successive recourse to several marabouts, she considers that, if the action of one of them has not satisfied her, it is because, in his case, he had either too particular a point of view, or inadequate skill, or lack of enthusiasm. But the recourse to another form of knowledge is never questioned. It would be false, though, to state that, either in a moment of lucidity or in one of weariness, she never voices a doubt, a wish for proof ('Is it working?'), questions to which by way of reply she can only get stories, that is to say interpretations through the prism of a culture and an individuality. Such, indeed, is her mental functioning that, it would seem, the reply is unimportant.

Why does she go to African marabouts? Apart from their large number in Paris and the ubiquitous and very personal character of their publicity, Africa has a place in Marie's life. Her father spent long years there and the man she loves was born there. Sufficient elements, perhaps, to suggest that there is in her orientation towards African marabouts a return towards part of her own history.

Relationship of client and marabout

When Marie consults marabouts, she is in a state of extreme urgency, and so of complete dependence on them. Doubt creeps sometimes into her mind, admittedly, and there are marabouts whom she doesn't hesitate to call 'charlatans'[4] either because one of them seems too purely commercial, or because she says she sees through the 'faking' carried out by another to see whether he can intervene, or because yet another seems to her 'not sure enough of himself' or 'not commanding respect'. But there is only one whom she has given up consulting.

Marie submits herself to all stages of consultation. She is indifferent to numerous divinatory techniques – chaplets, geomancy, casting of cowries, calls to genies, chiromancy, calabashes, stones and so forth. But she is straightaway sensitive to the gaze that the marabout fixes on her 'to understand'. A psychological relationship, then, but apparently entirely geared towards action because usually she starts the encounter by telling the marabout what brings her, rather than leaving him to guess as is often the custom.

As regards the interpretation that is given of her case, her attitude is the same. She yields to it, whether it is that her beloved does not want a woman for the moment, or that he has become infatuated with another woman, or that she is possessed by her own genie who is keeping all men away. If, deep down, she is able to refuse one or other of these explanations, she is nonetheless committed to entering the marabout's system: first, because beyond the interpretation, it is action that she has in mind, and, second, because in attributing to the marabout a 'power', she fears antagonizing this by any kind of opposition.

If, in the course of divination and interpretation, Marie involves herself as little as possible in what is called 'work', it does nonetheless become clear that her cultural relationship with the marabouts is one of conflict. This 'work' is secret, carried out when the client is absent according to ad hoc principles; the visible part is the prescription of certain rituals and the handing over of the *gris-gris* or amulet. Here there are two stumbling-blocks for Marie: the payment of the marabout, and the fixing of time-limits, which are two linked problems. As she considers, in fact, that marabouts are providers of services like others, Marie dithers between two attitudes: paying a large sum without discussion to reach her goals regardless of cost, or establishing a bargaining relationship – which some marabouts fit in with perfectly. But in both cases, for Marie payment of the marabout is binding him and obliging him to intervene. The logical consequence of this business relationship is that she feels herself justified in making certain demands, from which stems the second problem, that of time-limits.

It is clear that, for Marie, making a love come back when it is slipping away cannot be placed in an indefinite future. Many marabouts, for reasons internal to their work, refuse to fix estimates of time-limits, contenting themselves with the statement 'this will not go on'. That is why remuneration and time-estimates are linked: because she pays, she expects a sort of 'deus ex machina' coming from specialists that she thinks are all-powerful. Or again: there is no reason to pay for a hypothetical and distant result. Expecting a guarantee is part of the essence of a commercial relationship. Marie really harries some marabouts to extract a date from them. Again, in a moment of great distress, she may pay a high fee to a new marabout, contacted only because his publicity claimed 'results within a week'; and with another she wants to 'ask for a settlement'; she has paid, the result did not come, so he has done nothing.

However, if Marie fits well into this exchange relationship – analogous, for her, to paying a psychoanalyst – she appreciates that, sometimes, relations can be different, which shows the ambivalence of her attitude. Some marabouts, to whom she applied through one of their friends or relatives, ask for no remuneration, putting their personal loyalties before their livelihood. Another, to whom she explained her financial problems, went so far as to offer to lend her money. Marie, it seems, experiences the need – despite the commercial character of the relationship between her and the marabouts – to idealize what she calls the flow of sympathy that she says she finds only with marabouts.

Broadening the problem of the commercial relationship between marabout and client, we can advance the hypothesis that what is chiefly at stake is European notions of time. If marabouts fix estimates of time, which is contrary to their tradition, it is because their relationships have become commercial and because Europeans insist on being told *when* what they are paying for is to be achieved.

As regards observance of prescribed acts, Marie wavers between various attitudes. She accepts any sacrifices, whether in kind (lengths of white cloth, or fruits, or sugar) or in money. These may be of a certain sum to be given to the first person met in the street, or gifts to the marabout of a sum allowing him to buy a sacrificial animal, a cock or sheep. (Increasingly in France, marabouts take charge completely of animal sacrifice, seemingly wanting to save both themselves and their clients from too great a cultural confrontation.) For Marie, these sacrifices are a necessary step towards unravelling the problem facing her.

She receives the *gris-gris* – usually spells on sheets of paper tied or stuck up in a packet – without questioning their contents, even when the marabout does not inspire her total confidence. The secrecy, which is necessary to the marabout's strategy and to her own, she accepts totally; the meaning she leaves to the marabout. However, she observes the instructions fairly scrupulously: calling the name of her loved one so many times in such and such a situation, or putting the *gris-gris* somewhere. In her state of tension about the result, she breaks some completely intangible rules: for example, she fails to suspend the ritual during her menstruation, a suspension which for her would be bound to delay the result. Certain acts, whose performance makes her sceptical, she does feel the need to question. Thus the meaning of purification, essential to the 'bath' ritual, escaped her for a long time: this is to do with a liquid over which the marabout says his prayers, or a dilution of magical writings which the client must pass over her body or face. She cannot acknowledge the value of this practice, whose intangibility and lack of material effect on her she finds shocking. Finally there are the acts that she 'overdetermines'; such and such a *gris-gris*, which the marabout has said must be thrown in the Seine, will not in fact be thrown any old where: Marie creates an imaginary trajectory, according to which it is from this bridge and not elsewhere that the water should carry it away. Is it necessary to emphasize how totally Marie lives in the symbolic?

The meaning-system of the marabout, who is the one who deals the cards, goes by the way. But Marie creates her own code of conduct. Secrecy is desired, respected, adopted, but it is just because it exists that, paradoxically, it creates a system open enough for other codes to intrude. Outside the obvious meaning given to prescribed acts, it is clear that they mean something else too for Marie. In her search for a love which is fleeing, the marabouts are for her a hope which is indispensable even if it fades away. The amulets become viaticums, surrogate objects whose possession helps to overcome absence. In a complementary way, these constraining acts, rituals reintroducing order into her devastated daily life, provide a moratorium which is at time indispensable in that they constantly reactivate hope, and at times intolerable in that they constantly reactivate her anguish.

The personality of the marabout

Even if Marie says she is often clear about doubtful aspects of her relationship with the marabouts, it is true nonetheless that her attitude and her speech unfold an imaginary, completely idealized image of the marabout, certainly the construction of her own search. The marabout is part of the alternative group of 'gentle' therapies. She says of one marabout, who uses mainly plants and roots, that she imagines him as being a 'very gentle type', before even having seen him.

The marabout is charismatic. Those who make most impression on Marie are those with whom she experiences 'sureness', 'serenity'. In these alone is she able, that is to say willing, to 'believe'. The person of the marabout exhales a 'power' which she seeks to absorb. With others, she says, she is impressed by their 'great goodness', their 'purity'; one of them works outside Paris, in a 'little village' (which turns out to be St-Quentin) to escape the dross of the big city. Another one is not 'contaminated' by commercial society: he has no video recorder, no colour TV. This quasi-mystical being that she sketches is perhaps a response to her rejection of clairvoyants and psychics, whose associations are only too well-known to her. One could say that there is a double, non-simultaneous vision of the marabout: he is described as, and behaves like, a person decanted of all impurity, although his room is often invaded by consumer goods which place him without possible doubt in the commercial society, and this the client knows perfectly well. The marabout, like his client, plays when it suits him on one or other of these angles.

The marabout is a 'good sorcerer', a male version of the 'good fairy'. Marie immerses herself in her dream. In her very strong desire to return to a carefree childhood, she reconstitutes a utopia, a place where desires are still magically realized by the mediation of a good and powerful being.

The marabout is a mediator in whose hands she deposits her problem, leaving him to resolve it in her place. The consequences of this taking charge, indispensable to Marie, go well beyond an explicit request to take action. In so far as she gives them her confidence, Marie turns marabouts into a sort of safety-rail; they help her to take up a more normal life-rhythm. In their practice, an element necessary to their success is restoring calm to the client, 'cooling down the heart' to use the traditional expression; but it is clear that Marie is looking for psychological help. Paradoxically, the marabouts could well be steering Marie towards a working through of mourning, though they are certainly not wishing to. What she seeks from them is 'reassurance'. She creates a relationship of protection/dependence, going so far as to speak of the 'paternal' character of certain marabouts. Marie insists that this reassurance comes very little through words. She certainly feels, in their way of being, a conviviality which touches her. Certainly too this reassurance is due to the marabouts' 'taking action'. But above all they reassure her by refraining from putting into question either herself or her relationships with others. In short, the marabouts' words are accepted by her only when they echo her own. She can do without their interpretations. Moreover, when the marabouts' words are not just echoes, she rejects them. Here are two examples. One marabout could not refrain from expressing, as an African, his astonishment that she was so fixated on a single being. Another told her bluntly that any relationship that could be built up between her friend and her would inevitably be forced and not based on real feelings. This declaration the marabout was obliged by his own system of thought to make, because, if he builds up a relationship by violence, he puts himself in danger; he must therefore avoid as much as possible any recourse to what marabouts call 'malign magic'. In these two cases, the words which dared to be other than an echo resulted in Marie's simply breaking with the marabouts who offered them.

So what does the marabout's mediation mean? A relationship without any language other than an echo might seem to be the opposite of a therapeutic relationship, even if it can sometimes seem like one. But it's a necessary relationship at a time when Marie cannot hear anything accept her desire but equally cannot remain alone in total despair.

Ambivalence

Evidently the relationship between Marie and marabouts is ambivalent.

The lack of importance ascribed to interpretation, apart from the reasons discussed above, stems from the client's complete blindness to the material of divination. In African divination, the marabout is only an interpreter of messages from Allah or the genies or the angels, by means of cowries, prayers accounted for on chaplets, geomantic figures and so forth. Marabouts say explicitly that 'it is the sand' or 'it is the cowries' that speak.

Thus, contrary to the relationship that Marie establishes with the marabouts, they are not by their own lights all-powerful and cannot grant all requests.

The marabout, even more than the person he 'works' for, is constrained by a ritual: that is the meaning of the very closely defined sacrifice which is sometimes necessary to attain a truth that is hidden, and the sacrifice is laid down by those whom the marabout invokes. So it is not a question of a simple alms-giving, as Marie seems to translate it. It is significant that the four francs which a marabout asks her to give to a man in the street should be given by her to a beggar.

The marabout's 'work' is far from being a simple abstraction. Its essential condition is the state of purity, where physics and metaphysics join up. Marabouts say that often they put their very life at stake. By means of *khalwa* (mystical seclusion), they reach the world of angels and genies, even demons – confrontation with whom, if the marabout is not strong enough, or if he is not in a sufficiently pure state, can drive him or his descendants mad. Hence all the precautions, the patience required of the client to avoid precisely the use of dangerous 'malign magic'. Hence too the marabout's unwillingness to give time-estimates, for if Allah or the angels or the genies are going to take action it is arrogance to unveil what they alone know.

Finally and more generally, the 'constituent principles of personality among Black Africans' as Moussa Oumar Sy puts it[5] remain, even in a non-African environment, the definite reference-points for marabouts, and these escape Marie totally, just as does the cosmogony that they apply, with its principles of forces, fluids that constitute man and nature, the existence of a double, a genie that the marabout tries to capture and manipulate. Should one, then, conclude that there is nothing but a 'dialogue of the deaf'? This would be too hasty a judgment.

Beyond the cultural differences there are certainly, between French clients and African marabouts, constants of a kind. For both of them recourse to amulets has meaning within a tradition; for both, an insoluble difficulty can lead to appeals to unusual individuals. Perhaps the suggestions and actions of marabouts and the fantasies that they unleash have a special place in the French repertoire of finding solutions for difficulties? In looking for explanations we can point to the demand for pragmatism, to the need for treatment that works, to individualism, to the taste for new exotic mentors, but possibly above all to the rejection of fatalism and of the internalization of faults. Finally, it is through recourse to this other, through this detour to an elsewhere represented by the marabouts, that French clients try to reconstitute their own identities.

Notes

1   This article was first published in the proceedings of a conference *Vers des sociétés pluriculturelles: études comparatives et situation en France* held in Paris in January 1986 (ed. M. Piault, Éditions de l'ORSTOM, Paris 1987). The translation is by Jonathan Benthall.

2   The term 'marabout' is used here in a generic sense, which seems to be appropriate for most French clients. However, among the twelve marabouts consulted by Marie, one represents what some Africans call 'fetish-men', i.e. those not associated with Islam. He is in fact a Bambara from Mali.

3   I am specially grateful to the invaluable help of Khadidja Keita and Sada Mamadou Ba.

4   It is clear that when Marie speaks of 'charlatans', this expression cannot have the same referent as when it is used by Africans about some of their compatriots whose competence they are challenging.

5   Moussa Oumar Sy, 'Considérations sur les principes constitutifs de la personnalité chez les Négro-Africains', *Bulletin de l'IFAN* 33, Jan. 1971, pp. 14–63.

Chapter 26

Anne-Marie Brisebarre

■ THE SACRIFICE OF 'ID AL-KABIR:[1] ISLAM
IN THE FRENCH SUBURBS, *Anthropology Today*,
9.1, February 1993, pp. 9–12

Country in town

VERY EARLY IN THE MORNING of 11 June 1992, I stopped at a red
light in an avenue in one of Paris's eastern suburbs. In the neighbouring car was
a family of North African origin. A scene of daily life? Not quite, for in the back of
the vehicle there lay a sheep, a rural animal which does not pass unnoticed in this urban
setting. Today was the feast of *'Id al-kabir*, the Muslims' 'great festival', also sometimes called the sheep festival on account of the ritual cutting of a sheep's throat which
is performed in many families by the father in commemoration of Abraham's sacrifice. It takes place two lunar months and ten days after the end of the Ramadan fast.

The light went green, and the car moved off, taking the animal to its destiny.
Where would it be sacrificed? In the bathroom of a council flat, or in the cellar of
an ethnic minority workers' centre? Perhaps in the garage or little garden of a
suburban house. Or else the family and its sheep might move around desperately
in the suburb to find some place where this sacrifice would be permitted.

The day after the festival, people sometimes laugh about episodes arising from
the *'Id*, as if to forget the moments of anguish they have just lived through. One
example was a Tunisian-born family who, in June 1991, tried to carry to their
suburban flat, hidden in a large pan covered by a rug, the sheep that they had been
to buy from a farm on the outskirts of Paris. At each attempt, the bearers found
on the staircase an inquisitive neighbour accompanied by his dog, a German
sheepdog whose special interest in the situation one can well imagine. This only
intensified his master's suspicions. After several efforts, the family changed strategy
and asked a cousin who lived in a suburban villa to give them and their sheep hospi-
tality, out of range of the view of neighbours and the scent of dogs.

I have often, in the course of a seven-year research project, come across such
anecdotes, about the difficulty of celebrating *'Id al-kabir* when one lives in a town.[2]
Buying a live sheep, bringing it home, sacrificing it, skinning it, cutting up the

Figure 26.1   Children take their sheep for a walk before the sacrifice, Aulnay-sous-Bois, Seine-Saint-Denis, France, 1987.

carcass, getting rid of the waste matter, especially the blood – it is an obstacle course that hundreds of Muslim families begin again every year, often in an atmosphere of insecurity due to the secrecy surrounding a practice which carries with it such connotations of otherness.

The sale of sheep for *'Id al-kabir*: a lifebuoy for French sheep-farming

The Pastoral Alliance, a professional association to which many French sheepfarmers belong, acknowledged in its Bulletin for January 1990 that the direct sale of sheep to Muslims is 'a sure and durable outlet', capable of 'sustaining French sheep production in the years to come'. If such sales of live sheep are authorized, it is at the moment of slaughter that secular French norms impose a legal problem. In fact, the slaughter, even ritual,[3] of animals intended for human consumption is a technical action which must be carried out by a professional in the place reserved for animal deaths, the slaughterhouse. Family slaughter for 'Id al-kabir is categorized as illegal.

It is hard to say how old are the commercial links between professional French sheep-farmers and Muslims. The organization of these sales seems to have developed as the demand grew. Farmers and traders on the outskirts of big cities, informed about this occasional need of Muslim communities for live animals, saw here a direct commercial outlet, without the need for the usual intermediaries, allowing them to dispose of all or part of their stock.

Others, whether French or North African, have set up in the chief sheep-rearing areas the required networks for collecting rams that have not been castrated – the main requirement of this particular urban clientele. At the gates of Paris, but also in front of certain migrant workers' lodgings (known in France as *foyers*) or in suburban housing estates inhabited by large numbers of Muslim families, there can be seen on the morning of 'Id al-kabir lorries with several floors, registered in the West, Centre or South of France, unloading hundreds of sheep in places where there is no slaughterhouse. Where will they be sacrificed?

Organizing to control: collective places of sacrifice in the Paris area

The research project began in Cévennes with transhumant shepherds who do business with North Africans settled in Bas-Languedoc. These, mainly Moroccan, are employed as agricultural labourers in vineyards and fruit-farms. Living in villages, they have no problem in celebrating 'Id al-kabir: they buy a sheep from the nearest sheep-farm and cut its throat in their garden. Identified as a festive, religious and family practice, the sacrifice does not by any means disconcert country neighbours who are regularly confronted by the problem of slaughtering animals for family consumption. From 1987 onwards, I pursued my enquiry into urban areas, Paris and its suburbs, looking for 'collective' places of sacrifice. The density of the Muslim population in certain conurbations of the Paris periphery led during the 1980s to a number of attempts to organize and collectivize the 'Id al-kabir sacrifice.

These initiatives could be either public, emanating from veterinary or municipal authorities, or private, of a social or commercial character; but in any case they were, and are even more so today, at the heart of polemics on the place of Islam in secular France: the blood scattered in the sacrifice of the 'Id is one of the signs of the presence of the Muslim religion in France. This practice, which takes the animal's death outside the slaughterhouse, is denounced by the societies for the protection of animals as barbarous, violating not only the law but also the sensibility of the French people.

For a social anthropologist, who bases her research on direct observation, the decision to attend 'collective' places of sacrifice allows her to get round the difficulty which results from undertaking a study on the occasion of an annual festival: that is to say, the difficulty of observing at the same time and in the same place variants in the unfolding of the ritual such as the choice and treatment of the living animal, the mode of sacrifice, the treatment of the carcass and so forth.[4] However, by attending these collective and impersonal places one deprives oneself of a whole part of the festival, that which unfolds in the domestic sphere. This is why, among the researchers in our team, some have preferred another approach: working with a family and observing the festival as a whole, from the purchase of the sheep, which can take place several days before the festival, to the completion and consumption of the sacrificial meal. One can make a classification of the places in the Paris region where, over the last ten years, it has been possible to carry out the sacrifice of *'Id al-kabir*. The first criterion is then 'Who is the organizer?', a group or an individual, in a public or a private space, a professional of the meat trade or not.

The replies to these different questions about the status of the organizer(s) lead to the second criterion, the status of the place of sacrifice. This can be legal, tolerated or illegal. This classification has been called in question over the last five years. However, in 1981 a letter from Edith Cresson, then Minister of Agriculture, called on mayors of districts in the Paris region to take steps to make the *'Id al-kabir* sacrifice possible. She even envisaged applying to this ritual family slaughter a statutory dispensation similar to that which permits the slaughter of pigs for family consumption in French farms. At the end of some years, these arrangements resulted in political battles, such as those on the occasion of the multiple elections in 1988 (presidential, legislative and then municipal) which showed a strong drift to the National Front, the extreme right-wing party; but also in legal actions against the French government. The case of the commune of Aulnay-sous-Bois, in Seine-Saint-Denis, is typical.

The organization of *'Id al-kabir* at Aulnay-sous-Bois

In August 1986 and 1987, the health services of this commune had organized a place of sacrifice near the *Cité des 3.000*, a group of apartment blocks housing a large ethnic minority population, largely Muslim, and where in previous years numerous complaints from non-Muslim residents had been recorded on the day of the *'Id*, resulting in several interventions by the police and the fire brigade. This place of sacrifice – a grassy patch in an area of small businesses, specially arranged for the purpose – was to constitute a centre of attraction to allow control of the slaughter, as well as the collection and disposal of waste matter so as to avoid the 'pollution of the environment'. Authorization had been given by the office of Veterinary Services for the department. Five hundred sheep were killed with the help of a team of approved sacrificers, without any adverse incident.

However, a complaint against this arrangement was made with the Administrative Tribunal by the Oeuvre d'Assistance aux Bêtes d'Abattoir (OABA), a recognized non-profit society. In April 1991, this legal action resulted in the commune of Aulnay-sous-Bois being found guilty of having contravened the law which governs the slaughter of butchery animals, by organizing a killing outside a slaughterhouse.

From being tolerated by the office responsible for hygiene (the departmental veterinary services that report to the Ministry of Agriculture), this organization, whose aim was to prevent 'uncivilized slaughters', became, as a result of the judgment, illegal on the same footing as any slaughter carried out in secret.

The category of 'tolerated place of sacrifice' disappeared, leaving only two alternatives: the legal, that is to say the slaughterhouse, and the illegal, all other places.[5] Taking up the same argument, an article in the *Quotidien de Paris* for 10 June 1992, entitled 'Sheep sacrifices for *'Id al-kabir*: police commissioners disregard the law', criticized the position taken by certain commissioners of the Paris area who, alerted by the field staff of the veterinary services, and despite the Aulnay-sous-Bois decision, had preferred to make arrangements for slaughter for fear of the serious controversy that 'uncivilized' slaughters could have provoked.

From organization to bricolage: an encouragement to secrecy

If on paper it is easy to state that sacrifice in a slaughterhouse is the 'solution' to the problem of the *'Id* ritual sacrifice, a survey of the slaughterhouses in the Paris region makes such a proposition unrealistic and even a little hypocritical. After the closure of at least four, only four remain, all in the outer suburbs. The departments of Essonne, Hauts-de-Seine, Seine-Saint-Denis and Val-de-Marne contain no slaughterhouses.[6]

Except for the municipal slaughterhouse at Meaux, which in recent years has refused to take charge of sheep belonging to private citizens, these establishments have allowed hundreds of families every year to sacrifice their sheep, or rather have them sacrificed by approved specialists.

When Muslims do not go to slaughterhouses, because of living too far away or because they consider such a ritual out of place there (a point I shall come back to), what solutions, other than the killing of the sheep in the home, can be adopted in the Paris region? Here we encounter a system of odd jobs or 'managing somehow', where isolated people (those who belong neither to an associative network nor to a 'reconstituted' social group) pay a heavy price, financially but also socially.

In some suburban housing estates, but above all in *foyers*, are cellars and garages which become places of sacrifice. Their organization is usually internal to a Muslim community, often with an ethnic dimension corresponding to the history of each of these centres or to the ethnic mix in a housing estate.

Up till 1989, the Muslim cemetery in Bobigny welcomed Muslim families from Seine-Saint-Denis. After the prayer in the little mosque in the cemetery, a specially designed building, now disused, served as a room for the killing. Its small size, however, obliged the sacrifiers to officiate on the borders of the cemetery and in the garden next to the imam's house. This cemetery was founded about 50 years ago as an annexe to the Franco-Muslim hospital in Bobigny (now the Avicenne Hospital) for the burial of Muslims who died at the hospital without families. In the centre is a 'square of Muslims who died for France' under a French flag. Surrounded by industrial wasteland, this place has an ambiguous character, in that the religious and the military, France and Algeria, skirt one another without blending: it is frequented in the main by Muslims of North African origin, especially Algerians. At the time of the *'Id al-kabir* in 1988, I was impressed, comparing it with other places of sacrifice that I had visited, by the atmosphere of great freedom in which the ritual unfolded. This Muslim space seemed at that time to enjoy, at least symbolically, an extra-territorial status. But three years ago, the veterinary authorities of Seine-Saint-Denis forbade all ritual killings there, as in other places in the department.

In numerous farms on the outskirts of Paris, customers have the option of sacrificing the sheep that they have just bought, in the context of an exchange of services which satisfies the seller, whether farmer or trader, French or North African, as much as the Muslim purchaser. If many farmers dispose of part or even all of their stock at this time, that is to say several dozen animals, others have become industrialists in *'Id al-kabir* sheep: assembled especially for this occasion, thousands of sheep coming from various regions of France and even from abroad (England, Netherlands and Eastern Europe) will be resold and very often sacrificed on site.

Increasingly rare, for reasons I have explained, are places organized by the communes. For two years, the health officers of Mureaux (Yvelines) have been in discussion with representative Muslim associations about communal land with a view to controlling the *'Id* sacrifice by the organization of sheep sales, and then making available a location for the sacrifice 'out of people's sight and in the best conditions of hygiene possible'.

Sacrifices or ritual slaughters?

What remains of the practice of *'Id al-kabir* sacrifice in the conditions of immigration and urbanization that many Muslim families in France are familiar with?

The social anthropologist is not the only one to put this question. Muslims themselves ask it when they recall the festival in their own countries – via the childhood memories of those who have long lived in France, or stories told by the parents of the 'second generation'. For several years when *'Id al-kabir* coincided with the holidays, many families of North African origin returned home for the occasion.[7]

Among their regrets at not being able to celebrate the *'Id* with dignity, people speak of the impossibility of bringing the sheep into the family dwelling and integrating it into family life, entrusting it to children so that they will know the one who will take the place, as in the Abrahamic sacrifice, of the eldest son. Furthermore, is not the house the best place for the sacrifice? If it is carried out according to the rules, if the danger inherent in the spilling of blood is avoided, Allah's blessing lasts for the entire year.[8]

Our comparative observation of the *'Id al-kabir* sacrifice in different places has shown that the more its organization is alien to the Muslim community, and the nearer it gets to the legal killing of animals for butchers, the less the sacrificial ritual differs from a *halal* killing as it is practised in slaughterhouses for the day-to-day 'manufacture' of meat intended for the Muslim community.

Thus we have the 'sacrifice' in a slaughterhouse, carried out repetitively by the approved Muslim sacrificer with the family head reduced to the role of sacrifier (he who offers the sacrifice) and unable to see 'his' sheep have its throat cut. But there is a difference between the *'Id* sheep and a *halal* carcass bought from the butcher's: that is, the appropriation of the animal by the family head at the time of purchase. The sheep which will be consumed by the family during the *'Id al-kabir* meals is still often chosen by men according to criteria of sex, age and physiological state, to which will be added local physiognomic preferences pertaining to the presence of horns or an animal's colour.

This choice individualizes the 'Id sheep, which will thus have been seen, touched, integrated with the family, if only by a furtive laying-on of hands. A slight difference: but one which certainly establishes, in the eyes of some Muslims, the animal's status as a future sacrificial victim, and gives meaning to a festival which, in a context of immigration or cultural transplantation, finds or reinforces, quite apart from its religious character, other justifications relating to family and identity. 'The 'Id? It's like your Christmas, a festival for children and for the family' – that is a meaning already present in the countries of origin. 'But it's also like your 14th of July!'

It is precisely this dimension of identity which explains why the sacrifice has been maintained, and even resumed in some cases by Muslims who, when they lived in their original countries, did not sacrifice.

Wider implications

This study, undertaken in France, could be the starting-point for a comparison with other European countries with Muslim minorities. It would also be valuable to make a comparison with present-day conditions of sacrifice in big towns in Muslim countries such as Turkey or Tunisia. Ritual cutting of the animal's throat was originally part of rural practice and pastoral knowledge. Its transposition into an urban setting, albeit Muslim, brings with it numerous problems, including problems of hygiene.

Unfortunately we have come up against the poverty of literature concerning the 'Id al-kabir sacrifice not only in European urban settings but also in North Africa, where the descriptions both old and recent relate above all to traditional rural settings.[9]

From exchanges with European colleagues, it would seem that in certain countries such as Germany, Austria and Britain, ethnic minorities in cities have often grouped themselves into districts, whereas in France suburban housing estates are inhabited by families of the most diverse ethnic background and religions. If this mixing together has a positive effect on integration, for instance with regard to schooling, there is the negative consequence that particular cultural or religious expressions can provoke reactions of intolerance and the rejection of differences. By contrast, the existence elsewhere of quarters with an ethnic character can allow social groups to live out the strong moments in their calendar, like the sacrifice of 'Id al-kabir, in a more private manner.[10]

Notes

1   A first version of this article was published in French under the title of 'L'Islam des banlieues: le sacrifice de l'Ayd El-Kébir' in the *Journal des Anthropologues*, the review of the Association Française des Anthropologues, no. 49, autumn 1992. The translation is by Jonathan Benthall.

2   This research, still current, has been first carried out since 1986 as a personal study in rural areas of the Gard and Hérault departments of France, then in the Paris area. Later in 1990, a research team was set up with funding from the Fonds d'Action Sociale auprès des travailleurs immigrés et de leurs familles (FAS, Ministère des Affaires Sociales). The Muslims encountered were largely from North Africa (Algeria, Tunisia, Morocco) and West Africa (Senegal and Mali), all these countries being former French colonies. In certain areas of collective sacrifice, the study came across the sacrificial practices of Muslims who originated from the Comoro Islands, Mauritius, Indonesia and Pakistan. As well as the Paris area, the research team has worked in the towns of Amiens, Bordeaux, Grenoble, Lodève, Montpellier and Marseilles.

3   Everyday ritual slaughter – *halal* (= 'lawful') or *kosher* – i.e. that which results in the meat sold in Muslim or Jewish butchers' shops, benefits in France from a statutory dispensation dating from 1981 which allows for animals to have their throats cut without previous anaesthesia. It can be carried out only by an approved sacrificer in a slaughterhouse.

4   The legal time of sacrifice begins in the morning after the prayer of *'Id al-kabir*. Whereas sacrifice is forbidden in the evenings and at night, it is allowed during the two days following the festival. The most auspicious day is the first one after the prayer.

5   Our enquiry showed how difficult it is for Muslims to accept that a legitimate practice – the sacrifice of *'Id al-kabir* according to koranic rules – can be considered illegal.

6   National policy on slaughterhouses, since the closure of small establishments, tends today towards the closing of medium-size ones too, so that as the year 2000 approaches there will be only a few very big slaughterhouses all located in areas where the animals are bred. Now that the 'cold chain' is technically perfect, it is more rational to transport carcasses than living animals to urban consumers. The four slaughterhouses closed down were at Vaugirard, La Villette, Argenteuil and Couilly Pont-aux-Dames. The four surviving are at Ezanville to the north of Paris (Val d'Oise), Mantes-la-Jolie to the west (Yvelines) and Dammarie-les-Lys and Meaux to the east (Seine-et-Marne).

7   The Muslim year is lunar, 10 or 11 days shorter than our solar year, so that *'Id al-kabir* is a moveable feast in relation to our calendar.

8   In Islam, blood is the seat of life and the vehicle of the soul, for human beings as well as for animals. Only after giving the sheep's soul to God can one consume its meat. But the very sacredness of blood requires precautions to be taken when it is shed. One must slit its throat while saying the *Bismillah*, with a single blow of a sharp knife so as not to make it suffer. But the precautions also concern what happens to the blood, which risks being invaded by *jnoun*: one must avoid walking in it or even stepping over it, and it must be got rid of as soon as possible with large quantities of running water. In certain North African families, it is usual to mark with ceremonial blood a young girl ready to marry or a youngest son. Women have been seen to gather a little blood in a dish, to be dried for medicinal or magical purposes.

9   Cf. for instance the excellent work by A. Hammoudi, *La Victime et ses masques: Essai sur le sacrifice et la mascarade au Maghreb* (Paris, Le Seuil, 1988), which gives a minute description of the unfolding of the ritual in the Moroccan High Atlas.

10   Such is the conclusion, no doubt a little summary, that could be drawn from an interesting article by Pnina Werbner on sacrificial practice among Pakistanis in Manchester: '"Sealing" the Koran: Offering and sacrifice among Pakistani labour migrants', *Cultural Dynamics* 1.1 (1988).

Museums of the Underside

■ *Anthropology Today*, 9.2, April 1993

T HE RECENT ATTENTION GIVEN by anthropologists to museums is welcome, but too narrow in scope. All museums can be seen as museums of ethnography. Jonathan Webber, among the first to advance this argument, is currently exploring its implications with his dedicated fieldwork in one of the world's most agonizing museums, that which has grown up in the Auschwitz and Birkenau murder camp complex.[1]

In this strained but still intelligible sense of the word 'museum', large areas of northern France constitute open-air museums of the two world wars. There is much in the Somme area, particularly, to provoke meditation: the small German cemetery at Fricourt where the bodies of 17,092 soldiers were crammed after World War I, some of them with Jewish gravestones; the graves near Péronne of Indians, Egyptians and Africans. The scale of the British and French sacrifice is commemorated forever by Sir Edwin Lutyens' massive arch, the 'Monument to the Missing', engraved with 73,412 names. Intended to impress, it now seems the kind of building a child might have designed – perhaps because its two colours, brownish-red and white, recall those of Minibrix (which, for the benefit of younger readers, were a primitive rubber version of Lego); and is hence a particularly poignant reminder of the folly of statesmen.

Of a different order aesthetically is the Newfoundland memorial at Beaumont-Hamel, in a field of real, if grassed-over, trenches, where a bronze reindeer stands guard over a defensive casemate, carved with 800 names, looking out towards the stark remains of the 'Danger Tree' which still stands.

A new museum will open soon in Péronne, the 'Historial of the Great War', stressing its international aspects and the impact of new military technology. In the meantime, the nearby Delville Wood Commemorative Museum, which was finished in 1985, is, as well as a monument to the 25,000 dead South African volunteers, a piece of naked propaganda for the State of South Africa. It is a pentagonal fort based on the design of the Castle of Good Hope in Cape Town, with the Voortrekkers' double Cross of Consecration in the centre of the courtyard. It is the only site on the Somme where the visitor is given lavishly printed leaflets. Some visitors might be surprised to see a bronze relief panel in the museum, in which a group of white soldiers in battledress are apparently firing their guns towards a number of half-naked Africans. But no, the scene on the right is in fact a separate panel which records the foundering of the SS *Mendi* on 21 February 1917, when 600 black men who were to serve in labour battalions in France lost their lives.

Not far from the Somme, an English entrepreneur called Richard Boreham has started a museum to commemorate the French defeat at Agincourt, or Azincourt as they persist in calling it, in 1415. There are to be guided tours of the battlefield, and mediaeval tournaments. A village of 300 residents is throwing itself into trying to attract 20,000 English tourists a year, inspired by the cinematic heroism of Laurence Olivier and Kenneth Branagh. The mayor, chaffed by his friends for exploiting a French defeat, replies that one must live with one's own time: 'We are in the process of forming a great people: Europe'.[2]

Further south, Paris offers a wide range of great and well-funded museums. But does any other capital city boast a sewer museum? The Musée des Égouts de Paris is on the left bank near the Pont de l'Alma. You can learn much useful information about the development of the city and the principles of water supply. There are real functioning sewers to walk along, and you can even see a 5-ton flushing boat which plies the main sewers. The rat on display is a stuffed one. You can buy souvenirs and watch a video programme: but by this time my party could stand the smell no longer, and took the guidebook's advice to 'enjoy our lovely city of Paris up top'.

Having ascended the Eiffel Tower, that epitome of technological romanticism, earlier in the day, it seemed to me that the reason why Paris, and only Paris, has a sewer museum must be that Paris is the centre of structuralism. However, we must also remember the much older French tradition of Rabelais, who, as Anthony Burgess has written, rubs our noses in 'the remarkable fact that man is a kind of sewer with a holy spirit hovering over it'.

A number of anthropologists have written on the theme of 'Why Museums Make Me Sad' (the title of an essay by James Boon[3]). Perhaps more attention should be given to those museums which specialize in sadness, that is to say, in representing the underside of life rather than in what offers refreshment.

Notes

1   Dr Webber has published a preliminary account in 'The Future of Auschwitz: Some Personal Reflections', Frank Green Lecture, Oxford Centre for Postgraduate Hebrew Studies, Oxford, ISSN 0965 5913.

2   Jean-Claude Charles, report on Azincourt, *Le Monde*, 11 April 1992.

3   In *Exhibiting Cultures: The Poetics and Politics of Museum Display*, ed. Ivan Karp and Steven D. Lavine, Smithsonian Institution P., 1990.

Jonathan Benthall

PART SEVEN

Human Sciences in Authoritarian States

■   JONATHAN BENTHALL

AS DE WAAL SAYS ELSEWHERE in this collection, anthropology matters more than its practitioners often realize, and this section is devoted to its distortions under authoritarian regimes.

'The Schwidetzky Affair', excerpted from *RAINews* 1980–81, illustrates how it took German anthropology many decades to recover from the dominance of Nazism.[1] A physical anthropologist compromised – albeit fairly mildly compared to others – by her publications during the Third Reich, was still holding high office in an international representative institution, and sticking to an outdated view of racial essences, in the early 1980s. The editorial line taken in *RAINews* was perhaps less hard on the late Dr Schwidetzky than it should have been.

John Sharp's 1980 article on the two separate developments of anthropology in apartheid South Africa was one of the most influential published in *RAINews*, with the broad analogy it drew between official anthropology in Nazi Germany, Soviet Russia and Afrikaner-dominated South Africa. It provoked a nuanced reply from two anthropologists from the Potchefstroom University for Christian Higher Education (*RAINews* 37, April 1980, pp. 3–4), and a pained one from Tamara Dragadze, a British anthropologist of Georgian origin (38, June 1980, pp. 3–4), who warned against the injustice that might be done to Soviet colleagues if any association between their brand of ethnos theory and the kind promoted by the Nazis and the Afrikaner were to become generally accepted.

Sharp, then a lecturer in the English-medium and traditionally liberal University of Cape Town, is now head of the department of anthropology and archaeology at the University of Pretoria, which is Afrikaans-medium. Meanwhile, the two rival anthropology associations in South Africa have merged into one, Anthropology Southern Africa. He contributes an updating note.

I heard **Slawoj Szynkiewicz** give his paper 'Mythologized representations in Soviet thinking on the nationalities problem' at a conference in Poland. The date is important: October 1989, just before the fall of the Berlin Wall. Szynkiewicz is a senior Polish anthropologist, a specialist in the ethnography of Mongolia, with experience also of living and working in Moscow. Szynkiewicz reflects on the dilemma of anthropologists trying to survive intellectually when theoretical concepts were turned into officially petrified myth. The key point is that Lenin left the question of ethnic or national relations within international communism vague and open, leaving Stalin to establish his own theoretical model, which was later renounced by the Soviet rulers in favour of the supposed doctrinal authority of Lenin. Szynkiewicz's dry analysis is still immediately applicable today to the few surviving Communist states, but also suggests analogies with other forms of mythologized representations of social reality promoted by authoritarian regimes.

Whereas archaeology is regularly co-opted in many countries of the world for purposes of national propaganda and the promotion of tourism, **Gustaaf Houtman** records a particularly blatant and indeed ludicrous case in contemporary Burma, in defiance of the traditional teaching of the national religion, Buddhism, which refuses to privilege any one ethnic group. The Burmese military government seeks to make use of the discovery of some important primate fossils to substantiate the claim that human civilization began in Burma. Foreign scientific teams are required to liaise with the military intelligence authorities, and those that choose to do so, Houtman argues, are in effect lending support to one of the world's most oppressive governments.

These are all examples of social thought being distorted in societies where government seeks to impose a rigid party line. In all these societies, there have been scholars who have struggled to maintain their intellectual integrity and avoid indoctrination. In Burma, the strongest weapon of resistance is, according to Houtman, the Buddhist tradition of 'mental culture' or meditation, which is held to have more potency than any merely material heritage, and which is beyond the control of propagandists.

One might draw the conclusion that anthropology can only flourish in open and democratic societies. However, those of us fortunate to live in such societies must also recall that we are indoctrinated ourselves with some different 'mythologemes', such as the individual's absolute right to intellectual property, and that the hidden hand of the market stretches deeply into academic research and publishing so that packaging, novelty and gamesmanship often weigh more heavily than substance.

Note

1   For further information see the entry on German and Austrian anthropology, *Encyclopedia of Social and Cultural Anthropology* (London: Routledge, 1996); Dostal, W., 'Silence in the Darkness: German ethnology in the National Socialist period', *Social Anthropology*, 2(3), 1994, 251–62; Conte, Edouard and Cornelia Essner, *La Quête de la race: une anthropologie du nazisme* (Paris, Hachette, 1995).

Chapter 27

Jonathan Benthall

■ THE SCHWIDETZKY AFFAIR

Ilse Schwidetzky (1907–99) was a professor at the University of Mainz in former West Germany. She published prolifically on many topics of physical anthropology, especially the biology of skeletal populations and the classification and evolution of 'races', but came to international attention as recipient of the Broca Medal and as a senior office-holder of the International Union of Anthropological and Ethnological Sciences from 1978 to 1988.

RAINews 40, October 1980, p. 9 (News)

THIRTY-TWO FRENCH SCHOLARS – including Augé, Godelier, Le Goff, Le Roy Ladurie, Panoff and Vernant – have written an open letter dated 15 June 1980 to the organizers of a Centre National de Recherche Scientifique (CNRS) conference on Hominization, criticizing them for having invited to Paris, and honoured with the Broca Medal, Ilse Schwidetzky, the German biological anthropologist. According to the signatories, she collaborated between 1935 and 1944 with Professor von Eickstedt and was a main editor of the Stuttgart journal *Zeitschrift für Rassenkunde*. They claim that during the war this journal published pro-Nazi propaganda, and that Dr Schwidetzky is regarded as one of the practitioners of racial research under the Third Reich; also that in 1961 she published in the so-called 'overtly racist British journal' *Mankind Quarterly* an article on Racial Psychology which takes up some of the classical positions of post-1933 German anthropology.

'The idea', the letter continues, 'that a congress which gathers together the best world specialists in anthropology and palaeontology can tacitly admit, as part of the scientific heritage of humanity, theses which, in one form or another, have led whole populations to extermination, seems to us an insult to the victims and an offence to the scholarly world. It is not a question of condemning a person, but of avoiding giving the impression that racist anthropology is a legitimate part of scientific thought . . .' [. . .]

RAINews 41, December 1980, p. 13 (News)

. . . [W]e have heard from Dr Schwidetzky and take this opportunity to summarize her own position.

Dr Schwidetzky claims that *Zeitschrift für Rassenkunde* was not a racist journal. Egon von Eickstedt was internationally recognized as a scientist and the editorial panel included the French scientist H.V. Vallois. The journal appeared first in 1935, long after the development of Nazi racial theory, and von Eickstedt was known to be an anti-fascist; he is not attacked in the book by Karl Saller *Die Rasse im Nationalsozialismus* (1962) which attacks many other German anthropologists.

Furthermore, according to Dr Schwidetzky, she did not take part in research organized by the Rassenpolitisches Amt; in order to publish the results of some anthropological research in Silesia in the mid-1930s, she was obliged to accept some national-socialist bureaucrats as co-editors of the series, though they had no effect of any kind on the texts published.

Dr Schwidetzky writes that she has never written of Aryan, Jewish or Dravidian races, as she has been accused of doing. Her professor, von Eickstedt, wrote a chapter entitled 'The error of the Aryan race' in a book published in 1934 (for which reason he was attacked by the Nazis), and it was a basic rule of her scientific education not to confuse ethnological/linguistic notions with biological ones. She did indeed write on racial typology, but the pre-war period was one of classification: population genetics had hardly started, nor did multivariate analysis exist. The terms 'Nordic type', 'Alpine type', etc. were borrowed from a French anthropologist of Russian origin, Deniker (1852–1918), who gave the name 'Nordic race' in 1889 to the Northern European complex of high stature, fair pigmentation and mesocephaly [a head of medium proportion].

She doubts whether any Nazi politician ever read her work; and the anthropological institute at Breslau where she worked was mistrusted. Karl Saller has, according to her, been obliged to publicly retract a claim that she was a member of the Nazi Party.

Dr Schwidetzky admits that she had neither the vision nor the courage to denounce the Nazi regime:

> When politicians and journalists say that they did not know about the horrors of the camps till the end of the war, surely scientists may be allowed a certain political ignorance and naivety? As for courage, it is true that I did wish to survive with my family. I married at the beginning of the war and my three children were born during it. A wife – at the end of the war a widow – with three small children and all the anxieties of those years (such as getting food and clothing) is not very disposed to mount the barricades.

Dr Schwidetzky agrees with her critics that racism rests on the belief that racial groups can be classed along a scale of value, but she rejects the view that all classification of the human species into biologically homogeneous and differentiated groups is inevitably racist. This form of classification is a matter of scientific debate. Some anthropologists deny the existence of races or do not wish to use the word race for geographic/biological population groups. But there are many anthropologists [she argues in 1980] who do take races as a reality which must be studied in the same way as other phenomena of human biology; one reason for studying them is that the knowledge of biological phenomena could reduce the dangers of racism.

Dr Schwidetzky considers that, according to the following definitions, 'races' do exist: (1) the definition of population genetics, a race as a group of populations significantly distinguished from other groups by the frequency of hereditary characters (or the frequency of genes); (2) the statistical definition established by zoology, a 'race' or sub-species as a group in which 75 per cent of individuals can be classified correctly by means of distinguishing characters.[1]

Finally, Dr Schwidetzky writes that she never published in *Mankind Quarterly* [a journal committed to race-science], though that journal did publish an unauthorized translation of her article.

We did not report in our last issue that the CNRS congress on hominization was disrupted on 18 June by 'troublemakers' (to quote *Le Monde*) who criticized as racist not only Dr Schwidetzky, but also the whole of physical anthropology. A number of scientists have spoken up in Dr Schwidetzky's defence.

Albert Jacquard, a demographer and one of the 32 signatories of the letter mentioned in *RAINews* 40, has emphasized that the context of their protest is a disquieting tendency to 'normalize' or 'banalize' the actions of the Hitler regime; e.g. the claims that 6 million victims are the invention of the international Jewish plot, and that the gas chambers never existed.

RAINews 44, June 1981

Twitchings of the Third Reich

One of the first important decisions of the new Association Française des Anthropologues (AFA) has been to appoint a committee to report on whether or not Dr Ilse Schwidetzky's opinions on race published mainly before the end of World War 2 were sufficiently culpable for her to be considered unworthy of a French scientific honour today. [2] [. . .]

It is emphasized that the AFA's aim is not to hound an elderly scientist but to examine a chapter in the history of anthropology which demands analysis. In an article we published last year by Ulrich Braukämper, 'Ethnology in West Germany Today' (*RAINews* 33, August 1979), it was hinted – though not stated – that the development of German ethnology has still not recovered from the setback of Nazism. In some other countries today, the distortion of both physical and social anthropology for political purposes remains an urgent issue.

Even the anti-semitic fantasies of Nazi pseudo-science are still alive in extreme right-wing circles. For instance, Hans Günther's *The Racial Elements of European*

History is being serialized in English translation; no need to give details, because it appears that such 'journals' are helped to survive financially by those who collect them as curiosities. The AFA's decision to investigate *L'Affaire Schwidetzky* must be viewed in the context of the anti-semitic outrages committed in France last year.

Having read various extracts from Dr Schwidetzsky's writings we have not yet seen anything that disproves her explanation of her position as summarized in the December 1980 issue of *RAINews*. A full analysis would have to determine whether such a word as *Umsiedlung* (resettlement) must have had the same connotations of deadly euphemism for her in 1943 as for historians in 1981. The studied flatness of tone with which, in 1940, she reviews a book of so-called research on the Jewish question is in its own way peculiarly disturbing, as an abuse of academic objectivity. Whether or not she should have been given the Broca Medal is one thing: but it is too easy to assume that in Dr Schwidetzky's shoes one would have shown less frailty than she admits.

Notes

1   By the end of the 20th century, geneticists had ceased to use the word 'race' in Schwidetzky's first definition, preferring the term 'population' to refer to sub-groups of a species isolated by inbreeding. Her second definition has been discarded, replaced by a concept of 'social race', i.e. groups that are defined in a given social context on the basis of visible heritable attributes. *Editor.*

2   It seems no such report was produced. *Editor.*

Chapter 28

John Sharp

■ TWO SEPARATE DEVELOPMENTS:
ANTHROPOLOGY IN SOUTH AFRICA,
RAINews, 36, February 1980, pp. 4–6

THE UNSIGNED EDITORIAL in *RAINews* 35, December 1979, on Martin West's inaugural lecture as Professor of Social Anthropology at the University of Cape Town, calls for a rejoinder. In particular I query its gloss on Professor West's comments on the distinction between social and cultural anthropology in South Africa. We are told that this distinction is 'conceptually at least, rather artificial' so that it becomes 'ironical' that West, having set out the close connections between social anthropology and other social sciences, should see social and cultural anthropology in South Africa as 'distinct, even antithetical subjects'.

This interpretation rather suggests that it is Professor West who, for personal or idiosyncratic reasons, chooses to focus on divisions within South African anthropology, which are not, moreover, of any great significance. This implication is misleading to readers not wholly familiar with the South African situation.

I would argue, along with West, that there is an extremely wide divergence in South Africa between two styles of approach to the subject-matter of anthropology, that this divergence is of fundamental significance, and that, by and large, it is the English-medium universities which display one style and the Afrikaans-medium universities another. The qualification is important: there are individual anthropologists from both language categories who do not fit into a neat typology.

I shall attempt a preliminary explanation of the situation of Afrikaans-medium universities (in which I include both 'white' universities and, significantly, the 'tribal' institutions in the black homelands), both because it is an interesting case study of convergence between academic theorizing and state ideology, and because it raises certain issues with more general implications, as Gluckman (1975), indeed, suggested. In doing this, however, I do not mean to imply that local English-speaking anthropologists, given their own compromise with South African realities, have any grounds for complacency or self-righteousness when considering the work of their Afrikaans colleagues.

Most English-speaking practitioners would describe themselves as social anthro-pologists, in the tradition of illustrious predecessors such as Schapera and Monica Wilson but with an increasing interest in contemporary theoretical developments such as structuralism and neo-Marxism. Nevertheless, what West and others refer to as the distinction between social and cultural anthropology in South Africa has no valid parallel in the nebulous distinction between contemporary British social anthropology and American cultural (or social-cultural) anthropology. Many Afrikaans anthropologists are indeed wont to represent the situation in these terms, to explain their absolute rejection of all post-Malinowskian developments in British anthropology. But if their own version of the discipline has anything in common with an American approach it is with the anthropology of, for instance, Ruth Benedict rather than Sahlins, Kroeber rather than Geertz. And they are highly selec-tive in what they are prepared to take from Benedict and Kroeber. One must remember that 'cultural anthropology' is the unsatisfactory English rendition of the Afrikaans term *volkekunde:* in fact, 'anthropology' departments at the various Afrikaans-medium universities call themselves departments of *volkekunde.* This term they derive from the German study of *völkerkunde* without, one must say, any notice-able recognition of the 'state of insecurity . . . lack of clearsighted orientation, and . . . desperate search for new perspectives, which have dominated the scene in German anthropology' since the war (Braukämper 1979: 6).

A key concept in Afrikaans *volkekunde* is the notion of ethnos. The current doyen of Afrikaans anthropologists, P.J. Coertze of Pretoria University, defines his subject thus:

> *Volkekunde* studies people as complex beings as they lead a creative exis-tence, following their nature and character, in changing social-organic entities, called *etnieë* (ethnoses), which are involved in a process of active adaptation to a complex environment existing in space and time. (1973: 1, my translation)

Exactly what is meant by an ethnos as a 'social-organic' entity is rather hard to say, particularly because various Afrikaans authors differ in their interpretation of it. But, in general terms, all interpretations are guilty of the reification of culture: the emphasis falls not upon culture as the medium of human communication but upon cultures as closed systems into which individuals are born, in which they must live and from which only death can separate them. 'As many *volke* (peoples or nations) as there are, so many cultures are there' and 'human adaptation as a life process of *volke* has a particular characteristic: it occurs within an ethnic unit . . .' (Coertze *loc. cit.*).

There emerge differences in emphasis beyond these basic premises. Those, such as Mönnig (1978), who lay least stress on the organic nature of the ethnos are prepared to recognize that the ethnos's primary distinguishing characteristic – the consciousness of unity amongst its members – comes about through interaction with other ethnoses. On the other hand, Coertze and his followers (strongly represented at Potchefstroom University for Christian Higher Education) do not seem directly concerned with the implications of interaction between ethnoses: the consciousness of unity (*eenheidsbewussyn*) displayed by ethnos members appears as a product of

Figure 28.1   African women wait to vote for the first time in Libode, Transkei, November 1963, to elect representatives to the first Transkeian Parliament. Hundreds of Africans trekked to record their votes and thus create South Africa's first Bantustan.

common descent which leads, over time, to a genetic unit (Kies 1978), and as such is essentially a metaphysical notion.

These issues were openly debated for the first time ever (it is sad to admit) at the 1979 conference of South African anthropologists in Cape Town. Previous conferences (the first was in 1967) have been tame affairs, with participants coyly avoiding contentious political issues in the interests of sustaining a dialogue between English and Afrikaans universities. That a vigorous debate took place in 1979 was owing, in no small measure, to West's having tackled these issues head-on in his inaugural lecture, and several of Coertze's followers were constrained to elaborate upon the characteristics of the ethnos. They explained that, in addition to their sense of unity stemming from common origin, the members of an ethnos are taken to manifest characteristics – genetic, psychic and cultural – objectively differentiating themselves from others, which they are aware of as a common heritage. In the cultural sphere the chief demarcating characteristic is a common language, and there is, further, the dogmatic assertion that each ethnos is indissolubly linked to its own territory, although land is not, emphatically, seen as a political resource.

The several defining characteristics of an ethnos appear, in theoretical discussions, to be causally interrelated: it is, for instance, because members of an ethnos share genetic, psychic and cultural traits that they aspire to a common territory as a locus for self-expression. And the meaning of the concept becomes clear in the ethnographic practice of its users. Much research is designed to exemplify characteristics of an ethnos in its particular context ('land ownership and use among' or 'political and legal organization of' tribe 'x' in homeland 'y', cf. National Register of Research Projects 1976/7). Even when research is done into other areas – 'acculturation' (van der Wateren 1974) or applied anthropology and urbanization (Coertze, R.D. 1972) – the significance of the ethnos is invariably assumed as basic to the inquiry. No alternative ways of classifying the population under consideration are recognized to have potential precedence over ethnos allegiances.

The ethnoses that are discerned in the course of such study frequently fail to manifest all of the characteristics postulated as defining criteria. Coertze, for instance, notes (1973: 190–217) that traditional political boundaries in Southern Africa rarely corresponded with cultural, ethnos boundaries, and therefore that the territorial dimension of the ethnos was lacking in such cases. In contemporary vein, there is the problem that the geographical boundaries of any one homeland, whose determination was a matter of historical convenience, frequently include sizeable ethnic minorities, and many members of the dominant ethnos do not, and do not want to, reside in the territory to which they are 'indissolubly' bound. But observations of this kind do not appear to be cause for any re-examination of the theoretical status of the concept, which has been doggedly restated in the same form in publications and papers up to the present.

Let me say a little about the sources of the ethnos concept before looking briefly at the implications of its use. Most frequently cited by Afrikaans anthropologists in this connection are the works of Mühlmann (1938, 1948) and Shirokogoroff (1924). It seems that it is Mühlmann's earlier work, written at the height of Nazi power and pretensions, that enjoys greater currency; little cognizance is taken of what seems to me a subtle, but no doubt strategic, shift of emphasis in Mühlmann's later work.

Compare:

> We are turning back to a German heritage of intellectual development – Herder, the Romantics . . . the theory of national characters and its latest manifestation in Bastian's *volk*-ideas – when we consciously give *Völkerkunde* the task of once more becoming the science of the Volk (ethnos) (Mühlmann, 1938: 227),

with:

> Ethnos is always a political concept. The purely objective conception of *Volkstum* (people- or nationhood) which stems from the Romantics is, after the results of contemporary ethnographic sociology, no longer adequate. *Volkstum* is never a naturally given fact, but always a political achievement and therefore a purposive creation. (1948: 236–7)

Were this latter articulation of the issues to be pushed further than Mühlmann himself evidently cared to do, it might be possible for Afrikaans anthropologists to address themselves to contemporary theoretical concerns in this field, but they seem always more than content to fall back upon the explicitly metaphysical conception of Mühlmann's earlier book. Shirokogoroff's work receives favourable mention as well, although Afrikaans academics seem unaware that his ideas have continuing currency in contemporary Soviet ethnography where, as Dragadze's account (1978) makes clear, ethnos theory has been considerably developed. Language barriers are clearly to blame here, but one suspects that neither group of scholars would be particularly encouraged to know that they shared an interest in the ethnos idea.

It is, indeed, tempting to speculate about possible commonalities in the nature of those societies where ethnos theory has flourished – Fascist Germany, and contemporary South Africa and the Soviet Union. Clearly, in some sense the idea serves similar State-condoned or -encouraged ends, but one hesitates to pursue this line too far, given a measure of uncertainty about whether the use in the Soviet Union of the same term as in South Africa necessarily indicates an identical conception of its meaning and significance. In this context I note, with interest, Dragadze's observation that contemporary Soviet anthropologists attempt to accommodate their ethnos theory to their views on the development of class society, and her comment that Soviet contributions to the Burg Wartenstein conference on which she reports demonstrated a 'first-class knowledge of the international literature' (*op. cit.*: 124). In South Africa, however, the ethnos idea is something which is repeatedly and programmatically stated; it is not the subject of theoretical innovation, nor is there any rigorous attempt to subject it to competing perspectives. At the conference of South African anthropologists in 1978, mention of even the work of Barth on ethnic groups and boundaries was greeted by blank faces in many quarters. Part of the problem here is the self-imposed isolation of Afrikaans anthropologists. Apart from their annual foray to a conference open to representatives of all South African universities, most converse only within a closed, endogamous system of ideas. As West observed (1979: 7), few travel abroad to study; fewer have gained foreign qualifications; and many, but not all, belong to a professional society whose membership is limited to white, Afrikaans-speaking anthropologists.

A correspondence between the implications of the ethnos idea and the policy of separate development is patent. But, it seems to me, one must be cautious of portraying Afrikaans anthropologists as the intellectual architects of Apartheid. This is despite the past influence of a figure such as W.M. Eiselen (Verwoerd's confidant) and the fact that, for instance, P.J. Coertze has written an article explicitly entitled 'The necessity of separate development' (1976). It would seem, however, that *volkekunde* is not a highly prestigious subject at Afrikaans universities, possibly because of a professional concern which chooses to limit itself to the 'non-white' South African population; and the teaching of undergraduates seems a much more important activity than research and the elaboration of sophisticated theoretical perspectives. The latter is a characteristic common to all South African universities, but much more than their English-speaking counterparts, Afrikaans anthropology departments offer what amount to service courses, preparing their students for civil service posts – in the Department of Cooperation and Development (the current euphemism for the bureaucrats who control the lives of blacks) and, more recently, in the Defence force. In this respect they have an important function as agents of socialization, justifying, rather than initiating, developments in the policy of Apartheid and the homelands system.

In public, of course, Afrikaans anthropologists deny that their theories and studies have political significance. It is all 'pure' research, and Gluckman, indeed, did generously observe that there were Afrikaans anthropologists who 'emphasize[d] the beauty and harmony, and even the appropriate uniqueness, of each African culture' with a sincerity of motive (*op. cit.*: 22). Perhaps this is so, but one finds it hard to believe that there is no realization at all that these ideas serve as academic justification for continued Afrikaner, and generally, white domination over South Africa.

One of the most significant issues here, involving the future of anthropology in South Africa, is that at the 'tribal' universities in the black homelands almost all senior teaching positions are held by Afrikaans anthropologists: their particular brand of anthropology can be seen to have alienated a considerable number of black students who perceive the whole discipline as nothing more than a white man's ploy to keep blacks emmeshed in white perceptons of black traditional cultures. The black students have seen what their mentors refuse, overtly, to recognize: that the only group to which the ethnos idea applies in South Africa with any degree of accuracy is that of the Afrikaners themselves because the majority of them *want to be an ethnos*. The ethnos concept provides them with an easy rationale for their yearning for exclusivity by failing to address any of the real problems of sustaining power and privilege behind the overt issues. English-speaking anthropologists are not entirely guiltless here, for even if they were deemed acceptable by the authorities, few would consider taking a post at an institution devoted to Bantu Education.

Many of my Afrikaans colleagues will, I am aware, declare that this brief exposition is grossly unfair to them. Several, especially younger, anthropologists do read more widely than I have suggested and privately proclaim their opposition to ethnos theory. Many will argue that they do not use the 'ethnos' at all; but disclaiming the term is not enough if the ideas behind it are left untouched, and opposition to its present form will only be meaningful when it is made public. To my knowledge, however, no critique from within the fold has as yet appeared, and ethnos reigns supreme.

References

Braukämper, U. (1979). 'Ethnology in West Germany today', *RAINews* 33, August 1979: 6–8.

Coertze, P.J. (1973, ed.). *Introduction to General Volkekunde*. Johannesburg: Voortrekkerpers *(in Afrikaans)*.

Coertze, P.J. (1976). 'The Necessity of Separate Development', *J. Racial Affairs* 27(1): 11–24 *(in Afrikaans)*.

Coertze, R.D. (1972). 'The theoretical and philosophical bases of applied anthropology', *J. Racial Affairs* 25(2): 65–82 *(in Afrikaans)*.

Dragadze, T. (1978). 'A meeting of minds: a Soviet and Western dialogue', *Current Anthropology* 19(1): 119–28.

Gluckman, M. (1975). 'Anthropology and Apartheid: the work of South African anthropologists', in M. Fortes and S. Patterson (eds) *Studies in African Social Anthropology*. London: Academic Press.

Kies, C.W. (1978). 'The Coloureds of the northern Cape: aspects of nation-building', *S.A. Journal of Ethnology* 1(1): 23–8 *(in Afrikaans)*.

Mönnig, H.O. (1978). 'Developing a curriculum for volkekundiges' *S.A. Journal of Ethnology* 1(2): 1–7. *(In Afrikaans)*.

Mühlmann, W. (1938). *Methodik der Völkerkunde*. Stuttgart: Ferdinand Enke Verlag.

Mühlmann, W. (1948). *Geschichte der Anthropologie*. Bonn: Universitäts-Verlag.

Shirokogoroff, S. (1924). *Ethnical Unit and Milieu: A Summary of the Ethnos*. Shanghai.

van der Wateren, H. (1974). *Material Culture, Manufacture and Economic Life of the Bahurutshe of Motswedi*. Unpub. D. Phil. thesis: Potchefstroom University *(in Afrikaans)*.

West, M.E. (1979). 'Social anthropology in a divided society', Inaugural Lecture, University of Cape Town, New Series 57.

The more things change . . . : update by John Sharp

The 'Two separate developments' piece was the first – and, in retrospect, rather crude – attempt to consider the relationship between social anthropology and *volkekunde* in South Africa at the end of the 1970s. Adam Kuper pointed out that the two branches of the discipline had had much in common until the late 1950s, and I tried to build this insight into an enlarged version of the *RAINews* article (Sharp 1981), emphasizing that the two had grown apart during the 1960s and 1970s. The main differences were, however, political – social anthropologists and *volkekundiges* had divided along broad lines of opposition to and support for the ideology and practice of apartheid – and there were still significant areas of epistemological overlap in their scholarship.

Initial response (Booyens and van Rensburg, 1980) to these articles confirmed the political character of the divide, since a number of young Afrikaans anthropologists took the opportunity not to challenge my depiction of 'ethnos' theory, but to make it clear that they did not support the political system to which their more senior colleagues had given allegiance. This courageous stand cost some of these young scholars dearly, since their public repudiation of political orthodoxy contributed, at least indirectly, to the closing down of the anthropology department at one Afrikaans university in the 1980s.

Further articles in the 1980s and 1990s (Gordon 1989, 1991) explored and criticized the ways in which *volkekundiges* had placed anthropology in the service of the Afrikaner *volk* and the system of apartheid, particularly in the field of indigenous law, and in the attempts by the South African military to win 'hearts and minds' in Namibia and Angola by giving its troops lessons in indigenous etiquette and custom.

There was no serious attempt to defend, or explicate, the theoretical basis of apartheid-era *volkekunde* until the end of the 1990s, five years after the formal demise of apartheid. R.D. Coertze, retired by then from his position as Professor of Anthropology at the University of Pretoria, wrote an article entitled 'Comment on ignored criticism' (1999), in which he sought to explain his delayed reaction by arguing that the critiques by Gordon and me had not been worth responding to at the time on account of their inaccuracy and transparent animosity towards Afrikaners. But, he argued, he had been moved to belated rejoinder by the fact that works published in the 1990s (Hammond-Tooke 1997; Kiernan 1997; Schmidt 1996) were citing our arguments as received truth.

My response (Sharp, 2000) to Coertze rejected his allegation of anti-Afrikaner sentiment outright, but was deliberately more conciliatory towards his central plea that *volkekunde* had always embodied ideas and practices that were unique neither to South Africa nor to Afrikaner nationalism. Indeed, a more considered history of both branches of South African anthropology is now possible, given that the end of apartheid has ended the need for anti-apartheid struggle. Such a history should certainly explore the overlap between the two branches in detail, and situate the emergence of some of the core ideas of apartheid-era *volkekunde* in various strands of European scholarship.

This exercise should also be a collective endeavour, to which all anthropologists in South Africa contribute. The groundwork for the exercise has been laid by the recent amalgamation of the two professional associations – for social anthropology and for *volkekunde* (or 'cultural anthropology' as the latter was restyled in the 1980s) – into a single body under the new name Anthropology Southern Africa (ASA).

There are many new possibilities in South African anthropology, arising from post-apartheid realignments that include the fact that I now find myself teaching at the University of Pretoria – the former arch-bastion of Afrikaner nationalism – and filling Coertze's position as Professor of Anthropology. Yet one becomes aware that there are significant continuities within periods of great social and political change. As in the 1970s and 1980s, there is still a dearth of critical inquiry amongst professionals and students in the discipline, and the general intellectual climate in South Africa today is not a great deal more conducive to this kind of inquiry than it was then. The discipline may have escaped the shackles of having to take a position for or against a political tyranny, but its creative scope is now being compromised, insidiously, by neo-liberal insistence that it justify its existence by means of shallow outputs of practically orientated research, and shallow inputs of teaching students 'marketable' skills. But at least the struggle for a space for critical scholarship need not involve the two branches of the discipline in pointing fingers at each other.

References

Booyens, J. and N. van Rensburg, 1980. 'Anthropology in South Africa: reply from Potchefstroom', *Royal Anthropological Institute News* 37: 3–4.

Coertze, R.D., 1999. 'Kommentaar op geïgnoreerde kritiek [Comment on ignored criticism]', *South African Journal of Ethnology* 22(3): 81–96.

Gordon, R.J., 1989. 'The White Man's Burden: ersatz customary law and internal pacification in South Africa', *Journal of Historical Sociology* 2(1): 41–65.

Gordon, R.J., 1991. 'Serving the *Volk* with Volkekunde: On the rise of South African anthropology', in J.D. Jansen (ed.), *Knowledge and Power in South Africa*. Johannesburg: Skotaville Publishers.

Hammond-Tooke, D.H., 1997. *Imperfect Interpreters: South Africa's Anthropologists 1920–1990*. Johannesburg: Witwatersrand University Press.

Kiernan, J.P., 1997. 'David in the path of Goliath: Anthropology in the shadow of apartheid', in P. McAllister (ed.), *Culture and the Commonplace: essays in honour of David Hammond-Tooke*. Johannesburg: Witwatersrand University Press.

Schmidt, B., 1996. *Creating Order: Culture as politics in 19th- and 20th-century South Africa*. Nijmegen: University of Nijmegen Third World Centre.

Sharp, J.S., 1981. 'The roots and development of *Volkekunde* in South Africa', *Journal of Southern African Studies* 8(1): 16–36.

Sharp, J.S., 2000. 'One nation, two anthropologies? A response to Coertze', *South African Journal of Ethnology* 23(1): 30–3.

Chapter 29

Slawoj Szynkiewicz

■ MYTHOLOGIZED REPRESENTATIONS
IN SOVIET THINKING ON THE
NATIONALITIES PROBLEM, *Anthropology
Today*, 6.2, April 1990, pp. 2–5

SOVIET STUDENTS OF THE ETHNIC SITUATION were unpre-
pared to interpret recent developments. Many of them knew that the official
picture of uniform and harmonious modernization in faraway regions did not fit the
facts of life. However, particular discrepancies in the picture were seen piecemeal
as separate cases of non-application of the official model. This model was nevertheless generally accepted owing to its highly mythologized form which made it easy
to believe in. The requirement was imposed that this model of interpretation be
substantiated – which did not require thorough studies and thus kept scholars and
administration uninformed. The latter even preferred to stay ignorant and force
restrictions upon research.[1] Thus, a mythologized vision of nationality relations was
created. I shall give some cursory insight into the premises of that vision, leaving
aside its detailed applications.

The Soviet perception of the so-called nationality question was established by
Stalin. Lenin's ideas on the matter were vague and imprecise. They were not very
different from those of preceding reformers like M. Speransky in the 19th century,
though less precise; they were demonstrably more democratic, proclaimed self-
determination and criticized the policies conducted by the czarist administration.
He let his concepts be implemented by the Stalin administration with similar results.
Stalin, however, had an ambition to develop a theory of nationality relations, which
soon petrified into a set of mythologemes that is still alive in people's minds.

First, he established a verbal distinction which is still observed in academic and
political texts. This is a binary division between nations and nationalities (*natsii,
narodnosti*), that is big historical peoples capable of having their own political organization, and smaller or tribal and sometimes dispersed peoples with no state or
literary tradition. (It is worth mentioning that the Russian usage of 'nation' is not
an exact equivalent of the English word and denotes rather an ethnic majority of a
state or a republic.) The basic classification was not precise, but aspired to rigours
which are lacking in, for instance, the English terminology. A third category called

Figure 29.1   Working people of Baku greet Nikita Krushchev on his arrival in April 1960 to attend the celebrations of Soviet Azerbaijan's 40th Anniversary.

'national groups' is used marginally and refers to minorities of foreign origin like the Jews or Germans.

Definitional rigours soon turned into political ones, and became demonstrated in the state organization. Peoples who were accorded the right to enjoy the status of a Soviet republic became known as 'nations', while those rated lower were called 'nationalities'. Thus a discrimination was established with no regard for the actual history of the peoples in question, based only on arbitrary premises of terminology and federal organization. Since these last were practically constant, the system became caste-like and hierarchical. It was also vulnerable to exploitation in the sense of exerting negative pressures. One nationality – the Karelians, akin to the Finns – was elevated to the position of a nation only to be reduced again to its previous status, both changes being administered for political reasons. Similar pressures have been exerted also at the republican level. Some of the 15 Soviet big nations deny peoples living on their territories the right to separate identity: the Tadjiks treat the peoples of the Pamir highlands like this, as do the Georgians the Abkhasians, the Lithuanians the Poles, and so on.

The class of nationalities is further divided, according to political criteria, between those having the status of autonomy and others lacking such status. The former enjoy a somewhat secure position versus the host 'nation', which is not the case with the latter. The example of Karabakh proves that security is rather problematic. Each 'autonomy' is entitled by the constitution to some language freedom, as well as to its own representative law-making and executive bodies. These freedoms are token in character, very limited in practice, and their bare proclamation has been considered sufficient. In fact, autonomies are so constructed as to convey easily the orders and demands of centralized power.

Illustrative in this respect are definitions given by the *Great Soviet Encyclopaedia*, 1st edition. Autonomous republic is meant for nations 'not yet significant/sizable enough to be created a Soviet republic' (vol. 1, 1926: 381), while autonomous province has been designed for 'nations who in consequence of their underdevelopment . . . need a persistent assistance on the part of central power' (p. 380).

Such an autonomy appears to be a device for a veiled denial of self-government. Nevertheless, many ethnic groups have demanded lately to be granted it. Paradoxically, they aspire to a compartment within the structure responsible for their degradation, instead of trying to abolish it or turn it into a working self-governing institution. Thus they attest to the spell of the mythologized ethnostructure which originated with Stalin's ideas.

Again, establishing an autonomous republic is not subjected to any rule; there are no laws providing for conditions and procedures. During the early Stalin regime autonomies were created in a constant process which has never been repeated since. In the period 1924–37 there appeared at least 39 new or reformed autonomous units[2] as opposed to none in 1938–89 except those restored to a couple of formerly repressed peoples. These last had their status terminated arbitrarily, following a sort of canon consisting of a public accusation, indictment for alleged collective misbehaviour, renunciation of status, and exile. The final act of the sequence was in practice the original one and crucial to the process. Interestingly enough, the heavily ritualized Soviet political tradition did not elaborate on such cases. With some exceptions, neither the establishing nor the terminating of autonomies of various orders became subjects for celebration.

The initial period of the Soviet state saw an intense interest in ethnic diversity when particular identities were promoted or even revived. Some 50 groups were given for the first time the possibility to publish in their respective languages on the basis of specially designed alphabets. In the late 1930s, however, the development of national cultures came to a halt, although Stalin continued to believe that separate nationalities would persist in the near future until the world revolution won.[3] He did not want them, however, to play a political role in a totalitarian state. The new policy offered a type of relationship defined as the development of values national in form but socialist in essence. Thus a powerful restrictive measure was created, based on the imprecise but overwhelming mythologeme that national cultures have to evolve along a socialist and 'internationalist' path.

Republican authorities were constantly afraid of being held responsible for advocating nationalistic feelings. The term carries an intense negative flavour in the Soviet mythologized language and is opposed to the highly honoured 'internationalism'. The former equates to chauvinism or national egotism, the latter to altruistic and harmonious relations between various 'ethnies' careful not to stress their identity. 'Big family of nations and nationalities' has been another label for the Soviet peoples, introduced already in the Stalin period.

The socialist and internationalist essence of national cultures was being given an increasing emphasis until the new stage of unitarian trend produced an image of oneness known as the homogeneous Soviet nation, proclaimed in the 1977 constitution, thus outpacing the evolution envisaged by earlier leaders. Since then, references to cultural diversity were washed out and the idea of homogeneity flourished. New mythologemes were originated, one of linguistic unity (*yazykovoy soyuz*) based on the Russian grammar and lexicon, and another of spontaneously dissolving cultural identities. These two were added to the previously proclaimed Soviet or socialist amalgamated culture, and the three mythologemes were since then basic to the picture.

Academic researchers busied themselves studying bilingualism and mixed marriages in accordance with the assertion that language is the most sensitive indicator of cultural identity, while matrimonial alliances are placed next to language. A primitive theorem was formulated that the more people spoke two languages, the more Soviet or socialist they were. The republican authorities drastically limited teaching in national languages and almost completely closed the vernacular schools of small minorities. The resulting language unification became a convincing statistical index of heralded homogeneity. The American melting-pot of displaced and fragmented ethnic groups became an implied model for dissolution and eradication of cultural identities in their totality.

Accelerated assimilation, whether with the Russian or other Union nations, became a valued object of the late Stalin period up to our times. It was even more than that; the intention was proclaimed an accomplishment. Therefore population censuses reported decreasing numbers of peoples. The result was secured by providing census-takers with a list of licensed peoples reduced to around 100 out of the total of some 300. The latest census of 1989 provided for 114 ethnic units in spite of anthropologists' demands that the list be extended. In general, the expression 'nationality question' was used mostly in the sense of the process of assimilation or merging, about to be completed. Only recently has it acquired the meaning of frustration and conflict viewed as the real drive in the society.

Language is perhaps the most striking case of mythologization. The Soviet institutions have used almost exclusively Russian, even in situations when the constitution stipulated otherwise. At the same time there is no official language in the Union, while Russian is not formally authorized even in the Russian Republic. This derives from Lenin's dislike of a state official language as a means of degradation of minorities. Ideological disapproval of any language dominance stands in spectacular contradiction to the real state of affairs. The resulting inconsistency was alleviated by the thesis current in the 1950s and 1960s about two mother tongues including Russian. This formula led in fact to Russification and a resulting decline in status of other Slavonic languages, as well as some others. It became especially noticeable after World War Two, which demanded a concerted effort on the part of the multilingual army and society.

There developed a dogma of 'harmonious bilingualism', a sweeping generalization of a poor-quality Russian spoken mostly by the urban population in ethnic areas. It has not been reciprocal; the great majority of Russians living outside their ethnic territory do not speak local languages, which is resented as arrogance. But there is reciprocity in deterioration of the language usage. Most languages, including Russian, experience gradual erosion caused by lack of proficiency or primitivization on the part of bilingual speakers, and by restraints on education. Remarkable in this context are newly appearing complaints about degradation of the Russian culture and identity resulting from the overall Russification which leads to compromising of values.

Russification is indisputable, though rather incorrectly interpreted as a result of the Great-Russian chauvinism or drive to hegemony. It is primarily a consequence of the totalitarian policy of disregarding individual and group integrity and identity. The Russians themselves are victims of this policy. The process of Russification is assisted, though often also obstructed, by another dogma in ethnic relations. This is the constantly present mythologeme of the invariably 'progressive results' of incorporation of a particular people into the Russian empire or the Soviet Union, an incorporation which is invariably presented as voluntary. The thesis has lately been repeated by Gorbachev in the context of the Baltic republics. This again is not done in the interest of the Russians, but for the sake of the state as it is.

The most persistent mythologeme is the unique authority of Lenin's policy toward nationalities. It results from the renunciation of Stalin's disastrous methods and those of his successors. Another source of that long-lived myth is the inability to formulate any pragmatic programme adapted to the challenge of the time. Lenin's authority is constantly revived in order to rally public support for unpopular or difficult decisions.

In fact, there is no such thing as Lenin's policy in relation to the multi-ethnic state. He left some vague and sometimes contradictory declarations of a very general character which are useless in administrative practice. This is perhaps why they are not quoted in full, nor given a thorough scholarly evaluation – even by critical and investigative authors.[4] He is known as an advocate of equality of languages and nationalities, of their sovereignty, of federalism, of special attention to small ethnic groups, of 'awarding' autonomies down to the village level, etc. At the same time he spoke on the benefits of assimilation, though ignoring methods of achieving the goal. The only specific guidance he left is his rejection of a state official language, and this particular recommendation is being discarded now. Paradoxically enough, the law on the state language issued lately by the Latvian parliament mistakenly refers to Lenin in its support, thus adding a new mythologeme to the existing inconsistent mythology surrounding ethnic relations.

In closing, I shall specify some features of the particular language used in texts on the nationality question in the USSR.

1. *Representations are based on untested assumptions which are bound to stay unchanged, especially with regard to origins.* The case here is the alleged voluntary association of various peoples with Russia and the progressive consequences of that fact.

2. *The presence of a demiurge who solves problems and creates new reality.* In this case it is Lenin, whose ideas are binding and to be followed in the future.

3. *Causality is replaced by precedence; the facts are explainable solely by originating at the beginning, or due to the demiurge's intervention.* This applies to conservative thinking about autonomies which are continued because they have been established.

4. *Symbolization in the form of non-differentiation between words and things.* Autonomy is such because it is called so and not because of specific rights it provides for. A name decides the identity of a denoted thing; the example being three kinds of peoples: nations – nationalities – national groups.

5. *Conventional demonstration of benevolent and malevolent features* in binary oppo-
sitions of such values and counter-values as: internationalist vs cosmopolitan,
patriotic vs nationalist.

6. Finally there might be added an *anthropomorphous styling* found in such
expressions as 'family of nations' or 'elder–younger brother relations', revealing a
paternalistic manner.

Re-evaluation of current mythologemes has already begun, with particular
effect among the anthropologists and the linguists.[5] Nevertheless, it does not apply
to all those listed above. Besides, mythologized thinking on the subject continues
to persist among some scholars, politicians and the public. This has been proved
during the debates of the September 1989 plenary meeting of the Party Central
Committee, as well as in many letters published by papers and magazines. Those
who still profess the myth that the nationality question has already been solved are
apt to perceive current antagonisms as survivals of the past and acts of villains or
'unhealthy agents'.

Notes

1   Compare Yu. V. Bromley, 'Investigation of Ethnic Problems in the Light of the
    Resolutions of the 19th Party Conference' (in Russian), *Sovetskaya Etnografia* 1989
    No. 1, p. 5. A great part of the issue is devoted to the subject and carries very
    interesting comments.

2   Only republics and provinces are included in the count. There were also
    numerous local autonomies of village or lower district level, all of them abol-
    ished during Stalin's rule.

3   That was the old Leninist idea, inherited from the 19th-century Marxists. For
    Stalin it meant that the whole preceding stage of 'proletarian dictatorship' would
    have to cope somehow with an ethnically diversified and therefore less manage-
    able society.

4   Compare M.V. Kryukov, 'Reading Lenin' (in Russian), *Sovetskaya Etnografiya* No.
    4, 1989, who echoes a common misunderstanding about Lenin's alleged scepti-
    cism on autonomy, opposing him to Stalin in this respect (p. 17).

5   Last year there appeared a number of anthropological publications on the subject.
    I shall cite an English language paper as an example: V. Tishkov, 'Glasnost and
    Nationalities within the Soviet Union', *Third World Quarterly*, vol. 11 1989, no.
    4. A collection of contradictory views of linguists is also worth citing: V.P.
    Neroznak, ed., *Natsional'no-yazykovye otnosheniya v SSSR* (National-language rela-
    tions in the USSR), Moscow, Nauka, 1989.

Chapter 30

Gustaaf Houtman

■ REMAKING MYANMAR AND HUMAN ORIGINS,
Anthropology Today, 15.4, August 1999, pp. 13–19

IN 1988, THE BURMA SOCIALIST PROGRAMME Party (BSPP), built up after General Ne Win's 1962 coup, unravelled under popular protest. General Ne Win resigned and the experiment with military socialism lasting over a quarter century was over. In May 1990 democratic elections were held, in which the National League for Democracy, co-founded by Aung San Suu Kyi, over-whelmingly won the elections. However, by early 1991 it became clear that the military was in no hurry to hand over the instruments of government, for they grad-ually routinized themselves from a temporary committee running the country into a 'government'. Indeed, the generals today call themselves 'Ministers', and General Than Shwe, Chairman of the State Peace and Development Council and Minister of Defence, calls himself today 'Prime Minister'.

The regime systematically intimidates what it considers 'the opposition' with house arrest and imprisonment. It has closed down for the best part of the last decade the entire educational system, including for a time even primary schools, for fear of protests. Forced labour is used on a large scale. The outflow of Burmese citizens has caused a severe refugee problem with its neighbours. In short, the regime's international reputation sank so deep that its infamy eventually triggered the European and American economic and political boycotts around 1995. The 1997–98 Asian financial crisis scared many of its Asian backers. Though it was drawn within the orbit of ASEAN in 1997, the Indonesian democratic elections have deprived it of its greatest supporter within ASEAN. Furthermore, the Nigerian democratic elections deprived it of one of its principal role models. Thailand is re-evaluating its attitude to the regime of avoiding direct criticism. The regime retains a powerful ally in China, but internationally Burma is today regarded as a pariah regime comparable with Iraq.

Here I examine some notable features of this regime. Desperate for national and international recognition, it began the large-scale renovation and construction of pagodas, on the one hand, and museums, palaces and ancient monasteries on the other. These constructions have taken place rapidly on an unprecedented scale. It has decided to renovate and rebuild *all* the thousands of pagodas in the 11th century capital Pagan. It is furthermore collecting contributions for, and committing enormous funds to, pagodas all over the country. At least two dozen new museums have been built. These house ancient heritage, but also the history of the army and the Pondaung fossils that it claims represent the oldest humanoids of the world. The latter, it hopes, places the Burmese people on the world's map as the oldest civilization. It also is engaged in rebuilding all ancient palaces in the ancient capital of the Burmese (not the Shan or Mon polities). As the British deposed royalty as long ago as 1885, these initiatives to revive the architecture and symbolism of royalty suggest that the regime is attempting to bolster its legitimacy by taking on 'royal' airs. As I hope to show, these are all vital elements at the heart of the regime's 'new' ideology I have dubbed 'Myanmafication', after their decision to rename the country Myanmar in 1989.

Building a house

One of the regime's journalists explained that 'Myanmar resembled a house that tumbled down. The *Tatmadaw* [army] had to pick up the pieces and build a new one.' Indeed, General Saw Maung himself asserted that during the 1988 unrest 'the State Machinery had stopped functioning' and in the aftermath 'it is just like building a country from scratch'. A new house had to be built, and since 1989 museum building and the preservation of pagoda heritage have become the regime's substantive contribution to this new house.

However, there is much evidence that free-thinking people in Burma have no desire to live in this national house. As the Buddha said:

> I have passed in ignorance through a cycle of many rebirths, seeking the builder of the house. Continuous rebirth is a painful thing. But now, housebuilder, I have found you out. You will not build me a house again. . . . All your rafters are broken, your ridge-pole shattered. My mind is free from active thought, and has made an end of craving. (*Dhammapada* 153, 154)

These two quotations sum up two contrasting approaches to the institutionalization of tradition; the one compartmentalizes and the other does not, since compartments are seen as merely a product of ignorance. Aung San Suu Kyi expounds the latter view in her concept of the 'revolution of the spirit'. Taking the mind as its centre point, it contrasts the transcendent possibilities of mental culture with the bounded material cultural stance of the military.

History and archaeology

The Burmese term for history is literally 'pagoda history' (*thamaìng*). Museums and pagodas both deal with history. Indeed, they embody history. However, though surrounding often-similar objects (e.g. bones), the radically different circumstances and reasons for finding and displaying these mean that they are conceived very differently (fossils vs. relics). In short, they tell very different kinds of history.

Burma's military regime attaches much importance to history. The State Peace and Development Council (SPDC), or, as they were formerly called (until 1997), the State Law and Order Restoration Council (SLORC), sees itself playing a vital and honourable role in the history of the country. The late General Saw Maung, one of the current regime's founders, commented in 1990 that if American culture is 'very recent . . . only 200 years old', Myanmar history 'shows our culture has been here for tens of thousands of years'.[1] There was a great 'difference' between Burma and the rest of the world, and Burma had rubies and real jade that no one else had, and the Burmese did not need air-conditioning or winter coats. Such radically different and unique ancient culture could not permit itself to be enslaved by foreigners yet again.

SLORC inevitably had to show some spectacular reason that it was a legitimate government based on 'old' culture. It could only render this believable, of course, with proof. In the opinion of SPDC Chairman General Than Shwe the creation of Myanmar represents not so much fostering respect for the diversity of cultures within the union, but 'revitalization of a civilization'.[2] Civilization, as we know the concept from evolutionary anthropologists at the turn of this century, meant human beings historically emanating from a single family, hierarchically ordered depending on their ability to shake off nature through their cultural advances. This is convenient shorthand for a unified people all related to a single source, but some of whom are in greater need for civilization, and therefore 'development', than others. Today's military rhetoric of 'development' and 'modernization' goes hand in hand with this institutionalization of the past, and with the promotion of archaeology as the instrument for recovering it. The military pioneers recover the past so as to better control the present.

Burmese politicians sometimes express the origins of their political system, and of political, social and religious order, in terms of the Buddhist genesis myth. In this myth the Brahmas, the entirely spiritual and meditating celestial deities, came to earth only to be transformed into the first material human beings of flesh and blood as the result of partaking of earthly material food. Evacuation of human waste brought about gender differentiation and the ideas of shame and property. Having lost its radiance, society deteriorated due to greed to the extent that the first president and the first judge had to be elected to keep order. In the origin myth, political and legal office are thus entities elected by the people to help compensate for a disorderly society that, in turn, is the product of imperfect minds that have neglected the practice of mental culture.

Burman ethnic and national identity is ultimately taken back to this misty view of the past. For example, one popular etymology of Burma and Myanmar sometimes takes it back to Brahma. Furthermore, even modern political philosophy has been closely bound up with it. For example, Aung San, U Nu and later Ne Win, characterized socialism in terms of *byama-so tayà*, the social meditation practices that transcend embodiment. These prepare for the ultimate transcendence of *samsara* and the path to *nibbana*. Mythologically speaking, these practices also represent a return to the spiritual disembodied Brahma before mental defilements such as ignorance and

Figure 30.1   Discussing collaboration in the study and discovery of anthropoid primates in Myanmar: two professors from American universities holding discussions with the secretary of the State Peace and Development Council and chief of military intelligence, Lt. Gen. Khin Nyunt, of the Pondaung Fossils Expedition Team, 8 March 1997.

greed brought about human existence and the evil of private property. These practices seek to bring order to disorder and have been held up as ideal Burmese behaviour and as a vital ingredient to be practised by the country's political leadership.

Hitherto, entertaining such remote origins at the level of myth and exhortation to practise social meditation with a universal appeal (of loving-kindness and compassion) used to satisfy demands for identity. These practices conciliate identities and do not privilege one ethnic identity over another. The regime, however, concerned with Myanmar as a physical, strictly bounded, unity rather than a boundless product of the mind, is beginning to formulate the origination of humanity along a very different track based on physical archaeological evidence. It is impatient with mere 'ideas' about spiritual origination in the texts over which it feels it has insufficient control. It seeks to bolster the Myanmar State by transforming the status of Myanmar visibly in the eyes of the world, by locating, no less, actual proof of the origins of all mankind in Burma itself. If successful, it would, of course, represent a *coup de grâce* for the generals. Not only would their censorship have succeeded in extending 'Myanmar' as the preferred mode of self-identification right across the English speaking world (the country was renamed Myanmar in languages other than Burmese in May 1989), but they would be able to claim that the rest of the world (including its severest critics) is inferior and less civilized in the family of man.

The generals would appear to be subconsciously in pursuit of the etymological conjunction between Burma-Myanmar and the superior Brahma deities at the beginning of the world. Mental culture fulfilled this association perfectly adequately so far. Burmese ideas about political leadership continue to demand the practice of *byama-so tayà* social meditations and encounters with these Buddhist saints and hermits, and they continue to commemorate these in 'royal' style by building pagodas and by resolving to attain *nibbana*. Today, however, the generals go beyond pagoda building in the belief that culture must be unearthed by collecting physical archaeological evidence that must be housed in museums (and to some extent pagodas) placed under their control. In short, the regime looks for a more substantive and tangible impersonal pillar than the mind to tie their Myanmar *mandala* to.

Through this archaeological quest the regime hopes to restore to Myanmar its most impressive achievements and to locate the oldest forms of human life within its boundaries. It now weaves Pondaung into its summing up of its 'Myanmar culture and traditions' as follows:

> Myanmar's existence dates back to many centuries where under the rule of Myanmar kings and its own culture and traditions, civilization flourished. As part of the restoration of the rich cultural heritage of Myanmar, palaces and related edifices of Myanmar kings have been carefully excavated and renovated or reconstructed to their original designs. These magnificent structures clearly depict the once rich and affluent civilization of the Myanmar people.
>
> Moreover, in the Pon-Taung-Pon-Nyar region of central Myanmar, recent discoveries of some primate fossils dating back to some 40 million years may qualify Myanmar as the region where mankind originated. The findings, as recent as 13 April 1997, however, clearly indicate the existence of Myanmar culture and traditions since time immemorial. (Website, Myanmar Today, www.myanmar.com)

Buddhism has permitted a multi-ethnic polity to arise in the past exactly because it does not propose superior origins of any race or culture; this has been at the root of the Burman polity in the past. Invariably Burmese chronicles began with the story of the Buddha's enlightenment and the transformation of polities as the result of receiving his relics. However, the views that the regime currently proclaim no longer place the Buddha's relics central, but instead privilege the Pondaung fossils as the earliest origin for Myanmar, through which it unifies its 135 'national races' on the basis of some supposedly superior common regional physical origin.

I have described the regime's 'Myanmafication' projects as the attempt, since 1989, to attain to national unity without appealing to martyr and national hero Aung San. The regime's 'Aung San amnesia' was hastened when his daughter, Aung San Suu Kyi, reclaimed him for the democracy movement. If Aung San and Aung San Suu Kyi followed Burmese tradition by advocating universal and boundless loving-kindness meditation (*metta*), irrespective of ethnic identity, as a crucial ingredient to national harmony, the military now aims for a very different kind of national unity known as 'national reconsolidation'. In this, archaeology has become an indispensable instrument to localize and regionalize a substantively superior form of national identity. Through its newly discovered archaeological methods, the regime hopes to conquer prehistory and unify the 135 ethnic groups under one family umbrella now referred to as 'Myanmar culture'.

The archaeological quest is of such great importance that the more significant archaeological finds require nothing less than the Defence Services Intelligence Unit, namely the Office of Strategic Studies (OSS), which currently governs Burma under General Khin Nyunt, also Secretary 1 of the SPDC and *de facto* head of government. In this Myanmafication programme the archaeology and palaeoanthropology of Myanmar fall, as we shall see, within the realms of national defence.

National archaeology teams

Though the story has earlier beginnings, the contemporary evaluation of the Pondaung fossils as a public national treasure began in January 1997 when General Khin Nyunt learnt about them after an announcement of a discovery by a French team of the earliest primate fossils extant in Southern Thailand. He learnt that Burma also had very rare fossils from Pondaung, north-west of Mandalay, which had been discovered in 1978 by expeditions led by members of the Geology Department of Mandalay University. The potential of Pondaung had first been discovered as early as 1914 by a team from the Geological Survey of India. Both teams referred to the discoveries as *Pondaungia*.

After national independence archaeology was not considered a great priority, and the 1978 discoveries had even been suppressed by the Ne Win regime. However, theories had been floated that these included fossils of ancient higher primates and, with the regime's reputation at low ebb, General Khin Nyunt decided that these studies should be followed up, and in February 1997, after a discussion with some academics, Khin Nyunt directed his Office of Strategic Studies [OSS] and geologists of the Ministry of Education to explore and search for fossilized remains in Pondaung. By the end of February, the (Myanmar) Fossil Exploration Team was put together, including members of the OSS for 'full logistic support' and geologists from the Geology Department. Colonel Than Tun of the OSS was appointed leader of the expedition.

General Khin Nyunt ordered his team to go out on a 'mission' and to 'find evidence . . . since it would greatly enhance the stature of the country in the world'. He 'stated that it was necessary to search for and uncover further incontrovertible evidence that the fossilized remains of higher primates found in Myanmar could be dated as being 40 million years old, in order to advance the studies into man's origins'. The joint expedition team 'were being dispatched to search, explore and find such evidence' and he emphasized this mission 'was of vital importance since it would greatly enhance the stature of the country in the world' and he therefore 'urged the scholars to make every endeavour for the success of the mission'.[3]

In March and April 1997 numerous visits were made to different sites. Excitement mounted as finds were made including an elephant's tusk. In May, the team's geologists collected a variety of fossils, later presented to a gathering of government officials, scholars and media personnel, at the Defence Forces Guest House in Rangoon. On this occasion General Khin Nyunt gave the keynote speech alluding to the discovery as proof that human life and civilization began in Burma. The recent discoveries illustrated the origins of the great Burmese nationality and the superiority of Burmese culture. Should the academics be able to prove the claims, then Burmese people could definitely say that 'culture began in Myanmar'. Reports stressed that it was army officers who had heroically discovered some of the vital human remains in the fossil jigsaw, leaving little honour for Burmese civilian archaeologists and academics.

International validation

The military wished to be seen at the cutting edge. However, they had no clue how to interpret the evidence, and the next step was to invite foreign researchers to make sense of and legitimize these discoveries. Three different teams were invited to Burma.

An American team led by palaeontologist of Iowa University Dr Russell L. Ciochon studied the fossil specimens at the National Museum, Rangoon, in late 1997. Having previously been refused permission to continue his researches, he was reported 'highly gratified' at the leaders' keen interest and to be very pleased at being invited.[4] The American fossil exploration team then made a field trip to Pondaung with the Burmese team in December 1997 and January 1998.

A third field survey was undertaken by the Myanmar-France Pondaung Fossils Expedition, a team made up between the original Burmese team and a group of French palaeontologists, led by Jean Jacques Jaeger of France's Montpellier University. The French met the Burmese team on 31 March 1998 at a Defence Services Guest House, and carried out an expedition in April. When they assessed the finds displayed in the National Museum they concluded that these 'may belong to higher anthropoid primate[s] and to the Eocene, which is about 40 million years back', but somewhat disappointingly, they also said that they would need further evidence 'to determine the origin of man and that further study need be made'.[5] The Myanmar-France Pondaung Fossils Expedition Team held a press conference in conjunction with military intelligence sponsored by the OSS at the guest house.

The fourth academic team – the Joint Myanmar-Japan Pondaung Fossil Expedition Team – involved Japanese scholars from the Primate Research Institute of Kyoto University.

Pondaung revealed to the world

Subsequent to these initial explorations by the respective 'national' teams the military organized a seminar and an exhibition at the National Museum of Ethnology, Rangoon, in June 1998 to which geologists, palaeontologists, anthropologists, historians and archaeologists nation-wide were invited. At this seminar General Khin Nyunt urged that:

> just as an individual's worth depended on his heritage and his achievements, so also a nation's prestige could be measured in terms of its lineage and historical and cultural background. A nation that can provide historical evidence of its ancient roots and the emergence and growth of its culture, traditions and national traits is a nation in which national fervour and patriotism thrives. It is also a nation whose people will try to perpetuate its identity, sovereignty and independence. He said this was especially true of a country such as ours that had once been enslaved under an imperialist power and had had our history distorted and mis-

represented. To right this wrong, the Government of the Union of Myanmar had laid down social objectives which includes the uncovering of true historical records and the resolve to correct the warped and biased versions of Myanmar history as written by some foreign historians. He however acknowledged the fact that Myanmar historians, scientists and researchers had throughout the ages carried out research and study in their own capacity and had been custodians of authentic historical facts. Now however with full government support and sponsorship the results of isolated or individual research could be collated for a correct interpretation and presentation of a coherent authentic history of Myanmar.

General Khin Nyunt concluded by urging participants to prove on the basis of the significant and substantial finds of the primate fossils that 'The Myanmar people are not visitors who came from a faraway land and settled here. Life began here in this Myanmar environment of land, air and water. Their roots are here' (Kyi Kyi Hla, 'The Pondaung Fossil Expedition', *Myanmar Perspectives*, May 1998).

A seminar on these discoveries, co-sponsored by the OSS and the Higher Education Department of the Ministry of Education, took place at the Diamond Jubilee Hall, Rangoon University, on 2–4 June 1998. The Pondaung fossil expedition team attended this together with another team engaged in the study of ancient cultural evidence in Budalin Township, Sagaing. A number of historians, anthropologists and archaeologists were present at this event.

Pondaung's propaganda value and the National Museum

Evidently the Pondaung discoveries have implications well beyond the realms of science. They are portrayed in the regime's publicity as 'taken to indicate the origin of man in Pondaung Ponnyar area in the middle Myanmar', and are routinely introduced as a precursor to the political history of the Union and the regime's achievements.

General Khin Nyunt wanted a central location to place these findings for propaganda purposes. Construction of the five-floor National Museum at No. 66–74, Pyay Road, commenced in June 1990 and it was inaugurated on 18 September 1996. By December 1997 he had decided two things deserved pride of place, namely the Pondaung discoveries and the last royal throne. In the official museum report it is said that arrangements 'are under way to exhibit ancient Myanmar attire, other cultural objects of national races and fossils including fossilized primates excavated . . . by a research team led by Colonel Than Tun, Head of Department, Office of Strategic Studies, from the Pondaung area and others donated by the locals.'

> It can now be firmly said that there were living beings in Myanmar 40 million years ago and if Myanmar scholars can present with firm and full evidence to the world, it can be assumed that human civilization began in our motherland. (*Information Sheets*, 29 Dec. 1997)

This propaganda was taken up again at Exhibition '98 to Revitalize and Foster Patriotic Spirit, held on 1–30 November 1998 at the Tatmadaw [Army] Convention Centre.

A critique of Pondaung politics

In the course of exhibiting their finds, the regime displayed what was supposedly a fossil from the same region where U Thaw Tin and U Ba Maw had found fossils in 1978. Though these two Burmese academics had at the time tried to share their discoveries with the international community, they were arrested and the fossils were confiscated by the BSPP. Since that time, it was not known where these fossils were kept. General Khin Nyunt explained that at the time they had conserved the fossils in a secure place.

However, it would appear that the two who had originally discovered the fossils did not hypothesize that the human race or culture originated in Burma. Furthermore, in a paper delivered in November 1995, well before Khin Nyunt ordered his Pondaung missions into the field, Professor Than Tun, the most respected scholar in the field of Burma's historical research (not to be confused with OSS Colonel Than Tun who led the Pondaung Expedition), provided a serious critique of Ba Maw's early work on the Pondaung fossils during the BSPP era (1962–88) and urged that 'we shall have to wait for more discoveries'.[6]

Professor Than Tun found archaeological speculations about the origination of mankind in Burma to be quite ill informed and based on unsystematic research, causing unnecessary confusion in the archaeological world. He has furthermore criticized the general state of archaeological research in Burma. He says that, though the department of archaeology will celebrate its centenary in 1998, 'its operations are still being carried out in the early 19th-century style'. Stronger still, 'like the looters of old, they take what they want and leave what they don't want'. He encourages the keeping of records, the central reporting of all finds, research on them, and accurate dating. Undoubtedly, were there a free press, such criticism would have been amplified and joined by others to temper some of the regime's spectacular cultural and archaeological visions.

If this casts doubt on the regime's archaeological methodology, Win Thein, benefiting from living abroad and the freedom to say what he thinks, has indicated the Pondaung project merely represents regime propaganda to instil patriotism in the people, saying that though General Khin Nyunt and his colleagues have been working very hard in Pondaung, their attempt represents 'a new evolutionary theory which no one can accept' and he points out that there is no academic freedom in Burma and that 'the regime has previously coerced academics into writing history as they want it recorded'.

The generals are probably less interested in these finds than in the many magical ('mundane knowledge') myths about Pondaung. In the tourist literature it has been described as subject to 'tall tales and supernatural mysteries' where 'witches and sorcerers . . . molest visitors' and alchemists produced elixirs by powdering the strange fossils they gathered. The uniqueness of the archaeological finds, at a time when Burma is in such turmoil, may lift the spirits of some, but it also reveals how determined the army are to waste public resources, including its top intelligence officers, to track down culture, to detect components that may be used to help construct a new Myanmar in which the people are denied agency.

A critique of Pondaung archaeology

The generals strive for the mythological realization of 'Myanmar', and different national teams have clambered onto the bandwagon to attain privileged access to Burma's archaeological sites. As a result palaeoanthropologists have provided the regime with the credibility it craves in its cultural propaganda.

It may well be true that the earliest anthropoids originated in Burma. However, true or not, the seriousness with which the military pursues Myanmafication means, of course, that archaeology and culture have been placed, like the economy and ethnicity, and virtually everything else, into the realm of national defence and state secrecy. The most important archaeological objects were hidden from view and from all forms of inspection during the BSPP era (1962–88) because they were classed as national secrets. Today, however, these 'secrets' have been turned into national assets behind glass in the National Museum, where they supposedly, under the watchful eye of the statue of King Bayinnaung, the invader of Siam, engender the pride of race in the Burmese peoples and help unify the country. Dozens of museums have been built in the last decade to commemorate the regime's attempt to draw Myanmar civilization within its own controlled orbit.

It is well known that palaeoanthropologists who work in China have to tailor, to some degree, their public scientific opinions to the ideological and nationalist sensibilities of their hosts in order to retain access. However, what I would like to see is less emphasis on national teams in archaeological explorations, and a greater awareness by scholars from all disciplines of the ludicrous use to which their scientific discoveries are put. Archaeologists intent on interpreting archaeological finds from Burma should read *The Politics of the Past* (ed. P. Gathercole and D. Lowenthal, Unwin Hyman, 1990) and Bruce Trigger's 'Alternative Archaeologies' (*Man* 19, 1984). Above all, they should be careful when dealing with inexperienced Burmese military officers hosting and accompanying them about the finds.

Archaeology as an academic discipline is by and large a Western invention. The regime, in emphasizing archaeology as a military instrument for conquering the past, has exceeded its self-acclaimed prerogative to govern by means of indigenous values alone (exponents of the democracy movements are invariably characterized as 'foreign'). Yet Burmese claims to civilization and to national unity have historically been strongly rooted in and are legitimized by mental culture; it is the instrument of mind (*byama-so tayà*) that uproots the hard-edged selfish concepts of identity. The paradox is that the instruments of both enlightenment (mental culture) and archaeology (culture) negotiate the limits of civilization, reach out beyond the boundaries of human existence, relativize existence in time and space, and are also productive of super-beings (*arya*). They do so ultimately through the discovery and representation of human remains, which are used to stake claim to the land in which these rest.

However, that is where in my view their similarity ends, for *byama-so tayà* and Myanmar civilization address these limits through the intermediary of Brahma in very different ways. Mental culture has its own archaeology. *Ariya*, rather than refer-ring to Aryan, the Indo-European race that invaded India, in Buddhism came to mean 'the noble ones', namely those of whatever cultural or racial background who, by ridding themselves of mental impurity through spiritual practices (mental culture) will soon no longer be reborn in the cycle of life. Four stages are recog-nized, ranging from stream-winner, for whom there are still seven lives left, to *arahant*, for whom no rebirths remain. These are celebrated in the erection of pagodas built as part of the duty of charity, the first royal duty, in which saintly relics are housed and commemorated.

In this pre-modern model of the polity, *ariya* are counter-evolutionary for their centre-point is not culture, nation or museum, but cessation of being and the arrest of transmigration in *samsara*. *Ariya* cannot be confined by secular powers of the mili-tary as they have emancipated from their grasp. The regime therefore no longer regards building pagodas around relics of *ariya* as sufficient to unify Burma; it needs the Pondaung fossils within their grasp to become the corner-stone of a conserva-tive nationalism that centralizes and draws firm boundaries around ethnic identity from which no one can escape. The fossils are today guarded by soldiers behind glass. Mental culture unbounded has given way to archaeology imprisoned. Liberating hermit practice is giving way, once again, to insular Hermit State.

The regime hopes to silence its reflexive critics by pointing at the threat of the 'foreign' Trojan horse (i.e. all forms of political opposition) that only the military, as guardians of 'traditional civilization', can fight. In the process it is turning pagodas with their complex live histories into museums controlled by the military alone. This happened to the national Shwedagon Pagoda, where Aung San Suu Kyi launched her political career on 26 August 1988 when she gave her first major political speech at which she characterized the democracy struggle as 'the second national indepen-dence struggle'. Her father, too, gave his most inflammatory speeches against foreign colonial occupation at the Shwedagon. It is ironic that, with the aid of foreign archaeology, this commemoration of the Buddha's enlightenment and vibrant icon of Burmese ideas of political and personal freedom should today be turned into a museum, a representation of Burma's status as 'a prison without walls'.

From temple relics to museum fossils

The Burmese people are still deeply religious, and religious structures and values remain as the last avenues for phrasing political demands, for they preserve the last vestiges of local and personal agency. Unless one has superior armed forces, there is no longer a secular realm from which it is possible to engage in politics in Burma; the regime negotiates with armed drug barons but not with elected political leaders.

Museums have in the West become dominant institutions, absorbing palaces and churches and these modern state-sponsored structures are useful to govern-ment. The museum, as presently conceived, is a new political instrument in Burma introduced by the regime to enhance its national and international prestige while not committing itself to any kind of political reform. It has built exceedingly large museums to compete with pagodas. In Pagan, one of the largest structures is the new archaeological museum and Pagan is now commonly referred to as a 'veritable museum'. However, the museums seek to do two things: first, to selectively represent Burmese tradition for tourists in the hope of collecting dollars; and second, where they do address a Burmese audience, they are an attempt at sheer propaganda, and they seek to rein in any transcendental values there might be so as to confine their audience strictly within an invented Myanmar value system. They do not respond to the intellectual sensibilities of the Burmese peoples and do not open their eyes to their own history, nor to what is happening worldwide just in case they see how backward Burma is under military leadership.

In Burma, pagodas are vibrant and alive in local and national folklore. The regime wishes to control these places of independent worship. What better excuse than occupying and overshadowing these in the name of heritage conservation? Though it attempts to museumify the pagoda environment, it is unwilling to concede that it cannot control all aspirations of all people all of the time; people need independent institutions and practices that positively and independently stimulate their intellectual curiosity and religious sensibilities.

Today, regrettably, the only culture untainted by the regime's grasp is therefore mental culture, the culture produced in personal meditation that uproots the walls and partitions of the house, 'all your rafters are shattered – my mind is free from active thought . . .'. Behind prison bars these practices today are yielding new martyrs (*azani*) with fresh relics – such is the resilient politics of enlightenment. Fossils are no comfort and reproduce themselves differently in very different spheres of exchange. Meditation traditions are flourishing in Burma today, as never before.

Notes

This article has been slightly abridged for republication. A fuller argument will be found in pages 142–7 of Gustaaf Houtman's *Mental Culture in Burmese Crisis Politics: Aung San Suu Kyi and the National League for Democracy* (Tokyo: Tokyo University of Foreign Studies, Institute for the Study of Languages and Cultures of Asia and Africa), also downloadable from http://homepages.tesco.net/~ghoutman.

1   'General Saw Maung outlines goals for nation', 10 Dec. 1990. In: Weller, M. and National Coalition Government of the Union of Burma, 1993, *Democracy and politics in Burma: a collection of documents*. Manerplaw, Burma: Government Printing Office, p. 221.

2   State Peace and Development Council Chairman Senior General Than Shwe's message on the occasion of Golden Jubilee Independence Day. *New Light of Myanmar*, 4 Jan. 1998.

3   'The Pondaung Fossil Expedition', *Myanmar Perspectives*, May 1998.

4   *New Light of Myanmar*, 12 May 1997.

5   'French palaeontologists discover fossilized remains at Pondaung Region'. *Information Sheets* (published electronically by military intelligence on www.myanmar-information.net), 20 Apr. 1998. 'Myanmar-France Pondaung Fossils Expedition team meets the Press to clarify discovery of Pondaung primate fossils', *New Light of Myanmar*, 8 Dec. 1998.

6   Than Tun. 'Prehistoric researches in Myanmar'. In *Traditions in Current Perspective* (Rangoon: Universities Historical Research Centre, 1996), pp. 25–9.

Update by Gustaaf Houtman

By the end of 1999, the Pondaung fossils were impacting the conference circuit. Academic arguments were being formulated and presented about the anthropoid origins in Asia. It is argued, for example, that 'The occurrence of these forms (*Amphitipithecus, Pondaungia, Siamopithecus*) in the middle and late Eocene of Thailand and Myanmar supports the hypothesis that South Asia has been an evolutive centre for anthropoids and that North Africa should no longer be regarded as exclusive for the origin of that group', and that it 'gives support to the hypothesis of an Asian origin of anthropoids'. In the Burmese officials' view, the *Bahinia pondaungensis* they uncovered in Burma represented a new anthropoid primate species belonging to the Eocene, but also a more complete Eocene fossil than any of those found in China (see Jacques Jaeger and Stephane Ducrocq, 'The paleontology and evolution of Asiatic primates', paper presented at the International Symposium on the Evolution of Vertebrates, Lund, 21–23 Oct. 1999).

Since late 1999, also, the Pondaung fossils have been proclaimed by scientific bodies as indicating that these 'lend support to the idea that the ancestor of all monkeys and apes lived in Asia instead of Africa' and that 'this could mean that anthropoids migrated from Asia to Africa at some point'. Also, that the findings in Pondaung 'could mean that the anthropoid group has its roots stretching far back into time, possibly even into the late Paleocene (58–55 million years ago)'. In short, the Burmese officials' conclusion is that 'now we may have to change our whole story about anthropoid origins and evolution' ('Primitive primate makes the case for Asian anthropoid origins', Press Release, American Association for the Advancement of Science, 14 Oct. 1999).

These endorsements have encouraged the regime since early 2000 to place at the centre of the introductory homepage (http://www.myanmar.com) in large type a link to a page called Myanma Primates. This, in turn, leads to two articles and to a range of photographs of fossil-finds.

The Raw, the Cooked and the Marilynated

■ *Anthropology Today*, 10.6, December 1994, pp. 15–16

THOSE FORTUNATE TO HEAR Professor Marilyn Strathern's inaugural lecture 'The Relation: issues on complexity and scale' in Cambridge on 14 October are likely to remember it. Inaugural lectures usually select a topic for an analysis which, given the ceremonial character of the occasion, then has to be studded with allusions to institutional ancestors, intellectual peers, other friendly disciplines, and the impressive programme of departmental work which is being inaugurated. Strathern's topic was relationship itself, so that there was no disjunction between medium and message. Her guiding metaphor was the hologram, that mysterious visual model for post-Einsteinian physics. When the lecture is published by the university, it will not be the same with the addition of footnotes and bibliography, for it was in the nature of a musical composition.

Lévi-Strauss, that connoisseur of musical forms ranging from the Wagnerian leitmotiv to the piano étude, would surely have been delighted if he had been present. The form of Strathern's lecture was that of a fugue. If asked to summarize what she argued or criticize it, one would be in some difficulty. Schumann is said, when asked to explain a difficult piano piece, to have sat down and played it again. Reviewers of musical performances are much disparaged but can only do their best.

Marilyn Strathern spoke of the contribution of mid-century Cambridge social anthropologists to understanding social organization; of relations of kinship and affinity as biological givens and cultural constructs which demand analytical priority (assisted by Melanesian ethnography) over the mainstream Judaeo-Christian assumption of a discrete soul; of the twists given to these relations by the new reproductive technologies; of the gradual extension in English usage of the grammatical term 'gender' to a wider sense formerly deprecated by dictionaries as vulgar or jocular; of the infinite genealogical tree imagined for us by Darwin in *The Origin of Species*; of the institutional need to respect implicit, or understated, order which is now threatened by a dominant 'culture of enhancement' that insists on the Added Value of mission statements and quality control.

Figure PP7   Marilyn Strathern in Hagen, Papua New Guinea, 1976, photographed by Paula Brown.

It was relevant that the lecture was given to a massed audience in a smallish theatre – the 'Little Hall'. Strathern, like Blake, aims to see the world in a grain of sand. Holography, in its most general terms, is the means whereby patterns and messages generated by events in a particular area of space and time interact to generate new patterns, which represent the way in which the separate events inter-relate. These cross-correlations are read out when we inject into them a reference wavelength such as a laser beam, which has the property of imposing a kind of ordered set-structure. Strathern conveyed a conviction that an anthropology depart-ment with its nationwide and worldwide connections is quite able to take on the most seemingly daunting intellectual problems. Further, whatever a listener brings to the endeavour is valid. She offered such a plenitude of allusions that, just as no-one can have grasped them all, so no-one can have felt left out. If one had, earlier on a brilliant October afternoon in Cambridge, visited a microcosm of a mangrove swamp in the University Botanic Garden glass-houses, and later spotted Stephen Hawking being pushed in his wheel-chair, that was as germane to appreciating her lecture as the specialist knowledge brought by her fellow Melanesianists.

Strathern brings off this feat not only because of her admired academic achieve-ments but also because, as all her colleagues know, she practices what she preaches in everyday life by taking relationships seriously across the widest range, and by trying to optimize the work of institutions through releasing human potential and opening doors. In her commitment to registering the 'holomovement' (to borrow the late David Bohm's term) there is the same loss of sharp contrast and definition that we find in holograms as opposed to good photographs – but many find the gain worth the loss. As a further self-discipline, Strathern seems to eschew public emotionalism – whether celebrations of *communitas* or identification with suffering

– but her generosity of spirit leaves little doubt that behind this apparent austerity is someone who leaves space for feeling as well as thought.

As with a groundbreaking composer, her style of anthropology may become more familiar and understandable to us with the passing years. A doubt remains as to what happens when such a style is copied by others. When a hologram is broken, each piece can reconstruct the entire image, but the smaller the fragments the poorer the definition. And yet, if Marilyn Strathern is right in her choice of metaphor, there is no reason why knowledge should not be built up in her way in order to register the complexities of our world, rather than through the conventional analytical lens of one-to-one relationships – which would presumably subvert the basis of all those existing academic institutions whose ideal is a binary lucidity.

PART EIGHT

The Technology of Enchantment

■   JONATHAN BENTHALL

The smooth surface of cultured society is sapped and mined by superstition. Only those whose studies have led them to investigate the subject
are aware of the depth to which the ground beneath our feet is thus, as
it were, honeycombed by unseen forces. . . . The surface of society, like
that of the sea, is in perpetual motion; its depths, like those of the ocean,
remain almost unmoved.

THUS SIR JAMES FRAZER in his 1908 inaugural lecture at the
University of Liverpool, 'The scope of social anthropology'. He was thinking of
the 'grosser beliefs' of 'the vulgar'. For the late **Alfred Gell** – from whose lead
article, 'Technology and magic', the title of this section is borrowed – the truth is
even more vertiginous: irrationality haunts our most seemingly rational activities
like a shadow.

For Gell, magic is a way of getting something for nothing. It pervades our
modern technology so that the two are hard to distinguish. The 'technology of
enchantment' is mind-control, all the arts and creeds, advertising, public relations,
'spin'. A dangerously wide category, then, for it includes all the things which make
life worth living, as well as all the mechanisms, short of brute coercion, by which
people can be enslaved. But it was Gell's philosophy, as I understand it, that we
can protect ourselves from enslavement by means of play, willing submission to
enchantment and humour.[1] The articles chosen for this section are appropriately
diverse.

Mary Douglas contributes a very short report on a lively conference she organized in 1974 on the subject of 'lying and deceit'. I remember being struck at the
time by the unexpectedness of the theme and the variety of the speakers. It was a
relaxed weekend conference held at Cumberland Lodge in Windsor Great Park, of
a kind that rarely takes place any more. Well in advance of more ponderous debates

– whether on cognitive relativism or on the assertion of political power through brazenness in lying – the conference, of which this report is sadly the only trace, points a way in which anthropology could continue to serve as a convening discipline for specialist researchers to exchange and test one another's findings – especially on broad topics unearthed by anthropology which have not yet been done to death.

James Lewton-Brain asks why detective stories are so popular, and his answer is that they are essentially concerned with small communities such as an English village or country-house party, which are the breeding-ground for witchcraft accusations. The detective in an Agatha Christie novel, like the witch-doctor in a sedentary community, has the task of assigning responsibility for a malevolent act. In real life we hope to know better than to interpret misfortune by means of witchcraft accusations – we look for evidence and we accept the intervention of sheer chance – but we submit with pleasure to the enchantment of the detective story, the 'mousetrap' as in Agatha Christie's stage play which has run in London continuously for fifty years.

Real-life violent crime is deeply troubling and provokes a demand for magical expiation. **J. Anthony Paredes** and **Elizabeth D. Purdum** follow Frazer and Westermarck in considering capital punishment as a form of human sacrifice. After the execution by electric chair of a serial sex murderer, Theodore Bundy, in Florida in 1989, Paredes and Purdum carried out a study of a sample of local newspapers' handling of the story, and disclosed a flamboyant array of vernacular private rituals which appears to support the thesis. This is not a surprise to those who have read histories of public executions in eighteenth-century London. But whereas it is unlikely that capital punishment will be reintroduced in Britain, no politician can aspire to Presidential office in the United States without endorsing the continuation of capital punishment.

Declan Quigley's 1995 guest editorial on the paradoxes of monarchy was based on a talk he gave at a 'public seminar' on monarchy, in one of a series of such seminars that I organized in London in 1993 to mark the RAI's 150th anniversary. It was sparsely attended, and an immediate damper was put on the proceedings by the chairman, an anthropology professor, who began by stating that classical anthropological theories about kingship had no bearing on industrial societies. This was long before the tragic death of Princess Diana in 1997 and the birth of 'dianology' in academia. After 1997, Quigley's emphasis on scapegoating and sacrifice as a major constituent in the idea of monarchy seems less eccentric than it did to some of those who attended his talk.

Alex Weingrod discusses the symbolism of human bones and burials, with special reference to Israel – a country whose fascination with them he ascribes to the vulnerability of Israeli nationalism. This fascination intensified after 1967, with the military occupation of Palestinian territories and the growing influence of religious conservatives. Many other anthropological examples might be adduced (some of them, such as the Native Americans, mentioned by Weingrod), and indeed a concern for proper disposal of human remains is almost a cultural universal, reaching back deep into prehistory and surviving today into the most secularized societies.

In Gell's sense this concern is 'magical', a defiance of brutish mortality, whereas reason tells us that what separates human beings from the other animals is precisely the elusive stuff such as poetry and electronic bank transfers. Our cherishing of our animal remains is thus one of humanity's weakest points for ideological manipulation.

Note

1   Obituary of Alfred Gell by Eric Hirsch, Suzanne Kuchler and Chris Pinney, *AT* 13.2, April 1997, pp. 21–3.

Chapter 31

Alfred Gell

■ **TECHNOLOGY AND MAGIC**, *Anthropology Today,*
4.2, April 1988, pp. 6–9

'TECHNOLOGICAL' CAPABILITIES ARE one of the distinguishing features of our species, and have been since a very early stage in evolution, if not from the very beginning. It is no longer possible to claim 'tool using' as a uniquely 'human' characteristic, because there are distinct tool-use traditions among apes, especially chimpanzees, and rather more rudimentary examples of tool-use among some other species as well. Human beings, however, have elaborated 'technological' means of realizing their intentions to an unprecedented degree. But what is 'technology' and how does it articulate to the other species characteristics we possess?

The answers which have been suggested to this question have suffered from a bias arising from the misconceived notion that the obtaining of subsistence necessities from the environment is the basic problem which technology enables us to surmount. Technology is identified with 'tools' and 'tools' with artefacts, like axes and scrapers, which are presumed to have been imported in the 'food quest'. This 'food quest' has been imagined as a serious, life-or-death, business, and the employment of technology as an equally 'serious' affair. *Homo technologicus* is a rational, sensible, creature, not a mythopoeic or religious one, which he only becomes once he abandons the search for 'technical' solutions to his problems and takes off into the realms of fantasy and empty speculation.

But this opposition between the technical and the magical is without foundation. Technology is inadequately understood if it is simply identified with tool-use, and tool-use is inadequately understood if it is identified with subsistence activity.

Although it may be useful for certain classification purposes – especially in prehistory – to identify 'technology' with 'tools', from any explanatory point of view technology is much more than this. At the very minimum, technology not only consists of the artefacts which are employed as tools, but also includes the sum total of the kinds of knowledge which make possible the invention, making and use of tools. But this is not all. 'Knowledge' does not exist except in a certain social context. Technology is co-terminous with the various networks of social relationships which allow for the transmission of technical knowledge, and provide the necessary conditions for cooperation between individuals in technical activity. But one cannot stop even at this point, because the objectives of technical production are themselves shaped by the social context. Technology, in the widest sense, is those forms of social relationships which make it socially necessary to produce, distribute and consume goods and services using 'technical' processes.

But what does the adjective 'technical' mean? 'Technical' does not, I think, indicate an either/or distinction between production processes which do, or do not, make use of artefacts called 'tools'. There can be 'techniques' – for instance, the 'techniques of the body' listed by Mauss – which do not make use of tools that are artefacts. What distinguishes 'technique' from non-technique is a certain degree of *circuitousness* in the achievement of any given objective. It is not so much that technique has to be learned, as that technique has to be ingenious. Techniques form a bridge, sometimes only a simple one, sometimes a very complicated one, between a set of 'given' elements (the body, some raw materials, some environmental features) and a goal-state which is to be realized making use of these givens. The given elements are rearranged in an intelligent way so that their causal properties are exploited to bring about a result which is improbable except in the light of this particular intervention.

Technical means are roundabout means of securing some desired result. The degree of technicality is proportional to the number and complexity of the steps which link the initial givens to the final goal which is to be achieved. Tools, as extensions of the body which have to be prepared before they can be used, are an important category of elements which 'intervene' between a goal and its realization. But not less 'technical' are those bodily skills which have to be acquired before a tool can be used to good effect. Some tools, such as a baseball bat, are exceptionally rudimentary, but require a prolonged (i.e. circuitous) learning-process, in appropriate learning settings, before they can be deployed to much purpose. Highly 'technical' processes combine many elements, artefacts, skills, rules of procedure, in an elaborate sequence of purposes or sub-goals, each of which must be attained in due order before the final result can be achieved. It is this elaborate structure of intervening steps, the steps which enable one to obtain result X, in order to obtain Y, in order to (finally) obtain Z, which constitute technology as a 'system'.

The pursuit of intrinsically difficult-to-obtain results by roundabout, or clever, means, is the peculiar aptitude of the technological animal, *Homo sapiens*. But it is not at all true that this propensity is displayed exclusively, or even mainly, in the context of subsistence production, or that this aptitude is unconnected with the playful and imaginative side of human nature. Indeed, to state the problem in these terms is to see immediately that there can be no possible distinction, from the standpoint of 'degree of technicality', between the pursuit of material rewards through technical activity, and the equally 'technical' pursuit of a wide variety of other goals, which are not material but symbolic or expressive. From the Palaeolithic period on, human technical ability has been devoted, not just to making 'tools' such as axes and harpoons, but equally to the making of flutes, beads, statues, and much else besides, for diversion, adornment, pleasure. These objects had, without any doubt, their place in a 'sequence of purposes' which went beyond the elementary delight they afforded their makers. A flute, no less than an axe, is a tool, an element in a technical sequence; but its purpose is to control and modify human psychological responses in social settings, rather than to dismember the bodies of animals.

If a flute is properly to be seen as a tool, a psychological weapon, what is the technical system of which it forms a part? At this point I would like to offer a classificatory scheme of human technological capabilities in general, which can be seen as falling under three main headings.

The *first* of these technical systems, which can be called the 'Technology of Production', comprises technology as it has been conventionally understood, i.e. roundabout ways of securing the 'stuff' we think we need: food, shelter, clothing, manufactures of all kinds. I would include here the production of signals, i.e. communication. This is relatively uncontroversial and no more need be said about it at this point.

The *second* of these technical systems I call the 'Technology of Reproduction'. This technical system is more controversial, in that under this heading I would include most of what conventional anthropology designates by the word 'kinship'.

It must occur to anyone, nonetheless, who makes the comparison between human and animal societies, that human societies go to extreme lengths to secure specific patterns of matings and births. Once infants are born, their care and socialization is conducted in a technically elaborated way, making use of special devices such as cradles, slings, swaddling-boards, etc., and later on, toy weapons, special educational paraphernalia and institutions, and so on. The reproduction of society is the consequence of a vast amount of very skilled manipulation on the part of those with interests at stake in the process. Human beings are bred and reared under controlled conditions which are technically managed, so as to produce precisely those individuals for whom social provision has been made.

Of course, animals also engage in purposive action in order to intervene in reproductive processes, securing and defending mates, succouring their young, and so forth. Sometimes they seem to be quite cunning about it. I do not want to draw any hard and fast line between human and animal kinship here. But what I would suggest is that the really telling analogies between human and animal kinship systems are not to be found among wild populations of animal species, but among domesticated animals, such as horses and dogs, whose breeding behaviour, and social learning, human beings have learned to control using many of the same techniques as human beings use on themselves, with very much the same goals in view. We are (self-) domesticated animals; our animal analogues are the other domesticated animals.

Biologically, we possess the neotenous attributes (persistence of juvenile traits in the adult stage) which also often distinguish the domesticated variety of an animal species from its wild-type cousins (wolves vs. domesticated dogs, for instance). Domesticated varieties of animals are biddable, docile, creatures, because we have made them so. And so are we. The vaunted human attributes of teachability, flexibility – a kind of permanent childlike acceptance – are traits which have been evolved, not in the course of mighty struggles against the hostile forces of nature, but adapting to the demand for a more and more 'domesticable' human being. This is the phenotype which has been awarded maximum reproductive opportunities, and which now predominates, not because it has been 'selected' by nature, but because it selected itself.

The patterns of social arrangements which we identify as 'kinship systems' are a set of technical strategies for managing our reproductive destiny via an elaborate sequence of purposes. Accordingly, the whole domain of kinship has to be understood primarily as a technology, just as one would see horse-breeding and horse-breaking, or dog-breeding and dog-training, as 'technical' accomplishments. But how do we secure the acquiescence of horses and dogs in our intentions, apart from special breeding programmes, so as to secure a supply of tractable animals? Evidently, it is by exploiting natural biases in horse and dog psychology; in other words, by the artful use of whips, sugar-lumps, smacks, caresses, etc., all of which we can deliver because we possess hands, and know how to use them on animals all the better because we continually use them on one another.

Here we enter the domain of the *third* of our three technologies, which I will call the 'Technology of Enchantment'. Human beings entrap animals in the mesh of human purposes using an array of psychological techniques, but these are primitive by comparison with the psychological weapons which human beings use to exert control over the thoughts and actions of other human beings. The technology of enchantment is the most sophisticated that we possess.

Under this heading I place all those technical strategies, especially art, music, dances, rhetoric, gifts, etc., which human beings employ in order to secure the acquiescence of other people in their intentions or projects. These technical strategies – which are, of course, practised reciprocally – exploit innate or derived psychological biases so as to enchant the other person and cause him/her to perceive social reality in a way favourable to the social interests of the enchanter. It is widely agreed that characteristically human 'intelligence' evolved, not in response to the need to develop superior survival strategies, but in response to the complexity of human social life, which is intense, multiplex and very fateful for the individual. Superior intelligence manifests itself in the technical strategies of enchantment, upon which the mediation of social life depends. The manipulation of desire, terror, wonder, cupidity, fantasy, vanity, an inexhaustible list of human passions, offers an equally inexhaustible field for the expression of technical ingenuity.

My present purpose is not to explore the domain of the technology of enchantment, but merely to point out that it exists, and that it has to be considered, not as a separate province, i.e. 'Art' – opposed to technology – but as a technology in itself.

*   *   *

I have sketched the scope of the idea of 'Technology'. Now I want to consider the relationship between technology – defined as the pursuit of difficult-to-obtain objectives by roundabout means – and 'magic'. Magic is, or was, clearly an aspect of each of the three technologies I have identified, i.e. the technologies of production, reproduction and psychological manipulation, or 'enchantment'. But magic is different from these technologies, each of which involves the exploitation of the causal properties of things and the psychological dispositions of people, which are numbered, of course, among their causal properties. Whereas magic is 'symbolic'. Naturally, in stating this, I am conscious that there has been a prolonged debate about magic, and that not everybody agrees that magic is 'symbolic' at all; since it can be interpreted as an attempt to employ spirits or quasi-physical magical powers to intervene (causally) in nature. There is abundant native testimony to support this view, which is often the correct one to take from the standpoint of cultural interpretation, since nothing prevents people from holding at least some mistaken causal beliefs. However, from an observer's point of view, there is a distinction, in that efficacious technical strategies demonstrably exploit the causal properties of things in the sequence of purposes, whereas magic does not. The evolutionary survival value of the magical aspects of technical strategies is, therefore, a genuine problem.

I take the view that 'magic' as an adjunct to technical procedures persists because it serves 'symbolic' ends, that is to say, cognitive ones. Magical thought formalizes and codifies the structural features of technical activity, imposing on it a framework of organization which regulates each successive stage in a complex process.

If one examines a magical formula, it is often seen that a spell or a prayer does little more than identify the activity which is being engaged in and defines a criterion for 'success' in it. '*Now I am planting this garden. Let it be so productive that I will not be able to harvest all of it. Amen.*' Such a spell is meaningless by itself, and it only fulfils its technical role in the context of a magical system in which each and every gardening procedure is accompanied by a similar spell, so that the whole sequence of spells constitutes a complete cognitive plan of 'gardening'.

Magic consists of a symbolic 'commentary' on technical strategies in production, reproduction, and psychological manipulation. I suggest that magic derives from play. When children play, they provide a continuous stream of commentary on their own behaviour. This commentary frames their actions, divides it up into segments, defines momentary goals, and so on. It seems that this superimposed organizational format both guides imaginative play as it proceeds, and also provides a means of internalising it and recalling it, as well as raw materials for subsequent exercises in innovation and recombination, using previously accumulated materials in new configurations. Not only does the basic format of children's play-commentary (now I am doing this, now I am doing that, and now this will happen . . .) irresistibly recall the format of spells, but the relation between reality and commentary in play and in magic-making remain essentially akin; since the play-commentary invariably idealizes the situation, going beyond the frontiers of the merely real. When a child asserts that he is an aeroplane (with arms extended, and the appropriate sound effects and swooping movements) the commentary inserts the ideal in the real, as something which can be evoked, but not realized. But the unrealizable transformation of child into aeroplane, while never actually confused with reality, does nonetheless set the ultimate goal towards which play can be oriented, and in the light of which it is intelligible and meaningful.

The same is true of magic, which sets an ideal standard, not to be approached in reality, towards which practical technical action can nonetheless be oriented.

There is another feature which play and technology share. Technology develops through a process of innovation, usually one which involves the re-combination and re-deployment of a set of existing elements or procedures towards the attainment of new objectives. Play also demonstrates innovativeness — in fact, it does so continuously, whereas innovation in technology is a slower and more difficult process. Innovation in technology does not usually arise as the result of the application of systematic thought to the task of supplying some obvious technical 'need', since there is no reason for members of any societies to feel 'needs' in addition to the ones they already know how to fulfil. Technology, however, does change, and with changes in technology, new needs come into existence. The source of this mutability, and the tendency towards ever-increasing elaboration in technology must, I think, be attributed, not to material necessity, but to the cognitive role of 'magical' ideas in providing the orienting framework within which technical activity takes place. Technical innovations occur, not as the result of attempts to supply wants, but in the course of attempts to realize technical feats heretofore considered 'magical'.

Sometimes, ethnographers record technical procedures which seem magical in themselves, even though we are assured that they are entirely practical. In the Solomon Islands, and some adjoining parts of the Pacific, there used to be employed a technique of fishing using kites. This kind of fishing was done in lagoons. The fisherman would go out in a canoe, to which was fastened a kite, fashioned like a bird, but made out of pandanus leaves. From this kite, which hovered over the water, there descended a further string to which was attached a ball of spider's webs, which dangled just on the surface of the water. Fish in the lagoon would see the sparkling spider's web ball and mistake it for an insect. But when they bit into it the sticky spider's web would cause their jaws to adhere to one another, so that they could not let go. At this point the fisherman would reel in the whole contraption and take the fish.

This fishing technique exemplifies perfectly the concept of roundaboutness which I have emphasized already. But it also suggests very strongly the element of fantasy which brings technical ideas to fruition. Indeed, if one encountered 'kite-fishing' as a myth, rather than as a practice, it would be perfectly susceptible to Lévi-Straussian myth-analysis. There are three elements: firstly, the spider's web, which comes from *dark places inside the earth* (caves); secondly, the kite, which is a bird *which flies in the sky*; and finally, there is the fish *which swims in the water*. These three mythemes are brought into conjunction and their contradictions are resolved in a final image, the '*fish with its jaws stuck together*' just like Asdiwal, stuck half-way up a mountain and turned to stone. One does not have to be a structuralist aficionado in order to concede that here a magical, mythopoeic, story can be realized as a 'practical' technique for catching fish.

And there are innumerable other examples which could be cited of technical strategies which, though they might or might not seem 'magical' to us, certainly do so to their practitioners. I will cite only one. In the eastern highlands of New Guinea, salt is made by burning rushes and filtering the ashes through little retorts, made of gourds, which results in briny water, which can be evaporated to produce slabs of native salt. Technically, this procedure is rather sophisticated, since it is difficult to burn the rushes at the right temperature to produce the best ash, and difficult to concentrate the brine and evaporate it with minimum wastage. Needless to say, much magic is employed, with special formulae to cover each stage of the multi-stage process, and to provide 'corrective adjustments' if the process seems to be going wrong in any way. Jadran Mimica, who provided me with these details, and whose forthcoming study of Angan salt-making is eagerly awaited as an Australian National University thesis, has brilliantly analysed the indigenous conception of the salt-making process, which, in effect, recapitulates cosmogony in terms of trans-formations of bodily substances, approximately in the sequence:

> *food (wood) ⇒ faeces (ash) ⇒ urine (brine) ⇒ milk ⇒ semen (evaporated brine) ⇒ bone/shell valuables (salt)*

It would take much too long to indicate, even in barest outline, the manifold connections between salt-making and the mythological and cosmological context within which the Angan salt-makers have developed their particular expertise, and which, without a doubt, shaped it in the course of its development. The net result is that Angan salt is 'high tech' according to indigenous standards of evaluation, and has correspondingly high exchange value in local trade networks.

This leads me to one further observation on the relation between magic and technology. I have so far described magic as an 'ideal' technology which orients practical technology and codifies technical procedures at the cognitive-symbolic level. But what would be the characteristics of an 'ideal' technology? An 'ideal' technical procedure is one which can be practised with *zero opportunity costs*. Practical technical procedures, however efficient, always do 'cost' something, not necessarily in money terms but in terms of missed opportunities to devote time, effort and resources to alternative goals, or alternative methods of achieving the same goal. The defining feature of 'magic' as an ideal technology is that it is 'costless' in terms of the kind of drudgery, hazards and investments which actual technical activity inevitably requires. Production 'by magic' is production minus the disadvantageous side-effects, such as struggle, effort, etc.

Malinowski's *Coral Gardens and their Magic* – still the best account of any primi-tive technological-cum-magical system, and unlikely ever to be superseded in this respect – brings out this feature of magical thinking exceptionally well. Trobriand gardens were, no less than Angan salt-making sites, arenas in which a magical sce-nario was played out, in the guise of productive activity. Yam-gardens were laid out with geometrical regularity, cleared initially of the least blade of grass, and were pro-vided with complicated constructions described as 'magical prisms' at one corner, which attracted yam-growing power into the soil. The litanies of the garden magi-cian, delivered at the site of the magical prisms, have been recorded in their entirety by Malinowski, with detailed exegesis. They are full of metaphorical devices of some-times considerable obscurity, but, in effect, they consist of a prolonged series of descriptions of an ideal garden, the garden to end all gardens, in which everything occurs absolutely as it should in the best of all possible worlds. The pests which inhabit the soil will rise up, and, of their own accord, commit mass suicide in the sea. Yam roots will strike down into the soil with the swiftness of a green parrot in flight, and the foliage above will dance and weave like dolphins playing in the surf.

Of course, real gardens are not quite so spectacular, though the ever-presence of these images of an ideal garden must be a major factor in focusing gardeners' minds on taking all practical steps to ensure that their gardens are better than they might otherwise be. However, if one considers the litanies of the garden magician a little more closely, one realizes that the garden being celebrated with so much fine language is, in effect, not a garden situated in some never-never land, but the garden which is actually present, which is mentioned and itemized in very minute, concrete, detail. For instance, each of the twenty-odd kinds of post or stick which is used to train yam creepers is listed, as are all the different cultigens, and all their different kinds of shoots and leaves, and so on. It is apparent that the real garden and its real productivity are what motivates the imaginary construction of the magical garden. It is because non-magical technology is effective, up to a point, that the idealized version of technology which is embodied in magical discourse is imaginatively compelling.

In other words, it is technology which sustains magic, even as magic inspires fresh technical efforts. The magical apotheosis of ideal, costless, production, is to be attained technically, because magical production is only a very flattering image of the production which is actually achievable by technical means. Hence, in practice, the pursuit of technical efficiency through intelligent effort coincides with the pursuit of the ideal of 'costless' production adumbrated in magical discourse. And this observation can lead to a conclusion concerning the fate of magic in modern societies, which no longer acknowledge magic specifically, yet are dominated by technology as never before.

What has happened to magic? It has not disappeared, but has become more diverse and difficult to identify. One form it takes, as Malinowski himself suggested, is advertising. The flattering images of commodities purveyed in advertising coincide exactly with the equally flattering images with which magic invests its objects. But just as magical thinking provides the spur to technological development, so also advertising, by inserting commodities in a mythologized universe, in which all kinds of possibilities are open, provides the inspiration for the invention of new consumer items. Advertising does not only serve to entice consumers to buy particular items; in effect, it guides the whole process of design and manufacture from start to finish, since it provides the idealized image to which the finished product must conform. Besides advertising itself, there is a wide range of imagery which provides a symbolic commentary on the processes and activities which are carried on in the technological domain. The imagination of technological culture gives rise to genres such as science fiction and idealized popular science, towards which practising scientists and technologists have frequently ambivalent feelings, but to which, consciously or unconsciously, they perforce succumb in the process of orienting themselves towards their social milieu and giving meaning to their activities. The propagandists, image-makers and ideologues of technological culture are its magicians, and if they do not lay claim to supernatural powers, it is only because technology itself has become so powerful that they have no need to do so. And if we no longer recognize magic explicitly, it is because technology and magic, for us, are one and the same.

Chapter 32

Mary Douglas

■ LYING AND DECEIT, *RAINews*,
2, May/June 1974, pp. 1–2

I F ANTHROPOLOGISTS MEET to discuss immigrant communities or famine relief they obviously have a justified sense of relevance to the problems of the day. If they meet to talk about religious symbolism they may equally well be talking about remote places or about religious matters near home. Such are the times we live in that a conference on 'Lying and Deceit' seems unquestionably topical, relevant and important.

In a long slow swell for 200 years European thought has been rising to a new view of reality and hence of truth. Instead of belief in a concrete, universally apprehensible physical nature and unmistakable human nature as steady objects out there for anyone to touch and see, there is now a wary sophistication.

More and more, physiology, neuropsychology, and the behavioural sciences recognize that perception requires a heavy dose of subjective organization. The world as it is known at any time is recognized now as largely constructed by those who know it and who devise the measuring rods that extend their insights. Organizing knowledge means organizing the knowing subject at the same time.

These may be cryptic remarks, as esoteric as any anthropological musings upon kinship categories and bizarre rites. Perhaps it will be clearer to say simply that anthropologists are always faced by impossible problems of translation from an alien culture.

To recognize simply that each tribe creates its view of its own environment and leave it at that would be too easy. The universe a tribe finds itself in, part-peopled by ghosts or zombies, were-animals and humans, fits snugly to the social purposes of the people living in it.

Thus anthropologists slip into a relativism in which the truth of other people's beliefs cannot be discussed at all. Their peculiar statements arise from their peculiar perceptual scheme and that is it. And if this is valid from one tribe to the next, so it can be equally for one segment of society to another.

Figure 32.1 'The poker game' by Irving Sinclair, 1944, probably inspired by de La Tour's 'The Cheat' in the Louvre, Paris.

The thought that one man's truth is another man's lie often disables judgements of social policy. Many old-fashioned lies and deceits would have to be whitewashed clean as merely expressing different perceptual schemes. So it would seem that problems of truth and falsehood concern everyone, but concern anthropologists in a way in which they do not necessarily strike others.

The recent conference organized on behalf of the Royal Anthropological Institute by St Catherine's Society, Cumberland Lodge, was intended to range widely over the whole subject, with anthropologists exposing their reflections to the criticisms of philosophers, politicians, historians and poets.

Unfortunately, the pressure of political events prevented Michael Wolff, special advisor to the [Conservative] Government, from speaking to his title 'Lies, Damned Lies and Election Promises'. The sense of relevance in one obvious form would have been greatly enhanced by his presence.

Fortunately Richard Gregory, professor of neuropsychology at Bristol, provided another form of relevance. His presence ensured that the question of perception was not neglected.

Michael Gilsenan, an anthropologist, opened by describing a Lebanese society in which honour required bold lying and in which false claims were unmasked by lies, much in the spirit of the thriller where the villain is ensnared in an elaborately constructed lie by the detective. Peter Brown described Syrians of the fourth century AD who used similar judgements to sift valid miracles from demonic frauds.

At the beginning of the conference, self-deception and false consciousness were always threatening to fog or hog the whole discourse. But Mr D.F. Pears gave a sharp-edged philosopher's account of the paradoxes of self-deception and cleared the air.

As to the difficult concept of falsity generated by a social structure itself – something traditional anthropology has been helpless to deal with because of its static relativism – Roy Rappaport developed his own theoretical scheme by which true and false consciousness can be identified within an evolutionary cybernetics approach to religion; ambitious certainly, impressive too.

There were two high moments of the weekend. One was when Christopher Ricks took as his text: 'When my love swears that she is made of truth, I do believe her though I know she lyes.' He revealed an asymmetry between words for truth and words for lying in English. The truth terms are austerely isolated, with few puns or rhymes or double meanings; the lie terms are so enmeshed with others that ambiguities hinting at untruth continually press upon any neutral context.

Is this a peculiarity of English? Do the French have a different idea of truth? Anthropologists, taken off their guard by the lyrical poetry, were well outplayed at their own game. The other highlight came in the discussion about testing the truth value of miracles in the late Roman Empire: Richard Gregory focused on the Saints' problems of validating miracles by recalling the professional bother he had had once over a miraculous cure which only he and his assistants had witnessed – a case of restoration of sight to a man who had been blind for 50 years.

It is hard to say what came out of the conference: little in the way of results or conclusions, more in the way of perspectives and challenges and unexpected alliances. The new policy of the Royal Anthropological Institute is to open the windows and doors to encourage membership by non-professional friends. Its future conferences, on the anthropology of mourning, on the anthropology of science, on immigrants in Britain, on medicine and theology, and care of the aged, will probably follow a similar pattern, two or three anthropologists outnumbered by other specialists on a topic of common interest.

Chapter 33

James Lewton-Brain

■ A MURDEROUS FASCINATION,
RAINews, 65, December 1984, pp. 5–6

A RECENT PROGRAMME on the overseas service of the BBC, entitled 'Women and Mystery', was concerned with the detective story. In the final part of the series a number of persons – P.D. James, Elizabeth Ferrars *et al.* as writers, Anthony Storr as a psychiatrist – were asked why they thought the genre continues to be as popular as ever. A number of themes emerged: vicarious excitement, the spice of fear, a desire to remove oneself from the mundane and humdrum, a fascination with death, a pleasure in identifying scapegoats, the juxtaposition of the ordinary with the horrific.

In the following reflections, I refer to the 'classic' detective story, exemplified by writers such as Agatha Christie, Ngaio Marsh, Dorothy Sayers, or latterly, P.D. James. Comparable non-British writers would include Simenon with the Maigret novels or Carolyn Heibrun's alter ego Amanda Cross. What distinguishes the genre from more generalized adventure stories is the concentration on the small community, perfectly portrayed in the small English village or, in an even more circumscribed way, an English country-house party. Where the setting is the more diffuse one of the great city, the focus is narrowed to a club, a school, a theatrical company.

One point brought out on the BBC programme by a former police superintendent, and attested to in sociological studies, was that the reality of murder has little similarity to the dramatic portrayal of it in fiction: the banal reality is that over 90 per cent of murders are domestic crimes committed by rather unintelligent individuals who display a shabby hopelessness. And yet the fact that these crimes occur within the confines of the family circle relates to my hypothesis.

That there is an apparently inexhaustible market for murder mysteries, even though objectively one recognizes the fantasy nature of the events described, shows, it seems to me, that attraction to the genre has deep roots in the human imagination. It might be argued that because every human being does not feel this attraction, one cannot therefore claim for it any universality in a psychological sense. The same argument is raised in discussions about, for example, the universality of the incest prohibition or initiation rites. Two points may be raised to counter this view. First, as Fox observed, 'To put it paradoxically man's greatest instinct is to learn. It is therefore natural for man to be unnatural.' (1975: 54). In other words, because the human mind is so malleable, one will always find some combination of variables in society that can bring about a difference from what may seem a near-universal in human behaviour. Because some people in Western society are not attracted to murder mysteries it is probable that one could unearth reasons in their background to explain their deviance from the norm. Second, as Radin so sensibly noted regarding religious believers, 'we have three types: the truly religious, the inter-mittently religious, and the indifferently religious' (1937: 9–10). If this is true of a simple society how much more must it be true of a complex heterogeneous Western society? My hypothesis is that the fascination felt by those who turn to murder stories for entertainment is closely related to the explanation for death or misfortune often used by our ancestors: that they resulted from the evil doings of witches and sorcerers.

In many parts of the world today the fascination with and fear of witchcraft continues; indeed many writers have recorded a feeling that the situation has deter-iorated, that the threat has grown worse. As Mair noted, when there is no adequate knowledge of the causes of misfortune or techniques for dealing with them, 'a belief in witches . . . is not only not foolish, it is indispensable' (1969: 8–9). Except for a lunatic fringe in Western society today, few people take seriously the notion that one can be harmed by the ill-wishing or spells of others. Why this change in per-ception has taken place is not solely, I suggest, because of education and the secularization of society, but lies rather in increased social, economic and geographic mobility (cf. Brain 1975: 181–3; 1979: 214–15; 1983: 380–1).

For my present purposes, it is sufficient to note that beliefs about witchcraft seem to be a psychic response to living in a small, immobile, sedentary commu-nity. As Spicer once noted: 'As a result of the friction of living in almost any society at any time, there is a certain latent hostility that is likely to discharge on whatever target comes into focus' (1952: 239). The metaphor of static electricity is apt: where the community concerned is contained and circumscribed and where motion only takes place within it, then the generation of the emotions associated with witchcraft accusations – hatred, envy, jealousy, spite, malice, anger, lust – become imagin-able. As Mair so graphically and chillingly put it: 'The witchcraft explanation rests on the boundless possibilities of sheer human malevolence: it is easily acceptable because we all know the depths of our own hearts' (1969: 13).

In the small non-industrial community, wherever it may be in the world, the inability to express one's real feelings can take two paths: they can be repressed, turned inward, or they can be channelled into what *is* socially acceptable. In the former case – repression – the results may be a whole range of psychosomatic complaints – ulcers, colitis, asthma, migraine, severe depression – all of which may be diagnosed as being caused by witchcraft. In the latter case, the socially accept-able mode of dealing with one's emotions – or the psychosomatic results of their repression – may be the acceptance of the diagnosis of witchcraft, which in turn may lead to the making of an accusation.

The diagnosis of witchcraft to account for misfortune is, I suggest, the analogue of the diagnosis of murder following an unexplained death in a detective story. Today, few of us ascribe our ailments to the malevolence of others (though that we ascribe them often enough to our inadequate emotional relations with others is attested to by the flourishing industry of psychotherapy in all its manifestations). Where murder occurs, however, by definition the death *must* be due to someone's malevolence. Where witchcraft provides an adequate explanation for virtually all deaths, as well as a host of other lesser evils – those closely associated with the event and the witchdoctor diviner will ask the same question as the fictional detective – and the fiction readers: who could possibly have been responsible? Part of the pleasure of a good detective story lies in the gradual revelation that among the group of suspects many if not all of them are shown to have harboured malice towards the victim. The detective then has to establish which of the potential murderers is the actual one.

The witchdoctor, unconstrained by rules of evidence, since the physical presence of the killer at the victim's death is irrelevant, does, however, proceed by the same process as the fictional detective. In both cases it is assumed to be self-evident that the killer and victim were linked in a close emotional relationship which, according to the rules of society, should have had ascribed to it the qualities of love, respect, obedience or trust. A random, motiveless killing would seem unlikely to the diviner and hold little attraction to the fiction reader.

Frequently in both cases – witchdoctor or detective – the survivors, no longer bound by the normal rules of conduct, may reveal the evil and malign nature of the victim. While this may elicit sympathy for the killer, society cannot condone the assumption by a private citizen of the authority to dispense justice.

The fascination – and I use the word deliberately because of its etymology – of the detective story is, it seems to me, secure. Who has never wished ill of another for whom he/she should, according to society's rules, have love, honour or respect? Of course one realizes that in those societies where witchcraft is believed to be the cause of misfortune the belief is real, whereas in the case of the novel reader there is an awareness that the events described are fictional. However, the fictional events must often strike a responsive chord. The similarity of the fictional situation to the real one lies in the internal dynamics of a small community, with all its inevitable stresses and tensions.[1]

Note

1   The BBC programme mentioned a fascination with death as a continuing reason for the genre's success. It is common knowledge that death and sex have been linked poetically and in verbal play. I have suggested elsewhere (1977, 1979) that there is a subconscious linking between death, putrefaction, faeces, genitals and sex; the verbal play being the superficial manifestation of this subconscious link. If this is correct then any engagement with death – or violence – will provide a sexual frisson.

References

Brain, J.L. 1975. 'Witchcraft: a hardy perennial', in *Colonialism and Change: Essays presented to Lucy Mair*, ed. M. Owusu. The Hague: Mouton, pp. 179–201.

—— 1977. 'Sex, incest and death: initiation rites reconsidered', *Current Anthropology* 18(2): 191–208.

—— 1979. *The Last Taboo: Sex and the Fear of Death*. New York: Doubleday.

—— 1983. 'Witchcraft and Development'. *African Affairs*, 83: 371–84.

Fox, R. 1975. *Encounter with Anthropology*. New York: Dell.

Mair, L.P. 1969. *Witchcraft*. New York: World University Library.

Radin, P. 1937. *Primitive Religion*. New York: Viking Press.

Spicer, E. 1952. *Human Problems in Technological Change*. New York: Russell Sage.

Chapter 34

J. Anthony Paredes and Elizabeth D. Purdum

■ 'BYE-BYE TED . . .': COMMUNITY RESPONSE
IN FLORIDA TO THE EXECUTION OF
THEODORE BUNDY, *Anthropology Today*, 6.2,
April 1990, pp. 9–11

IN 1985, WE PRESENTED at the American Anthropological Association meeting in Washington, DC, a paper comparing capital punishment in modern-day Florida to Aztec rituals of human sacrifice in 16th-century Mexico. Finding the usual explanations for capital punishment and its widespread support in the contemporary United States incomplete at best, we hypothesized that capital punishment in contemporary America functions as the ultimate validator of law, serving 'to reassure many that society is not out of control after all, that the majesty of the Law reigns, and that God is indeed in his heaven', in much the same way the Aztec rituals reassured the population that the state was healthy and the Sun would remain in the heavens.

The idea of human sacrifice as a means of reaffirming the power and control of society as a whole is of course not new. Sir James Frazer in *The Golden Bough* chronicles a variety of customs whereby a person or an animal is killed, often after being both treated well and tortured, in order to rid society of its accumulated ills.

Bronislaw Malinowski observed that 'there are no peoples however primitive without religion and magic'; neither are there peoples so civilized that they are devoid of magic. All peoples turn to magic when knowledge, technology and experience fail (Malinowski 1954). In the face of evidence that capital punishment does no more to deter crime than the rituals of Tenochtitlan did to keep the sun in the sky, we concluded 'that modern capital punishment is an institutionalized *magical* response to perceived disorder in American life and in the world at large, an attempted magical solution that has an especial appeal to the beleaguered, white . . . God-fearing men and women of the working class. And, in certain aspiring politicians they find their sacrificial priests.'

In a 1987 revision (see Radelet 1989), we cited as 'emic' verification of our validation-of-law hypothesis a popular bumper sticker expressing resentment of a new Florida statute requiring automobile passengers to wear safety belts: 'I'll buckle up when Bundy does; it's the law'. The momentum was building for notorious, serial sex-murderer Theodore Bundy to become the central character in a contemporary

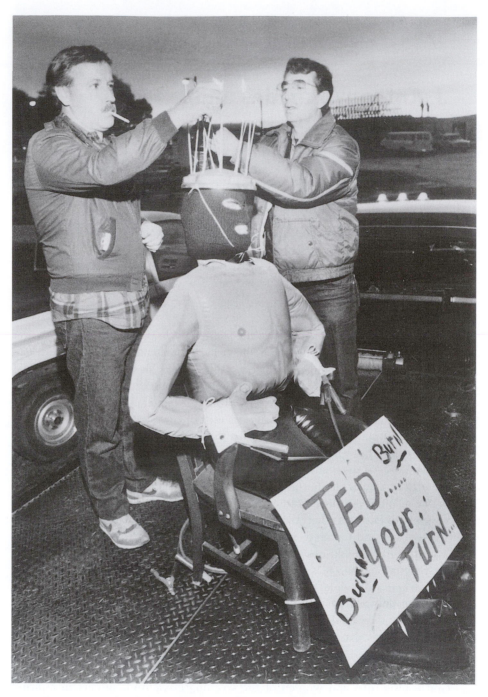

Figure 34.1   From the *Tallahassee Democrat*, 25 January 1989, captioned: 'Butch Pearse, left, of Starke, and Bob Reaves, of Gainesville, light up Bundy effigy at prison'.

mass-media morality play. When Bundy was executed in the electric chair on 24 January 1989, for the murder of a 12-year-old girl, public reactions to his execution seemed to confirm our ideas about capital punishment. Given the enormity of Bundy's crimes and the celebrity status he had received, his execution became a dramatic extravaganza casting into high relief the underlying psychological and social currents that swirl around capital punishment as a cultural trait.

It seemed a natural follow-up to our earlier paper to analyse newspaper data on the Bundy spectacle for evidence that might test our general hypothesis that 'capital punishment . . . serves the psychosocial function of reassuring members of society that law reigns.' Once we began work on this present paper we realized we had seriously underestimated the attention Bundy's execution had received in the Florida press.

There are 49 daily newspapers in Florida (Boyden 1989: 289–333). For purposes of the present essay we rely upon a sample consisting of only the Miami, St Petersburg, Orlando and Tallahassee newspapers. Together, these account for approximately one-third of the total circulation of all Florida daily newspapers. The papers were selected to represent political points of view as well as location. The *Orlando Sentinel* is one of the most conservative metropolitan newspapers in the state, the *St Petersburg Times* is the most liberal. The *Miami Herald* falls between the two. The *Tallahassee Democrat* is also rather middle-of-the-road, but Tallahassee is also the state capital, the site of the Chi Omega sorority house murders, and near the site of the murder for which Bundy was executed.

The sheer volume of items dealing with Bundy is impressive. During 20 January to 28 February 1989, some 280 Bundy-related items were published in the four newspapers. The *Tallahassee Democrat* published fourteen Bundy items on 25 January, the day following Bundy's early morning execution on 24 January; the other newspapers published ten to twelve items on the 25th. By contrast, the *New York Times* and the *Washington Post* carried only one Bundy-related item each on 25 January. The newspaper from the nearest major metropolitan area outside Florida, the *Atlanta Journal and Constitution* carried only two items on Bundy. Even the newspaper from nearby Mobile, Alabama, less than 50 miles from the Florida border, published only two items on the day after Bundy's execution, albeit both on the front page. The Bundy story was front-page stuff in Florida for a week, but fascination with Bundy may not have been so pronounced elsewhere, despite national TV coverage. Nevertheless, our survey of four Florida newspapers has produced a rich corpus of data for anthropological analysis.

We have only skimmed the surface of the complex and many-faceted themes found in 280+ items on Bundy from 40 days' worth of newspapers. What we present here is, perforce, rather broad,[1] but, as we had hoped (we won't pretend otherwise), there is in the material much confirmation of our views on the psychosocial functions of capital punishment. Many other themes are represented as well.

Not all Floridians support the death penalty. This is amply evident in the newspaper data; even so, some early reports and commentaries claimed that capital punishment opponents were less active in connection with Bundy's execution than with others. Some of those opposing capital punishment did admit to having difficulty in remaining true to their position, faced with the heinousness of Bundy's crimes and noted, for example, 'if ever a defendant met the criteria for Florida's death penalty, he [Bundy] did'.[2] Even so, the number of death penalty opponents attending the customary post-execution protest in the state capital the day after an execution was, in the Bundy case, three times the usual number.[3]

In the last few days before Bundy was executed the story was dominated by two themes: legal manoeuvres to save Bundy from execution, and Bundy's confessions to murders in the far west. The latter were widely seen as a ploy to save his life. Bundy was portrayed by the state governor as trying to bargain over the bodies of his victims.[4] Briefly, the governor and Bundy seemed locked together as mythic combatants, the governor standing firm to execute his duty – 'it's the law' – and, incidentally, realizing a significant political credit. One state legislator declared that if Bundy were executed on schedule the governor would be 'viewed as an archangel of justice'.[5] One columnist drew a parallel between the Governor and Jimmy Stewart in the role of the 'Man Who Shot Liberty Valance'.[6]

There was in those final days some uncertainty about whether there would be an execution: 'they ain't going to do nothing'[7] declared the father of the girl for whose murder Bundy was to be executed. There was in various accounts a running theme of last-minute appeals being 'an abuse of the process',[8] 'a mockery of the legal system',[9] and a general complaint that too much time had passed without carrying out Bundy's sentence[10] – in fact, Mello (1989: 2–3) argues that 'the legal process created a series of "Bundy exceptions" to the rule of law . . . that despite the outward appearance of heightened due process . . . in reality the legal system failed in this case'.

The final days before Bundy's death provided an opportunity for one last cliff-hanger of whether good would triumph over evil, whether the collective force of society would prevail over that deepest structural threat to social order: the categorical anomaly. Here was the bright, articulate, college-educated, handsome, former law student crisis counsellor, who looked 'like a professional tennis player',[11] but who was also a murderer, rapist and sodomizer who beat his human prey with a club, tore at their flesh with his teeth, and tossed the remains of his last victim, a girl of twelve, into a 'pigsty'.[12] In these terms, Bundy was that ultimate Judaeo-Christian anomaly of anomalies who, like the serpent in the Garden of Eden, is the creepiest of creeping things – truly Lucifer among us, according to one close observer.[13]

With less and less chance that Bundy would win another reprieve, newspaper coverage shifted to accounts of the throng of news reporters converging on the 'cow pasture'[14] across from the Death Row prison. As if to heighten the drama, newspapers recounted details of Bundy's grisly crimes, of the anticipated execution procedures, of Bundy's mental condition, of his final interviews, of his turn to religion – 'Bundy prays and reads Bible'.[15] In these final hours the stage was also set for the epilogue that was to follow.

A born-again Christian lawyer who had got to know Bundy through a prison ministry visited the condemned at length, urging that he confess his other crimes, and that he be given time to do so. But the lawyer had just been elected a district prosecutor, so his actions stirred great controversy among his constituents. Only when the prosecutor pressed for the death penalty in another case, weeks after Bundy's execution, did he seem to cleanse his reputation.

Bundy himself laid the groundwork for the subplot of another public discourse following his death, by claiming that pornography and alcohol fuelled his evil deeds.

* * *

Figure 34.2 From the *Tallahassee Democrat*, 25 January 1989, captioned: 'Man reaches out to touch hearse bearing Bundy's body as it leaves prison'.

Once the sentence was carried out and Bundy's body was borne away – in one dramatic photo, a man reaches out to touch the hearse as if it were a passing icon in a religious procession – there followed a flood of sentiment giving native expression to the function of capital punishment as a validator of law. These sentiments were succinctly summarized by the frequently used phrase: 'The system works',[16] often accompanied by reference to Bundy's 'manipulation' of the system.[17] 'Bundy loomed as an evil genius . . . who . . . play[ed] games with a judicial system that promises to protect us from the dark',[18] declared one newspaperman. 'Now people know that our system works'[19] said one witness to the execution. Responding to a Boston criminal justice professor, one letter writer said that those 'opposed to capital punishment need to be reminded that this is a nation of laws, not of men whose feelings distort justice; that laws form a basis of order, freedom, and the citizens' protection from criminals'.[20]

One of the most frequently recurring words to describe feelings after Bundy's execution was 'relief', relief as simple as respite from constant speculation about Bundy's execution, to relief that the system 'really works',[21] to a Hegelian sense of closure for the families of victims, to catharsis of a classic sort – 'purging ourselves',[22] as one columnist put it.

Not unrelated to the oft-cited sense of relief was a surprisingly unabashed release of vengefulness. 'Hundreds celebrate execution',[23] announced one news story. In the 'cow pasture' on the morning of Bundy's death were many revellers – singing, drinking, carrying frying pans, selling 'Burn Bundy Burn' T-shirts,[24] and producing a genuine carnival atmosphere – like Mardi Gras,[25] said one reporter. Another writer, as if wanting to play into the hands of an anthropological analysis, described the celebrants as 'acting in a savage manner'.[26] Even more pointed was an effigy execution carried out by some in the crowd, as if by magical emulation they, too, could participate in the killing of Bundy. Similarly, in some cities disc jockeys played requests for songs celebrating Bundy's execution, especially 'Bye-Bye Ted Bundy'[27] sung to the tune of Don McLean's early 1970s popular work 'American Pie', a selection for parody in itself thick with symbolism. Among the most peculiar identifications with the execution was the Tallahassee bar-owner who presided over an execution party wearing a halo-like contraption representing Bundy's brains being burned.[28]

One of the more surprising aspects of the Bundy spectacle was the extent to which some used the event to display their creativity – trying to 'out comic'[29] one another as one writer put it. Often these expressions played on elements of popular culture of the most innocent genres – 'Bundy Bar B Q' on short-order menus, a bawdy parody of 'On top of old Smokey',[30] and, in reference to the sorority house murders, a chilling play on Walt Disney's seven dwarfs: 'Chi O, Chi O, It's off to hell I go'.[31] Adding to the surreal quality of it all was the announcement of Salvador Dali's death juxtaposed to Bundy execution stories on the front page of several newspapers, including photographs of Dali's impish, mustachioed countenance.

Afterwards, execution celebration was a frequent subject for condemnation by both supporters of the death penalty and by those opposed. Much of the celebration did appear to be, as critics claimed, a tasteless expression of vengeful glee. Nonetheless, even among the more sober there was an implication that by his slaughter of innocents Ted Bundy had placed upon society a collective moral obligation to exact vengeance and retribution. As one headline announced, 'Bundy Pays the Price'.[32] Vengefulness is not surprising given that, according to one account, the governor issued the final telephone order to kill Bundy 'on behalf of the countless victims of Theodore Bundy both dead and living, across Florida and the nation'.[33]

Even in their condemnation, though, some tried to find an explanation for the macabre celebration surrounding Bundy's execution. One veteran reporter wrote, 'perhaps it was an eruption of hatred for a criminal justice system that is too slow to right wrongs'.[34] One correspondent defended the cheering at Bundy's death saying, 'The people of Florida and the rest of the United States did not cheer when Ted Bundy was electrocuted because they were bloodthirsty. They did so because justice finally prevailed over a flawed judicial system . . .'[35] One of the more off-beat defences of post-execution revelry was the letter to the editor comparing those events to the jubilation of the Munchkins in the Land of Oz after Dorothy's house squashed the wicked witch of the East![36]

Many subthemes were woven around the central drama of the events of 24 January. Columnists, letter writers and public figures used Bundy's execution as an opportunity to declaim on topics as varied as the venality of the legal profession, the arrogance of the 'liberal elite',[37] God's ordination of earthly governments, state pride for Florida having executed Bundy, alarm that the state's image would be damaged by having executed Bundy, the dedication and bravery of police officers,[38] the certainty that whatever else may be said an executed murderer never kills again, loss of civic innocence (echoing lines of Thorton Wilder's *Our Town*), apprehension that even in death Bundy was mocking society by his wish to have his ashes scattered over the Cascade Mountains where bones of many of his alleged victims were found, the abortion debate (those cheering the execution were probably pro-abortion, a writer suspected;[39] another linked supporters of the death penalty to the 'pro-lifers'),[40] the pros and cons of the death penalty itself, the need for reform in the appeals process, the need to understand and protect ourselves from truly malevolent forces in our midst, and much more. At least two items even challenged Florida motorists to 'buckle up',[41] now that Bundy's sentence had in fact been carried out.

While we are far from a conclusive analysis of the drama surrounding Ted Bundy's final days, these preliminary observations suggest that many do take special comfort in the affirmation of authority and order which capital punishment seems to provide – especially when the executed is such a vile smart-aleck as the likes of Ted Bundy. Ironically, such an execution provides the stage for some to act out their own private rituals of rebellion and disorderliness.

Ding, dong the witch is dead.

Notes

We wish to thank Jorge Zamanillo for his assistance in compiling the data and Janet DuPuy, Erica Esan and Bridget Beers for their tireless typing of various drafts of this paper. This is a revised and slightly expanded version of a paper first presented in the Association for Political and Legal Anthropology Session, 'The Death Penalty and Other Socially Sanctioned Killings', at the 88th Annual Meeting of the American Anthropological Association, Washington, DC, 15–19 November 1989.

1   We give here citations only for quoted materials and specific narrow points of information, rather than attempt full documentation of every statement. Even in some of the citations, though, several different sources sometimes could have been used but only one was selected as an example. Abbreviations for newspaper titles are introduced after first mention in citation.
2   *St Petersburg Times* (ST), 1–25–89, p. 12A.
3   *Tallahassee Democrat* (TD), 1–26–89, p. 1-B.
4   ST, 1–21–89, p. 1-A.
5   TD, 1–22–89, p. 1-B.
6   Ibid.
7   TD, 1–23–89, p. 2-A.
8   TD, 1–20–89, p. 2-A.
9   ST, 1–23–89, p. 8-A.
10 TD, 1–23–89, p. 2A.
11 TD, 1–24–89, p. 1-C.
12 TD, 1–21–89, p. 14-A.
13 TD, 1–23–89, p. 5-A.
14 *Orlando Sentinel* (OS), 1–24–89, p. 4-A.
15 OS, 1–24–89, p. 1-A.
16 OS, 1–24–89, p. 8-A.
17 ST, 1–25–89, p. 4-A.
18 TD, 1–29–89, p. 9-A.
19 ST, 1–25–89, p. 4-A.
20 OS, 2–6–89, p. 10-A.
21 TD, 1–25–89, p. 4-A.

22   OS, 1–25–89, p. 9-A.
23   OS, 1–25–89, p. 5-A.
24   TD, 1–24–89, p. 5-A.
25   ST, 1–29–89, p. 5-D.
26   ST, 1–27–89, p. 4-D.
27   ST, 1–25–89, p. 4-A.
28   TD, 1–25–89, p. 4-A.
29   ST, 1–25–89, p. 4-A.
30   OS, 1–24–89, p. 1-A.
31   ST, 1–25–89, p. 1-A.
32   TD, 1–25–89, p. 1-A.
33   OS (4 Star edition), 1–24–89, p. 1-A.
34   ST, 1–29–89, p. 5-D.
35   OS, 1–29–89, p. 2-G.
36   TD, 2–24–89, p. 12-A.
37   ST, 2–1–89, p. 17-A.
38   *Pensacola News Journal*, 2–17–89, p. 8-A. Although the Pensacola newspaper was not in the sample analysed for this article, it was also examined (as was the *Jacksonville Times Union*); Pensacola was the site of Bundy's arrest leading to eventual execution.
39   OS, 1–31–89, p. 8-A.
40   ST, 1–30–89, p. 13-A.
41   OS, 1–29–89.

References

Boyden, Donald P., Ed. 1989. *Gale Directory of Publications* (Formerly *Ayer Directory of Publications*), 121st Edition, Volume 1, Catalog of Publications. Detroit: Gale Research Inc.

Frazer, Sir James. 1959 (originally 1890). *The New Golden Bough: A New Abridgement of the Classic Work*. Edited by Theodore H. Gaster. New York: Criterion Books.

Hegel, G.W.H. 1952. *Philosophy of Right* (originally 1821, translated by T.M. Knox). Oxford: Oxford U. P.

Malinowski, Bronislaw. 1954. *Magic, Science and Religion*. Garden City, New York: Doubleday Anchor Books.

Mello, Michael. 1989. Death Row as Mirror, Death Row as Metaphor: Theodore Bundy and the Rule of Law. Paper presented at American Anthropological Association Meeting, Washington, DC, 15–19 November 1989.

Radelet, Michael L., Ed. 1989. *Facing the Death Penalty: Essays on a Cruel and Unusual Punishment*. Philadelphia: Temple U. P.

Chapter 35

Declan Quigley

■ THE PARADOXES OF MONARCHY,
Anthropology Today, 11.5, October 1995, pp. 1–3

MEDIA ACCOUNTS OF THE British monarchy tend to focus on a depressingly limited number of themes and particularly, of course, on the marital and extra-marital relationships of the younger royals. The most prevalent explanation of the declining public estimation of the monarchy is not so much in terms of what they do, however, but how it is reported. Royal dalliances, after all, hardly constitute historical novelty. The real harm, monarchists lament, is done by the instant and detailed publicity afforded by modern communications, since legitimation of the crown demands that it retain an aura of mystery, and mystery sits uneasily with tabloid headlines screaming out the latest royal peccadillo.

Arguably the more damaging demystification is brought about by the ensuing statements of the aggrieved parties, followed by those from a succession of PR agents, solicitors, in-laws, 'close' friends, former nannies and so on. It is the sheer numbers who now have the opportunity to invade the royal domain through the media which strips the monarchy of the illusions of dignity so categorically. Of course it is not only the royals who are sacrificed in this way for the benefit of society: any public figure is open to the same fate, and the more public, the greater and more humiliatingly invasive the scrutiny.

But is this all there is to it, a question of exposure? Is royalty simply one victim among others in the modern addiction to open up what was previously hidden? Anthropologists have had curiously little to say about monarchies in modern democracies, given the huge and extraordinarily rich literature on traditional kingship (rather less on queenship) ranging across the globe and encompassing societies of every size – from the smallest Pacific islands through the classic cases of sub-Saharan Africa to the complex city-kingdoms of South and South-East Asia.[1] This demographic and geographic spread is paralleled by an exciting range of theoretical questions revolving around the nature and functions of political ritual (and indeed of ritual in general) and the social roles of myth and symbolism, particularly those relating to transcendence and the sacred. Perhaps less obvious to the non-initiate,

Figure 35.1   King Letsie III of Lesotho acknowledges his people at the Maseru stadium after his coronation in Lesotho, October 1997. This was the country's first coronation since 1963, following decades of political upheaval.

but also central in analysis after analysis of the institutional devices of kingship, are questions relating to scapegoats and sacrifice as well as to royal reversals of 'ordinary' social codes, most famously those concerned with incest avoidance. Even a relatively superficial survey of royal ritual gives one the impression of a microcosmic study of some of the core themes in the emergence of social anthropology as an academic discipline.

Two figures stand out in the development of the comparative explanation of kingship: Sir James Frazer and A.M. Hocart.[2] Earlier attempts to belittle their respective contributions by focusing on their theoretical weaknesses (Frazer's evolutionism, Hocart's diffusionism) now seem rather shallow, given the suggestive richness of their observations and the comparative scope of their approaches. Recently Frazer has been championed by a number of Africanists, while Hocart's insights have tended to figure most prominently among those working in the Pacific and in the caste-organized societies of South Asia. But the two approaches are closer than is commonly acknowledged, and one should not be misled into believing that geography somehow dictates the essential qualities of royal formations. The most striking feature to emerge from the literature is how consistently the same elements

Figure 35.2   On 1 September 1997, the day after Princess Diana's death, mourners queue to sign one of the books of condolence at St James's Palace, London.

appear, albeit with different permutations, in societies which have no obvious historical connection.

In a spirited defence of Frazer which draws on a wide range of recent ethnography, Luc de Heusch has pointed out that *The Golden Bough* contains two explanations of the common phenomenon of the scapegoat king which, though different, complement each other nicely.[3] In the first (often mistakenly identified as Frazer's only theory of kingship), the king or a surrogate must be sacrificed, or simply removed, before his physical degeneration endangers the health and continuity of the kingdom and cosmos, since their well-being is identified with the monarch's bodily perfection. In the second, which in fact appears to be the more frequently reported in the ethnographic literature, the king is held to embody the sins and evil of his subjects and he is therefore made the vehicle for carrying these away in the time-honoured tradition of scapegoated functionaries or marginalized groups.

The main emphasis in Hocart's approach is on kingship as a form of ritual, rather than political, organization.[4] Drawing parallels between traditional Fiji and the caste societies of South Asia, he argues that 'the king's state is an organization for prosperity by the due observance of traditional rules'.[5] Primary among these rules is the repetitive performance of sacrificial rites the purpose of which is to regenerate the kingship by removing any pollution which accumulates at the royal centre.

There is a great deal of dispute among the specialists on caste regarding the relative positions of priests and kings. Until recently the prevailing view has been that priestly purity is the paramount principle around which the primary features of caste societies are organized. Hocart's position, as I have argued elsewhere, is that the underlying principle of caste organization and ideology is rather that those who *rule* must be pure.[6] From this perspective, the priest is always a vessel for removing the pollution of kings and nobles (those members of dominant castes who have always replicated the kingship on a lesser scale). Without the purificatory mechanism of his priests, the Hindu king simply accumulates the evil and death of his people to become, as the Sanskritist Jan Heesterman so vividly puts it, 'as great an abomination as ten brothels or even as the keeper of ten thousand slaughter houses'.[7]

At stake here is legitimation, and the capacity of a particular figure to secure this by transcending the ordinary rules of kinship so that he represents all lineages before the gods through the repeated sacrificial re-creation of a perfect, timeless centre. Those who prefer materialist certainties like to portray caste as a peculiarly rigid form of stratification where the central problem, as in all systems of inequality, revolves around the wielding of temporal power. It is much more revealing to view caste as a particularly complex manifestation of kingship where, as in all forms of kingship, ritual and temporal functions are collapsed.

* * *

If Frazer and Hocart are correct, there would appear to be an irresolvable ambiguity at the heart of kingship. On the one hand it represents the most auspicious social qualities – the 'exemplary centre' as Geertz and others have termed it, typically given material form in the regal appurtenances of thrones and palaces. On the other hand it embodies the most inauspicious social qualities which can only be expiated through sacrifice, paradigmatically a real or symbolic regicide which, interestingly enough, is often enacted during the very rites of enthronement. The idea is captured brilliantly in Hocart's stunning statement that 'The first kings must have been dead kings'.[8] To be made king through the transformative act of an installation ritual is to be made into a figure who is at the very centre of society and yet must be removed from it, who, as Durkheim might have put it, collapses 'good sacred' and 'bad sacred'.

In his 1991 lecture, de Heusch argued that all of the ethnographic variations on the intensely problematic status of the sacred king derive from his unique function among humans of articulating the social order and the natural order. Of course, monarchs in modern democracies are no longer expected to harmonize the natural and social worlds, though residues of this remain, particularly in the association between monarchy and death – the required presence at national ceremonies of remembrance of the war dead, for example, or the way in which a royal death is often likened to a natural calamity. Such vestiges notwithstanding, the prevalent modern perception is unquestionably that monarchs are not responsible for general fertility, health and prosperity in the way which is widely reported in the anthropological literature.

In comparative terms, it is the rupture of this association which appears to be at the core of their current predicament. Where kingship is genuinely indispensable, the awe-inspiring identity of natural and social generally permits the exemplary centre to re-establish itself with ease against the carnivalesque rituals of rebellion which commonly punctuate monarchical reigns, and which feature more prominently still in periods of interregnum. In such societies, kings are scapegoated because this is demanded by their ritual centrality and because the kingship itself will comfortably survive the passing expiation. In modern democracies, however, royals are scapegoated because of the marginality of their ritual function to society's welfare and to the symbolic devices of political legitimation. For this reason, the contemporary rituals of rebellion of the tabloids threaten to push the institution over the edge rather than reinvigorate it (as their hollow pieties would sometimes have us believe is their aim). *Some* scapegoat mechanism remains an intrinsic element of all modern political systems, but we all know it need not be kingship. The redundancy of monarchy easily lends itself to savage ridicule both of royals themselves and of those who would attempt, through the symbolic paraphernalia of kingship, to insist on its universal indispensability when comparison shows otherwise.

With the abolition of the princely states in post-colonial South Asia we see a social formation which might be labelled 'kingship without kingdoms'.[9] The supreme figureheads have gone, but the institution of kingship is retained and replicated through the practices of the 'little king' members of dominant castes. Conversely, in the modern industrial democracies we may often have kingdoms without kingship in all its full-blown sacrificial ambiguity. Nevertheless, the paradoxes that persist may well ensure the survival of a number of monarchies well into the next millennium. If, as some have argued, one of the central purposes of ritual is to make time stand still and if, as others have argued, the essential ingredients of all ritual are to be found in the heightened contrivances of royal ceremonies, then royalists may be right that we lose something very fundamental when we abolish the monarchy. In any case (for those monarchists who need consolation), whether one looks at the installation rituals of republican presidents the world over, or the more mundane workings of caste systems where ritual centralization remains an everyday political necessity, it would appear that many ostensibly non-monarchical systems live (prosper?) only by surreptitiously proclaiming: 'The kingdom is dead; long live the kingship.'

Notes

My thanks to Elizabeth Tonkin, who made a number of useful comments on an earlier draft.

1   An excellent series of bibliographies can be found in J.-Cl. Galey (ed.) *Kingship and the Kings*, 1990 (Chur and London: Harwood Academic P.)

2   See especially Frazer, J.G., *The Golden Bough* (London, Macmillan, 1978 [1922]) and Hocart, A.M., *Kingship* (Oxford U. P. 1969 [1927]) and *Kings and Councillors: An essay in the comparative anatomy of human society* (ed. R. Needham, U. of Chicago P., 1970 [1936]). E. Kantorowicz's *The King's Two Bodies* (Princeton U.P., 1957) is more often drawn upon by historians but its impact on anthropologists is as yet limited – though see B. Schnepel, *Twinned Beings: Kings and Effigies in Southern Sudan, East India, and Renaissance France* (1995, Gothenburg: Inst. for Advanced Studies in Social Anthropology).

3   The presentation was made to mark the 50th anniversary of Frazer's death, at the School of Oriental and African Studies, London, on 22 June 1991. A number of

the same themes were again elaborated on by de Heusch at a public seminar on monarchies organized by the RAI in October 1993, also at SOAS, as part of the special events during the Institute's 150th anniversary year.

4   For a useful summary of Hocart's material on kingship, see B. Schnepel, 'In quest of life: Hocart's scheme of evolution from ritual organization to government', *Eur. Jnl of Sociology*, 29, 1988, pp. 165–87.

5   Hocart, *Caste: A Comparative Study* (Oxford: Clarendon P., 1950 [1938]).

6   Quigley, D., *The Interpretation of Caste* (Oxford: Clarendon P., 1993).

7   Heesterman, J., *The Inner Conflict of Tradition: Essays on Indian Ritual, Kingship and Society* (U. of Chicago P., 1985).

8   Hocart, *Social Origins* (London: Watts, 1954), p. 27.

9   Nepal, the last Hindu kingdom, offers invaluable comparative material for this reason.

Chapter 36

Alex Weingrod

■ DRY BONES: NATIONALISM AND
SYMBOLISM IN CONTEMPORARY ISRAEL,
Anthropology Today, 11.6, December 1995, pp. 7–12

Introduction

THAT HUMAN BONES[1] AND BURIALS are intimately related with modern nationalism can hardly be doubted (Mosse 1979, 1990). As new and often flimsy creations, nations require symbols of power, past glories and awe that can overcome the roars of discord and contention which periodically appear to threaten their existence. What can provoke emotions of identification more powerfully than shrines devoted to the bones of ancestral heroes, just as state-sponsored burials provide occasions for dramatic collective events that continue to be celebrated in future years? Examples come quickly to mind: the post-World War I 'tombs of the Unknown Soldier' that Inglis recently described (1993), or Lenin's Tomb and Mao's Mausoleum, two instances that signify nationalist identifications in addition to expressing revolutionary ideologies. As these examples suggest, the bones themselves may be treated in different ways: they may be placed into the ground in single or mass graves, or else the body may be preserved and displayed in a special structure.

Not surprisingly, bones and burials have had a prominent place in contemporary Israeli nationalism. The Zionist movement has been largely nationalist by definition, and in addition, the Holy Land and its ancient sacred history provided an especially fertile setting for bones to become prominent features in the nationalist creed. Burial and reburial, the use of bones as a means of connecting the past with the present, have been repeated themes accompanying the will to rebirth of this old-new people in its old-new land.

There are many different dimensions to this complex motif, and several have been examined in earlier studies. For example, Sivan (1991, 1993) analysed the emergent forms of memorializing Israel's war dead (the '1948 generation'); writing of the cultural format commonly chosen to commemorate the 'fallen soldiers' — published remembrances written by comrades and family members — he concludes that whereas the contents are typically secular and nationalist, they follow a traditional Jewish religious form of memorialization (the 'yizkor books') that reaches back to the thirteenth century. Almog (1992) studied a different aspect of recalling dead heroes – the many stone and metal monuments that have been erected throughout the country – and he adopts a semiotic theory of analysis as a means of interpreting their message. Levinger (1993) also examined Israeli war memorials, although her analysis focuses more on topics of ideology and aesthetics. Finally, Aronoff (1993) has taken a different direction, one that is closely related to the topics developed in this article: his focus is on the bones themselves and the uses to which they are put in present-day Israeli culture and politics. Bones, burials and reburials, he argues, are intertwined with complex issues of contemporary Israeli collective action and the process whereby socio-political legitimacy is created and used.

These previous studies begin to indicate the scope of the Israeli interest in bones.[2] And indeed, it is hardly an exaggeration to state that bones have become a kind of Israeli obsession: repeatedly, and in various different contexts, public issues involving bones and burials leap into prominence. Why this is the case, and how this focus upon bones is connected with Israeli ideologies and social divisions, is the central theme of this article. I shall briefly describe and then analyse a number of events that illustrate my claim of an Israeli obsession with bones. Most of these events are recent, and they were selected in order to emphasize the continuing, repeated fascination. I shall also consider why this theme has been emphasized, and how bones relate to basic controversies within Israeli society.

Bones as issues of public concern

Take then, as examples, the following three events reported by the Israeli media in a single week in January 1993. The first involves bones, archaeologists and Jewish religious fundamentalists. Early in 1993, ultra-religious Jewish zealots clashed with archaeologists and construction crews who were building a new road on the northern edge of Jerusalem; the work was suddenly stopped when the construction crews and the archaeologists accompanying them were accused by the zealots of defiling Jewish bones buried in a third century Jewish cemetery that had been uncovered by the bulldozers (*see* Figure 36.1). As in previous instances, this dispute quickly escalated and became a national issue, and it was resolved only after the intervention of cabinet ministers and an appeal to the High Court of Justice. (According to the Court's decision, the archaeologists had proper legal claim to the ossuaries and their bones, and at considerable additional expense the roadway was shifted away from the ancient burial ground.)

The second case that week involved different issues: the media reported that the President of Israel, in discussions with the visiting President of Ukraine, proposed that the bones of a famed nineteenth-century Chassidic rabbi, Reb Nachman of Bratslav, whose grave is located in the Ukrainian city of Ouman, be dug up and re-interred in Israel. The Israeli President's suggestion was immediately followed by an angry outburst of disclaimer by Reb Nachman's followers; they did not want their Rebbe's bones to be transferred to Israel, nor were they the least bit pleased by the President's involvement in their affairs.

Figure 36.1 Jewish zealots rush to an ancient Jewish burial cave in northern Jerusalem on 27 January 1993, following a ruling by the Israeli supreme court allowing the excavation and demolition of the cave to make way for a new road. The zealots created civil disturbance which resulted in a reversal of the ruling by an appeal court.

The third issue had still different nuances. Later that same week, in a speech to the Knesset, the Israeli Minister of Education recalled an incident in which a military curfew had been imposed upon the Palestinian residents of Shechem, a town in the West Bank, in order that politically right-wing politicians and rabbis could celebrate what they claimed to be the grave of the Biblical figure of Joseph – although, as the (left-wing) Minister caustically remarked, this site was in reality a Muslim holy place dating from the Ottoman period that had no connection whatsoever with Joseph or his bones.

Three raucous, well-publicized incidents involving bones in a single week! Can there be any doubt that there is an Israeli obsession with bones? To be sure, incidents such as these are not necessarily repeated each week: the passion over bones is not *that* total and dedicated. However, these were by no means isolated or atypical events: there is a lengthy list of similar occasions – all of them with bones as their central theme – that can be cited. Three additional instances are particularly useful for interpreting the meanings attributed to bones and how they have been used. In common with the cases already described, these incidents were widely publicized and, in some instances, controversial and contested.

In December 1992, the bones of 23 Moroccan Jews were transferred from Morocco to Israel for reburial. These were the physical remains of Jewish immigrants who, in 1962, left Morocco illegally by boat on their journey to Israel; their boat sank in a storm near Gibraltar, and the bodies that washed ashore were buried in a Jewish cemetery located outside of the Moroccan town of El-Huseima. Recently, after many years of protracted negotiation with the Moroccan governmental authorities, the bones were dug up and flown to Israel where they were reburied on Mount Herzl, the Jerusalem burial ground that is reserved for the remains of Israel's national heroes. To cite another recent instance in 1990 the bones of four Moroccan *zaddikim*, holy men or saints, were transferred from Morocco to Israel and re-buried in the cemetery of Kiryat Melanchi, a small town located about sixty kilometres south of Tel Aviv. A shrine was built covering their graves, and it has become the site of a yearly *hilloula*, or pilgrimage.

The last event to be described is, once again, quite different, and it took place more than a decade ago. In May 1982, the then Israeli Prime Minister Menachem Begin presided over a bizarre ceremony in which bones that were deemed to be those of followers of Bar Kochba, the first century Jewish rebel against Roman rule, were given a state funeral and re-buried in a remote site in the Judaean desert. Participating in the ceremony were government ministers, high army officers, the Chief Rabbis and Supreme Court justices, all of whom were flown to the site by army helicopters; the reburial provoked an angry controversy, and a small band of critics mocked the ceremony by dressing in Roman togas and demonstrating on a nearby hill (Aronoff 1986).

How can this Israeli fixation with bones be explained? Why do public events involving bones and burials appear with such frequency, and why too have they become issues in dispute? These six cases are clearly very different from one another, so that explaining them and their meanings will require different frames of reference to be introduced.

Human bones seem always, whatever their particular context, to be exceedingly powerful representations. The force of this claim can be measured by the great attention that bones, burials and mortuary customs have received in the anthropological literature (Bloch and Parry 1982; Palgi and Abramovitch 1984; Kan 1992). Indeed, bare, disconnected bones – femurs, skulls, rib-cages, limbs – seem almost inevitably to produce emotions of fear and awe. They are profound images of the past and the future, and have the power to conjure primeval visions of mystery, frailty and death. What is more, bones are the past, the ancestors, and whoever controls them can thereby exercise some measure of control over the past. Here nationalism and the sacred, politics and culture, are close to the root of this particular Israeli passion. To be sure, this focus also resonates with a host of other cultural motifs: the brooding Israeli concern with death, the Holocaust and memorials, to cite one related theme, or again, the paradoxes that inhere in establishing a new nation in its ancient land (Handelman 1990: 191–223; Zerubavel, Y. 1990).

Bones in Jewish religious tradition

The bones of Jewish dead are the central topic of this analysis; and it is therefore important to understand how bones are perceived and related to within Jewish religious tradition. With Tukchinsky's (1946) well known primer on Jewish mourning customs as guide, a series of basic principles can be briefly stated. The topic is obviously much more complex then the summary presented here, but the following axiomatic statements indicate some fundamental Jewish religious beliefs and practices regarding death and burial.

First, upon the onset of death the body must quickly be buried in the earth. This is a biblical injunction of great force, and no other method of disposing of the body (such as cremation or exposure to the elements) is permitted. Second, bones in any form or condition represent the body in its totality: that is, bodily remains (such as portions of a rib or a foot) are perceived and dealt with as if they were the entire body. It is for this reason that particular remains, just like the body as a whole, have to be buried. Third, man has both a body and a soul (in Hebrew *nefesh*, *neshama*, *ruach*), and the soul that is released from its body at death remains near to the body's place of burial or wherever the bones have been kept. This is yet another reason why bodily remains that were buried previously, and subsequently uncovered, must be reinterred: the soul is unable to rest if some bones were removed and have not as yet been returned to the earth. Fourth, as a general rule reburial is not permitted; there are exceptions, however, including temporary burials when it was known beforehand that the body would later be reinterred, as well as reburial in the Holy Land of Jews who died in the diaspora. Fifth, the dead as well as their remains – that is, the bones of the dead – are polluting and therefore inherently dangerous; although this is particularly the case for males who are in the category of *Kohen*, or priest, it extends equally to all Jews. Sixth, the dead and their remains must be honoured (in Hebrew, *k'vod ha'meth*). This is a broad-scaled, fundamental matter and rests upon various basic principles. For example, the dead must be honoured since man was created in God's image, and therefore dealing improperly with the dead is analogous to an act of defilement perpetrated upon man in his lifetime, and, ultimately, a sin against God. Bones and bodily remains must also be honoured since they are destined to be resurrected when the Messiah comes. Thus, to sum up briefly, according to Jewish law not only must bones be kept in the earth, in so far as it is possible (and with the exception of reburial in *eretz ha'kodesh*, the Holy Land) they should remain intact at the place where they were initially buried.

These religious prescriptions are critical for understanding both the different, frequently conflicting interests in bones, as well as ways in which they are dealt with and used. The reasons for this should be clear: these particular religious traditions of act and thought are not merely a backdrop to behaviour, but are directly influential in everyday affairs.

The cultural-political contexts: the uses of bones

We can now return to the issues of bones in present-day Israeli society and culture. How should the previously presented cases be interpreted or explained?

The case of the burial site in Jerusalem, and the recurring conflicts between Israeli state authorities, archaeologists in particular, and Jewish religious zealots, represents one set of instances in which bones are a central topic. Jerusalem and its environs has been the location of many previous disputes. However, since this entire region has been settled for millennia, bones and conflicts regarding them develop practically everywhere. Not only do archaeologists often dig in ancient inhabited sites and mounds where burial grounds are likely to be found; practically every new road or construction project undertaken anywhere in Israel (as well as elsewhere in the immediate region), is likely to uncover a Canaanite, Second Temple or Byzantine site with its associated refuse, burials and, inevitably, bones. This immediately poses problems. Bones are crucial elements in the archaeological project: they reveal important clues regarding population size and composition, basic physical features, disease and medical treatment, cultural beliefs and practices, and potentially a great deal more. Archaeologists therefore may wish to remove bones to a laboratory or other place so that their scientific work may proceed.

However, if the bones are deemed to be those of Jews then a problem and likely dispute immediately arises: as we have seen, according to religious tradition the bones of the Jewish dead must be kept in the ground, and they must also be properly 'honoured'. Whenever burial vaults or graves are uncovered or discovered, archaeologists eagerly look forward to examining the bones – while the *haredi*, or ultra-orthodox guardians of Jewish burial sites, just as eagerly insist that the bones must be reburied.

As has frequently been remarked, archaeology in Israel is not only a national pastime and passion, but also an integral part of Zionist nation-building (Elon 1971). Organized and funded by the state and the universities, archaeology has been a major vehicle for tying the present with the past, and thereby (among other matters) seeking to validate the Jews' historic claim to their land. It is, therefore, a serious pastime that has powerful political and cultural implications. What is more, archaeology is displayed as a 'science', and the need to exhume bones and bring them to a laboratory for analysis is explained as an essential part of the scientific project. This is, then, one of the contesting ideologies, and it has been labelled or identified as a part of the 'secular religion' or 'civil religion' that developed within the Zionist movement throughout this century (Leibman and Don-Yehiya 1983).

The other viewpoint, or ideology, is religious, and although the main actors are associated with the small *haredi* community of ultra-orthodox zealots, it finds broad support within the entire religious Jewish community. The religious or orthodox view is that bones should remain in the earth, and that there is no cause or reason to tamper with them for so-called 'scientific purposes': digging up bones dishonours the dead, is an affront to the soul, and it may also complicate the process of resurrection. It is for these immediate reasons that religious zealots and the *haredi* burial society, the *atra kadisha*, maintain close scrutiny on archaeological sites and seem to appear mysteriously whenever bones or burial places are uncovered.

Even though archaeological projects and what is to be done with bones (as well as the other objects that are uncovered) are specifically referred to and legislated for by Israeli law, during the past several decades clashes between the state, archaeologists and the religious community have repeatedly taken place. Clearly, what is at stake are different visions and understandings of the past – the one secular and nationalist, the other religious and traditionally Jewish – and consequently not only over who controls the past but also who may shape the present.

The burial ceremony and shrine commemorating the bones of Bar Kochba's warriors, as well as the purported burial place of the Biblical Joseph, strike several parallel chords. Bones in these instances are mainly part of the political-cultural processes that unfolded following the Six Day War in 1967 and Israel's occupation of the West Bank. This period has been characterized by an explosive growth in religious-nationalist ideology as well as in dedicated nationalist activities (Sivan and Friedman 1990). Land occupied in the war, and the West Bank in particular, has been imbued with a holy status by some of the Jewish settlers and their political supporters. No wonder then that the Ottoman tomb outside the town of Shechem was already in 1967 identified as the grave of Joseph, and the band of religious zealots who initiated the idea also established a *yeshiva*, or religious seminary, at the site itself. Their message was clear: 'we have reclaimed our ancient land, and there can never be a thought of again leaving the bones of the Patriarchs'. The reburial of bones of what were purported to be Bar Kochba's warriors served the same purpose: the ceremony was conceived and staged by the then Prime Minister, and the melodrama bore the message that Israel would never retreat from lands where the bones of its ancient heroes were buried.

In contrast with those instances (such as those involving archaeologists and religious fundamentalists) in which bones are dug up and removed, in these two latter instances bones of a real or imaginary kind are being placed in the ground. There is a conscious attempt to establish new mythologies: bones are used as sacred symbols of the past, and they become a key element in a broad-based political and cultural process of legitimating claims to territory. It is important to note that these deliberate projects have had mixed results – the attempt to create new shrines and mythologies are not always successful. 'Joseph's Tomb' has not received widespread recognition as a 'real' site for prayer and pilgrimage, and following the ceremony that was held in 1982 the desert location of the 'grave of Bar Kochba's warriors' literally disappeared from view. Neither has become an 'authentic' sacred or national site. Whether this is because Shechem's location on the West Bank is dangerous for Israeli travellers, and the Judaean desert far off the beaten track, or because of a deeper sense that these are contrived places, invented and manipulated for partisan purposes, the bones placed in the ground have not been transformed into widely recognized national or religious shrines.

The two cases involving the bones of Moroccan Jews represent the continuing efforts to redefine the Moroccan Jewish presence in Israel. Briefly summarized, Moroccan Jews who migrated to Israel in large numbers during the 1950s and early 1960s found themselves placed in a low-status position vis-à-vis the reigning Ashkenazi elites, and since that time they have designed new forms of collective mobilization that resulted in both group and individual upward mobility (Weingrod 1990). Transferring the bones of the 23 immigrants is a part of this process. They were defined as *maapilim*, illegal immigrants to Zion who were willing to court danger in their efforts to reach the shores of Israel. Until then, the term and its associated prestige had been reserved for European Jewish immigrants who strove to reach Palestine-Israel during the 1930s and 1940s (Aronoff 1993). Indeed, the Israeli Moroccans who negotiated the transfer and reburial of the remains were consciously aware that they were engaged in an effort to redefine the status of their *eda*, or ethnic group. There was, in fact, a good deal of rivalry between Israeli political figures (including Moroccans) as to who would finally arrange the transfer of bodily remains during the decade in which negotiations took place, the boat was given a Hebrew name (it had been the *Pisces* but was renamed *Egoz*), and the North Africans who drowned were recognized and celebrated as *maapilim*: their graves on Mount Herzl are a dramatic demonstration that they too had taken a heroic part in creating the new state, and that members of their ethnic group had also made the ultimate sacrifice.

Transporting the bones of *zaddikim*, saints or holy men, from Morocco to Israel, is another dimension in this overall process. Since the 1960s a series of new saints and their shrines have been established in a number of outlying, peripheral Israeli towns; in all of the cases the *zaddikim* are Moroccan or Tunisian in origin, and members of these ethnic groups have also taken the leading role in organizing large-scale pilgrimages to the new holy shrines (Ben Ami 1984; Bilu 1987; Weingrod 1991). Digging up the remains of revered holy men in Morocco and reburying them in Israel is a recent innovation: the bones were reburied, a shrine was quickly built, a yearly pilgrimage is planned and the town-fathers have hopes that this will be a spur to tourism and local development. Morocco – in the form of bones and traditional shrines – has been transferred to Israel and is publicly displayed there, and in a paradoxical fashion this has lead to a heightened sense of their legitimacy and rooted status as Israelis.[3]

Finally, there is the case of the bones of the Bratzlaver Rebbe, and the anger of his followers at the suggestion that his bones be brought from the Ukraine to Israel. Why did his *hassidim*, or followers, reject the suggestion? The issues are complicated, but what is certainly involved are conflicts in traditions, both nationalist and religious. The Bratzlaver are an anomalous Chassidic sect: unlike the others, there has never been a successor to the group's founder, and his personality continues to play a central role within their particular tradition. Reb Nachman chose to be buried in Ouman (he previously had journeyed to the Holy Land, but returned from there to Eastern Europe), and over the years his followers have developed a tradition of pilgrimage to his grave. They were undoubtedly perplexed by the 'Zionist president's' attempt to intervene in their affairs: like all Jews, *zaddikim* and others, Reb Nachman will appear on the Day of Redemption; but until then, or until his Chassidim decide otherwise, his bones will remain in the Ukraine (Green 1979).

Each of the issues or cases analysed here is distinctive and nuanced: they represent, in effect, an array of contrasting symbolic expressions. At the same time, however, comparing them reveals some important similarities and contrasts. Most notably, these issues or cases can be seen to represent different, contesting Israeli political-cultural ideologies. Leibman and Don-Yehiya (1983) distinguish between what they term 'Israeli civil religion' and the 'new Israeli civil religion': the former is associated with the secular, state-socialist, nation-oriented Labour Zionist ideology that dominated Israeli politics and culture since the turn of this century, while the latter also incorporates and places special emphasis upon traditional religious as well as nationalist motifs. Analysed in these terms, the cases of bones and burials can be grouped into different types or categories. Both the archaeologists' project of constructing the nation's past, and the transfer and reburial of the bones of the Moroccan *maapilim*, can be seen as expressions of the 'Israeli civil religion': bones in these cases are indications or celebrations of the nation's past and present, and they represent traditions whose outlook is fundamentally secular. By contrast, 'Joseph's tomb', where religious motifs are intertwined with nationalism is linked with and expresses the 'new Israeli civil religion'. Burying the bones of Bar Kochba's warriors seems to be intermediate between the two: the major themes are nationalist and historical, although traditional religious themes are incorporated.

The most instructive contrast, however, is between the bones of the Moroccan rabbis and those of the Bratzlaver Rebbe: why, in the one case, were their bones dug up, transferred to Israel and reburied, whereas in the other instance the Rebbe's followers insisted that his bones continue to be buried in Ukraine? This comparison reveals two deeply different religious ideologies. According to the Moroccan interpretation, burying the bones of revered rabbis in the soil of the Holy Land is part of the process in which their community, or *eda*, is united with the Jewish people in its land; moreover, bringing the remains of the holy men from Morocco to Israel is permissible and proper, since it is a statement of Israel's sacredness and primacy. The Bratzlaver interpretation is almost precisely the opposite: in common with other *haredi* ultra-orthodox groups, the Chassidim do not recognize Israel as the sacred centre, nor do they wish to minimize their cultural and ideological separateness from other segments of the population. On the contrary, the Rebbe's grave in Ukraine continues to be the sacred centre and consequently it is only with the coming of the Messiah that Reb Nachman's bones will be transported to the Holy Land. These bones are differently conceived for reasons that are both theological and eschatological (Weingrod 1993).

Conclusion

The interpretations presented thus far have been particular, and seek to explain why in each instance bones have had such a lively fascination: they are addressed to the specifics of a broader political-cultural trend. Finally, I suggest some general reasons why bones have repeatedly become a focus of interest, and turn to several points of comparison between the Israeli and other contexts.

How may the recent Israeli fascination with bones be explained? Two related trends were significant. First, bones and burials became prominent in the post-1967, post-Six Day War and Greater Israel, period of time. During these decades 'nationalism of the right', as well as religious fundamentalism and mysticism, flourished and became influential. Second, as this new ideological structure became established, making use of bones came to be viewed as acceptable and proper: bones, burials and shrines became recognized themes or features of the new political-cultural system (the 'new Israeli civil religion') that was asserting its claim to hegemony.

This should not be taken to mean that events involving bones and burials were absent during previous decades; on the contrary, there are a number of well-known earlier instances in which the remains of leading Zionist figures, or martyrs killed by the Nazis, were reburied in public ceremonies.[4] Yet 1967 can reasonably be seen to mark a turning point in Israeli culture. Nationalism developed new themes and became more exuberant in the period following the Six-Day War and the Israeli occupation of the West Bank and Gaza: the sudden expansion into new lands, as well as the stream of violent incidents that followed, were accompanied by a new rightist nationalist rhetoric. This was commonly expressed in near-sacred tones and celebrated in slogans, songs, codes of speech as well as a certain sensibility that emphasized 'the people of Israel in the land of Israel' (Leibman and Don-Yehiya, 1983). While the electoral victory of the right-wing Likud Party in 1977 gave new impetus to these features, they were already blossoming during the previous Labour government. What is more, religious fundamentalism and mysticism were also growing in force; traditional religious groups became 'more observant', new groups that emphasized fundamentalist belief and practice also emerged, and, in addition, they became more insistent, vocal and public as their sense of self-confidence and success grew. Religious mysticism, with its emphasis upon the efficacy of holy persons and places, also drew wider followings. Each of these trends had its own inspiration, inventions and internal development, but they also interacted and thereby influenced each other.

It is within this intense, highly creative mixture of ideology and activity that the focus upon bones grew and became magnified. As was pointed out earlier, displaying and celebrating the bones of heroic ancestors is conducive with ideologies of nationalism, just as the heightened feeling of power and purpose among some religious-fundamentalists led them to actively challenge the archaeologists' project. Moreover, making public use of bones and burials became more reasonable and acceptable in the new 'reigning cultural climate', or hegemonic system, that was being fashioned. This is a key point: in a period which sacralized 'the People of Israel in the Land of Israel' a concern with bones was perceived to be proper and legitimate. Moreover, each instance in which bones became public issues had implications for others; for example, burying the remains of Bar Kochba's ancient warriors made the reburial of the ill-fated Moroccan immigrants an acceptable, culturally reasonable act. The process, in brief, was one in which bones became recognized as proper representations of an ideological system that was asserting its control.

Finally, the disputes previously described between archaeologists and religious fundamentalists also point to a number of comparative topics. As has been emphasized, conflict over the possession and burial of bones is a contest regarding who exercises control over the past, and therefore a struggle over the nature of the Israeli culture and society. From the viewpoint of the religious zealots, as well as the Israeli religious minority, the past and the present are encompassed by God's will and design. The past beginning with Creation is known, and the archaeologists' claim of 'science' poses a false issue since there can be no purpose in 'studying the past' that is determined by God's will. What is more, those who died in previous generations must have been 'religious Jews', and consequently the zealots are simply guarding their remains as they, the dead, would have wished in their own life time. Of course, the archaeologists' viewpoint is totally different. For them, as well as for the majority secular population, the bones of Jews and others must be respected, but the past 'is history' and consequently a scholarly problem which should be interpreted 'scientifically', and which has, moreover, considerable relevance to contemporary political issues.

This debate has many parallels with on-going disputes in the United States between archaeologists and Native Americans. The major issues in this controversy include access to sacred burial places, the control and disposition of bones and the artefacts uncovered in association with them, and consequently whether the Native American past will be constructed by archaeologists or by the Native Americans (McGuire 1992). The bones of Indian ancestors are 'their bones', say the Native Americans, and they therefore have the natural right to deal with them according to their own tradition and belief. The fact that until recently archaeologists and others could control their project without challenge does not mean that this will continue in the future; indeed, the issues are not only legal and political, they also pose serious ethical dilemmas and divisions within the scholarly community (Goldstein 1990).

Even though there are differences in what is actually being disputed and the topics in debate (for example, the Israeli zealots are interested in bones and not in the artefacts found with them, while the Native Americans wish to control both; in addition, the controversies between *haredim* and archaeologists have been legal and political, but not 'ethical') there is a great deal of similarity in these two instances. The conflicts in both cases are between different religious or ideological viewpoints, and they involve the objections of minority groups who oppose the activities of what previously had been usual practice by state authorities. Moreover, in both instances the objections grew increasingly insistent as the minorities became more self-confident and assertive. The issues are therefore not limited and parochial, but rather, as Benedict Anderson and others have lately demonstrated, of great scope and consequence: the past is a valuable resource, and it is likely that conflicts regarding its control will continue and grow (Anderson 1983; Friedman 1992).

Dry bones? By no means dry: these bones are, if anything; richly filled with meaning.

Notes

1   My title alludes, of course, to the Prophet Ezekiel's apocalyptic vision ('O ye dry bones, hear the word of the Lord') of worldly desolation and redemption (*Ezekiel* 37). In a contemporary context, the Israeli cartoonist Kirchen has also drawn upon Ezekiel and calls his wry parodies of everyday Israeli life 'Dry Bones'.

   Earlier versions of this article were presented to the 'Workshop on Nationalism and the Sacred' that took place in Leipzig, Germany, in July 1993, and to a symposium titled 'Anthropologists and Controversial Issues in Israeli Society', held at the Annual Meeting of the American Anthropological Association in Washington, DC, during November 1993. My special thanks to Mike Aronoff, Shlomo Deshen, David Leiser, Robert Paine and Steven Sharot for their helpful critique and comments.

2   The contemporary Israeli interest in burials and bones extends to at least two other topics: recovering the bodies of soldiers missing in military action, and controversies over where to bury the bodies of Israeli soldiers who are Christians or Muslims. An example of the concern with recovering bodies is the continuing attempt to locate the *Dakar*, an Israeli submarine that was lost at sea with all of its crew thirty years ago. Regarding where soldiers are buried, Israeli military

cemeteries are divided according to religious affiliation, and controversies rage
when the authorities order that 'comrades in arms' must be buried in separate
sections. While related to the subject of this study, these topics require detailed
separate consideration and therefore have not been included.

3   Interestingly, all of the saints newly transferred to Israel have their origins in
North Africa. There are complex explanations for this, but an important reason
is that Egypt and Morocco are the only Arab countries with which Israel has formal
or informal political relations. One supposes that if, in the future, similar relations should be established with Iraq, Yemen and Iran, a parallel process of
transferring bones and establishing shrines, both religious and national, is likely
to begin. Eastern Europe and the United States are the other areas from which
the bones of religious and other figures may be brought to Israel. The Holy Land,
it appears, may in the future become even more cramped with holiness.

4   Aronoff points out that already in 1930 the bones of Moses Hess, a nineteenth-
century socialist Jewish visionary thinker, were brought to Palestine by the
reigning socialist-Zionists and reburied on the shores of the Sea of Galilee (1993:
54). In 1950 the remains of Theodore Herzl, the founder of the modern Zionist
movement, were reburied on the Jerusalem hill-top that bears his name; and in
yet another well-known case, in 1963 the bones of Vladimir Jabotinsky, the
founder of the right-wing nationalist Revisionist Party, were given a state funeral
and reburied on Mount Herzl. These acts were designed to mark the Zionist vision
of Israel's primacy, as well as to confer legitimacy upon different secular Zionist
political-ideological groups. Moreover, following the establishment of Israel the
remains of various heroic figures (such as Hanna Senesh, who was killed by the
Nazis after having parachuted into Hungary during World War II) were brought
to Israel and reburied.

References

Almog, O. 1992. Israeli War Memorials: A Semiological Analysis (in Hebrew),
    Megamot. 32.2, 179–210.

Anderson, Benedict. 1983. *Imagined Communities*. London: Verso.

Aronoff, M. 1986. 'Establishing Authority: The Memorialization of Jabotinsky and the
    Burial of the Bar Kochba Bones in Israel Under the Likud', in M. Aronoff, ed.
    The Frailty of Authority, New Brunswick: Transaction P., 105–30.

——— 1993. 'The Origins of Israeli Political Culture', in: E. Sprinzak and L. Diamond,
    eds. *Israeli Democracy Under Stress*. Boulder: Lynne Rienner.

Ben Ami, I. 1984. Folk Veneration of Saints among Moroccan Jews (in Hebrew).
    Jerusalem: Center for Folklore Research, Magnus Press.

Bilu, Y. 1987. 'Dreams and Wishes of the Saint', in H. Goldberg, ed. *Judaism Viewed
    from Within and From Without*, Albany: SUNY P.

Bloch, M. and Parry, J. 1982. *Death and the Regeneration of Life*. Cambridge: Cambridge
    U.P.

Cohen, Eric. 1983. Ethnicity and Legitimization in Contemporary Israel. *Jerusalem
    Quarterly*. 24, 21–34.

Elon, A. 1971. *The Israelis: Fathers and Sons*. New York: Penguin.

Friedman, Jonathan. 1992. The Past in the Future: History and the Politics of Identity.
    American Anthropologist, 94, 837–59.

Goldstein, L. and Kintish, K. 1990. Ethics and the reburial controversy. *American Antiquity* 55: 585–91.

Green, Arthur. 1979. *Tormented Master: A Life of Rabbi Nahman of Bratslav*. Tuscaloosa:, U. of Alabama P.

Handelman, D. 1990. *Models and Mirrors: Towards an Anthropology of Public Events*. Cambridge: Cambridge U.P.

Inglis, K. 1993. Entombing Unknown Soldiers: From London and Paris to Baghdad. *History and Memory* 5, 7–31.

Kan, Sergei. 1992. Anthropology of Death in the Late 1980s. *Reviews in Anthropology*. 20, 283–300.

Leibman, C. and Don-Yehiya, E. 1983. *Civil Religion in Israel: Traditional Religion and Political Culture in the Jewish State*. Berkeley: U. of California P.

Levinger, E. 1993. Socialist-Zionist Ideology in Israeli War Memorials of the 1950s. *Journal of Contemporary History*. 28, 715–46.

Mosse, G. 1979. National Cemeteries and National Revival: The Cult of the Fallen Soldiers in Germany. *Journal of Contemporary History*. 14, 1–20.

—— 1990. *Fallen Soldiers: Reshaping the Memory of the World Wars*, Oxford, Oxford U.P.

McGuire, R. 1992. Archaeology and the first Americans. *American Anthropologist* 94(4): 816–36.

Palgi, Phyllis and Abramovitch, H. 1984. Death: A Cross-Cultural Perspective. *Annual Rev. of Anth.* 13, 385–417.

Sivan, E. 1991. *The 1948 Generation: Myth, Profile, Memory* (in Hebrew). Tel Aviv: Ministry of Defence.

—— 1993. To Remember is to Forget: Israel's 1948 War. *Journal of Contemporary History*. 28, 341–59.

Sivan, E. and Friedman, M. 1990. *Religious Radicalism and Politics in the Middle East*. Albany: SUNY P.

Tukchinsky, Y. 1946. *The Bridge of Life* (in Hebrew). Jerusalem: Slomin P.

Weingrod, A. 1990. *The Saint of Beersheba*. Albany: SUNY P.

—— 1991. 'Saints and Shrines, Politics and Culture: A Morocco-Israel Comparison', in D. Eickelman and J. Piscatori, eds. *Muslim Travelers*. Berkeley: U. of California P., 217–35.

—— 1993. Changing Israeli Landscapes: Buildings and the Uses of the Past. *Cultural Anthropology*. 8(3).

Zerubavel, Yael. 1990. 'New Beginning, Old Past: The Collective Memory of Pioneering in Israeli Culture', in Laurence J. Silberstein, ed. *New Perspectives on Israeli History: The Early Years of the State*. New York, NYU Press, 193–215.

Hard-wired Human Science, or Cognitive Fluidity?

■ *Anthropology Today*, 14.3, June 1998, pp. 1–2

I have included this piece partly to illustrate the difficulties of finding bridges between cultural and biological anthropology, and partly because it is rare for a great foundation such as Novartis, with its extensive powers of patronage, to be publicly criticized. This Novartis conference in London and the publication resulting from it were, in my view, scientifically substandard.

L OOKING BACK AT Robert A. Hinde's edited collection, *Non-Verbal Communication*, published in 1972 – the result of a Royal Society study group with contributions by Leach, Gombrich and Jonathan Miller as well as leading ethologists and psychologists – it is tempting to conclude that interdisciplinarity in the human sciences has made little headway in the last quarter-century, at least as regards the relationship of cultural anthropology to biology. Whereas during this period cultural anthropology has earned many friends in history, philosophy or religious studies, also for rather different reasons in the medical world, it has for the most part embraced an epistemology – one focused on meanings, values and experiences – which differs sharply from that of biology. And whereas some anthropology departments in the UK, most conspicuously Durham, try to keep channels of cooperation as open as possible, this is not a high priority for the majority of cultural anthropologists at the moment.

That the fault is not entirely theirs is exemplified by a state-of-the-art edited collection, *Characterizing Human Psychological Adaptations*, published last year[1] for the highly respected Ciba Foundation – which has since changed its name to the Novartis Foundation – as the proceedings of a symposium held in London in October 1996. Contributors include the celebrities Leda Cosmides, Richard Dawkins and Steven Pinker, and the chair was Martin Daly of the psychology department of McMaster University, Canada.

Once upon a time the Ciba Foundation published human science symposia of genuine catholicity – *Caste and Race*, published in 1967, remained on reading lists for many years – but the current policy seems to be to invite only participants who share a common approach, in the interest of academic peace. (Another example is the 1996 symposium on 'Genetics of Criminal and Anti-social Behaviour', to which the only cultural anthropologist invited – though he did not in fact show up – was Napoleon Chagnon, who is far more sympathetic to genetic explanations than most of his colleagues.) The only cultural anthropologist invited to 'Characterizing Human Psychological Adaptations' was, admittedly, a particularly brilliant one, Dan Sperber, and several of his interventions in the discussions are published in the proceedings. However, these are all couched in the idiom of psychology, with two exceptions. First, he claims it is more likely that matrilineal inheritance systems promote a relaxed attitude to paternity doubts than that (as is argued by the speaker) 'the preference for matrilineal inheritance would emerge in societies where doubts about paternity are greater'. Second, Sperber draws briefly on his own fieldwork in Mauritania and Ethiopia to point out the cross-cultural variability of beliefs regarding the duration of pregnancy. These are sound enough points, but half a page in a 300-page book does not redress the balance. (Can it be that Sperber is conducting participant observation of evolutionary psychologists, and wishes to disturb the object of his study as little as possible?) It is true however that the chair, Martin Daly, does not seem to be against cultural anthropology in the way that he is against Freudian theory, which he considers to be now lingering on only in 'pop psychology and literary criticism'.

A critique of evolutionary psychology such as the archaeologist Steven Mithen's[2] – deploring over-emphasis on 'hard-wired' domain-specific intelligence as opposed to the 'cognitive fluidity' celebrated by cultural anthropologists – is not cited. Furthermore the book raises serious problems both at the level of quality of data and at a more philosophical level.

To take an example of poor data (Mithen has given others from earlier publications in this discipline), one contributor, Randy Thornhill, tells us as a fact, citing his own five-page article in *Trends Ecol Evol*, that greater lifetime mate number and 'sexual advertisement' are found 'in women who are reared and live in social environments of reduced paternal investment'. This 'adaptation' is presented as analogous to the callusing of the skin from friction, or the formation of antibodies against a parasite. At no conference in cultural anthropology would a speaker get away with such a statement without being asked, at the very least, for more context and particularization.

As regards philosophy, it is true that some of the contributors worry a little that the principle of 'reverse engineering' – inferring specific Darwinian environments and selection pressures from the analysis of observable adaptations – could be a circular form of argument. But a more searching approach is needed. Daly takes as an epigraph for the book a dictum by a 1960s pioneer of these studies, George Williams, 'Is it not reasonable to anticipate that our understanding of the human mind would be aided greatly by knowing the purpose for which it *was designed*?', and Daly adds: 'The workings of the psyche *are obviously organized* to achieve various ends' [emphases added]. Scientists should surely try to avoid the imprecision of the floating passive voice, which is well described by Arabic grammarians as *al-majhul*, 'the unknown'. We are all indeed trapped by the constraints of language, as Darwin was when he originally advanced the concepts of 'natural selection' and 'fitness'. But a measure of humility is called for and when Daly attacks 'the same old hostility, ignorance and foolishness' of those who do not yet appreciate evolutionary psychology (but without citing critics), it is clear that he is a missionary as well as a researcher, and that his cause risks becoming what Stephen Jay Gould has called 'ultra-Darwinism'. Or as the anthropologist Tim Ingold – who, like Mithen, has made efforts to integrate the arguments of evolutionary psychology with his own discipline – has written, 'Despite the claims of evolutionary theorists to have dispensed with the archaic subject/object and mind/body dualisms of Western thought, they are still there, albeit displaced onto the opposition between the scientists, to whose sovereign imagination is revealed the design of nature, and the hunter-gatherer whose behaviour is interpreted as the output of innate dispositions installed by natural selection, and of which he or she has no conscious awareness.'[3]

Many suggestions made by contributors to this volume – about cheater detection, different animals' awareness of numbers, monogamy, or risk assessment – are of great interest. Foundations such as Novartis should be on the lookout for the equivalents to Robert Hinde, an outstandingly successful interdisciplinarian, among the middle generation of practising scientists, who could find a way of orchestrating these neo-Darwinian approaches with the more seasoned tools of philosophy and cultural anthropology. They should be able to afford the risk of inviting to the party not only those cultural anthropologists who broadly accept the neo-Darwinian paradigm, but also those of Tim Ingold's persuasion, which is that neo-Darwinism with its insistence on genetic traits does not do justice to the all-pervasiveness of sociality. Researchers who refrain from examining their own preconceptions fall short in this essential aspect of scientific method.

Notes

1   John Wiley, £55.
2   'Understanding mind and culture: evolutionary psychology or social anthropology?' *AT*, December 1995. This followed a British Academy/Royal Society conference in April 1995 on 'The evolution of social behaviour in primates and men', attended by both Cosmides and Mithen. Mithen's book *The Prehistory of the Mind: A Search for the Cognitive Foundations of Art, Science and Religion* was published by Thames and Hudson in 1996.
3   See his essay 'The Evolution of Society' in the recently published *Evolution: Society, Science and the Universe* (ed. A.C. Fabian, CUP, £16.95).

PART NINE

War and Civil Strife

■ JONATHAN BENTHALL

'**H**ISTORIANS ARE TO NATIONALISM', wrote E.J. Hobsbawm in 1992, 'what poppy-growers are to heroin-addicts: we supply the essential raw material for the market.'[1] Anthropology has long been justly proud of its record in decisively refuting the biologistic racism which was once used to justify slavery in the United States and later the Nazis' programme of genocide. But perhaps it was only in the 1990s that anthropologists came to realize how much they, like historians, are often unwittingly the primary producers of theories of primordial identity that turn out to be dangerous and addictive. As for genocidal projects, it has become increasingly clear that it is intelligentsias that promote these, not the uneducated.

Alex de Waal, who through his provocative writings on famine and humanitarian relief has had an exceptional practical impact on the work of aid agencies, wrote a guest editorial in 1994 on the Rwandan genocide, criticizing anthropologists for not doing enough to rebut misleading press coverage which assumed the cause to be 'age-old tribal animosities'. An exchange of views with **Johan Pottier** followed – Pottier claiming that de Waal had exaggerated and that his article was a betrayal of anthropology (and Pottier contributes an updating note to this anthology). A full-length article by the Belgian anthropologist Luc de Heusch (not reprinted here) followed in the August 1995 issue (11.4), and much has been written since about the Rwandan genocide. De Waal's reply to Pottier shifts the gravamen of his charge from the present generation of anthropologists to the earlier generation that devised a racial classification which was adopted by others for the purposes of anti-Tutsi propaganda. By the 1970s, no serious Africanist anthropologist was still promoting these ideas, yet an old text such as Charles Seligman's *Races of Africa*, which expounded them, was still being republished with all the authority of Oxford University Press as late as 1979. De Waal's concluding remark is: 'Anthropology deals with issues of immediate importance, and its practitioners have a greater role than they may realize.' Khazanov makes the same point in his article at the end of this section.

Whereas the 1993 decennial conference in Oxford of the Association of Social Anthropologists was generally an involuted affair, a last-minute extra session on ethnic violence was packed out and since then the warnings of Hobsbawm, de Waal and others have been gradually absorbed.

Going back to 1985, we reprint an article by **Veena Das**, the prominent Indian anthropologist, on the anti-Sikh riots in Delhi in November 1984 following the assassination of Indira Gandhi by one of her Sikh bodyguards. At that time, few other anthropology journals would probably have printed the article, since it eschews the academic tone of voice. It is marked by spontaneity and passionate commitment, for Das was herself part of the community of concerned citizens who, in default of action by the official services, took major responsibility for providing relief to victims of violence. Das asks questions which still resonate. For instance, how should social scientists describe the details of carnage which may be used to inflame more violence, but which if censored out may protect society from discovering the truth about itself? How can relief workers avoid the infantilizing of victims? How can an anthropologist studying such a crisis maintain an intellectual understanding of it, while also being emotionally involved? Das concludes with the prediction, which has been sadly been proved correct, that 'development will bring in its wake more rather than less of these crises'.

Julie Taylor's article 'Argentina and the "Islas Malvinas"' was published in the October following the Falklands/Malvinas war in 1982. Taylor had written a pioneering study *Eva Peron: the Myths of a Woman* in 1979. A correspondent in the February 1983 issue of *RAINews* criticized her for ignoring the rights of the Falklands inhabitants. In her (and the Editor's) defence, it might be mentioned that the rights of the Falklands inhabitants had been vigorously defended in nearly all the British press before and during the war. Taylor's article neatly articulates the Argentine point of view, though it needs to be said that many of us in Britain were just as surprised as the rest of the world to see the naval Task Force setting out in the spring of 1982 to fight a colonial war. The article makes no claims to scientific objectivity, yet it may be argued that the cause of objectivity is served by allowing a dissenting voice to be heard as a counterbalance to the majority view, which was essentially that of British nationalism.[2]

Anatoly M. Khazanov, writing in 1996, addresses the role of anthropologists amid the outburst of ethnic tension and conflict in the former Eastern Bloc. He aptly warns them against the temptation to identify goodies and baddies too readily, as a result of personal affiliation or preference. He notes the risks to anthropologists' personal safety, and also to their professional integrity when working in regimes where state intelligence services are ubiquitous. His article will resonate with anthropologists who work in other parts of the world, such as the Middle East.

Perhaps the deepest question is one which Khazanov only hints at, which is that which arises at the conclusion of an ethnic conflict. Yes, the perpetrators of war crimes must be punished, and often are – if and when they have lost the war. But, as Renan wrote, every nation-state begins with an act of forgetting so that it does not tear itself apart. Anthropologists have had more to say about the need to remember than about the need to forget.

Ending this selection with Khazanov's article is not intended as a sign of pessimism. The impression which we may sometimes form, that the world is becoming more turbulent in general, may be due to skewed media coverage and a willingness to forget how violent the last century was. However, fieldworkers nearly everywhere are going to have to become more politically sophisticated and more alert to the spread of surveillance and espionage, with its undermining of the local trust which, when it is earned and maintained, is the fieldworker's strongest asset.

Notes

1   'Ethnicity and nationalism in Europe today', *Anthropology Today*, 8.1, February 1992, pp. 3–8.

2   No similar defence was articulated of the right of the 1,200 former agricultural workers of Diego Garcia in the British Indian Ocean Territory not to be displaced by the British government between 1967 and 1973, to make way for a British and American naval base; and not until 2000 did the British High Court revoke their exclusion.

Chapter 37

Alex de Waal

■ GENOCIDE IN RWANDA, *Anthropology
Today*, 10.3, June 1994, pp. 1–2

JOURNALISTS HAVE DESCRIBED the current mass killing in Rwanda
as the expression of age-old tribal animosities. There has been no public
protest from social anthropologists. This is not only a source of shame for the discipline, but a missed opportunity to help stop the carnage.

The genocide in Rwanda is a crime, perpetrated by a known group of individuals associated with two extremist political parties, the National Republican Movement
for Development and Democracy (MRND) and the Coalition for the Defence of the
Republic (CDR). The first targets were members of opposition parties, journalists
and human rights activists, both Hutu and Tutsi. As the killing spreads to the rural
areas, it has become a programme of genocide specifically targeted at the Tutsi, who
before the killing represented about 10 per cent of Rwanda's 7 million people. Over
200,000 have died so far, and the killing continues.

A crime requires motive, means and opportunity. The motive of those responsible was to continue to monopolize power and seek a 'final solution' to the political
opposition, both civilian and armed. Attempts by President Juvenal Habyarimana
to stall on the implementation of agreements for power sharing were not succeeding, owing to domestic and international pressure.

The primary means for perpetrating genocide is mobilization of the militias that
had been established by the MRND and CDR since late 1991. Use of the civil administration to encourage ordinary people to participate in killings is a supplementary
strategy. Army units, especially from the Presidential Guard, and death squads have
also helped direct the killings, especially in the towns. Radio broadcasts have been
used to incite the population.

The genocide against rural Tutsi in Rwanda is particularly traumatic because
the killers are largely people from the same community as their victims. People are
murdered by their neighbours, their schoolteachers, their local shopkeepers. Such
mass mobilization of killers was necessary because of the particular nature of
Rwandan society.

Figure 37.1   A Rwanda Patriotic Front (RPF) rebel looks at a painting of the late President of Rwanda, Juvenal Habyarimana, at the entrance to the presidential residence near Kigali near the international airport, 23 May 1994. Habyarimana was killed on 6 April when his plane crashed. Both the residence and the airport were captured by the RPF army.

Rwanda has long been known as a true nation in Africa, containing three groups: Twa, Hutu and Tutsi. German and Belgian colonists characterized them as respectively aboriginal Pygmies, Bantu peasants and Nilo-Hamitic aristocrats. The truth is that they were three different strata of the same group, differentiated by occupational and political status. There is some analogy with the Indian caste system, though individuals could and did move with difficulty between the categories; and the Twa are victims of some of the worst discrimination in Africa.

The reciprocity in Hutu–Tutsi relations that had diluted the latter's dominance in pre-colonial days was destroyed by Belgian rule. Instead, a rigid system of tribute and exploitation was imposed, creating deep grievances that underlie today's violence. In the north-west, formerly an anomalous region of Hutu kingdoms, the Belgians dismantled the pre-colonial political system and imposed Tutsi overlords. The modern Hutu extremists – the late President Habyarimana and his clan – derive from this area.

The differences in physical stature between the groups have been wildly exaggerated: it is rarely possible to tell whether an *individual* is a Twa, Hutu or Tutsi from his or her height. Speaking the same language, sharing the same culture and religion, living in the same places, they are in no sense 'tribes', nor even distinct 'ethnic groups.'[1]

Two things enable one to identify an individual as Twa, Hutu or Tutsi: knowledge of the person's ancestry, and the possession of an identity card which, since 1926, has by law specified which group he or she belongs to. The latter is a legacy of Belgian rule: those with ten or more cows were classified as Tutsi, those with less as Hutu – and a tiny minority of those 'recognized as Twa' had their status as an ethnographic curiosity confirmed in perpetuity. But checking every identity card is time-consuming, and the killings needed to be carried out rapidly to be successful, so those planning the killing needed to mobilize militiamen from every community in the country, who knew every Tutsi family personally. In 1991, the government began to implement a system known as 'Nyumba Kumi' (literally 'ten houses') – one man from every ten households was mobilized and armed. Such are the logistical challenges facing those who contemplate genocide.

The killers were able to practise their methods on various occasions since 1990, killing perhaps 3,000 people, mainly Tutsi. This is well-documented in the 1993 report of an international human rights commission.[2]

The opportunity was provided by a conjunction of circumstances, which allowed the hardliners to confuse the international community for sufficiently long to be able to perpetrate the crime with extraordinarily little international response. This sowing of confusion was the key to the killers' success. Because President Habyarimana himself was the first casualty, his acolytes were able to present themselves as victims of the plot, rather than the perpetrators. The deaths of ten Belgians serving with the UN force focused international attention on the plight of foreigners. The renewed offensive by the Rwandan Patriotic Front (RPF) – motivated in part by the desire to rescue Tutsi civilians from the militias – enabled the government to speak of aggression and the need for a ceasefire. But above all, the killers portrayed the situation as one of uncontrollable spontaneous ethnic violence.

Prompt international condemnation of the coup in Burundi in October 1993 prevented political extremists from seizing and holding on to power. The absence of such condemnation in Rwanda last month allowed the killers to carry out their task undisturbed. This was largely because the crime of genocide was misdiagnosed as a spontaneous outbreak of ethnic violence. The Secretary General of the United Nations, Boutros Boutros-Ghali, spoke in late April of 'Hutus killing Tutsis and Tutsis killing Hutus' and proposed sending troops to bring about a ceasefire between the (Tutsi-dominated) RPF and the (Hutu-dominated) army. This was precisely what the militias wanted: a chance to stop the RPF advance so they could complete the genocide of unarmed Tutsi away from the battle lines.

The United Nations is now putting forward more modest proposals. But the international diplomatic ball game moves more slowly than the speed of the killing.

The more perceptive journalists are now retreating from their earlier characterization of 'random tribal killing', but they have yet to explain what is happening, politically or anthropologically.

The great majority of Rwandans are, of course, appalled by the cataclysm that has engulfed their country. They, and the opposition forces, are not implicated in the killing. The ability to stop the genocide and build a peaceful future for Rwanda lies ultimately with these Rwandese people. But the absence of an incisive analysis of the crime, and the failure to condemn the criminals responsible, is leaving these people demoralized and embittered. This is dangerous: it inhibits a positive reaction from Rwandan people, and makes it more likely that there will be indiscriminate violence in revenge.

Even a modest anthropological appraisal of the nature of Hutu–Tutsi identity, and of the nature of genocide in a country such as Rwanda, could rebut the misleading press coverage and the irrelevant and even damaging proposals for international intervention that have followed.

Notes

1   Chrétien, Jean Pierre. 1985. 'Hutu et Tutsi au Rwanda et au Burundi', in J.-L. Amselle and E. M'bokolo, eds, *Au Coeur de l'Ethnie: Ethnies, Tribalisme et État en Afrique*, Paris, Éditions La Découverte.
2   International Commission of Inquiry into Human Rights Violations in Rwanda, *Report*, Human Rights Watch, New York, 1993.

Chapter 38

Johan Pottier and Alex de Waal

■ **CORRESPONDENCE AND COMMENTARY**,
Anthropology Today, 10.4, August 1994, pp. 28–9

Genocide in Rwanda

Journalists have described the current mass killings in Rwanda as the expression of age-old tribal animosities. There has been no public protest from social anthropologists. This is not only a source of shame for the discipline, but a missed opportunity to help stop the carnage (*AT*, June 1994).

BY THE TIME THE JUNE ISSUE of *AT* circulated, Alex de Waal himself had appeared on TV to discuss the planned circumstances of the genocide. In his 'public protest' (or whatever it was), he indirectly joined other Africanists, all with research experience in Rwanda, who were helping to achieve clarity. Some wrote or spoke publicly (Chrétien on TV5; DesForges on CNN; Lugan in *Le Figaro*; 30 Belgian Africanists in an open letter to the Belgian authorities, the EC and the UN), while others exchanged information on Internet. Some, to be fair to them, were unable to comment publicly, sometimes because they did not wish to endanger the lives of friends or relatives in Rwanda.

Yes, de Waal is right, initially journalists (even some very senior ones) erred in talking about age-old tribal conflicts. Some continue doing so. But others, aware of their knowledge gaps, took the trouble to read through recent anthropological writings (Richard Dowden, *The Independent*, pers. comm.). De Waal himself, incidentally, has failed to do this in depth, and anyone with any knowledge of Rwanda's history will find his interpretation of the past (in which Twa, Hutu and Tutsi become 'different strata of the same group') quite naive.

Questions need to be asked about how anthropologists and journalists can improve their rapport, and Rwanda is a lesson in this respect. But we must not exaggerate, as de Waal does, when guessing what might be achieved by closer professional cooperation. He refers to Boutros Boutros-Ghali, who in late April still spoke of 'Hutus killing Tutsis, and Tutsis killing Hutus'. Flagrant misrepresentation indeed. But is it right to blame journalists and anthropologists for errings by the Secretary General of the UN? The reason for Boutros-Ghali's misrepresentation surely lies within the UN itself. If the UN send an 'International Commission of Inquiry into Human Rights Violations in Rwanda' (January 1993), which concludes in its report that Habyarimana and his entourage are orchestrating political murders dressed up as ethnic murders (a conclusion recently restated in *Le Figaro* by Jean Carbonare, one of the Commissioners), then surely the UN Secretary General should have known better. Why did he not know about this report in detail? Whatever the answer, it is unfair to blame either the media or anthropologists.

De Waal's justification for accusing his colleagues in anthropology, together with journalists, is contained in the following statement:

> Prompt international condemnation of the Coup in Burundi in October 1993 prevented political extremists from seizing and holding on to power. The absence of such condemnation in Rwanda last month allowed the killers to carry out their task undisturbed. This was largely because the crime of genocide was misdiagnosed as a spontaneous outbreak of ethnic violence.

This bizarre statement puts anthropologists, who failed to organize a 'public protest' against the misrepresentations of planned genocide, in the dock along with the international forces (arms-dealers, politicians, military advisors) who set up and activated Rwanda's killing machine. Bizarre? Yes. For it cannot be a footnote that the 'promptly condemned' coup in Burundi resulted in the death of between 50,000 and 100,000 people.

That genocide in Rwanda should be an occasion for stabbing colleagues in the back and implicating them (it seems all anthropologists are implicated) in this genocide is absurd, intriguing and very painful.

Johan Pottier
School of Oriental and African Studies,
University of London

Is it bizarre to lump together anthropologists with arms dealers as bearing responsibility for the genocide in Rwanda?

In the context of Rwanda, perhaps not entirely (though it is chiefly an earlier generation that should be put in the dock). The killers have been driven by Hutu extremism – a weapon more powerful than any fragmentation grenades.

Hutu extremism is a bland name for a genocidal ideology, which has drawn deeply on racial theories, notably the Hamitic hypothesis, that were developed by anthropologists. Standard texts such as Seligman's *Races of Africa* (reissued as recently as 1979) gave academic respectability to systems of racial classification, which continue to have common currency in political discourse in central Africa.

Should the profession be responsible for the abuse of theories it spawned in earlier days but which it has now discredited? I would argue that it cannot absolve itself entirely. At least we should popularize our refutations of our ancestors' errors.

Moreover, some contemporary scholars have also been less constructive; for example, Jean-Luc Vellut recently coined the term 'people's genocide' to explain the killing in Rwanda (letter in *TLS*, 15 July 1994). This unfortunate diagnosis plays right into the hands of the genocidal criminals.

When the genocide was unleashed on 6 April, central to the extremists' strategy was a smokescreen of confusion and disinformation. There was a mass assassination of political opponents (mostly Hutu), followed by a rolling policy of massacres throughout the countryside over the following weeks and months. This was deliberately presented by the killers as uncontrollable ethnic violence, about which nothing could be done. Blowing away the smokescreen could have helped to bring the violence to an end much more rapidly; those who started the killing could have been pressured to order it to stop. In Burundi, when there was international condemnation, the killers rapidly stopped their killing. Tens of thousands died, but had the world reacted as it was to do with regard to Rwanda, the figure might have been far higher.

Could academics and journalists have contributed to dispelling the confusion, and helping to stop the genocide? Perhaps they could.

Contrary to Pottier, the 1993 International Commission of Inquiry had nothing to do with the United Nations; it was put together by a group of non-governmental human rights organizations at the invitation of Rwandese human rights organizations. There was no failure of communication within the UN. Dr Boutros-Ghali responded as he has always done, to pressure from the United States and France, to the (inaccurate) picture painted by his Special Representative in Kigali, and to the *New York Times* and American network television. In late April, when he proposed re-enlarging the UN force in Rwanda, it was largely in response to public outcry. But the analysis was still woefully deficient.

By May, to be sure, the better informed journalists were revising their accounts of the killings. As usual, radio and newspaper correspondents were ahead of their TV colleagues. Some social anthropologists have indeed played a role in illuminating the media; these colleagues are to be warmly commended. But the damage had been done: several hundred thousand people were dead.

It is of course not possible to condense the history of ethnicity in Rwanda to a paragraph or two; I would rebut Pottier's caricature of my views by referring readers to the African Rights paper 'Rwanda: Who is killing, who is dying, what is to be done' (May) and to my piece in the *TLS* (1 July).

I was disappointed in Pottier's defensive reaction to my piece as a 'stab in the back'. It was certainly, in crude language, meant as a kick on the backside. Anthropology deals with issues of immediate importance, and its practitioners have a greater role than they may realize.

Alex de Waal
African Rights, 11 Marshalsea Road,
London SE1 1EP

Update by Johan Pottier, September 2001

The most important piece of evidence regarding the UN's unwillingness to act upon information coming out of Rwanda in early 1994 is the fax by UN General Romeo Dallaire to Lt-General Baril on 11 January 1994. Sent to Baril at the UN Department of Peace-Keeping Operations (DPKO) in New York, this fax gave reliable details of the preparations for genocide, but was ignored. When the killings began, the US, through its representative Madeleine Albright, argued persuasively that the UN had no business being in Rwanda. For an illuminating account of how the UN reached this consensus, and of the disregard for area expertise within the UN bureaucracy, see Michael Barnett's (1997) 'The UN Security Council, Indifference and Genocide in Rwanda', *Cultural Anthropology* 12(4): 551–78.

It is important that readers put the correspondence between de Waal and myself in a fuller, ongoing context, which must include Rwanda's occupation of part of the eastern region of the former Zaire. Important in this respect is that the RPF-led post-genocide Government of Rwanda has crafted its own version of Rwandan history, an activity in which it has been assisted by (mainly anglophone) anthropologists and social scientists who had little or no familiarity with the Great Lakes prior to the genocide. For details of their contribution to how Rwandan society and the economy needs to be understood today, see my 1995 article in Obi Igwara (ed.) *Ethnic Hatred* (London: ASEN Publication) and my forthcoming book *Re-Imagining Rwanda: Conflict, Survival and Disinformation in the late 20th Century* (Cambridge: CUP). The book focuses on the contemporary production of ethnographic knowledge regarding Central Africa, a production to which not just anthropologists, but other social scientists, journalists, aid and development workers, and diplomats have all contributed.

Chapter 39

Veena Das

■ ANTHROPOLOGICAL KNOWLEDGE AND
COLLECTIVE VIOLENCE: THE RIOTS IN DELHI,
NOVEMBER 1984, *Anthropology Today*, 1.3,
June 1985, pp. 4–6

MANY SOCIAL SCIENTISTS have made the observation that human
nature is, perhaps, encountered in the raw in the midst of a riot. As a discipline, however, anthropology has not generated a collective body of knowledge
which could help us in formulating problems of anthropological ethics when engaged
in the understanding of collective violence, nor has it reflected on problems of
theory and method pertaining to societies caught in the savage brutalities of mass
murder, arson, looting and rape. The following observations were formulated while
I was engaged in the tasks of rehabilitating riot-victims. The issues have not been
thought through, and if one is drawing attention to them at this stage, it is only in
order that one may turn to the professional collectivity for enlightenment and for
the fighting of personal despair.

Let me briefly describe the context within which the riots took place. Following
the assassination of the Indian Prime Minister, Indira Gandhi, in Delhi on 31
October 1984, there was widespread violence against the Sikhs for three days. The
assassins were from the Sikh community and it was initially assumed by many that
the riots were an expression of the spontaneous anger of crowds against a dastardly
act. Initially it was thought that the number of people killed in Delhi would not
exceed a hundred. Whereas many people were completely bewildered by the
violence for the first two days, it was still assumed that the police would take charge
and law and order would be restored.

By 3 November, it became clear to civil rights groups, university teachers and
students, retired bureaucrats, journalists and other concerned citizens that they
had to take the major responsibility for establishing relief camps, procuring food
and medicines, and collecting information about the number of people dead or
missing. The police were either partisan or passive. Even the army, which was called
in on 3 November, and which did a commendable job in restoring confidence,
was not expected to take any responsibility for the running of camps or bringing
criminals to book. Although the administration and the police became much more

co-operative later, the entire burden of collecting and collating information about the crimes, of which the evidence was disappearing every day, as well as the organization of camps, fell entirely on the voluntary efforts of citizens.[1]

It is in this context that my colleagues and I decided to enquire into the pattern of riots by going into the affected localities rather than restricting ourselves to relief camps.[2] Other voluntary organizations and some journalists had been rendering help as well as collecting information earlier. The locality that seemed to be in need of immediate help was Sultanpuri, the scene of one of the worst carnages in the city. We have already described elsewhere the sequence of events, the connivance of the police and criminal elements in perpetrating violence, and the conditions in which the lower caste Sikhs from Rajasthan became the targets of brutal violence by other members of lower castes.[3] In contrast, the upper castes and the affluent Sikhs escaped with loss of property and were mostly helped by their upper-caste Hindu or Muslim neighbours. My purpose now is to draw attention to those kinds of problems which invite sustained research of an anthropological nature and are important for the profession as well as the wider society.

The first issue that we encountered on 8 November, when we visited the locality, related to our responsibility as social scientists to the urgent request of the victims that the truth about their suffering be recorded and made public.

In the locality as a whole, the number of people killed exceeded 200. The S.H.O. at the Police Station assured us that not more than twenty people had been killed. Clearly it was important to collect the names of the people killed if official figures were to be challenged. However, when we went into the locality we expected that providing for the physical needs of the victims would take priority over all other matters. The people were, indeed, hungry. But more than their need for food, we discovered, was the need to tell us all that had happened to them. In fact, as soon as they discovered that we were university teachers, they impatiently brushed aside all other questions and took us from house to house insisting that we immediately record the names of the dead, the sequence of events during those two days of violent outrage, and the names of the criminals and the police officials involved. One man, whose two sons had been killed, offered to raise fifty rupees later if we could have an account of their suffering published in a newspaper. We discovered thus that being subjected to brutal violence for two consecutive days had not been successful in stripping men of their cognitive needs, nor could it blunt their desperate need to have the truth recorded and communicated.

Our report on the Sultanpuri carnage was published in the *Indian Express* on 16 November. It recorded the events, our estimates of the number of people killed and the manner of their killings and also gave a list of all the names of police officials, criminals and politicians who were seen in various roles during the carnage by the victims. Immediately, it raised a controversy about whether the publication of such a report was ethical during such a turbulent period. A senior professor of history of the Jawaharlal Nehru University stated during a seminar that he was shocked by the irresponsible behaviour of some academics who had published a blow-by-blow account of the violence. Others expressed the concern privately that such reports may fan passion and lead to vengeance. In a recent court-hearing, two judges of the Dehi High Court described the authors of the report as 'worse than wretched' and stated that such gory details did not add anything to that which was generally known.

To my mind, all this raises a general question: which standards of descriptions shall we evolve in recounting events of this nature? To the victims, the horror of the violence consisted in the details. They wanted their suffering to become known as if the reality of it could only be reclaimed after it had become part of a public discourse. On the other hand, the intellectual community wanted to stop at the process of labelling it as 'communal violence' or 'state violence'. I suspect that there was a need here to suppress detail, for that would bring us face to face with the necessity of explaining why men use certain styles of violence, a fact that we in Indian society have not been prepared to face since the days of the communal holocaust of 1947.

From the point of view of anthropological understanding, it seemed to me that we need to listen to the ethnographic voice, rather than dismiss it as either 'gory' or even 'trivial'. Let us take two examples. As the events of the riots were recounted in detail, it impressed upon me that the murder and looting had not been done in silence and that the speech of the perpetrators of violence had provided important signs to the victims who were in a continuous process of interpreting it. One man explained to me why he had run away, even as he was being beaten by sticks, leaving his wife behind, and how he had since used his wife as a messenger between the different relatives. 'As we came out of our house', he said, 'a crowd attacked us. My wife fell on me to protect me from the blows of the *lathis* (staves). Some men addressed her as *bahenji* (sister) and asked her courteously to move away. So, I thought, they are not going to harm her and I then ran. My interpretation was correct and she has, since, moved quite freely, collected rations, information, and even gone to the police station to report the death of my brother.' In another locality a woman was ravaged by guilt because she felt she had read the signs wrongly and condemned her son to death. 'I should have taken my son out with me. I learnt only later that they were only killing men. I had hid my sons in a neighbour's house and locked it. They burnt that house.' Attention to detail is necessary if we are to understand the spatial picture of the body as an object of violence, the prevalence of black humour when collective death is treated as a macabre spectacle, the manner in which survivors internalise guilt and begin to blame themselves as responsible for the carnage; and, finally, the intense need of survivors to make their experience part of collective knowledge. Perhaps the dismissal of detail by the intellectual community of historians, political scientists and legal scholars is a mechanism by which we hide the truth of our society from ourselves. Anthropological research should help us in understanding how the very constitution of knowledge in these disciplines performs a hiding rather than revealing function. The unconscious censorship which is so typical of folklore is not necessarily absent from scholarly discourse.

Most accounts of the conditions of fieldwork rest on the assumption of reasonable normality. If one is working among victims of a collective tragedy, one's movements are naturally determined by the sole criterion of the needs of the people. Procuring rations, arranging for medical help, filling in forms and establishing liaison with police officers and administrators – these are the activities that define the trajectory of one's existence. Yet one feels that space, time and relationships have become so compressed that what would take months to unravel in ordinary circumstances suddenly lies exposed. Since fieldwork depends so heavily upon the empathy that one is able to establish, we need to produce more accounts of fieldwork under such conditions and the manner in which the normal barriers between insiders and outsiders are suddenly overcome. Obviously, the rhythms of society have a good deal to do with what aspects of social life will be revealed to the researcher. Perhaps, along with describing the methods of fieldwork in which the researcher has complete control over his field, we should also draw attention to the opposite pole: when society seems to take control of the researcher, who simply has to lend himself or herself to become the anonymous space on which the hitherto suppressed knowledge of society inscribes itself.

A related area in which we need to generate comparative description as well as to evolve analytical tools is in relation to the language of the victims. Police investigations as well as court-hearings depend a good deal upon eye-witness accounts and upon assumptions of logical consistency. As far as we can tell, the capacity to relate incidents in a connected manner can get impaired in survivors. If we had enough research on the nature of this impairment, anthropology could have provided expert knowledge on the relation between the event and its representation. For instance, we found that many accounts tended to place equal importance on a brutal event such as a murder and a trivial but contiguous event such as the theft of a particularly nice garment. In other cases the fear of an attack became a recurring theme, and people could hallucinate about voices of mobs that they claimed to have heard. In still other cases, there was a propensity to use theatrical expressions and a profusion of metaphors (e.g. rivers of blood were flowing), as the only means through which the inner horror could be given expression. None of these modes of representation and expressions meant that the people were not capable of providing witness. What it did mean was that standards of interpretation needed to be flexible enough to take into account the circumstances of the events and their recall.

Lastly, we would like to know how general is the tendency to infantilize victims. The assumption of relief-agencies, including well-meaning ones, is that victims are unable to take control of their lives.[4] As a young historian, Radha Kumar, noted, even the language at the disposal of relief-workers distances them from the victims. Everyone referred to those staying in relief-camps as inmates, thus making prison-wardens out of the relief-workers. The tendency of survivors of collective disasters to either complete stasis or exaggerated movement provided difficulties of comprehension to many. For instance, it was assumed that the constant running after rations, sewing-machines, work-kits and bicycles, by people after they had returned to their localities, was a sign of their inability or refusal to return to normal work. In contrast, I found that when we provided knitting-machines and a skilled tutor in one of the streets, the women abandoned their constant search for new sources of 'relief' and began to concentrate upon development of knitting-skills.

A discussion between some of the iron-smiths, and a relief agency that had done otherwise commendable work, highlighted this tension and also provided comic relief. The agency wanted to distribute work-kits to the iron-smiths whereas they thought that it would be better if they were provided with money. The point made by the iron-smiths was that they were themselves *lohars* and they saw no reason why they could not buy iron and forge their own tools. The relief agency was, perhaps, a little suspicious of their intentions. This was brought out into the open when one of the men said 'you are afraid, we will spend the money by getting drunk. Maybe one or two will; but ultimately you either have to trust us or leave us'. There was shrewd economic sense here for while the relief agency was engaged in discussions, forging of tools, distributions, at least thirty working-days were lost. The economic loss was greater than if some of them had, indeed, made a celebration of the money and blown it up in a drunken evening.

In the last few years research on disasters has grown and was ably summarized by D'Souza in the February 1985 issue of *Anthropology Today*.[5] However, in the case of collective destruction brought about by one set of human beings upon another, the issues become more complex than if people were facing disasters brought about by nature. The greatest difficulty of studying a situation such as this is that the anthropologist cannot remain uninvolved, for his or her own anxieties about death, evil and suffering are constantly aroused. The temptation to either flee from the situation or become completely submerged in it, abdicating in both cases the responsibility to provide an intellectual understanding of it, are overwhelming. In such a situation, we found great intellectual support in the writings of Bruno Bettelheim on survival in a concentration camp,[6] and Lifton on the survivors of Hiroshima,[7] for their sensitivity to language and the narrative enterprise of human life. Perhaps the modern world calls for a far greater collaboration between anthropologists, linguists and psychologists towards an understanding of human behaviour (including linguistic behaviour) under crises rather than normality, for, unlike D'Souza, I feel that development will bring in its wake more rather than less of these crises.

Notes

1   Excellent documentation on the riots was produced in the form of reports by *Indian Express, The Statesman, Illustrated Weekly of India, Manushi, Economic and Political Weekly* and *Lokayan*. The report produced jointly by the People's Union for Civil Liberties and People's Union for Democratic Liberties was the first comprehensive account of the riots and was followed by the reports of People's Commission, Citizens for Democracy, and Nagrik Ekta Manch.

2   These colleagues were Professors Ranendra Kumar Das, Manoranjan Mohanty and Ashis Nandy. Subsequently, consistent help has been provided by teachers and students of whom I would like to make special mention of Dr Mita Bose and Sanjiv Dutta Chowdhary.

3   See Das, Veena *et al.,* 'Only widows and orphans left', in *Indian Express*, 16 November 1984, and 'A new kind of riot', in *Illustrated Weekly of India*, 23–29 December 1984.

4   I would like to acknowledge here the great support we received from the Indian Express Relief Fund. The enlightened attitude of the Steering Committee of this fund and their empathy with the suffering victims will be long remembered by all who had the privilege to be associated with them.

5   D'Souza, Frances, 'Anthropology and Disaster Relief', *Anthropology Today*, 1985, Vol. 1, No. 1, 18–19.

6   Bettelheim, Bruno. *Informed Hearts*, New York, 1966.

7   Lifton, Robert J. *Death in Life: The Survivors of Hiroshima*, New York, 1976.

Chapter 40

Julie Taylor

■ ARGENTINA AND THE 'ISLAS MALVINAS':
SYMBOLISM AND THE THREAT TO
NATIONHOOD, *RAINews*, 52, October 1982, pp. 1–3

MANY ARGENTINES JOINED OUTSIDERS to criticize the junta in
Buenos Aires for using the repossession of the Falkland/Malvinas Islands to
manipulate popular sentiment and unite support for an increasingly disliked leadership. Yet they, with most of Latin America, have stood behind the military
government's claim to the islands. The junta's success in mobilizing Argentina
depended, not on support for the government's members or for their military move,
but on the unanimous Argentine feeling that claims to the 'Malvinas' are central to
Argentina's claims to national identity. Many Argentines – perhaps most – have
been committed not to their government, but to the cause which the government
is exploiting. Nevertheless, in both diplomatic and military confrontations that
government can count on Argentine popular sentiment and on widespread Latin
American sympathy for it. The failure of the British and their American allies to
assess the depth of the Argentines' unanimous dedication to recovering their sovereignty over the islands has resulted from an inability to assess the cultural context
and historical experience which form Argentine and Latin American public opinion
in this crisis.

For the Argentines, the 'Malvinas' symbolize their relationship with world
powers and therefore their identity as a nation. They represent Argentina's experience as a colonized and dominated culture, an experience shared with the rest of
Latin America. Long before the recent conflict, the islands figured in political
discourse and daily conversation as a focus of resentment against the high-handed-
ness Argentina had come to expect from the British in particular, but from others
like them as well. The crisis itself convinced the Argentines in their interpretation
of years of delay in the talks over the islands as an intentional humiliation of their
nation by Britain, confirming the suspicion that the British never gave credence to
negotiations or to the Argentine negotiating position. Events since April have also
linked the 'Malvinas' with the Argentine tradition of attempting to establish a position and an identity independent of the larger powers. And in the interaction of the

Figure 40.1   An Argentine man reads the latest edition of *La Razón* in Buenos Aires on 14 June 1982, during a demonstration in front of the Casa Rosada after Britain and Argentina reached an informal ceasefire agreement in the Falklands/Malvinas conflict.

symbolic messages being created by the British and Argentine governments for their peoples, the subtle imperialism to which Argentina is subject has emerged translated into the simplistic terms of 19th-century colonialism.

The British, not the Spanish, are perceived by Argentines as the threatening imperial power in their past. The story in Argentina goes that the British made three Argentine invasions. In the first, they sent their troops and were repulsed by the Argentines. In the second, they again sent their troops and were again repulsed by the Argentines. In the third, they sent two businessmen who immediately took over. British financial influence was predominant in the area before Argentina gained independence from Spain, and the British did in fact invade and occupy Buenos Aires in both 1806 and 1807, when troops and citizens dislodged them. In 1828, the British Foreign Office's pressure finally led to the establishment of Uruguay as a buffer state between Argentina and Brazil in response to demands for peace and markets for British commerce. And in 1833, the British seized the 'Malvinas'. The episodes of the British invasions and the creation of independent Uruguay closed with the signing of formal agreements. But there was no resolution of the confrontation over the 'Malvinas'.[1]

Argentina's ill-fated colonization of the 'Malvinas' had begun in 1829 when Governor Louis Vernet initiated his systematic plan for long-term development. The British consul at the time described Vernet as impressively knowledgeable and prepared for the task he had set himself. Vernet thought the islands could become a provisioning point for sealers and whalers in the area. American sealers, however, preferred not to have to pay for their provisions. In protest, Vernet seized an American sealing vessel, only to find his colony destroyed by American gunboats and surviving colonists taken off to be tried as pirates. The next year the British moved in, confident that the Argentines recognized it would be futile to oppose them, not least because Britain was a major power behind the current Argentine government. Their assessment was correct, but the Argentines never accepted British occupation of the 'Malvinas'. It was not the result of an unpopular treaty or an unsuccessful war. There was no settlement with which Argentina could be dissatisfied. No basis other than force was offered for the claim to the islands at the time: no battle was ever won, no treaty signed, no negotiation made.

As the century passed, the British, their investments, and their customs established themselves in a flourishing commercial community in Buenos Aires and brought with them the painful ambivalence of any relation between a subordinated people and the power which dominates them. Argentines are not unmindful of benefits the British bestowed upon them, but they point out that these benefits often worked more to the advantage of the British than of the Argentines. The railroads constructed in the 1870s and thereafter, for example, were built in a fan-like pattern converging on Buenos Aires, not to facilitate communication or stimulate markets within Argentina, but to move resources to the port for shipment to England and its trading partners. In the 20th century, increasingly after the world depression, commercial agreements seemed to Argentines to repeat a similar message of subjugation. Argentines still recall the 1936 riots which broke out to protest against the concessions which the English demanded in order for Argentina to retain its English markets in the face of Commonwealth competition.

Meanwhile, British technology, British business and British fashion were everywhere the highest standard, but for Argentina, as for much of the world, that standard too often proved unattainable. In Argentina, the British examples are given a poignant vitality by the elegant and prosperous elite community of Argentines of British descent. Some ethnically British Argentines make a concerted effort to identify with their South American homeland. Others, however, give substance to their countrymen's suspicions that Anglo-Argentines deprecate Argentina's culture. For example, an Argentine whose family had arrived from England in the 1850s mentioned laughingly that he could not remember ever having read a book in Spanish. A Cambridge educated *estanciero* of British descent insisted on sending his son to Scotland for training in farm management, despite neighbours' remarks (and the son's bitter laments) that he was being ill-prepared for pampa conditions. Further, few members of other groups define themselves in such a way, as Franco-Argentinos, Italo-Argentinos, Asturiano-Argentinos and so on, even though they may belong to a club or association of people from their place or origin. Stories circulate about Anglo-Saxon and Celtic grandmothers exhorting their grandchildren not to marry 'the natives' – counsel which I heard administered more than once.

The English, and those who have supported or replaced them, have consistently seemed to act as though Argentine culture and even Argentine geography do not exist. Like other Latin Americans, Argentines are born into a Western world that denies any value to their culture, and consequently denies them an identity. A Brazilian professor who had been part of a delegation to convince European banks that his country would be a trustworthy recipient of loans summed up the treatment they had received by observing, 'We are just Indians to the rest of the world.' In a similar vein, an Argentine sociologist referring to the 'Malvinas' crisis said, 'The English are treating us like natives.'

But Argentina has virtually no pre-Columbian heritage to which they can turn for an identity. In this, they are an extreme case of a condition shared by all Latin American national cultures, even in areas where pre-Columbian civilization flourished. Precisely because non-Western culture has never been entirely accepted in the West, an indigenous American identity has commanded little respect. Neither has it been easily adopted by Latin Americans who have been able to obtain an education only in systems built on European cultures and values or an indigenism planned in this context. Attempts to claim an identification with Amerindian civilizations have demanded re-education of large groups, a task that makes gargantuan demands on the imagination as well as on the pocketbook. Latin America faces the same problems as would, for example, the United States in this respect. Which regional cultures should be stressed? What combination of those cultures would fit into a national education system without further marginalizing a nation's population in today's world? Not only marriage between Spaniard and Indian, but prejudice and systematic repression intervened between most Latin Americans and revivals of their pre-Columbian identity even in nations such as Peru and Mexico. Latin American national cultures have virtually no experience with which they can identify directly 'before' colonization to contrast with experience 'afterwards'. Europeans displaced Indian cultures, leaving little room for native tradition in mainstream Latin American civilization as it is known today, a synthesis which began with conquest and immigration. It is not easy for members of national cultures (as contrasted with enclaves of native societies removed from what is thought the mainstream) to resort to indigenous traditions without reconstructing them first, giving identity an inevitably arbitrary quality. Only in a very few cases have leaders consciously chosen to revive indigenous cultures long after colonization. In Argentina, for the nation and for most individuals, returning to an 'original' culture is not even an option.

At the same time, however, the powers that dominate the Western world negate Latin America's claims to a European heritage. They do this through ignorance of Latin American intellectual and material culture as well as through apparent disdain for their politics and disregard for their needs. Argentines are aware of international admiration for Borges, but Borges' renown is perceived as an isolated phenomenon, unaccompanied by deeper appreciation of his Argentine cultural context. Latin Americans participate in a Western culture which, in their reading of world opinion, as reflected in the media, in academia, in the arts, and in politics, acts as if they are not there.

In such a context, national identity becomes an obsessive problem, but one that is all but impossible to solve. The 'Malvinas' represent for the Argentines many aspects of the struggle for the identity which eludes them as a nation.

The years of negotiations over the islands incarnate the Argentines' bitter experience as a non-entity in the minds and policies of others. As Argentines see it, the islands have evidently been an insignificant matter for the British, who have not felt the need to decide the question in over 100 years of negotiation. Over the decades following the British takeover of the archipelago, the Argentines continued to send notes of protest and to append their reservation to all relevant treaties.

In the 1940s and 1950s conflicting claims to the Falklands/Malvinas flared up once again. The English responded by proposing to take the matter to the International Court of Justice, which Argentina repeatedly refused to do. The underlying causes of the refusal lie in widespread feeling in Latin America and the Third World in general that The Hague has been dominated by the larger powers and could only give a biased decision. This unwillingness to resort to The Hague is in my opinion well grounded in the composition of the court and the consequent basing of its opinions exclusively on Euro-American sources. The cases in which court members from the Third World have asserted themselves, refusing to be intimidated, have been few.[2]

Later, negotiations were begun in the United Nations, also to no avail, although the Argentine claims to the islands were recognized by the United Nations. In 1976 the Shackleton Commission submitted to Parliament its assessment of the economic viability of the Falklands under British rule. The report made it clear that either a major financial commitment from an unwilling United Kingdom or increasing dependence on Argentina, already responsible for many essential services to the islands, including their mail and air links, was necessary. Nothing was done. In 1981, when Britain proposed a 25-year freeze on further negotiations, Argentina refused to agree to another generation of waiting. Argentines have assumed that decades of delay on a matter so important to Argentina can only mean that the British are intentionally humiliating their country. If the affront is unintentional, it is doubtly insulting as yet further evidence that Argentina and its claims mean nothing to Britain.

At the same time, the clash over the 'Malvinas' has once again heightened the Argentines' *image of themselves* as pawns in the games of the larger powers. Argentina's response to this perception in other contexts has been a series of attempts to establish an alternative position. Its neutrality during World War II, for example, was less a reflection of fascist influence on its leadership than an expression of a particular type of nationalism within the international balance of power. A similar statement of independence may be in the offing as economic sanctions and prolonged military conflict in the 'Malvinas' crisis force Argentines to turn definitively to the USSR. The ideological implications of the East–West confrontation will remain primary only for parties in the East and West. For people in the South, the overwhelming consideration will be how to survive in a world in which the significant confrontation, in their view at least, pits the powerful against the powerless.

Finally, the recent Argentine military occupation of the islands was a statement cast in the idiom of imperialism as territorial conquest. This language of 19th-century colonialism had all along provided the terms in which the 'Malvinas' symbolized imperialist threat to Argentine national identity. While the government had specific political ends in mind, for many Argentines the gesture itself was symbolic, bloodlessly enacting for the rest of the world the implicit violence of the situation. In Argentine minds the British had defined the confrontation as military with the landing of their marines in 1833 and their failure to follow through negotiations to legitimise what was, for the Argentines, a usurpation. Argentina now dramatized the violent ingredient of the bucolic presence of the kelper shepherds. There was a chance that 20th-century Britain would recognize the confrontation as anachronistic and would break the stalemate which it had imposed on negotiations.

Ironically, the British government chose to respond to the Argentine initiative in the same symbolic idiom which, because it was valued quite differently in the British context, was similarly politically useful. The sailing of the British fleet, which surprised much of the world and astounded many Argentines, became (for the latter) predominantly an image of a classic imperial power chastising troublemakers on its outlying borders. The gurkha troops sent into battle added to this symbolic statement: a very common Argentine expression for one who sells out his own fatherland (*vendepatria*) is sepoy *(cipayo)* with many of its connotations intact derived from the Indian troops famed in the Sepoy rebellion whom the English had hired to fight against their own countrymen. Because Argentines see the repossession of the 'Malvinas' as the redress of an illegal action after more than a century's search for a solution through legal channels, the British armada and its troops were, to them, the incarnation of disregard for international laws and conventions.

British military rhetoric reiterated the idea of 'turning the screw', gradually escalating violence with the explicit end of using an armed threat to force the Argentines to the negotiating table. This emphasis of military strategy over diplomatic negotiations confirmed for Argentines that they were dealing with an imperialism based on the domination of territory by force. When England turned so quickly to its gunboats, and actually used them to torpedo the *General Belgrano*, killing hundreds of Argentines outside the war zone, they confirmed in the Argentine mind that they were as committed to might perpetrating right as they had been in 1833. In the flurry of events and imagery, it was lost to view that might cannot be said to be an attribute of England in the 1980s. Britain, once again Great in the symbolic logic of the situation, became a worthy enemy.

If the Argentines are indeed fighting for their identity, we can assume that military reversals will make them the more determined. In this particular cultural context, the policy of turning the screw was able to solve nothing. A battle which denies Argentine sovereignty over the 'Malvinas' also denies, in the eyes of the Argentines, that Argentina exists. Argentina cannot admit to its own symbolic annihilation by admitting that the battle of the 'Malvinas' is over. This logic will force the state of war to continue, transforming not only the South Atlantic but the Western Hemisphere in its wake.

Notes

Parts of the above article have appeared in a different form in the August 1982 issue of *Atlantic*.

1   Events building towards this confrontation had begun centuries earlier with disputed claims to the discovery of the archipelago. Neither Spanish nor English records of voyages in the South Atlantic, including those of Davis and Hawkins, yield sufficient evidence to establish which nation first sighted the islands (Goebel, Julius, Jr: *The Struggle for the Falkland Islands: A Study in Legal and Diplomatic History*. Kennikat: Port Louis and London, 1971, p. 42).

Further, popular opinion notwithstanding, sovereignty has to do with possession, not discovery, a tenet accepted by Spain in 1646–48, but with a venerable tradition in English common law. It was in fact the French who first settled on the archipelago in 1764 under Bougainville, one year before John Byron claimed the islands for Britain and two years before the British managed a settlement at Port Egmont. The French settlement was ceded to the Spaniards in 1767, which allowed them legally to claim occupancy prior to the British by virtue of succeeding to the French title (Goebel 1971: 269) as well as according to Article 8 of the Treaty of Utrecht. The interpretation of the latter was disputed by the English, incorrectly according to Goebel (1971: 246).

In 1770 a new agreement avoided war between England and Spain, handing over the islands to the Spaniards while allowing the English to maintain their fort on the condition that they abandon it in the near future. The legal status of the promise of evacuation and of the subsequent abandonment are difficult to determine, but it seems fair to assume that British claims to the Falklands/Malvinas after abandonment depend on the validity of their claims to Port Egmont in the first place.

Finally, a definitive step to confirm recognition of Spanish sovereignty in the Falklands/Malvinas was taken in the Convention of Nootka Sound in 1790, where England and Spain pledged not to establish new colonies in the South Pacific and South Atlantic. What was already occupied, and that presumably included the Falklands/Malvinas with no Englishmen on them, was to remain in status quo.

*Editor's note: The edition of Goebel referred to by Dr Taylor is a reprint of the original edition by Yale U.P. in 1927. Yale have now issued a new edition containing new material (see the review by H.S. Ferns in *TLS*, 2 July, which questions Goebel's conclusions).

2   Falk, Richard. *Reviving the World Court*. Charlottesville: University of Virginia Press [1986].

Chapter 41

Anatoly M. Khazanov

■ ANTHROPOLOGISTS IN THE MIDST OF
ETHNIC CONFLICTS, *Anthropology Today*,
12.2, April 1996, pp. 5–8

THE COLLAPSE OF THE COMMUNIST REGIMES in the Soviet Union and Eastern Europe and the emergence of new states there are accompanied by an outburst of ethnic nationalism, territorial disputes, tension in interethnic relations and, in the worst cases, by direct ethnic conflicts.[1] This brings to the fore the position of anthropologists and other scholars toward these conflicts, their professional responsibility and moral standing on the issue. To many of our colleagues in the East this is not a purely academic dilemma. Their attitude and behaviour directly affect their professional career, social reputation, livelihood: it may literally become a matter of life and death. I know at least four cases when anthropologists in the ex-Soviet Union fell victim to assassinations, apparently because they were advocating policy that did not suit some extreme groups in their societies. However, even Western anthropologists, particularly those who are doing fieldwork in the regions affected by ethnic strife, often face similar problems: whether they should remain neutral or take a side in the conflict. Again, in making their choice they have to take into account practical considerations, including the very possibility of continuing their work in a given region.

However, the very nature of ethnic tension and strife not infrequently makes it impossible to form categorical judgments about who is right and who is wrong. Often, in such conflicts there are no good guys at all. In one respect or another all guys are bad; it just happens that some bad guys are stronger than others and use their strength to relegate their adversaries to the position of underdogs. Of course, ethnocide, ethnic cleansings, pogroms and other similar actions are crimes and should be condemned as such irrespective of the reasons for the conflict. Their instigators and perpetrators should be prosecuted, and it is unfortunate and shameful that in most of the case they remain unpunished. The very fact that they so often manage to come out unscathed often only encourages others to follow their step.

Still, if one studies the roots of ethnic conflicts, one often finds out that arguments for each side are not without reason. It is difficult to deny that the Bosnian

Figure 41.1   Chingiz Iskanderov, right, weeps over the coffin containing the remains of his brother as other family members grieve in the background at a Muslim cemetery in Agdam, 5 March 1992, during the burial of Azerbaijani victims killed during fighting in and around the embattled Armenian enclave of Nagornyi-Karabakh in Azerbaijan. The city of Agdam is outside the Armenian enclave but suffered gravely during the war.

government did not take into account the interests and concerns of its Serbian citizens when it unilaterally declared the independence of the republic. Likewise, not only the Armenian side but also their Azerbaijanian adversaries have some strong points in their conflict over Nagornyi Karabakh. The same can be said about Georgians and Abkhaz, Georgians and South Ossetians, Ossetians and Ingush in corresponding disputes, or about Moldavians and Slavs in the conflict in Transdniestria.

Usually, ethnic strife invokes a number of conflicting principles: the principle of majority rule, the principle of minorities' and indigenous populations' rights, the principle of territorial and historical continuity, and several others. Wherever ethnic strife exists, any argument triggers two more by the opposing side, and so on *ad infinitum*, where each side has its own notion of justice. Even international law is often powerless in this respect, since it is itself ambiguous in the extreme. The right of nations and peoples to self-determination essentially contradicts the principle of inviolable state borders and the state's sovereign rights to its territory.[2] Likewise, essentially similar movements are often arbitrarily characterized either as national-liberation movements (with plus signs attached), or as secessionist ones (with implicit minus signs). If Algeria had a right to secede from France, why is the same right denied to Chechnia?

Regrettably, outbursts of extreme ethnic nationalism have affected a significant number of anthropologists and other scholars in the ex-Communist countries. Not only do they identify their standing with the interests of their own nationalities;

sometimes they extend this identification to an overt or tacit support of any a ction undertaken for the sake of the so-called national interests. To the best of my knowledge, very few Azerbaijanian scholars revealed the desire, or courage, to condemn the pogroms in Sumgait and Baku, and very few Armenian scholars raised their voices against the ethnic cleansing in Shusha and Khodjaly. I do not know any Georgian anthropologist who protested against the policy of the Georgian government in Abkhazia that clearly violated the human and ethnic rights of the Abkhaz minority, or any Abkhaz scholar who protested against the ethnic cleansing and atrocities conducted against the Georgian population during the Abkhaz counter-offensive.

Sometimes the same scholars do not disdain the racist and xenophobic statements that add fuel to the fire of ethnic strife and hatred. Thus, one prominent Armenian scholar characterized his Azerbaijanian and Turkish colleagues as wild Turks whose heads are filled with 'nomadic instincts which revive now and again, influencing their theories',[3] while no less prominent Azerbaijanian scholars published a special volume of articles on the allegedly negative role played by Armenians in the history of Trans-Caucasus in the nineteenth to early twentieth century.[4] The volume contains a separate section called 'Memorial publications', a series of deliberately selected anti-Armenian articles written by pre-revolutionary authors, often Tsarist colonizers displaying chauvinistic and even openly racist attitudes. Thus, the editors quote with approval and sympathy excerpts from articles by V.L. Velichko who announced at the start of the century: 'Armenians are the extreme instance of brachycephaly; their actual racial instinct make them naturally hostile to the State'.

Such is the style and the level of argumentation employed by both sides. Complex issues of ethnic history again become the battlefield of national rivalry.

In ethnic conflicts in the ex-Soviet Union, and elsewhere in Eastern Europe, not only territory and ethnic status but also anthropology and history became an arena of contestations. The famous Soviet Marxist historian of the 1920s, Mikhail Pokrovsky, openly announced: 'History is the present projected into the past.' This statement was widely criticized by the official Soviet historiography yet usually followed in practice. Unfortunately, it is still often followed. This situation reflects a certain deeply rooted political culture according to which modern political and ethnoterritorial claims can be justified by scientific, or rather pseudoscientific arguments going far back into the past.[5] In the USSR autochthonous and ancient origins were viewed as a matter of ethnic and national pride and advantage (cf. numerous attempts to lengthen the history of Eastern Slavs, the special domain of B.A. Pybakov, for many years the head of Soviet archaeologists). In the post-Soviet period, anthropology, archaeology and history still are often perceived as a way to increase one nationality's self-esteem by diminishing the stature of others.

No wonder that for many years the Georgian scholars tried to prove that the Abkhaz are but alien and late arrivals on the territory of Abkhazia. The same tactics are applied to the Ossetians. Before the outbreak of the military conflict over South Ossetia the Georgian scholars held that the Ossetians had settled on the territory of Georgia in the thirteenth century; afterwards they began to claim that the Ossetians had come to Georgia only in the seventeenth century, or even in the beginning of the twentieth century.[6]

It is no wonder also that the Armenian and Azerbaijanian scholars seek to justify their respective people's claim on Nagornyi Karabakh by trying to prove that from time immemorial the region was populated by Armenians, or, on the contrary, by the alleged Albanian ancestors of Azerbaijanians.[7] It would seem that the question of whether Karabakh's indigenous population spoke Armenian or Albanian should be of a purely academic interest. The indisputable fact remains: at present the overwhelming majority in this region are Armenian (regardless of their ethnic and linguistic ancestry) who seek to join Armenia. Neither can this fact be changed by the two conflicting versions: the Armenian one claiming that the Turkic-speaking population appeared in Nagornyi Karabakh only in the late Middle Ages, or the Azerbaijanian one arguing that the Armenians came to Karabakh from Iran as late as in the 1830s. However, Caucasian nationalism has its own logic. Indeed, why only Caucasian? Didn't Hitler and Stalin resort to similar arguments while carving up the map of the world?

Under the circumstances, serious scholarship is perverted, and the ridiculous aspects of the disputes are overshadowed only by their tragic implications. 'The best things about history', Goethe wrote, 'is the enthusiasm it arouses'. I would add: and this is the worst thing too.

Unfortunately, some Russian anthropologists also became prone to nationalistic fervour. One of the most striking examples is the case of Victor Kozlov from the major Russian anthropological institution, the Institute of Ethnology and Anthropology, who lent direct support to an outspoken racist and anti-Semite. This story was described, though one-sidedly, by Tamara Dragadze.[8] The debate which 'has raged on both sides of the Atlantic' was based not on the excerpts from Kozlov's expertise published in the Russian liberal newspaper *Izvestiia* but on a complete text of this expertise which is at the disposal of the American and West European anthropologists. This debate was not confined to 'Russians and Russian immigrants and visitors to the United States'. It involved many American, British, German and other Western scholars, and several anthropological organizations. Besides, to the best of my knowledge neither a few Russian anthropologists who exposed the incident to their Western colleagues,[9] nor the vast majority of those Western scholars who take alarm about the situation in the Institute of Ethnology and Anthropology, call for international funds to be withheld from the Institute, or for Kozlov, or anybody else, to be dismissed. The only exception is a very few individual letters to the director of the Institute, Valery Tishkov.

The main point is not a danger of 'trivializing the matter into personal attacks', as Tamara Dragadze sees it. The problem is whether our Russian colleagues, or any other for that matter, should follow, not only in their declarations but also in their writings and other publications, the norms of professional ethics adopted by the international community of anthropologists? Personally, I think that there is no room for indulgence in such matters, however so far Kozlov's views and actions have not been condemned by his colleagues in Moscow in any unambiguous way.

While we are debating, Kozlov is acting. Recently he has published an anti-Semitic book.[10] To prove it I have to provide but a few quotations from it preserving specific features of the author's style and grammar:

> The remarkable similarities in the emergence of anti-Semitism in very different countries of the world makes one also look for its causes in the very essence of Jews who are intrinsically linked to their religion –

Judaism. Jews are raised in this religion with an attitude of arrogance toward *goyim* (those who are not Jews or profess Judaism) and [seek] open separation from them. As is well known, such an attitude never promotes good relations with neighbours.

The arrogance of Jews-Judaism stems from those tenets of their religion that claim they are the only people loved by God and chosen by Him to implement His Testaments in this world. For this purpose, Jews are called upon to reign over other peoples ruthlessly exterminating those who do not obey them. (pp. 75–6)

It is quite possible that Lenin's Russophobia to a large extent reflected the views of people who were the closest to him. Jews with their long-standing, almost traditional antipathy to Russians were the most salient among them. (p. 113)

By the way, the deadly hatred towards Jews of Hitler's National Socialists was in large a measure caused precisely by an irreconcilable clash of two extreme nationalist ideologies: one of them elevating Germans, and the other elevating Jews. (p. 138)

The behaviour of Russia's Jews, who during the 'restructuring' years undertook destroying the Soviet system with the same zeal they revealed when creating it . . . has its reasons. This behaviour is rooted in the orientation of Judaism to destroy everything that Jews cannot dominate, be it Russia of the Czars that gave shelter to Jews ousted from the countries of Central and Western Europe, or the Soviet Union that provided them with a rapid ascent into the elite groups and protected them from complete extermination by the Nazis. Still, it failed to awaken in them any widespread feeling of patriotism, as is demonstrated by their growing emigration, mainly to the USA and Israel. (pp. 232–3)

I could continue to quote from Kozlov's book but it seems to me that its character is clear enough. I should only add that the book does not contain (deliberately?) any reference to a publisher, however it is printed in the same way as many other recent publications of the Institute of Ethnology and Anthropology, and the same Institute is the only place in Moscow where this book can be purchased.

Just like elsewhere, an atmosphere of ethnic strife and tension does not facilitate the work of Western anthropologists in the ex-Communist countries or in those which still remain Communist. Being dependent on the benevolence of local authorities, assistance of indigenous anthropologists and striving to win the trust of their informants, they are sometimes too eager to become their advocates and/or please them by sharing, or pretending to share, their prejudice.

If one turns to the ex-Soviet Union, one may ask: is it accidental that many Western scholars working in Azerbaijan tend to accept and to support the Azerbaijanian claims on Nagornyi Karabakh, while those working in Armenia take the Armenian side? Or that the scholars who are doing research in Georgia or in the Baltics are often trying to justify the policy of corresponding governments toward the ethnic minorities in their countries? Do they sufficiently take into account that information they are provided with may be one-sided and biased, sometimes even deliberately distorted?

Nowadays, ethnic tension and conflicts are usually accompanied by a kind of propaganda war. Each side is trying to justify its position and to win the support of the public opinion abroad. Under the circumstances, a Western anthropologist may easily become a victim of manipulation, blackmail (for example, a threat to make one's further fieldwork impossible), and even bribery.

Three years ago my Azerbaidjanian colleague explained to me why, to his mind, one Western scholar is a staunch supporter of his country in the conflict with Armenia. He cynically remarked: 'Of course, he is and will remain on our side. The Azerbaijanian government allowed him to take out of the country a lot of old carpets. Other foreign visitors are forbidden to do this. Moreover, he was allowed to take these carpets without paying the export duty.' I hope that the position of this scholar was in no way influenced by the opportunity to buy the normally expensive carpets at a cut-rate price. However, he certainly had to be more scrupulous in his behaviour and had to care more about his reputation in the country of his study.

Honesty always brings better results. During my fieldwork in different parts of the ex-Soviet Union I am meeting with many people who are active in various nationalistic movements, including extreme nationalists. I never hide that I disagree with them on many issues, and I always stress that my sympathy with the plight of any discriminated ethnic group ends at the moment when they start to discriminate the other ones. Still, I am on good personal terms with most of these people who despite our disagreements continue to provide me with valuable information.

My last warning concerns the necessity to protect informants and sometimes even the confidentiality of their information. Not infrequently, Western anthropologists, particularly graduate students, do not pay enough attention to this extremely important issue. The degree of democratization in many ex-Communist countries should by no means be overestimated. I know for certain that some people in these countries after their meetings with Western anthropologists were approached by various governmental offices, including secret services, that inquired about the nature of their contacts, and even suggested what kind of information they should or should not convey to them. Thus, one of my graduate students, while doing his field research in Uzbekistan, discovered that his host and the most trusted informant regularly reported to the local secret police office about all his contacts and activities.

I have to give up my strong desire to resume fieldwork in Uzbekistan and Turkmenistan, hopefully only for the time being, because I do not wish to be watched while doing it or to create problems for my contacts there. I want to stress that this is a matter of personal choice, connected with my background, my relations with friends and informants in these countries, and some other reasons. In no way am I going to recommend that anybody follow my example. Surveillance by the police and other governmental institutions happens in many other countries, especially in the Third world, and it would be detrimental to anthropology if research were done only in liberal democratic societies. However, let us have no illusions. The Big Brother of the former Communist world begot the numerous Smaller Brothers who continue to watch us, and this should be taken into account very seriously.

In all, the work in the Communist and post-Communist countries poses many professional and even moral problems for Western anthropologists. One of them is their obligation to always protect their informants. As to their position in ethnic conflicts, they should not hurry to take sides. Certainly, they must expose all kinds of ethnic and racial discrimination and all violations of human and ethnic rights, but at the same time they should describe ethnic conflicts objectively, whenever possible suggesting ways to alleviate the tension.

Notes

1   See Anatoly M. Khazanov *After the USSR: Ethnicity, nationalism, and politics in the Commonwealth of Independent States*. Madison, WI: University of Wisconsin press, 1995.

2   Cf. Articles I, II and 2, IV of the United Nations Charter.

3   A. Mushegian. 'Albanofily' i Pravda Istorii, *Kommunist,* Erevan, 2 October 1988.

4   Z. Buniatov (ed.). *Izvestiia Akademii Nauk Azerbaidjanskoi SSR*. Seriia istorii, filosofii i prava. No. 3, Baku, 1988.

5   V.A. Shnirel'man. Zlokliucheniia odnoi nauki: etnogeneticheskie issledovaniia i stalinskaia natsional'naia politika. *Etnograficheskoe obozrenie*, No. 3, 1993: 52–68.

6   O. Vasilieva. *Gruzia kak model' postkommunisticheskoi transformatsii*. Moscow: Gorbachev-Fond, 1993: 46.

7   Cf. G.A. Galoian and K.S. Khudaverdian (eds.) *Nagornyi Karabakh*. Erevan: Izdatel'stvo AN Armianskoi SSR, 1988: F. Mamedova. *Politicheskaia istoriia i istoricheskaia geografiia Kavkazskoi Albanii*. Baku: Elm. 1986: A.S. Sumbatzade. *Azerbaidjantsi-etnogenez i formirovanie navoda*. Baku: Elm, 1990.

8   Tamara Dragadze. Politics and anthropology in Russia. *Anthropology Today*, vol. 11, 1995: 1–3.

9   An open letter from Russian anthropologists to the colleagues abroad. *Society*, vol. 32, No. 6, 1995: 7–8.

10   V.I. Kozlov. *Russkii vopros. Istoriia tragedii velikogo naroda*. Moscow, 1995.

Anatoly Khazanov – Afterword, November 2001

We have entered the twenty-first century and the 'age of globalization' but contrary to the rather widespread wishful thinking, there is no reason to assume that ethnic and national identities will become vague and utterly meretricious in the foreseeable future. The postmodernist concept of the world as a huge global supermarket, in which customers voluntarily choose from a wide range of identities, just as they choose consumer goods, is far from reality.

Actually, globalization divides as much as it unites. It is but a new stage of modernization, and just like modernization in general, it is uneven and differential. This situation alone in a time of rapid changes may transpose cultural, economic, social and political competition in plural societies to the ethno-national plane. Another factor that should be taken into account is the illusion of the universality of the nation-state. While the world as a whole may be becoming less diverse, individual states are becoming more heterogeneous. Multi-ethnic and multinational identities often oppose the striving of a state for homogenization.

The continuing salience of ethno-national identities, both territorialized and transnational, and corresponding tension and conflicts, seem to be inevitable at the current stage of globalization. The best that can be hoped for in this respect is not to eliminate their underlying reasons, but to prevent their most extreme forms, especially violence and bloodshed. This brings to the fore once again the problem of the responsibility borne by anthropologists and by intellectuals in general in ethnic conflicts.

Some of these are members of the ethno-national groups directly involved in the conflicts. To demand that they remain absolutely neutral in such a situation would be unrealistic, especially – and this bears repeating – since in most of these conflicts there are no absolutely right or wrong sides. After all, anthropologists are humans, and as such they have their own identities and allegiances. However, we may expect them to at least avoid adding fuel to the fire, and thus aggravate the conflicts. To a large extent, all nationalist ideologies are based on ethnocentric narratives, 'collective memory', and mythology constructed, perpetuated and propagated by intellectuals. It is worth remembering, however, that myths cease to be merely myths and become social reality when people are ready to kill and be killed in their name.

And what about those who are not participants, but observers and scholars of these conflicts? First, we should continue to expose crimes committed by all sides in such conflicts, be they mass destruction, executions, rape, looting, ethnic cleansing or terrorist activities. At present, international public opinion matters, and sometimes it matters very much. Otherwise, all sides involved in conflicts would not strive so hard to win its moral support. This allows us to exercise a certain deterrent influence. We must insist that freedom of information and its collection, as well as the activities of international truth-seeking and reconciliation bodies, should be guaranteed and become the *sine qua non* of conflict resolution.

Second, it seems that all of us are unanimous in understanding that there is no military solution and, in the long run, no clear winner in ethno-national conflicts. Likewise, it is much better to prevent conflicts than to deal with their disastrous consequences. As a rule, politicians do not much listen to the warnings of experts in academia, and even when they do listen, they pay much more attention to their current worries than to worries-to-be. The possibility of outbreaks of violence in Kosovo, or Indonesia, had been predicted long ago, but were largely ignored, just as the Kurdish problem is largely ignored today. Still, our warnings are worth repeating time and again.

Index

Note: Very general terms such as 'anthropology', 'culture', 'religion' have been omitted from the subjects indexed.